D0162600

SUMMA PUBLICATIONS, INC.

Thomas M. Hines
Publisher

William C. Carter
Editor in chief

Editorial Board

Orders:
 P.O. Box 660725
 Birmingham, AL 35266-0725

Editorial Address:
 2530 Mountain Brook Circle
 Birmingham, AL 35223

Touched by the Graces

[...] comme Virgile nous fait reconnaître Vénus à l'odeur d'ambroisie qui s'exhale de la chevelure et des vêtements de la déesse; de même, quand nous venons de lire Quinault, il nous semble que l'Amour et les Grâces viennent de passer près de nous. (La Harpe, *Cours de littérature*)

Philippe Quinault
Auditeur des Comptes   de l'Académie Françoise

Touched by the Graces

The Libretti of Philippe Quinault in the Context of French Classicism

Buford Norman

SUMMA PUBLICATIONS, INC.
Birmingham, Alabama
2001

Copyright 2001
Summa Publications, Inc.
ISBN 1-883479-35-5

Library of Congress Control Number 2001 135905

Printed in the United States of America

Cover photo, "Vénus dans sa gloire," by Michael Hudson from
Opera Atelier's production of Lully's *Persée*, North American Premiere,
November 2000. Toronto, Canada.
Reproduced with permission.

Libretti pages from *Atys*, *Thésée*, and *Armide* courtesy of the Harvard Theatre
Collection, Houghton Library, Harvard University

Cover design by Susan Dendy

for Elizabeth

O trop parfait modèle
D'une épouse fidèle!
O trop parfait modèle
D'un véritable amour.
(*Alceste*, III.v)

Contents

List of Illustrations

Frontispiece: Portrait of Quinault by Edelinck, from Charles Perrault, *Les Hommes illustres* (Paris: Antoine Dezallier, 1690-1700).

Page 124: Quinault, *Thésée,* act II, scene i (Paris: Ballard, 1675; Harvard Theatre Collection, TS 515-22).

Page 184: Quinault, *Atys,* act I, scene iv (Paris: Ballard, 1676; Harvard Theatre Collection, TS 515-22).

Page 352: Quinault, *Armide,* act V, scene v (Paris: Ballard, 1686; Harvard Theatre Collection, TS C17 v2).

Preface

Le phénix de la poésie *chantante* renaît de ses cendres; il a vu mourir et revivre sa réputation en un même jour. Ce juge même si infaillible et si ferme dans ses jugements, le public, a varié sur son sujet: ou il se trompe, ou il s'est trompé. Celui qui prononcerait aujourd'hui que Q** en un certain genre est mauvais poète, parlerait presque aussi mal que s'il eût dit il y a quelque temps: *Il est bon poète*.

La Bruyère, "Des Jugements" §13

There has never been a book in English on Philippe Quinault, and the latest books in French (Gros, Buijtendorp) were published in 1926. Yet Quinault was probably the most frequently performed and the best remunerated playwright of the age of Louis XIV. What other author could say that he had been chosen to be the successor to Molière and that he had succeeded in a "certain genre" where such giants of French classicism as Racine, La Fontaine, and Boileau, had failed?[1] Voltaire considered

---

[1] Quinault received 3,000 livres from Lully for each libretto and an annual pension from Louis XIV of 3,000 or 4,000 livres. In comparison, Racine had a pension of 1,500-2,000 livres and rarely received more than 1,500 livres for the publication of his plays. See the introduction, p. 8, on the frequency of performance of the Quinault-Lully operas and chapter 4 (*Thésée*), 127-30, for more details on Quinault's pension and on the attempts by other writers to furnish Lully with libretti. See also La Gorce, "Un proche collaborateur."

Quinault to be "le second de nos poètes," yet all that most students of seventeenth-century French literature remember about him is that Boileau contrasted him to "un auteur sans défaut."[2] Such contradictions are difficult to understand even given the vagaries of literary history, which has consigned many a once-admired author to the ash heap and given new life to others, and it is no wonder that La Bruyère chose the example of Quinault for his comment on the fluctuations of taste. Ridiculed by Boileau in the 1660s, by the 1680s "le phénix de la poésie chantante" ruled supreme in the creation of texts to be set to music.[3] He would retain this reputation throughout the Ancien Régime, and in 1777 Gluck would not consider himself to have achieved true success as a composer of French operas until he had reset Quinault's *Armide* with only a handful of minor changes to the text. Quinault's texts suffered the same neglect as did Lully's music during the nineteenth and most of the twentieth centuries, but the situation has begun to change.

In writing today about Quinault, Lully, and other librettists and composers of the French seventeenth and eighteenth centuries, we have the advantage of great advances in research and of being able to see and hear many of the operas of what musicologists call the French baroque. Much of this research and many of these performances have come since 1987, the 300th anniversary of Lully's death, which saw, in addition to a flurry of scholarly activity and an outstanding international colloquium, the hugely—and, for many, surprisingly—successful production of *Atys* by William Christie and Les Arts Florissants. *Atys* was soon revived for an international tour, and a revival of interest in seventeenth-century French opera was well under way. Indeed, when the Théâtre des Champs-Élysées staged a cycle of three Quinault-Lully operas—*Alceste, Armide,*

---

[2] "Je le regarde comme le second de nos poètes pour l'élégance, pour la naïveté, la vérité et la précision" (Voltaire, *Correspondance* 126: 259; letter 19759, to Mme du Deffand, Nov. 26, 1775). "Si je pense exprimer un auteur sans défaut, / La raison dit Virgile, et la rime Quinault" (Boileau, *Satire* II (1665), 19-20). Boileau wrote in the preface to the 1683 edition of his works: "[...] dans le temps où j'écrivis contre lui, nous étions tous deux fort jeunes, et [...] il n'avait pas fait alors beaucoup d'ouvrages qui lui ont dans la suite acquis une juste réputation."

[3] La Bruyère's comment on Quinault's recent success was first published in the fourth edition of *Les Caractères*, which appeared in 1689, a few months after Quinault's death and three years after his last libretto. In the 1689 edition, the last sentence contains neither the parenthetical "en un certain genre" nor the qualifier "presque."

and *Roland*—one could actually see people scalping tickets. The new opera house in Lyon opened in 1993 with the same *Phaéton* that had been the first opera performed in the old house in 1688. There have been concert versions of *Amadis, Isis, Persée,* and *Thésée,* and the latter two have been performed in Toronto and Boston, respectively, in the 2000-2001 season. At the same time, our knowledge of the history of French opera and of how it was performed is growing by leaps and bounds: a new edition of Lully's complete works is under way, and the Centre de Musique Baroque de Versailles has celebrated its tenth anniversary. It is only fitting that Quinault, whose libretti provided what was universally considered the crucial component of any opera, receive some of this attention.

§ § §

However, if the Sirens call, Scylla and Charybdis guard the way. We hear the beauties of Lully's music, yet to understand exactly why his *tragédies lyriques* were so successful we need to understand the texts by Quinault to which most of them were set. These texts remain relatively unknown partly because the esthetic and poetic theory behind them are misunderstood, but this theory remains misunderstood largely because the texts are not well known. Should one concentrate on the theory, referring to the texts only when illustrations are needed? Or should one concentrate on the texts, referring to theoretical issues when necessary even though the theory has not been spelled out in detail?

When discussing a well-known author, one would probably choose the former approach, assuming that the reader would be familiar enough with the texts to know whether the references to them were accurate and well chosen. In the case of the *tragédie lyrique,* however, the theoretical issues at hand are better known than the texts—a reader who has read some of the major authors of seventeenth-century France is more likely to be familiar with *vraisemblance,* the *merveilleux,* and classical versification than he/she is with Quinault's *Thésée* or *Armide,* even if he/she has not considered the specific qualities required for a text written to be set to music.

I have thus chosen to concentrate on the texts, in this case the eleven libretti that Quinault wrote from 1673 to 1686 for *tragédies lyriques* by Lully.[4] An introduction will nonetheless be necessary to establish the context in which the *tragédie lyrique* began and to lay out the most important theoretical issues at stake in seventeenth- and eighteenth-century discussions of this new type of theater. After a chapter devoted to the prologues that begin each opera, the eleven chapters that follow—one on each libretto—will include a discussion of the traditional literary elements such as plot, characterization, and style plus a second section devoted to an issue that is more specific to musical theater. Many of these issues are open to a variety of often conflicting interpretations, and I will not hesitate to borrow from a variety of critical approaches as I emphasize in turn the structural, stylistic, ideological, or sociological aspects of Quinault's texts. I will also take into account the general principles of musico-dramatic structure, though without going into details that would be more appropriate in a musicological study than in a literary one.

It is my hope that this combination of the traditional with an eclectic, more modern approach will serve both to introduce Quinault's texts to a wider public and to facilitate further investigation. Quinault made a major contribution to works of great emotional power and of great beauty, and, as Nathan Edelman put it so well, "Beauty is not so low that it need not be understood" (165).

§ § §

---

[4] Another reason for beginning with the texts rather than with theoretical issues is the publication of Catherine Kinztler's fundamental study of the philosophical and esthetic elements of the *tragédie lyrique*, *Poétique de l'opéra français de Corneille à Rousseau*. Though her book is not primarily a literary study, her analysis of the classical "esthémé" and the "système poétique" of classical theater in general and of the *tragédie lyrique* in particular is essential for understanding the underpinnings of the literature during the glory years of the reign of Louis XIV. Kintzler's book is especially helpful on the relation of the *tragédie lyrique* to other types of theater and on such questions as *vraisemblance, bienséance, nécessité*, plot structure, and the ethics of fiction and theater.

This book has been several years in the making, and I could never mention all the people and institutions who have helped me bring it to fruition. A sabbatical leave from the University of South Carolina and a National Endowment for the Humanities Grant for University Teachers allowed me to complete the first chapters, and countless librarians, especially at the Bibliothèque Nationale de France divisions of Musique and Opéra, helped me consult and understand an often bewildering array of old books, manuscripts, and scores. Jean Duron, Corinne Daveluy, and all the wonderful people at the Atelier de Recherches at the Centre de Musique Baroque de Versailles have been unflagging in their support. I am also indebted to all the musicians who have brought Lully's music to life, confirming and/or challenging what I saw on paper.

I would like to acknowledge my gratitude to the late James Anthony, "Mr. French Baroque Music," who many years ago encouraged a young literary scholar to delve into the wonderful world of French Baroque Music and who, on paper and in person, was a faithful guide until his deeply regretted death shortly before this book went to press.

Of the dozens of colleagues who have shared their insights with me, I am especially grateful to William Brooks and Jérôme de la Gorce, whose knowledge of Quinault and Lully are second to none. I would also like to thank my colleague Georgia Cowart for reading an early draft and for countless brainstorming sessions; Louis Auld for a careful reading of the chapter on *Thésée;* Michèle Vialet, a rigorous yet understanding collaborator; Lise Leibacher Ouvrard, on whose printer and monitor the early chapters first saw the light of day; Claudine Pellerin, Alain Durel and his assistant Anna Takahashi, and Lionel Sawkins for copies of performing editions of scores of *Alceste, Roland,* and *Isis;* Tom Hines and Bill and Lynn Carter, expert and prompt editors and warm friends.

Mostly, I want to express my gratitude to my wife, Elizabeth Joiner, to whom this book is dedicated and whose love, support, and critical judgment have contributed to every page.

And finally, I would like to recognize someone I have never met, Willie Mays, whose marvelous gifts and consummate showmanship in center field and on the base paths first revealed to me how talent and spectacle work together to create emotion.

§ § §

Some parts of this book have been published previously, though in considerably different form. Parts of the introduction and of the conclusion appeared in "The *Tragédie Lyrique* of Lully and Quinault: Representation and Recognition of Emotion," in an issue of *Continuum* (vol. 5, 1993, 111-42) devoted to literature and the arts. I developed some of the ideas in section 2 of chapter 6 for the volume *Lully Studies* edited by John H. Heyer (Cambridge University Press, 2000), 57-71, and for "Opera as Drama, Opera as Theater: Quinault's *Isis* in a Racinocentric World," *Cahiers du 17ᵉ* 7.2 (2000): 57-71. An earlier and expanded version of section 2 of chapter 7 can be found in "A Woman's Fate in the Balance: The Persephone Myth in Quinault and Lully's *Proserpine*," co-authored with Michèle Vialet, in *Images of Persephone: Feminist Readings in Western Literature* (Gainesville: University Press of Florida, 1994), 45-74. French versions of parts of section 2 of chapters 3 and 6 appeared in the proceedings of two conferences: "Les Styles d'*Alceste*," *Papiers du Collège International de Philosophie* 16 (1993): 39-54, and "La Tragédie lyrique, déca-danse ou apothéose? Le cas d'*Isis*," *La Pensée de la danse à l'âge classique: écriture, lexique et poétique*, ed. Catherine Kintzler, Cahiers de la Maison de la Recherche (Lille: Université Charles-de-Gaulle—Lille III, 1997), 35-46.

§ § §

References to Quinault's libretti are to my edition (Toulouse: Littératures Classiques, 1999). Quotations are identified by act, scene, and line. For example, act one, scene one, line one is abbreviated I.i.1, the first line of a prologue as P.1, and the first line of a dedicatory epistle as E.1. Line numbers followed by a 'd' indicate stage directions that precede the line. For other works by Quinault, and for the published Boscheron biography, references are to the 1715 edition of his complete theater; however, for the sake of convenience, I give page numbers from the much more widely available reprint of the 1778 edition; the text (but not the spelling and punctuation) is the same in both editions, unless otherwise indicated.

Quotations from Ovid's *Metamorphoses* are from the Humphreys translation. References to Racine's theater and poetry are to the new

Pléiade edition by Georges Forestier, which gives the text of the first edition of each work (the one Quinault was most likely to have known). Line
numbers, however, are those of the more frequently reproduced 1697 text,
which Forestier gives as well as those of the original editions when
Racine's changes involved the addition or deletion of entire lines.

References to the Parfaicts' manuscript *Histoire de l'Académie
Royale de Musique*, 1645-1742 are to the Beffara copy. I will refer to this
work as *Académie Royale*, to avoid confusion with their *Histoire du
théâtre françois depuis son origine jusqu'à présent*.

I have used short titles (usually the first word or two) of other
works I cite frequently. The use of abbreviations has been kept to a
minimum: *O.C.* for *Œuvres complètes*, *O.D.* for *Œuvres diverses*.

French quotations reproduce the spelling of the edition quoted. As
a result, quotes from Quinault's libretti and from major authors such as
Racine, Boileau, and Sévigné have been modernized, while many others
have not.

Musical examples from *Atys* are from the facsimile edition of the
1686 Ballard score, published by Broude Bros. Ltd., to whom I am grateful for permission to reproduce them. The four examples on page 29 are
in a modern transcription, for greater clarity of presentation.

Introduction

Issues and Contexts

- I -

THE OPERAS THAT JEAN-BAPTISTE LULLY, the creator of French opera, and his librettist, Philippe Quinault, created between 1673 and 1686 were so successful that special ordinances were passed to control the crowds. It was not unusual for spectators to see the same opera at least ten or fifteen times in a season, and Quinault's libretti were widely published and eagerly discussed. What were these "tragédies lyriques" that were so popular, that were performed far more often than Racine's tragedies? Why has literary history tended to neglect them, and the lyric stage in general, to the point that the standard account of neoclassical esthetics and of French culture during the reign of Louis XIV is seriously incomplete? These are some of the questions that I hope to answer in the pages that follow.

§ § §

Quinault had been the author of numerous successful tragedies and tragi-comedies from 1653 to 1671, but in the 1670s it was Racine who dominated the tragic stage. Thanks in part to Boileau who, in his *Satires*, denigrated Quinault and other rivals of Racine, the public came to appreciate plays such as *Bérénice* and *Phèdre* in which the action was concentrated on the sufferings of lovers far less heroic and *galant* than those of Quinault. The taste of the public was not changing, however, as much as Boileau would have us believe. If plays such as Quinault's *Astrate* (1665) were too "doucereux" for the public that admired the tragedies of Racine's maturity, this same public shed floods of tears over the plight of the young lovers in the latter's *Iphigénie* (1674) and flocked to the Académie Royale de Musique to hear Quinault's words set to music by Lully. Rather than say, like La Bruyère (see preface, p. i), that either the public of the 1660s or that of the 1680s was wrong, I would say that both knew how to enjoy Quinault *and* Racine. And if we can say that today Quinault is once again rising from the ashes of obscurity, it is because the public of the late twentieth century discovered, as did that of the 1670s, that it can enjoy—and learn from—both Racinian tragedy and the Quinault-Lully *tragédie lyrique*.

In 1989, the first issue of *Continuum* was, appropriately, devoted to the theme "Rethinking Classicism." The volume contains, among a number of excellent articles, essays by Jules Brody and Robert Nelson that challenge the "Racinocentric" notion of French classicism. For Brody, the seventeenth-century French classical doctrine

> is at best a crude, inorganic extrapolation of a neoteric, pseudo-Aristotelian theory of tragedy, modulated around such abstractions as imitation, reason, nature, unity, decorum, and verisimilitude, and designed to account teleologically for the mature production of Racine, the only "classical" writer, as it turns out, whose works betray any palpable connection with the doctrine. (53)

Brody may be exaggerating to make his point, but the fact remains that our view of what Alain Viala calls "une réalité ambivalente, instable et conflictuelle" ("Galanterie et classicisme" 134) is Racinocentric, or, more precisely, it is our-idea-of-Racine-ocentric. We have understandably built our image—for it is, and could hardly be, little more than that, an image, a mental construct—of classicism around its greatest writer. It is problematic enough that such an image may not fit many other writers of the period; if the image is not accurate to begin with, our view is seriously skewed.

It is not my goal in this book to propose a new interpretation of Racine, and certainly not to suggest that he does not deserve his lofty place in the literary firmament, but it will help understand how the same public could enjoy Racine and Quinault if I point out two examples of fairly commonly held opinions about Racine that do not really stand up to close scrutiny. First, he is known as the portrayer of strong, often violent emotions in characters such as Phèdre and Hermione, torn between right and wrong, reason and passion, yet he was known to his contemporaries as "le tendre Racine." I suspect that many members of his audiences were as moved by the declaration of love between Hippolyte and Aricie (II.2) as they were by Phèdre's famous avowals (I.3, II.5).

Second, we often emphasize the order, the reason, the classical decorum of Racine. A critic as perspicacious as Roland Barthes—controversial as it may be, his *Sur Racine* contains numerous useful insights— could write in *Le Degré zéro de la littérature* that the words of "le langage classique,"

> neutralisés, absentés par le recours sévère à une tradition qui absorbe leur fraîcheur, fuient l'accident sonore ou sémantique qui concentrerait en un point la saveur du langage et en arrêterait le mouvement intelligent au profit d'une volupté mal distribuée. (66)

How could someone who has obviously read *Phèdre* closely not remember the almost magical yet ominous sounds of "La fille de Minos et de Pasiphaé" and not find "saveur" or something beyond "intelligent movement" when the /a/ and the /é/ of "Pasiphaé" return in "C'est Vénus toute entière à sa proie attachée" and "L'avare Achéron ne lâche point sa proie" (I.i.36, I.iii.306, II.v.626)? Does Racine the poet not linger over these unusual words, these striking combinations of sounds? There is more to Racinian tragedy than carefully constructed plots, psychological analysis, "transparent" discourse, and "regular" alexandrines. There is *tendresse* in Racine and there is a concern for the sonorous side of poetry, for the effect that words can have independently of their meaning. These two characteristics—and they are only two among many—are in fact to be found in many seventeenth-century authors, and if we were more familiar with the *tragédie lyrique,* or, as it is often labeled on title pages, *tragédie en musique,* we would be more aware of them and we would have a more complete understanding of Racine and of the seventeenth century in general.

It is in such a spirit that Kintzler, in her *Poétique de l'opéra fran- çais,* has demonstrated that, in spite of a tradition that calls seventeenth- century music "baroque" and seventeenth-century literature "classical," the *tragédie lyrique* is part of the same poetic and philosophical system as spoken tragedy, of which Racine is the quintessential representative. The Quinault-Lully operas share the Aristotelian goals of Racinian tragedy (imitation of the passions and catharsis through rather formal and stylized means) and many of its principles (order, restraint, verisimilitude, neces- sity, propriety, and the dominance of the written word) but take a rather different approach. In their operas the noble tone of tragedy alternates with celebrations, merrymaking, and even comedy. Almost all of the ac- tion is staged, usually quite elaborately, whereas in Racine's tragedies there was only one simple set, many key events were narrated, and vio- lence and the supernatural were forbidden. Tragic drama is generally un- derstood in the seventeenth century to feature the inability of heroes and heroines to fulfill all their desires; in contrast, the mythological plots of "lyrical tragedies" often have endings that exalt heroism and true love. Reason is sometimes mocked, characters give in to weaknesses without necessarily being punished, and the pursuit of pleasure is rarely thwarted.

As almost all the writers of the period insist, the rules exist only to help attain the overall goals of instructing, pleasing, and moving audi- ences, and especially the last two. Since spoken and sung tragedy reached these goals, but in different ways, it makes less sense to follow Boileau and view opera as an exception to classical rules and restraint[1] than it does to see classicism as a temporary narrowing and focusing that occurs within a broader, more varied esthetic framework that privileges heroism, pleasure, spectacle, and accommodation to the taste of the literate public. The *tragédie lyrique* is one of the most complete manifestations of this

---

[1] Spielmann points out that the "projet classique" is not a "fait accompli" (80) and that "le genre esthétiquement dominant, à partir des années 1670, c'est justement l'opéra" (82). Zebouni (14) argues that Boileau's *Art poétique* is more of a manifesto than an art of poetry, that he is trying to impose a new, minority point of view. See also Biet, *Tragédie* 52. I will return to the question of coexisting esthetics during what is known as the classical period in chapter 10 (*Amadis*), 298-300.

framework. The individuality and exuberance of the first half of the century, along with its "baroque" esthetic, were still very much alive in the
1670s, as was the "galant" esthetic of the 1650s and 1660s, and in literature one still finds a reflection of a taste for adventure, heroic deeds, and
noble love. At the same time, other important changes were taking place,
including the gradual demise of this heroic ideal, the rise of absolutism
and of capitalism, and the increasing influence of women. It is hardly
surprising, then, that a major literary debate developed over the merits of
this new type of theater, a debate that can be regarded as a major round of
the Quarrel of Ancients and Moderns. The standard date for the beginning
of the Quarrel is 1687, yet in 1674 Racine felt threatened enough to
devote half of the preface to his tragedy *Iphigénie* to an attack on the
"modernes" who defended Quinault's libretto for *Alceste,* which had
appeared earlier in the year. Racine would end his public theatrical career
with his next play, and it seems clear that the success of his rival Quinault
was one of the main factors in his decision to give up the theater for
historiography.

I will discuss several of these issues more fully in the chapters that
follow. First, however, it is important to take a close look at just what a
tragédie lyrique is and at how it fits into a larger tradition of musical
theater.

- II -

French efforts to mix music, dance and theater can be traced back
at least as far as Beaujoyeulx's *Ballet comique de la royne* in 1581, "the
most important attempt to date in France to unify poetry, dance, music
and decor within one continuous action" (Anthony, *French Baroque Music* 41). The next ninety years saw an impressive variety of combinations
of these arts—*ballet de cour, pastorale dramatique, tragédie à machines,
tragédie de collège, comédie-ballet, tragédie-ballet*—and if some of
these, such as the *tragédie-ballet*, were fairly short-lived, others, such as
the *ballet de cour*, have a long and complex history that reveals a constant
experimentation with "total theater."[2]

What sets these works apart from opera is that they have no extended passages of dramatic poetry (*ballet de cour, pastorale dramatique*)
or that the music and dance are added to, rather than integrated with, the
dramatic poetry (*tragédie à machines, comédie-ballet, tragédie-ballet*).
They can be, for example, a "comédie mêlée de musique et d'entrées de
ballet" (Molière, *Les Amants magnifiques,* 1670), but they are not a
"tragédie *en* musique." What we now know as opera—a dramatic work
sung from beginning to end—was first staged in France by Italian troupes

---

[2] For an overview of the history of French musical theater before the *tragédie lyrique,* see Powell, *Music and Theatre;* Auld, *Lyric Art* 1: 69-88; Louvat, "Théâtre musical"; and Brooks, "Perrin, Corneille, and the Beginnings of French Opera." I will discuss
this history in more detail in the opening pages of chapter 2 (*Cadmus et Hermione*).

It is impossible to cite here all the works that contribute to our understanding of
these types of musical theater. Anthony (*French Baroque Music,* chaps 1-6) discusses
each, and there are useful articles by La Gorce, Niderst, and McGowan in Mamczarz,
ed., *Les Premiers opéras en Europe.* The books on tragedy by Biet (44-46) and Delmas
(30-39, 56-58) give a good brief description of the *pastorale dramatique, tragédie de
collège,* and *tragédie à machines.* On the pastoral, see also Marsan; Durosoir, "Pastorales avec musique"; Kintzler, *Poétique* 197-204; and Louvat, "L'Opéra français avant
Lully" 90-96. Delmas's *Recueil de tragédies à machines* contains a useful introduction.
On the *ballet de cour,* see the standard works by Christout and McGowan and the edition of Benserade's libretti by Canova-Green. The especially abundant bibliography on
Molière's comedy-ballets includes Auld's *The Unity of Molière's Comedy-Ballets,*
Abraham's *On the Structure of Molière's Comedy-Ballets,* Mazouer's *Molière et ses
comédies-ballets,* Fleck's *Music, Dance, and Laughter,* several articles by Powell and
his recent *Music and Theatre in France*; Fajon, "La comédie-ballet, fille et héritière du
ballet de cour," compares the two genres. On Molière's *Psyché,* which is the best known
example of a *tragédie-ballet,* see Delmas, "Le Théâtre musical et *Psyché* de Molière."

invited by Mazarin in the 1640s and 1650s. The honor of being the first French opera should probably go to La Guerre and Beys's *Le Triomphe de l'Amour sur des bergers et des bergères* (1655) or to Perrin and Cambert's *Pastorale* (1659), works that were successful enough to encourage Perrin to found his Académie de Musique et de Danse in 1669 and to make Lully envious enough to take over Perrin's monopoly on musical stage productions in 1672. Lully engaged Quinault as his librettist, and they quickly patched together the pastoral *Les Fêtes de l'Amour et de Bacchus* from scenes that Lully had written with Molière.

Still, if French opera had been invented, it had not yet found the form that would make it a true rival of spoken theater.[3] Credit for this form belongs to Lully, but one could wonder why it was only in 1673, with *Cadmus et Hermione,* that he found it, after twenty years of experience with the *ballet de cour* and the *comédie-ballet* and extended collaboration with writers as talented as Benserade and Molière. There are examples of most of the musical forms that characterize the *tragédie lyrique* in Lully's works before 1673 (*air, récit,* chorus, overture, *ritournelle, récitatif,* for example); what is lacking is extended passages of recitative, and these require a full-length dramatic text that has literary merit (something almost universally denied to Perrin's libretti) and can also be set to music. It is this text that Quinault supplied, and it is this contribution that his contemporaries recognized when they often referred to what we today call "the operas of Lully" as "les opéras de Quinault."[4]

Quinault certainly had the experience. He could write to Louis XIV in 1684 that, in addition to having written sixteen comedies, tragicomedies and tragedies between 1653 and 1671, he had been contributing

---

[3] "Lully n'est pas le créateur de l'opéra français, si l'on réduit la définition de l'opéra à celle d'une pièce de théâtre où la musique est présente en continu." From another point of view, however, Lully can be considered the inventer of opera in the sense that he finally found "la formule exemplaire de la tragédie lyrique" (Louvat, "L'Opéra français avant Lully" 82).

[4] See, for example, Lecerf 1: 8-9 and Anthony, *French Baroque Music* 95. In the eighteenth century, Cahusac wrote that it was Quinault who "réunit avec la vraisemblance suffisante au Théâtre la Poësie, la Peinture, la Musique, la Danse, la Méchanique" (3: 71).

to royal *divertissements* for 24 years.[5] He must have been thinking of the pastoral *Lysis et Hespérie* (lost) that he wrote in 1660, which was followed by numerous contributions to court ballets (especially the *Ballet des Muses* of 1666), the *Églogue de Versailles* (1668), and, most recently, the verses that were sung between the acts of *Psyché* in 1671. Except for *Lysis et Hespérie,* all of these works involved collaboration with Lully, and it is hardly surprising that

> [v]ers 1672, quand l'idée de créer la tragédie en musique se précisa dans le chef de Lully, le nom de Quinault dut lui apparaître comme une évidence: le poète avait démontré sa capacité à écrire de bons vers pour le chant, il était bien en Cour et ses deux dernières tragédies venaient de rappeler qu'il avait autant de propension à versifier les « tendresses amoureuses » que le Florentin—et Sa Majesté—en pouvaient souhaiter. (Couvreur, "Collaboration" 34)

I would add only that it is by no means certain that it was only, or even primarily, in the head of Lully that this new spectacle took shape. If it was only after he hired Quinault as his librettist that Lully created the *tragédie lyrique,* the influence of Quinault on Lully's thinking must have been considerable.

The success of the new *tragédie lyrique* was immediate. New productions followed each season until Lully's death in 1687, and the form of the *tragédie lyrique* remained basically the same throughout the Ancien Régime.[6] Based on the number of performances and the number of libretti sold, this new type of theater was more popular than the traditional spoken theater, even though Racine was at the height of his career. A new opera could have a run of as many as 150 performances, at least three times a week over a period of almost fifty weeks. By comparison, Racine's tragedies rarely had a first run of much more than thirty, and the

---

[5] See Couvreur, "Collaboration" 9. On Quinault's career in the spoken theater, see Brereton 220-22, 240-51. For a brief overview of the types of tragedy and tragi-comedy from 1640 to 1660, see Delmas, *La Tragédie* 13-17.

[6] I have preferred the term "tragédie lyrique" to "tragédie en musique" because of its more common modern use, in spite of the use of the latter on title pages of Quinault's libretti. I use "opera" to refer to this type of musical theater as a whole, from the early seventeenth century to the present.

greatest box office success of the century, Thomas Corneille's *Timocrate,* only had about eighty.[7]

The creation of each new opera was an impatiently awaited event, both in Paris and at court where, especially during the 1670s, they were performed fifteen or twenty times during Carnival, before opening in Paris after Easter. Both the preparation of a new opera and its perform-ances were the subject of considerable discussion. Sévigné's correspon-dence—which is only the best known example—contains ninety-one references to Lully operas (compared to seventy-four to Racine's plays), and forty-six of these contain a quotation from a Quinault libretto.

Such popularity of course made Lully and Quinault their share of enemies, including Boileau, Racine, La Fontaine, and Saint-Evremond, and the dismay of these rivals constitutes one of the most eloquent testi-monials to the success of the new opera. La Fontaine summarizes their reaction: "Hiver, été, printemps, bref, opéra toujours" ("A M. de Niert, sur l'opéra," *O.D.* 619).[8]

A literary quarrel, one of the most important salvos in what be-came known as the Quarrel of the Ancients and Moderns, broke out al-most immediately, following Quinault and Lully's second opera, *Alceste,* in 1674. Charles Perrault defended his "modern" colleague in his *Critique de l'opéra, ou examen de la tragédie intitulée Alceste, ou le Triomphe d'Alcide* (1674), and Racine took Perrault to task in the preface to his *Iphigénie.* The major quarrels about music would not develop until early in the eighteenth century, but numerous texts in the 1670s and 1680s show that the *tragédie lyrique* quickly took its place among other types of theatrical productions.[9]

---

[7] See Picard, *Carrière* 91, and the edition of *Timocrate* by Giraud, 13-14.

[8] On the popularity of the *tragédie lyrique* see also Gros, *Quinault* 647 and the quotations from the *Gazette de France* (April 29, 1673) and Du Tralage in Anthony, *French Baroque Music* 93-94.

[9] In addition to works by La Fontaine, Racine, and Perrault already mentioned, see Boileau, "Fragment d'un prologue d'opéra," and works in the bibliography by Bauderon de Sénecé, Callières, Rapin, and Saint-Evremond. On the role of opera in the Quarrel of Ancients and Moderns, see chapter 3 (*Alceste*), 96-101. Opera was also included in quar-rels about the morality of theater, such as the debate between Caffaro and Bossuet in 1694; see Barras for an overview of the subject. On the efforts by Boileau, Racine, and La Fontaine to replace Quinault as Lully's librettist, see chapter 4 (*Thésée*), 127-31.

As Kintzler has shown, there was a natural, logical place in 1673 for a musical theater alongside the spoken theater:

Poésie dramatique

AU THÉATRE	A L'OPÉRA
tragédie	tragédie lyrique
pastorale dramatique	pastorale lyrique
comédie	comédie lyrique[10]

In short, the *tragédie lyrique* is a successful form of theater that pleased public and critics for more than a century and that is having an important revival today. Lully and Quinault's solution to the challenge of combining words and music is not the one adopted by composers of today's best known operas, from Mozart to Puccini, but it is nonetheless a very viable one. Those of us fortunate enough to have seen some of a series of remarkable productions since the 1987 *Atys* by Les Arts Florissants know what beauty and what emotion can be attained in the combination of words and music that seem simple when compared to those of nineteenth-century opera. For example, the words and the music of Sangaride's "Vous me perdez, Atys, et vous êtes aimé" (I.vi.181) are not especially remarkable in themselves (at least not in the sense that we think of the words of Mallarmé or the music of Strauss as remarkable), but the emotional effect is striking.[11] Furthermore—and this is why the *tragédie lyrique* must be understood from a literary point of view as much as from a musical one—the effect depends on the words; it is only when one

---

[10] The *pastorale dramatique* disappears around 1660. The first major example of a *comédie lyrique* is Rameau's *Platée* in 1745. I have combined the two charts in Kintzler, page 204. Like Kintzler, I prefer not to call the *tragédie lyrique* a genre, but rather a form, or type, of theater. As she says (*Poétique* 41), the *tragédie lyrique* fills a slot in an already existing grid of theatrical forms and constitutes an "espèce poétique à part entière" that can be subdivided into genres. See also Biet, *Tragédie* 44, for whom tragedy is "un code général composé de genres variés qui peuvent admettre le chant, la danse et les machines."

[11] This is not just my personal reaction—I have witnessed similar reactions in friends, students, and audiences. Similarly successful combinations of simple words and fairly simple music are found in "Atys est trop heureux" (I.iv) and "Espoir si cher et si doux, / Ah! pourquoi me trompez-vous?" (III.viii). These and the other examples from *Atys* that I refer to in the text have been recorded by William Christie and Les Arts Florissants.

understands the implications of Sangaride's last word that one is struck by the full poignant effect of the musical phrase. Words do not interfere with music, and understanding enhances feeling rather than hinders it. If some people today would argue with these two statements, no one in seventeenth-century France would have.

- III -

Before describing the *tragédie lyrique* in some detail, it is important to understand it as part of the larger category of stage productions in
which the entire text is sung.[12] Consider the components that go into an
opera: text, action represented on stage, instrumental and vocal music,
costumes, and decor (including machines and lighting) are a part of every
opera, and most—especially early opera and later grand opera—include
dance as well. Each component can be broken down into subdivisions, or
elements, and some components (text, action and music) can be divided
into two groups of elements. In the following brief overview of some of
the key issues involved in interpreting opera, there will not be room to
give a full treatment of each element, but it will be useful to list some of
them here:

> text (prose[13]): plot, structures, themes, myths, characterization,
>   passions, ideologies, esthetics.
> text (poetry): figures, images, rhythms, sounds.
> action (types of discourse, means of representation): recitative,
>   aria, ensemble, chorus; narration; spectacle.
> action (acting): movement, gesture, declamation, appearance.
> music (vocal): melody, harmony, rhythm, articulation, pronuncia-
>   tion, phrasing, voice quality.
> music (instrumental): melody, harmony, rhythm, theme, leitmotif
> dance: choreography, pantomime, costumes.
> costumes: style, fabric, color, makeup, wigs.
> decor: materials, style, size, degree of abstraction; machinery,
>   lighting.

---

[12] For a brief overview of the need to understand opera as a special form of drama
and the *tragédie lyrique* as a special form of opera, see Turnbull.

[13] I use "prose" and "poetry" in the sense that Eliot does in *Poetry and Drama* (42-
43; quoted in Kerman, p. 5). For Eliot, prose is capable of expressing "classifiable emotions [...] when directed towards actions." Poetry expresses "a fringe of indefinite extent,
of feeling," and music expresses feelings at "moments of greatest intensity." Eliot deals
briefly with one of the main goals of opera: the representation of order in life through art
and a combination of the musical and the dramatic.

If one is to describe opera, one must consider all of these components. Defining opera, distinguishing it from other types of theater, is another matter to which I will return shortly, since it involves the relations between words and music, as well as the overall "literariness" of opera, key issues for any study of libretti.

Since opera always involves words being sung, there must be a text, or libretto. Almost all libretti before the twentieth century are in verse, often in traditional lyric meters. In the best of all possible worlds, lyric poetry is, as its name implies, poetry intended to be sung, and the sounds and rhythms are chosen accordingly. The rub, of course, is that since opera always involves action represented on stage, the words must (to put it very simply) help tell a story. The text thus tends to become dramatic poetry, which is not always compatible with lyric poetry; words are often chosen for their meaning and effect with little regard for their sound and rhythm, and compromises must be made. Indeed, the development of opera can be understood as a struggle between the demands of lyric and dramatic poetry. As Kerman aptly puts it, for Orpheus, the supreme lyric artist and the subject of several early operas, "the crisis of life becomes the crisis of his lyric art: art must now move into action, on to the tragic stage of life" (20).

It is the glory and curse of opera—and of writing about opera—that it brings an art form such as music, with its mathematical abstraction and emotional immediacy, into direct contact with real life situations; glory because opera works, curse because its components are constantly interacting with each other, making it difficult to talk about one without neglecting or oversimplifying another. For example, the history of opera is characterized by a debate over the relative importance of music and words.[14] In the beginnings of opera in Florence in the first years of the seventeenth century, and in France in the second half of the century, poetry was the "mistress" of music as composers and librettists sought to produce emotional effects similar to those of ancient Greek music and tragedy. As opera developed, however, composers—and usually the public—preferred to give a larger role to music, and as a result the words and

---

[14] There is an excellent discussion of this duality in the third chapter of Lindenberger's *Opera: The Extravagant Art*, pp. 108-27. See also histories of opera such as those of Grout and Donington (*Rise of Opera*), and Poizat 19-20, 65, 77.

action became less and less important until a "reform," such as those of Metastasio, Gluck or Wagner, brought about a change (usually fairly brief) in direction. These reforms were usually justified as efforts to return to Greek tragedy (Lindenberger, *Extravagant Art* 97-101).

Since the words of a libretto are meant not only to be sung but also to be the basis of staged action, it is not surprising that the role of the action represented, of plot, on the operatic stage has gone through cycles similar to those of the role of words—important at the beginning, then a mere excuse for beautiful singing, then more important thanks to a reform, and so on. Even in periods when action is considered important, many operas have more than enough verisimilitude-stretching situations to make it clear that their success depends on more than the plot, that the words are there to do more than tell a story.

Acting on the operatic stage has also gone through cycles of formality and realism. Many early performers relied more on stylized gestures than on "realistic" acting, while more recently performers have often been expected to be "singing actors." Such creatures are extremely rare, and even Maria Callas, for many people the best singer-actor of our time, has numerous detractors who do not like her voice. Most singers today are happier to go through the motions and save their energy for the music, well aware that their fame and income depend more on their singing than on their acting. As a result, many operagoers develop a remarkable ability to put up with what any theatergoer would consider bad acting. This is not just a sign of bad taste among opera-lovers, however, and I will return several times to the idea that the essence of opera, and especially of the *tragédie lyrique*, transcends our current notions of good acting and of realism. A genre where everything is sung abandons any claim to a strict imitation of exterior reality and carries the spectator toward a more interior world of feeling and nonverbal expression. More than in any other genre, the disparate multigenericity of opera helps to dislocate the focus of attention from the object represented and representing (why are these people singing instead of talking? why all this unnatural acting?) to its effect on the subject (why am I here?). It is ultimately the effect on the spectator of all the components of opera—verbal, musical, visual—that makes opera the unique art that it is.

§ § §

If, when describing an opera or a *tragédie lyrique*, one must take into account all of the components I have mentioned, it is useful to give the main role among these components to music when defining opera.[15] There are other genres that feature many of its components (ballet), feature all of them except music (straight theater), or feature all of them without giving music the major role in producing the effect to which the text, acting, and other necessary components contribute (comedy-ballet, machine plays). In opera, as music and text struggle for preeminence, the key is often what Anthony calls "musico-dramatic organization" (*French Baroque Music* 100). Robert Donington's definition in *The Rise of Opera* makes this clear:

> To stage human characters in human situations so that they develop through their own inherent tensions and conflicts towards some sort of an inevitable resolution: this is drama [...].

> It is opera when a verbal text articulates a drama intended to be staged with full theatrical décor, to music which does as much as the words to develop the characters and situations all the way through to their final resolution. (18, 19)

An important distinction completes his definition:

> Drama is the essence of opera. Not, indeed, as drama happens (without benefit of music) in the great world outside; but as drama unfolds in those inner moods which so condition our experience of the outer world. (17)

---

[15] As Kintzler puts it, the world of opera "n'est pas définissable par le dénombrement des éléments qui le composent" (*Poétique* 186). Her approach is to go beyond an enumeration of ingredients to "une véritable recette," to find the way to "incorporer les ingrédients de l'opéra à la structure même de l'œuvre théâtrale, de leur donner une fonction poétique à part entière" (189). The "recipe" developed by Kintzler is part of her masterful demonstration of the place of the *tragédie lyrique* in the classical "moment poétique," independent of yet parallel to spoken tragedy, thanks to a "transformation poétique" (218).

Such definitions call attention to the difficulty of writing about opera when they borrow a literary term ("drama") as they try to show that opera creates drama more, or at least as much as, through musical than through literary means.[16] The understandable insistence on the words "drama" and "dramatic" to *define* opera often leads to a more problematic use of them to *interpret* opera, taking one away from a consideration of the overall effect of all the elements of an opera and leading to a concentration on plot, events, and actions. Such a narrow concentration can bring one to conclude that a well-constructed opera, like a well-made play, that contains built-up and released tensions, surprises, and a well-prepared denouement, could be considered successful even if it had no effect on the emotions of the audience. In a more balanced view, all of the components carry what Paul Robinson calls an "aesthetic weight" and must be taken into account (331). The weight can vary, and music can have an integral role without always having the main one.[17] This is obvious when one considers the semiotics of a genre where the spectator must observe and interpret words (their literal and figurative meanings, influenced by the delivery of the actor/singer), singing, instrumental music, actors (body movement, facial expression, gesture), sets (changes, machines), lighting, costume (changes, disguise), and dance. It is hard to imagine that music, even the combination of vocal and instrumental, can always capture 50 percent of the spectator's attention and thus be considered the principal element.

While this disproportionate emphasis on narrative, on plot and events is unfortunate when applied to any dramatic genre, it is especially so when applied to opera, because there are so many nonnarrative components that help create the total effect of opera: costumes and décor, for example, often dance, and many aspects of music, such as the difficulty of a vocal part and the beauty of a melodic line.[18] As Lindenberger

---

[16] See, for example, Kerman's *Opera as Drama:* "A work of art in which music fails to exert the central articulating function should be called by some name other than opera" (xiii).

[17] By "integral" I mean present from beginning to end of the work and contributing to the same effect as the other components.

[18] These components are nonnarrative (though one can certainly speak of narrative types of dance and music, such as pantomime or recitative) but certainly not nonrepresentational. They make a major contribution to the spectator's perception and conception of what is happening on stage (of the drama in its basic sense) but are related more to

suggests in a dual definition of "dramatic" that at first seems contradictory but is quite indicative of how the term is often used, those who invoke the analogy of music to drama "tend to stress the dramatic aspect of literature: music as expressive of strong emotion or as a dramatically conceived sequence of frequently unspecified narrative events."[19] It often happens that the part of his definition before the "or" is forgotten while the part after it is retained, perhaps because it is more difficult to analyze emotion than plot.

The various components that make up opera are there precisely to contribute to the emotional effect which has been the main goal of opera since its beginnings in Florence around 1600. The stated goal of opera's "inventors" was to create a music that would move the audience as much as the music of the ancient Greeks did (according to their writings). The emphasis was on the emotions, on the inner world, on representing the effects of the passions rather than external reality.[20] The reforms mentioned earlier, which were intended to return the emphasis of opera from virtuoso singing to its original goals, could be exaggerated and displace the emphasis too much toward the dramatic in the sense of the second part of Lindenberger's dual definition—a sequence of events, at the expense of strong emotion. Or rather, and especially in the nineteenth century, strong emotion came to be associated with action and a more realistic portrayal of characters. It is not that nineteenth-century opera neglects the emotional response of the audience—far from it—but that it often assumes that the simpler and less "realistic" means of the *tragédie lyrique* were insufficient to create a strong emotional response. And since most opera performed today is from the nineteenth century, our view is

---

responses to specific events than to the working out of the plot. It is ironic that it is critics with a background in music, such as Donington and Kerman who, in order to play down the importance of the words, deemphasize so many aspects of music as they insist on its dramatic aspects.

[19] *The Extravagant Art* 65. Spiegelman makes a similar distinction between "human drama" and "plot, conceived as a piece of narrative architecture."

[20] Kivy argues in chapter 1 of *Sound and Semblance* that it is more accurate—and probably a better translation of Aristotle—to speak of music as representing the emotions rather than imitating them. See also his *Osmin's Rage,* chapter 3. In what follows, the term "representation" should be understood in the context of mimesis, of what is often called imitation.

distorted and we are led to believe that early opera is not "dramatic" and thus not successful.[21]

Operatic drama involves tension and resolution not for their own sake but for the resulting emotional reactions. Just how the actions and characters are presented is of secondary importance so long as the audience feels the tension, becomes involved in the situation or tension and experiences an emotional reaction when it is resolved.[22] This is where the analogy between musical drama and literary drama is best, since both arts have their own kinds of resolution of established tension—melodies return to the tonic pitch, harmonic progressions reach an anticipated point of repose, a theme returns in a new context; questions are answered, identities revealed, misunderstandings removed. When music and literature work together successfully, the main point is not that each is dramatic in its own way, but that audiences react in similar ways to each kind of drama, that literature and music, along with the other components that make up opera, contribute to the same emotional effect. If they do, the opera is successful, and dramatic.

---

[21] Kerman, in his chapter on the "dark ages" of opera, says that "French opera was a stilted entertainment combining baroque excesses with the driest neoclassicism" and that its dramaturgy was "naïvely rigorous" (40). I have discussed his concept of drama more fully in an earlier version of this chapter, "The *Tragédie-Lyrique* of Lully and Quinault: Representation and Recognition of Emotion," pp. 117-18, and I will return to it in section 2 of chapter 6 (*Isis*).

[22] Rosen, who illustrates brilliantly in *The Classical Style* how much more interest there is in working out fairly simple musical material than in the materials themselves or in what "happens" at the end, makes a similar point about La Fontaine's *Fables:* "The morals of Aesop are not in themselves interesting today, and they were almost equally unimpressive in the seventeenth century, although people still had a taste for serious epigrams. What holds our attention in La Fontaine is how he arrives at the final banal significance" ("The Fabulous La Fontaine" 43). See also Rosen's discussion of drama in baroque music, *Classical Style* 69-80.

- IV -

The word *dramatique* in the seventeenth century was used only in
its literal sense, "en parlant de la poësie de téâtre" (Richelet), but the notion of expressing the emotions and of evoking an emotional response in
the audience with or without a tightly constructed plot was very present.
Ménestrier, discussing the "caractère de la Musique Dramatique" in his
1681 treatise on "Représentations en musique," described the principal
effect of the music in Greek tragedy and the desired effect of modern
"musique dramatique" as the expression of "les passions et les mouvemens de l'ame par les paroles, les inflexions de voix, les gestes, et les
images des choses" (81). There are similar statements about the goals of
such works throughout this treatise, making it clear that all the components of a dramatic musical work should contribute to the expression of
the passions and the moving of the audience.[23]

These components (*paroles, voix, gestes, images, actions, chant,
récit, mouvements du corps*) are much the same as those discussed in section 3—text, action, music, costumes, decor, dance—and they are also
those of the *tragédie lyrique* as Lully and Quinault developed it between
1673 and 1686. A brief overview of this new kind of theater will help understand its special nature and the reasons for its success, its similarities
to and differences from spoken tragedy.

Quinault's eleven libretti for Lully *tragédies lyriques* were read as
independent texts throughout the seventeenth and eighteenth centuries
and published frequently as "tragédies" either separately, in collections of
libretti, or in Quinault's collected works. In eighteenth-century editions of
Quinault's works, such as his *Théâtre [...] contenant ses tragédies,
comédies et opéra* of 1715, eight of the eleven libretti are introduced by a
title page with the descriptor "tragédie en musique," but there is a title at
the top of the page on which the first act begins which reads "Tragédie."
Even when printed as the text of an opera, Quinault's libretti were

---

[23] For Perrault, a great supporter of Lully and Quinault in the *Critique d'Alceste*, a
work is good "si elle divertit, si elle touche, si elle émeut" (100). Callières, though he
dislikes Lully's music and would prefer recitative recited by actors rather than sung,
offers a similar definition of the goals of dramatic music: "animer par des sons appro-
priées [sic] au sujet les grands traits de passion que le poëte doit y jetter dans ces sortes
d'ouvrages destinez à estre chantez" (269).

considered to belong to the same general category as the tragedies of
Racine.[24]

The subjects for the first eight Quinault-Lully operas were taken
from classical mythology, those for the last three from chivalric romances. According to Lecerf, "Quinault cherchait et dressait plusieurs
sujets d'Opéra. Ils [Lully and Quinault] les portaient au Roi, qui en
choisissait un" (2: 212). The best known examples of royal choice
involve the last three Quinault-Lully operas, but even if there was no
standard process for the approval of the subject of the earlier operas, the
subject of each new libretto was known well in advance, and Louis would
have had ample opportunity to object.[25]

The most typical plot involves a noble hero (Theseus or Perseus,
for example) who overcomes many obstacles, often with supernatural
help, and marries his beloved. One often finds the same relationship
among the main characters that William Brooks has discerned in Quinault's later tragedies and tragicomedies, where the two lovers are opposed to a jealous and vindictive rival or rivals ("Quinault Criticism" 44).
To take an example with well-known characters, Perseus is in love with
Andromeda, saves her and her country—with the help of Venus—from
Medusa and a sea monster, and wins her from his rival Phineus.[26] The heroes are usually able to reconcile their two main concerns, love and glory,
but there are notable exceptions, especially in the last two libretti, *Roland*
and *Armide*.

---

[24] The title pages of *Cadmus et Hermione, Alceste,* and *Persée* contain "Tragédie"
rather than "Tragédie en musique." Complete or selected editions of Quinault's theater,
which include libretti, were published in 1715, 1739, 1778, 1791, 1811-17, 1824, and
1882. The Ballard *Recueil général des opera* (1703-1745) contains all of Quinault's
libretti, as do the two *Recueil des opera [...]* published in Amsterdam by Wolfgang in
1690 and 1699. There were numerous collections printed outside of Paris—mostly in
Amsterdam—that bound together previously printed or reprinted libretti in order to meet
an increasing demand for these texts. See Brooks, *Bibliographie critique* B06-B09, C01-
C04, and Schmidt, *Livrets* xviii-xx and 484-551.

[25] For the choice of the subjects of *Amadis, Roland,* and *Armide,* see the opening
pages of the chapters devoted to each of these libretti, below. See pp. 131-32 of chapter
4 (*Thésée*) for a discussion of the approval of Quinault's libretti as he wrote them.

[26] There are important exceptions to this type of plot, especially in the three chivalric libretti where the hero is rather different from the mythological ones of the earlier
libretti, but these differences are of lesser interest here, since my emphasis is on the esthetics of the *tragédie lyrique* in general rather than on its evolution and its connections
with reigning ideologies.

It is obvious from this brief description of the plot of *Persée,* and especially from the fact that all the events mentioned are seen on stage, that the *tragédie lyrique* does not observe all the rules that classical tragedy does. Events that are found only in *récits* in spoken theater of the seventeenth century, such as the appearance of a monster or of a divinity or the descent of Hercules into Hades, were among the mainstays of the *tragédie lyrique,* especially in the *divertissements.* Machines were required to transport these nonhuman characters, and a different set was expected for each act. Unity of place was thus impossible, and the multiple exploits of the heroes—much busier even than Corneille's Rodrigue— made unity of time equally unfeasible. Unity of action was sometimes observed, but not in the first three Quinault libretti, which featured a servant—and often comic—couple parallel to the heroic one. It is not that the *tragédie lyrique* has no rules; Kintzler (281-97) has shown convincingly the importance of a "vraisemblance du merveilleux"—founded on a concept of nature and leading to *nécessité* and *propriété*—in the creation of a theatrical world that is recognized as fictional but nonetheless characterized by an order analogous to that of nature (as conceived by seventeenth-century science). It is not the world of Racinian tragedy, but it is certainly a world that existed parallel to that of Racine.

Quinault's libretti contain a prologue and five acts and average 1,039 lines and 6,121 words in length.[27] The five acts, with their diverse characters and events, present considerably more variety than one finds in spoken tragedy, though the basic types of scenes are similar: a character alone, two or more in conversation, or a group that reacts to what is said or is happening. Quinault used several forms and styles, not just to supply appropriate text for Lully but also to provide structure for the text.[28] He used varying rhyme schemes and combined alexandrines, associated with dramatic poetry, with the shorter lines associated with lyric poetry,

---

[27] Of the 1,039 lines, an average of 97 make up the prologue. By comparison, Racine's nine profane tragedies average 1,653 lines and 14,692 words (Bernet 40). In counting words, I have not included those in lines that are sung more than once, even though they are repeated in the libretto.

[28] See section 2 of chapter 3 (*Alceste*) for a discussion of the different styles that Quinault uses. As I will discuss in chapter 5 (*Atys*), the structure of a *tragédie lyrique* is both literary (length of lines and passages; tone; register) and musical (length; keys; recurring motifs).

including every length from two to eleven syllables. The words for the first two types of scenes (recitatives, dialogues, and monologues, for example) were written before the music, but always in collaboration with Lully and with careful attention to sounds and rhythms that could be sung with ease and effect.[29] The music never kept the words from being understood, but served to enhance the meaning and effect of the text.

The delivery, being sung, was formal and stylized, as was the acting. Most of the action took place at the front of the stage, and was expressed as much through standard rhetorical gestures (called "*action*" in the seventeenth century) as through what we would consider a realistic portrayal of what was happening. This stylization is hardly naive, but rather a sign of a keen awareness of problems of representation.

As Du Bos (1: 482), Turnbull (33), Gros (*Quinault* 587), and others point out, the *tragédie lyrique* "is designed to be seen as much as to be heard." Each of the five acts had a different set, and each act contained a *divertissement*, representing some spectacular action such as the descent of a god or a celebration. The staging and costumes—often complemented by elaborate machines[30]—were particularly lavish, and the text was no longer the "mistress" of the music. Quinault usually had to set words to music already composed by Lully, to be sung by soloists or choruses and, even more importantly, to be danced.

We think today of opera as being a combination of music and words, yet a *tragédie lyrique* is incomplete and indeed inconceivable without dance, an art that was probably more familiar to—and certainly more frequently practiced by—any well-born seventeenth-century person than literature, painting, architecture, or sculpture. It was not only a noble pastime and a reflection of universal harmony, but a way to show one's exterior and interior worth. To take a famous example, in *La Princesse de*

---

[29] Lully supposedly made Quinault rewrite many scenes, but for reasons more literary than musical; it was only *after* he finally accepted Quinault's text that he began to set it to music (Lecerf 2: 215). See section 5 for more details on the collaboration between Lully and Quinault; the discussion of the *divertissements* at the end of section 5 gives examples of the third type of scenes (groups), in which the music was written before the words.

[30] Detractors of opera suggested that the public was more interested in impressive machinery than in the music and action, and that much of the music was there only to cover up the noise of the machinery. This attitude is present at least as early as Corneille's *Examen* of *Andromède*.

Clèves Lafayette chose a ball for the first meeting between M. de Ne-
mours and Mme de Clèves, a scene carefully prepared from the beginning
of the novel. When they meet and become an instant object of admiration,
they are dancing, and not as one of many couples as in a modern ball, but
alone, under the careful scrutiny of the entire court.[31]

Quinault and Lully's accomplishment is not only to have developed a combination of music and poetry that can sustain a five-act drama,
but also to have made dance an integral part of this drama, an "expressive
medium and a legitimate dramatic tool" (Anthony, *French Baroque Music* 132). They did this by including, along with the fixed forms of noble
dance (minuet, gavotte, sarabande, etc.), expressive dances, including a
kind of pantomime, that represented the actions and emotions contained
in the libretto.

---

[31] McGowan's summary of the importance of dance in seventeenth-century France
is not exaggerated: "Ainsi, la danse selon les théoriciens du XVIIe siècle dépasse les
possibilités d'imitation des autres arts; elle peut tout exprimer, et représenter dans son
miroir de gestes et de mouvements la vie d'une époque dans toute sa complexité: sa
philosophie, sa politique et ses mœurs" (15). For more information on dance see Bonnet,
Cahusac, and Ménestrier, as well as more recent works such as Anthony, *French Baroque Music*, esp. chap. 8; Christout; Ellis; Harris-Warwick; Hilton; Kintzler, *La Pensée
de la danse à l'âge classique;* Lancelot; Marsh. Kintzler (*Poétique* 267-68) gives a good
summary of the arguments in favor of dance as an integral part of the *tragédie lyrique*,
as *vraisemblable* or necessary aspects of the action and as "moments de trouble et de
suspension," of joy before fear or anxiety before calm.

- V -

    Several important aspects of the *tragédie lyrique* have been mentioned briefly in this overview and merit further development: the text and the relationship between words and music, the plot and its socio-ideological implications, *vraisemblance* and the *merveilleux*, stylization, and the *divertissements*. For the texts (*livrets*), Quinault chose words that would be easily understandable when sung. He has frequently been criticized for his ordinary and limited vocabulary but as Perrault, in his *Parallèle des Anciens et des Modernes*, and many others were quick to understand, his vocabulary met the requirements of a text that is to be set to music, requirements that are quite different from those of spoken tragedy. According to Perrault and the Moderns, those who criticize Quinault do not know what music is, do not realize that one cannot understand all the words of a piece of vocal music. A word meant to be sung must be understandable even if a syllable is lost, and a sentence must be understandable even if some words are lost. To make this possible, the words in a libretti must be "fort naturelles, fort connuës, & fort usitées." This is exactly the type of vocabulary Quinault uses—"expressions ordinaires" and "pensées fort naturelles" (3: 237-42). Quinault's libretti are not simplistic and badly written but, as Voltaire and many others recognized, they are perfectly suited to the needs of opera as it was understood before the Revolution.[32]

---

[32] A comparison of the richness of the vocabulary of Quinault's libretti to that of Racine's tragedies, using the method developed by Bernet, reveals *Alceste* to be of about the same richness as *Bérénice* and *Alexandre*, richer than *La Thébaïde* and *Andromaque*, but less rich than *Iphigénie* and, of course, *Phèdre*. See also Giraud, "Quinault et Lully" 202.

    See Gros, *Quinault* 743-68 for praise of Quinault's style by Voltaire, Marmontel, La Harpe, and many other eighteenth-century critics. A passage from Eliot's *Adam Bede* (chap. 50) presents an interesting defense of "ordinary" words: "[...] the finest language, I believe, is chiefly made up of unimposing words, such as 'light,' 'sound,' 'stars,' 'music,'—words really not worth looking at, or hearing, in themselves, any more than 'chips' or 'sawdust': it is only that they happen to be the signs of something unspeakably great and beautiful."

Words and music

Quinault's texts were ideal for a composer such as Lully not just because they were understandable when sung but also because they provided suitable words for each situation, the appropriate sounds and rhythms, and phrases of the right length; there is, as Poizat points out, a "musique du livret" (223). I will discuss in more detail in the conclusion how Lully composed very much in the Platonic-Aristotelian tradition of the Florentine creators of opera in which music represents behavioral manifestations of various passions (see also Kivy, *Osmin's Rage* 29-30). These manifestations are largely linguistic, and Quinault and Lully wanted their characters to sound much as a person would in certain situations, that is, to use words and sounds that would be appropriate to the situation. As Lecerf put it, Quinault and especially Lully excell at writing "certaines réponses qu'il fait faire à ses chanteurs du même ton [...] que les feroit une personne du monde trés-spirituelle" (2: 196).[33] A few examples will suffice to give an idea of this complex interaction of words and music in a period when music was expected literally to fit the words.

First, however, it is necessary to offer a brief description of the different types of music used by Lully.[34] The most common, found in almost every scene, is recitative (*récitatif*), which can perhaps be best described as heightened declamation.[35] It follows the rhythms and intonations of the French language quite closely, featuring some melodic and rhythmic variety but falling short of true melody. The simplest type is

---

[33] Racine's son Louis makes a similar statement in his *Traité de la poésie dramatique,* adding the important distinction that Lully and other composers were more likely to base their music on the speech of actors ("habiles déclamateurs") than on the speech of certain members of society: "la déclamation est la première imitation des tons de la nature, au lieu que la musique est l'imitation des tons de la déclamation. L'habile musicien, quand il met des paroles en chant, cherche les tons que prendrait un habile déclamateur, et y ajoute ses modulations. La musique est donc une imitation plus éloignée de la nature que la déclamation; elle n'est que la copie d'une copie" (chap. X, 6; quoted in Regnault, "Que me parlez-vous de la musique?" 81).

[34] The best overall discussions of these "moyens du discours" are Duron's "L'Instinct de M. de Lully" 97-118 and Anthony's *French Baroque Music* 106-20. Duron's examples of *récitatif sec, d'action,* and *lyrique* are from *Alceste:* III.vii.635-40; II.ii.308-15; II.vi.422-24. See also Bouissou, *Vocabulaire de la musique baroque.*

[35] See Barnett, "La Rhétorique de l'opéra" 336-37. He cites the anonymous *Idées sur l'opéra* of 1764, "le récitatif n'est qu'une déclamation notée et embellie," and Bérard's *L'Art du chant* (1755), "le Chant n'est qu'une déclamation plus embellie que la déclamation ordinaire."

often called *récitatif sec;* in its most basic form it consists of a series of notes on the same pitch leading up to a different pitch at the end of the phrase, but it can—especially in Lully's later works—take on considerably more melodic freedom.[36] It is used for most conversations, from simple passages of exposition to the most serious discussions and disclosures.

When Lully—probably in conjunction with Quinault—decided he needed something more than basic recitative, the nexts steps were what Duron calls *récit d'action* and *récit lyrique.* The former is used for more animated discussions, calls to action, exclamations, and other such moments that stand out in a conversation. Musically, these moments are characterized by stronger rhythms, melodic leaps, and a greater sense of movement (at least temporary) toward another key.[37] The *récits lyriques* are also used for moments that stand out, but for reasons related more to emotion than to action. They allow the expression of a feeling, a brief pause on an *état d'âme,* and are almost like an *air,* though they never abandon the rhythmic structure of the text to take on a melody of their own.[38]

A special case of this song-like recitative is what I will call monologues, even though the character singing a monologue is not always alone;[39] they are sometimes found, for example, at the beginning of

---

[36] Lully's *récitatif sec* is quite different from the *recitativo secco* of Italian opera. One rarely finds in Lully's scores more than four consecutive notes in the same phrase on the same pitch, although some passages in the early operas, such as act IV scene iii of *Thésée,* contain five or six in a row. Italian recitative can contain as many as ten or eleven (be it Monteverdi's *L'Incoronazione di Poppea* or Verdi's *Nabucco),* and as many as six is quite frequent (Mozart, *Don Giovanni,* for example).

[37] "L'Instinct de M. de Lully" 101. "Le récit d'action [...] vit [...] sur la mobilité, sur une rythmique plus enlevée [...], sur un mouvement harmonique plus subtil cherchant à souligner un affect particulier."

[38] "L'Instinct de M. de Lully" 104-06. "Ce type de récit prend des contours très proches de ceux du petit air; des lignes se profilent, les angles s'adoucissent. Mais le rythme général demeure toujours tributaire du débit de la parole, et on n'y peut voir aucune reprise ou organisation intérieure fermée." This form is sometimes called *arioso* (Beaussant, *Lully* 576).

[39] Schneider ("Monologues") reserves the term for scenes when the character is completely alone. There is a variety of terms to describe these passages: "air-récitatif en rondeau" or "rondeau/récitatif" (Beaussant, *Lully* 567, 577), "monologue écrit dans une écriture récitative" (Duron, "*Atys*" 63), "recitative-monologue" (Newman 98-99). They are often labeled *récit* in Lully's scores, but this term can refer to any passage sung by a single singer. I avoid this term and its possible confusion with *récits* in spoken theater of

a scene with a confidant. The most obvious differences between mono-logue and *récit lyrique* are that the former have fuller instrumental ac-companiment and that they contain repeated lines, usually the first, which gives them a rondo structure, such as ABA or ABACA.[40] Monologues are usually reserved for key moments, such as "Espoir si cher et si doux" in *Atys* (III.viii), when Cybèle realizes that her love for Atys is hopeless. In this sense they are similar to arias in more recent opera; musically, however, they remain heightened recitative, for it would have been un-thinkable to interrupt these moments of emotional intensity for a song that departed from the rhythms and intonations of the text to create its own musical structure. A more apt comparison is to the great monologues in Corneille and Racine, which let out all the rhetorical stops but retain the basic form of the alexandrine.

Airs, which are full-fledged songs, as opposed to lyrical recitative, are found most often in the *divertissements* or in scenes with secondary characters. Duron calls the *airs* in this second type of scene "petits airs," and they are especially prominent in the comic scenes of the first three Quinault-Lully operas, where they add considerable variety to the recita-tive of the dialogues. When a main character does have a *petit air,* it is rarely at key emotional moments.[41] These *airs* have easily recognizable—and hummable—melodies and regular rhythms; in the *divertissements* they are often sung to the music of a dance one has just heard.

The collaboration between Quinault and Lully, as they prepared words and music for these various types of music, was very much a two-way street. In the librettist's "direction," words that a character would be likely to say needed music that would reflect, in a heightened way, the patterns of ordinary speech. For recitative, Quinault wrote the words and

---

the period, such as the "récit de Théramène" in *Phèdre,* used to describe action that has taken place off stage. Since events that are only described in classical tragedy are often shown on stage in the *tragédie lyrique,* there is little need for a *récit* in this sense.

[40] In a classic case of the exception that proves the rule, Armide's "Enfin, il est en ma puissance" (II.v), the most famous of all of Lully's monologues, is accompanied only by the continuo and contains no repeated lines.

Lully often repeated lines, or parts of lines, that Quinault did not repeat. This is par-ticularly common in the songs of the *divertissements,* but also in some passages that he treats as *petits airs.*

[41] In *Alceste,* for example, they occur at moments of temporary happiness for Ad-mète (III.iii.554-58) and Alceste (II.vii.438-42).

discussed them with colleagues before taking them to Lully. Lully suggested—or mandated—numerous corrections and, once he was finally
satisfied with the text of the recitatives, set it to music that followed
closely the rhythm and intonation of Quinault's words.[42] In French this
normally involves, among other things, pitches that rise until just before
the end of a phrase and slightly longer note values on key syllables in
phrases, in addition to less specifically French characteristics such as a
higher pitch at the end of a question or on an exclamation. Rhythmically,
the final syllable of a word or group of words would receive a relatively
longer note value than the words preceding it. The following two examples from act I scene vi of *Atys* show a phrase of simple recitative—at the
beginning of the scene, Atys is trying to conceal his emotion—and a *récit
lyrique,* a moment of emotional climax appropriate for much greater
melodic variety:

> ATYS: Sangaride, ce jour est un grand jour pour vous,
> SANG: Nous ordonnons tous deux la fête de Cybèle. (I.vi.141-42; fig. 1)

> Vous me perdez, Atys, et vous êtes aimé. (I.vi.181; fig. 2)

In the composer's "direction," words with appropriate sounds
were needed to match the rapid sounds of the speech of an agitated person
or the slow, languid tones of one of Lully's famous "sommeils" (sleeping
scenes). Compare the long notes and vowels of Le Sommeil in act III
scene iv of *Atys* to the rapidly rising and falling notes, wide leaps, and
phrases ending on an *e muet* as Atys is temporarily insane (act V scene iii,
an example of a *récit d'action*):

---

[42] Lecerf 2: 212-16. It is unclear just who Quinault's colleagues were; various
sources mention the Académie Française, the Petite Académie, Perrault, Boileau, Boyer,
and Mlle Serment; see chapter 4 (*Thésée*), 131-32, and Gros, *Quinault* 106-07, n. 9 and
174, n. 7.
    A tradition, which there is no reason to doubt, has it that Lully based his recitative
on the declamation of the actress La Champmeslé (Lecerf 2: 204) who, according to
another tradition, rehearsed her lines with Racine down to the appropriate *ton* for certain
words (Louis Racine, *Mémoires* 1146; Du Bos 3: 334). Singers were expected to be
aware of vowel length and to recognize which syllables in a phrase should be lengthened; see Bacilly, part 3.

Sangaride ce jour est un grand jour pour vous.

Nous ordonnons tous deux la Feste de Cy - bele,

Figure 1.

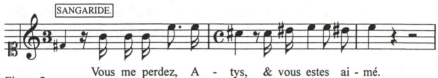

Vous me perdez, A - tys, & vous estes ai - mé.

Figure 2.

Dormons, dormons tous, Ah! Ah! que

le repos est doux! Ah! que le repos est doux!

Figure 3.

Quel desordre ? quel bruit ? quel éclat de ton -

ner - re ?

Figure 4.

Dormons, dormons tous;
Ah! que le repos est doux! (III.iv.456-57; fig. 3)

Quel desordre! quel bruit! quel éclat de tonnerre! (V.iii.920; fig. 4)

There are also physiological considerations, since each vowel is easier to produce at some pitches than at others and certain combinations of phonemes are easier to sing than others.

Plot

An emphasis on representing in music how a character would react in a given situation results in a conception of opera in which what happens to a hero or heroine is less important than how he or she sounds in reaction to an event. With few exceptions, operas are settings of an existing story, and audiences normally have at least a summary of the action before the performance begins; libretti were available throughout the seventeenth and eighteenth centuries and there was enough light for audiences to read them during a performance. Furthermore, rare is the operagoer, in the seventeenth or twenty-first centuries, who will not see several performances of the same work. What is going to happen to a character is a foregone conclusion in many plays and in almost any opera, especially those of Quinault and Lully, which were based on myths or romances familiar to the audience. Audiences are moved by the expression of emotion, and a "dramatic" performance obviously develops its tension, conflict, and emotion in other ways than by making the audience wonder what is going to happen at the end.

The public went to the Académie Royale de Musique not so much to be caught up in a suspenseful plot as to have their souls "alarmed"; this last word comes from Mme de Sévigné, who wrote on January 8, 1674, concerning *Alceste,* "il y a déjà des endroits de la musique qui ont mérité mes larmes. Je ne suis pas seule à ne les pouvoir soutenir; l'âme de Mme de La Fayette en est tout alarmée" (1: 661). This reaction is typical of most spectators—they were not there to gain deep psychological insights into the actions of the characters, but to be moved by their plights. In true Aristotelian mimesis, the spectator shares the feeling that the character—aided by words, music, staging and the other elements of the *tragédie lyrique*—represents. As Kivy points out, Aristotle is especially interested in how mimesis arouses appropriate emotions in the audience, just as Plato felt that "the spectator had as much to gain or lose from a musical imitation as did the composer and performer" (*Osmin's Rage* 34, 32). One does not have to hang on every twist of the plot to experience true musical drama.[43]

This relative lack of importance given to the plot is confirmed in seventeenth-century discussions of opera, such as Bauderon de Sénecé's *Lettre de Clément Marot à M. de *** touchant ce qui s'est passé à l'arrivée de Jean Baptiste de Lully aux Champs Élysées,* one of two satires written in 1688, one year after the death of Lully, which pit Ancients against Moderns and describe Lully's arrival in the Champs-Élysées to less than unanimous critical acclaim. Unlike Callières, the author of the other satire, Sénecé is willing to discuss "musique représentative" on its own merits. When he talks about opera, about the "assemblage" which makes up the *tragédie lyrique* (*chant, danse, décor,* etc.), there is no mention of plot.

Similarly, among Ménestrier's "ornemens des autres pieces de Theatre" are "le choix d'un beau sujet, une agreable disposition" (*Représentations* 167), but they are only two among the many means by which the opera expresses "les divers mouvemens de l'Ame," such as "de beaux vers, des sentimens tendres, des décorations propres, des changemens de scene, des voix rares, des accords de divers instrumens, & d'entrées de ballet." The action of an opera is different from that of a spoken tragedy:

> Il n'en est pas de ces actions [de la tragédie lyrique] comme des Tragedies où les sujets Historiques sont les plus propres avec des intrigues bien conduites & un enchaînement de Scenes qui se lient les unes aux autres [...]. (*Représentations* 239; see also Gros, *Quinault* 647 ff.)

---

[43] As Lindenberger puts it, going back to Longinus, the emphasis in opera "falls not on a work's relation to whatever reality it is imitating but on its ability to communicate its sublimity to its audience" (*Extravagant Art* 26; see also p. 132 and the quote from the entry on opera in Rousseau's *Dictionnaire de musique*). The terror that Aristotle insists on as one of the two principal aims of tragedy is the fear that something terrible may happen to *us* (*Poetics* 95; page 1453 in the standard Bekker edition).

Perrault also emphasizes the differences of genre. Toward the end of the *Critique d'Alceste* (99-100) he suggests placing opera in a separate—and modern—genre (which would include machine plays such as *Andromède* and *Psyché* as well as opera) "qui n'admist que des évenemens extraordinaires et surnaturels," in which spectators would pardon the absence of a tightly knit plot and in-depth development of character in return for being pleased, and especially for being moved, by effects generated by means other than complex words—gesture, pantomime, music, dance, machines, spectacular decor and costumes, etc.[44] In short, opera does not achieve its emotional effects so much by building carefully to an emotional conclusion as it does by expressing various emotions in loosely connected scenes. Precise plot details are less important than the opportunity to express "the essence of a narrative situation in musical terms" (Lindenberger, *Extravagant Art* 40), and the presence of an aria—or a Shakespearian soliloquy—that does not advance the plot is by no means a structural weakness. The *tragédie lyrique* does not paint emotions "dans toute l'étendue qu'elles demandent," as Boileau ("Fragment d'un prologue d'opéra," *Œuvres* 262) and most modern critics suggest tragedy should do, but expresses, represents recognizable emotions that affect the spectator.[45] As Batteux summed it up a half-century later: "Ce qui intéresse le plus n'est pas le fond même de l'action, mais les sentiments qui sortent des situations amenées par l'action" (303).

---

[44] Perrault returns in the *Parallèle* to the idea of a separate genre for opera and for tales such as that of Psyche, which "fournissent les plus beaux sujets, & donnent plus de plaisir que les intrigues les mieux conduites et les plus regulieres" (3: 283).

[45] This emphasis on the audience's perception of, reaction to a scene rather than on the place of the scene in a series of events is similar to what Todorov calls the "gnoséologique" type of "organisation du récit," as opposed to the "mythologique" (54). See also Labie's characterization of the *tragédie lyrique* as the "apothéose du lieu commun," a system designed to evoke in the spectator "un processus d'identification et de reconnaissance automatiques" (131). Forestier's remarkable *Essai de génétique théâtrale* shows convincingly that the Aristotelian notion of giving priority to plot in constructing a tragedy does not result in an emphasis on the psychology of the characters (63, 70) or in a neglect of creating emotional reactions in the spectator (13, 16, 66, 101).

Ideology

An important aspect of the Quinault-Lully *tragédies lyriques* is that their contemporaries often recognized specific court intrigues or general situations in the plots of these works.[46] The best known example is *Isis* (1677), in which Mme de Montespan thought she saw herself portrayed as an excessively jealous and vindictive Juno and persuaded Louis XIV to have Quinault replaced as Lully's librettist for the next two operas.[47] It is limiting, however, to read the Quinault-Lully *tragédies lyriques* only as a "simple reflet de l'image du prince" (Canova-Green 260) or as what Philippe Beaussant calls a "miroir encore plus exact" of the king (*Versailles opéra* 102). One definitely finds reminders of Louis XIV's power everywhere, especially in the prologues and *divertissements* (see the end of this introduction), but the presence of king-like gods and weak kings, of heroes who are sometimes invincible (Theseus, Perseus) and sometimes quite flawed (Roland, Phaeton; see chap. 9, 263-64), makes the political aspects of the *tragédie lyrique* extremely complex. For example, a literal reading in which Quinault's kings and/or heroes represent Louis XIV is not at all satisfactory. The image of the prince is far from always being positive (Brooks, "Lully and Quinault" 107)— Admète (*Alceste*) is an extremely weak king who takes second place to Alcide, and Célénus's vengeance on his rival-in-love Atys seems insignificant when compared to the tragedy of the two lovers. Nor is a literal reading in which the hero represents Louis XIV satisfactory—Louis is no longer a young hero embarking on great adventures, and Quinault's operatic heroes are often potential successors to the reigning ruler (*Thésée, Phaéton*).

As Jean-Marie Apostolidès suggests in *Le Prince sacrifié*, the *tragédie lyrique* should be understood not as a direct reflection of current events but as part of a changing "epistémé" and "esthémé."[48] Any ideological interpretation of the Quinault-Lully operas must take into account

---

[46] Girdlestone, *Tragédie en musique* 331, 336; Gros, *Quinault* 118-22.

[47] See chapter 6 (*Isis*), 186-89.

[48] Pp. 9-10, 128, 181, 58, 62, 80; see also his entry in the Hollier *New History*. The term "esthémé" is Kintzler's (*Poétique* 30-31, 522-26). For a discussion of relations between hero and king in epic poetry, see Jackson, Miller. I have dealt with this complex issue in more detail, but certainly not exhaustively, in "Le Héros contestataire dans les livrets de Quinault: politique ou esthétique."

the much larger issue of changing social, political, economic and esthetic systems in the 1670s and 1680s, in particular the relation between king and hero as both capitalism and the absolute monarchy of Louis XIV threatened the traditional feudal system. Few of Quinault's characters are able to realize the ideal presented in Racine's *La Thébaïde* (1664): "Régnez et triomphez, et joignez à la fois / La Gloire des Héros à la Pourpre des rois" (IV.iii.1141-42), and if young heroes such as Theseus and Perseus are definitely the center of attention in many of the Quinault-Lully *tragédies lyriques,* noble spectators must have viewed them nostalgically as a carryover from the heroic, feudal ideal of the preclassical period. This ideal no longer had its place under Ludovican absolutism, and mythological plots were less calls to action than a rethinking of values or, more generally, a manifestation of the universal theme of the hero on a solitary quest for meaning, individual fulfillment, and the benefit of society.[49] The heroic image that Louis and his court would like to present is thus present, but so are some of the problems already apparent by the end of the second decade of his personal reign, such as the dissatisfaction of many nobles and the struggles for succession to various European thrones. As Apostolidès suggests, "au niveau imaginaire [il] règne une pluralité de solutions," and classical theater "met constamment en scène l'origine de la situation présente" (*Le Prince sacrifié* 10; see also Marin 243 and Biet, *Œdipe en monarchie* 421-24 and *Tragédie* 108-09).

Another reason not to impose a limited ideological reading on the *tragédie lyrique* is that it remains primarily an esthetic phenomenon; too much insistence on ideology can introduce a "lien trop contraignant avec l'actualité" (Vuillemin 240), a "réalisme gênant" (Sweetser 658). No matter how much these works served to enhance the glory of the king and the nation, they reflect even more the esthetic and social changes that were taking place in the 1670s. The *tragédie lyrique* was of course designed to please the king, but also to please a public whose taste was greatly influenced not only by the slow-to-die feudal ideal of the aristocracy but also by the increasing presence of intelligent, well-read women.

---

[49] For more information see Gros, *Quinault* 664-78; Zweig; and Delmas's introduction to Corneille's *Andromède,* lxxxi and xcix-c. Bury (*Littérature et politesse*) offers an excellent presentation of the connections between heroism, nobility, *honnêteté,* and *galanterie.*

As Faith Beasley points out, in female-authored texts such as Villedieu's *Les Désordres de l'amour* (1675) and Lafayette's *La Princesse de Clèves* (1678), the king yields his central role to his subjects, often to women. Very much the same thing happens in the *tragédie lyrique:* the king is rarely the strongest character, love and gallantry become as important as heroic deeds, and sentimental motives become as important as political ones.[50]

Questions such as those of the ideological nature of the *tragédie lyrique* and of the influence of women on this new type of theater are complicated by the differences between the tragedies themselves and the prologues that precede them. While there are thematic links between the tragedies and their prologues, in most cases there is little connection between the plot of the prologue and that of the tragedy, and the prologue represents an obvious—if often pastoral, mythological and allegorical— glorification of Louis XIV and/or celebration of recent victories. One is thus tempted to conclude that the *tragédie lyrique* as a whole is devoted to the glorification of the king. I suggested above that this is not the case, and the discussions of individual works in the following chapters will furnish numerous examples of how this obviously propagandist mode of the prologues does not continue into the tragedies themselves.[51]

I will discuss the prologues in more detail in the next chapter; here, one example must suffice to show the dangers of interpreting the *tragédie lyrique* as simple royal propaganda or as a "school for royal mistresses" (Howard 198). In addition to glorifying Louis XIV, the prologue of *Cadmus et Hermione*, as well as those of several other Quinault-

---

[50] Beasley, *Revising Memory* 168. Kathleen Wine discusses the importance of exterior displays of *galanterie* in "Romance and Novel," p. 152. I will return to some of these changes in section 2 of chapter 10 (*Amadis*).

I would like to think that this preeminence of the esthetic value of the *tragédie lyrique* is obvious, but if it is not, the tremendous revival of interest in the music of Lully, Rameau, and other composers for the lyric stage of the Ancien Régime should suffice to make the point. For some important observations on this revival, see the comments by William Christie in part 2 of Labie. Christie insists, as do all seventeenth-century commentators, on the emotional aspects of the *tragédie lyrique*.

[51] See, for example, Ferrier-Caverivière 116. However, Apostolidès suggests that after *Phèdre* tragedy is supplanted by opera, which presents "un mythe conciliateur, unificateur dans lequel la notion même de conflit se trouve évacuée" (*Prince sacrifié* 181). Such a statement, while true for the prologues, does not hold for most of the tragedies, unless one neglects all the conflict that precedes the final resolution.

Lully operas, criticizes his wars.[52] Whether it is another example of the
growing influence of women or a more general expression of discontent,
the glorious image of the benefactor/king is somewhat tarnished when
Apollo/Louis XIV slays a monster (Python) that he has created himself
and is then too busy to stay for the celebration of his victory. Furthermore, even though Quinault insists that "Le sens allégorique de ce sujet
est si clair, qu'il est inutile de l'expliquer," can one take the allegorical
representation of Louis XIV at his word when he says "Ce n'est point par
l'éclat d'un pompeux sacrifice / Que je me plais à voir mes soins récom-
pensés"? Louis was hardly one to turn down praise; even in the prologues, a literal reading will not do.

La vraisemblance, le merveilleux
      The difficulties one encounters in trying to present a literal, overly
ideological interpretation of the *tragédie lyrique* can be seen as a consequence of its emphasis on the expression of emotion rather than on the
expression of ideas. Another consequence of this emphasis is that a conception of action and plot, which sometimes concentrates more on the
emotional content of individual scenes than on the sequence of events,
implies a similar conception of verisimilitude: one may find the action
invraisemblable, but not the emotions.[53] The plots of *tragédies lyriques*
often violate the most common type of *vraisemblance*, that which is concerned with the plausibility of the plot, with the probability of an action

---

[52] This criticism is even more obvious in the dedicatory epistle "L'Académie Royale
de Musique, Au Roi" that prefaces *Cadmus et Hermione* (see below, p. 52):
> Grand Roi, dont la valeur étonne l'Univers,
> J'ai préparé pour Vous mes plus charmants concerts;
> Mais je viens vainement Vous en offrir les charmes;
> Vous ne tournez les yeux que du côté des armes;
> [...]
> L'Empire où Vous régnez, sans chercher à s'accroître,
> Trouve assez de grandeur à Vous avoir pour Maître,
> Votre règne suffit à sa félicité,
> Souffrez qu'il en jouisse avec tranquillité. (1-4, 23-26)

[53] Denis de Rougemont makes a similar point about medieval romance: "[...] what
shall be verisimilitude in any given piece of literary fiction depends on the nature of the
passions which this piece of fiction is intended to please. In short, a reader pays no need
to distortions or to twistings of the 'logic' of current observation so long as the licence
thus taken produces the *pretexts* necessary to the passion which he longs to feel" (36).

taking place; this probability is based on the expectations of the audience, which in turn are based on shared cultural assumptions. To take the example of *Alceste,* spectators at the opera would certainly not find many of the actions of mythological heroes, heroines or divinities in conformity with what they ordinarily do or see happen, but they could recognize expectable emotional situations. Few wives choose to die for their husbands, yet Alceste's desire to sacrifice herself to save her husband is a recognizable emotional response. Even fewer wives are rescued from Hades by a doting Hercules, yet seeing such great virtue rewarded rarely fails to move an audience.[54]

Eighteenth-century writers are quite explicit about this "emotional *vraisemblance.*" For Du Bos, for example, "Il est donc une vérité dans les récits des Opéra; et cette vérité consiste dans l'imitation des tons, des accents, des soupirs, et des sons qui sont propres naturellement aux sentiments contenus dans les paroles" (1: 470).[55] Seventeenth-century practice and theory reveal the presence of this type of *vraisemblance,* even though discussions are less explicit than those of Du Bos and other eighteenth-century writers. In spite of the more or less obligatory references to the rules and to the utility of the theater and other arts, the seventeenth-century emphasis is on *plaire,*[56] *toucher,* and *émouvoir,* which means that

---

[54] See Perrault's discussion in the *Critique d'Alceste* of the reactions of contemporary spectators and Regnault (*Doctrine* 106): "Ce qui arrive à Phèdre ne nous arrivera jamais. Elle n'est pas un cas. Aussi pouvons-nous nous identifier à elle [...] sans problème". Parts of this paragraph are taken from my "Actions and Reactions: Emotional *Vraisemblance* in the *Tragédie-Lyrique,*" in which I discuss the *vraisemblance* of the Quinault-Lully operas in more detail.

A rather extreme statement of this combination of emotion and *vraisemblance* is found in Catherine Bernard's 1696 novella, *Inès de Cordoue:* Élisabeth de France, queen of Spain, who loved "les Vers, la Musique, & tout ce qui avoit du rapport à la galanterie" (6-7), proposes the telling of "contes galans" with two principal rules: "Que les avantures fussent toûjours contre la vray-semblance, & les sentimens toûjours naturels," since "l'agrément de ces contes ne consistoit qu'à faire voir ce qui se passe dans le cœur" (7-8); see Delmas, "Mythologie et mythe" 49-50.

[55] See Lecerf 2: 196, quoted above (25), about Lully's ability to find the appropriate tone.

[56] The classic statement of this esthetic is in Racine's defense of "le plaisir de pleurer et d'être attendris" in his preface to *Bérénice.* Writing to spectators who liked the play but thought it did not follow all the rules, he said: "Je les conjure d'avoir assez bonne opinion d'eux-mêmes pour ne pas croire qu'une pièce qui les touche, et qui leur donne du plaisir, puisse être absolument contre les règles. La principale règle est de

a tragedy or a *tragédie lyrique* must above all be *emotionally* plausible, *vraisemblable*. Even when writing about the spoken theater, theorists did not insist on the *vraisemblance* of a plot just out of a concern that the events of the plot seem real; they were concerned that a spectator would not have the appropriate emotional reaction if he/she did not find the events in conformity with the "sentiment ordinaire des hommes" (d'Aubignac 76-77).

Any consideration of the *vraisemblance* of the *tragédie lyrique* must also take into account the presence of the *merveilleux* which, as Kintzler has shown, has its own special *vraisemblance*.[57] All the Quinault-Lully operas included mythological or legendary characters, divine intervention and/or magic. As we have seen earlier (p. 32), Perrault suggested the creation of a new genre to include works such as opera and machine plays where the *merveilleux* plays such an important role, since he understood that *vraisemblance* in such genres is in reference to the accepted norms of mythology (*Critique* 99-100). Lecerf (1: 30-33) also pointed out the special *vraisemblance* of opera, not "en soi même" but "par l'usage": the poet "traite les sujets de la Fable, comme s'ils étoient véritablement historiques." Once again, the point of opera is definitely not to be true to "real" life, so there is no reason why the presence of the divine or the extraordinary should keep a work from moving the audience. Their presence certainly did not bother the spectators of ancient Greek tragedy, which was, after all, one of the models for seventeenth-century opera.

---

plaire et de toucher. Toutes les autres ne sont faites que pour parvenir à cette première." I will return to this passage in the conclusion, pp. 354-55.

Georges May's study of Galland reveals the presence of an "esthétique du plaisir" at the end of the seventeenth century, where creating pleasure for the audience becomes at least as important as the traditional didactic goals of literature; such an esthetic is clearly implied in the *tragédie lyrique*. May quotes Du Bos as one of the first to favor this esthetic explicitly (196-215, passim; see Du Bos 1: 77, 2: 339, 2: 381).

[57] See p. 21 above and *Poétique* 281-97, where Kintzler shows that the "vraisemblance du merveilleux" in the *tragédie lyrique* is as rigorous as "ordinary" *vraisemblance* in tragedy. Its limits are based, by analogy with "expérience réelle," on an "expérience pensée comme possible et représentable" (296). The result is a "visible jamais vu" (520).

Stylization

The emphasis on familiar and recognizable words, on reactions to recognized emotions, on how a person would sound in a given emotional situation, and on the *merveilleux,* together with the lack of emphasis on what we consider today to be a realistic plot, makes it hardly surprising that acting styles would be more emphatic, stylized, and rhetorical than realistic. Our knowledge of styles of acting, declamation, and singing in this period is unfortunately quite sketchy, but it is safe to say that Lully's singing actors preferred to use standardized rhetorical gestures, similar to the ones in paintings by Le Brun and others, rather than offer "realistic" portrayals of individuals.[58] I place "realistic" in quotes because, while such portrayals may not be realistic by our standards, they did reflect real emotional situations and responses. They were codified and, if you like, artificial, but they were based on recognizable physical reactions that accompany specific emotions. As a sign, as a representation, an arm raised in astonishment, for example, is no more removed from the object of its representation than is the exclamation "ciel!" or a leap to an unusually high pitch by an actor or a singer.[59] Most important, these gestures successfully conveyed a message while retaining dignity and formal beauty, what Biet calls a "noblesse du port" (*Tragédie* 59). In this way they were the ideal partner to Lully's music, suggesting to the audience what a person in a given emotional state would look like while the music suggests what he or she would sound like.

Foucault and others have shown that one of the main characteristics of the seventeenth-century world view is an acute awareness of the artificiality of our systems of representation. To express that observation in the terms of the the debate about opera, one could say that the words

---

[58] See Regnault, "Que me parlez-vous de la musique," for an excellent overview of the importance of rhetoric for seventeenth-century French theater and for important distinctions between singing and tragic declamation; he draws on documents from the papers of Racine's son Jean-Baptiste, published in Vaunois 199-211. Forestier, in the "Lire Racine" section of the introduction to his edition of Racine, insists on "l'irréductible *distance* de la représentation théâtrale," on perfecting the artificial in order to imitate nature (lxviii; his italics). See also Apostolidès, *Le Prince sacrifié* 38, 45-46; Barnett, "La Rhétorique de l'opéra" 344-48; Verschaeve; Fumaroli, "Le Corps éloquent."

[59] According to Du Bos, Racine taught La Champmeslé to lower the pitch of her voice in *Mithridate,* III.v.1112, so she could declaim the second part of the line an octave higher (3: 157).

and ideas of the language we speak do not necessarily represent reality any more than operatic mimesis does. Given the gap between us and the world, which no one system of representation can bridge, an art form like the *tragédie lyrique* that denies a realistic mode of mimesis is right on the mark; stylization is not naive but rather an effort to reach the essence of reality in a concentrated way, "plus stylisé et plus chargé" (Kintzler, *Poétique* 73).

The *tragédie lyrique* is also far from naive in that as it denies a realistic mode of mimesis it opts for an emotional one. The well-known, predictable plots created situations in which spectators could recognize familiar emotions, even if they did not find the situations familiar. The *vraisemblance* of the emotional situations and reactions is more important than that of the plot, the paradigmatic is more important than the syntagmatic. When one is more concerned with an inner reality found beneath the surface, with feelings more than with events, the presence of the *merveilleux,* of stylized acting, of singing kings and dancing soldiers need not be shocking.

Divertissements

The use of text, music, acting and staging to represent—in a stylized, often schematic way—emotional states and to move the audience was by no means the only goal of the *tragédie lyrique*. Each act had its scenes, much like those of spoken tragedy, in which characters reacted to events and to actions of other characters, but it also had its *divertissement,* in which the main characters were usually spectators to large-scale events involving many secondary characters. Here Lully took advantage of all the spectacular resources at his disposal—instrumental music, airs and choruses, dance, lavish costumes, machines, "changements de théâtre"— and created music that was quite different from that of the *récitatifs, récits d'action,* and *récits lyriques* described above (p. 26), where Quinault wrote the words first and Lully set them to music that followed closely the rhythm and intonation of declaimed French.

For the *divertissements* Quinault often had to fit words to music Lully had already written, often following a *canevas,* "certaines notes d'un maître de musique qui marquent au Poëte la mesure des vers de la chanson qu'il doit faire" (Richelet; see Anthony, "Lully" 317 and Lecerf 2: 218-19). In many cases the words were sung to a dance tune already played by the orchestra, and several stanzas were often set to the same music. Obviously, in passages such as the one below from act IV scene v of *Atys,* the music and words do not match as well as they do in the various types of recitative (see figures 1-4, p. 29).

> La Beauté la plus severe,
> Prend pitié d'un long tourment
> Et l'amant qui persévère,
> Devient un heureux amant. (IV.v.772-75)

La beauté la plus fevere   Prend pitié d'un long tourment,
Et l'Amant qui perfevere   Devient un heureux Amant;

It is here, of course, that Quinault's words often seem less than original, but this is part of the give-and-take involved in the collaboration between composer and librettist.[60] Furthermore, he was composing words for set, stereotypical situations where action and characterization were secondary. The point was for Lully's music to provide appropriate embellishment for the spectacle on stage and to provide the catchy tunes that were whistled all over France for a century.

    Here, music is no longer the slave of poetry. Just as the great *fêtes* at Versailles suggested a time and place outside of the unfolding of everyday events, so these *divertissements* often stood somewhat outside the developing events of the other scenes of a *tragédie lyrique.* This may seem like a weakness from the point of view of dramatic unity, but it was not necessarily so for Quinault and Lully's audiences, who appreciated pomp, ceremony, and the embellishments of their orators (even if they did not always agree with what was beneath this exterior splendor). Furthermore, just as the royal *fêtes* showed Louis XIV as a monarch above all others, so these *divertissements* showed Lully very much in charge of his

---

[60] Perrault said in his *Hommes illustres* that Lully especially appreciated Quinault's ability to write words for dance melodies he had already composed, "qui y convenoient aussi bien & souvent mieux que si elles avoient esté composées les premieres" (81).

collaborators. Whatever one thinks of the esthetic and dramatic role of the *divertissements* of the *tragédie lyrique,* they were necessary ideologically, a reminder of the power of the monarch and of his musician.

The *divertissements* were also necessary as a means of introducing dance into an art form in which "la danse va de soi [...]. Son évidence est telle que l'on ne songe même pas à s'interroger sur sa fonction poétique propre au sein de l'opéra" (Kintzler, *Poétique* 189). The first Italian operas produced in France, under Mazarin, often brought more glory to the French composers who wrote the music for added ballets than to their Italian counterparts, and nineteenth-century French audiences demanded ballet scenes in French operas and even in Italian operas produced in France, including such tightly constructed masterpieces as Verdi's *Otello.* These ballets were more or less well integrated into the action of the operas, but it is clear that in many cases the importance of the ballet scenes themselves often outweighed that of any contribution they might make to the plot (until, of course, "reformers" insisted that action was paramount and that dance, like music, could be admitted only if it contributed to a narrow notion of dramatic effect).

The esthetic and dramatic role of dance in particular and of the *divertissement* in general is certainly not negligible. That their staging and the music pleased the audiences is without doubt, and the following chapters will show how carefully Quinault and Lully constructed them to serve their needs. Quinault always found a way to relate these spectacular scenes to the plot, though their purpose was not always to advance the action—if the arrival of a monster who threatens the hero or the people increased the tension in addition to moving the action quickly forward, the celebration of a marriage or a victory served more to relax tension.[61] The music is more tuneful, more diatonic, less full of unexpected tones and harmonies, easier to remember. At the same time the hero can have a moment of respite before confronting his next obstacle, the lovers can have a moment together before jealous rivals threaten their happiness. As

---

[61] Kintzler, in her excellent discussion of how the general laws of theater apply to *divertissements* (*Poétique* 281-97), points out that "Les lois du contraste et de la progression dramatique croissante sont donc subordonnées à celle de la nécessité du merveilleux dans la tragédie lyrique" (285). For a good, brief example of a *divertissement* "combining the functions of spectacle and dramatic agent" see Anthony, "Lully" 321. Anthony also discusses the key structure of the *divertissement.*

in so much of baroque esthetics, the overall effect is one of opposing masses.

In this sense a *divertissement* that would seem to interrupt the development of the drama can be understood as part of a series of juxtaposed scenes of tension and relaxation that make up the drama on a larger scale. Furthermore, in an art form that placed more emphasis on the emotional reaction of the spectator than on the plot, these scenes have a direct effect on the audience's emotions, evoking not just feelings of joy (weddings, celebrations) or fear (monsters, charms of evil magicians) but usually admiration as well, an essential element of the "programme" of the first century of the *tragédie lyrique:*

> représenter de façon spectaculaire des passions enjouées et lamentables afin de produire chez le spectateur une passion primitive sans laquelle aucune autre passion ne serait possible: l'émerveillement, l'admiration. (Kintzler, *Poétique* 221)

For Descartes, admiration is "la première de toutes les passions" (*Les Passions de l'âme,* Art. 53), the passion we feel when we encounter something surprising or new, which is precisely the reaction of an audience when confronted with suddenly appearing divinities or impressive set changes. Many contemporary accounts express not only enjoyment of the music, dance, and staging but also astonishment at the technical achievements and novel artistic effects. As I argued at the end of section 3, it is the emotional reaction of the audience that is paramount, and from this point of view the *divertissements* are hardly the superfluous graftings that so many critics/gardeners would prune.

Descartes says that admiration has no opposite passion, since we consider the unsurprising "sans passion." It does have a counterpart, however, in the sense that much of the effect of the *tragédie lyrique,* and of the arts in general, is in the representation of easily recognizable emotions (passions). These emotions may be unsurprising and the characters' reactions to these emotional situations may be as predictable as the mythological plots, but the audience's recognition of these emotions and reactions is one of the principal goals of the *tragédie lyrique,* a key notion in its esthetic. *Divertissements* can thus be seen as forming an esthetic and emotional counterpart to the scenes that advance the action, an appeal to another type of audience reaction, to surprise more than to recognition. I will return in the conclusion to some of these key issues related to the effectiveness of musico-literary genres, such as imitation, representation, recognition, and in particular the audience's recognition of the emotions represented by the various components of the *tragédie lyrique*, but first it is important to take a closer look at how these components work together in Quinault's *livrets*.

1

Prologues

The King Comes First

- I -

THE PROLOGUES OF THE QUINAULT-LULLY OPERAS are at the same time separate from and linked to the five acts that follow. On the one hand, being devoted almost exclusively to the evocation of specific contemporary events and to praise of the king, they rarely contain more than a passing reference to the subject of the opera.[1] On the other hand, they introduce myths and themes that will occur in the tragedy itself and prepare the spectator for indirect allusions to Louis and his court. Though they are an integral part of the complex world of the *tragédie lyrique* (Cornic 48), their conception and orientation are quite different from those of the rest of the work, and they require a different approach for a satisfactory analysis (Reckow).

Much of their interest lies precisely in this ambivalent nature, in the way they allow a smooth transition from the everyday world of the spectator—seventeenth-century, twenty-first-century, or in between—to the special world of the *tragédie lyrique*.[2] It is difficult enough, in the

---

[1] Six prologues do not mention the subject of the opera at all, and those to *Atys* and *Persée* do little more than announce the name of the hero. Only the prologues to *Amadis, Roland,* and *Armide* establish thematic links between the prologue and the opera that follows. I will discuss these prologues later in this chapter, in section 3.

[2] See Duron, "Instinct" 65: "Le prologue permet la transition du réel au spectacle"; Néraudau, "Du Christ à Apollon" 21: "[...] les prologues, qui marquent le passage entre

spoken theater or cinema, to enter immediately into the world that one sees and hears on the stage or on the screen. The difficulty is compounded when the actors not only sing and dance but also represent larger-than-life heroes or divinities. In particular, the words are harder to understand, and it takes some time to become attuned to the multiplicity of systems of communication that reach our eyes and ears, all of which are to some degree removed from what we experience in the "real" world. Vocal and instrumental music, dance, costumes, machines, decors, all of these components convey messages that require decoding.

In this rather complex version of the mimesis that characterizes the esthetic of early modern France (whether one calls it classical or baroque), there are several levels of imitation at work. To take but one rather simple but basic example, between the spectator and his or her emotional reaction there is an actor using words to represent objects or ideas, plus poetic sounds, rhythms, and images and the melodies and harmonies of a vocal line to reinforce the representation. At the same time, instrumental music supports and/or supplements the vocal line, as do the actor's gestures and costume. Furthermore, the actor is in front of an elaborate set, designed not only to help situate the action but also to give esthetic pleasure and evoke admiration. It is also quite possible that the actor will be dancing, or surrounded by dancers, and perhaps transported by an elaborate machine. It is a lot to take in and to process, and the period of transition created by a prologue allows sufficient time for this processing to take place.

In this general sense, the prologue of a *tragédie lyrique* has much the same function as the preliminary moments of any linear art form—the preamble of an address, the opening pages of a Balzac novel, the introductory section of the first movement of a classical symphony, or the credits of a film. What sets Quinault's prologues apart is, to a large extent, the explicit allegorical encomium of Louis XIV—praise of the king because the king expected it (and was paying for it), but also because it was important to remind the spectators of the existing political situation

---

le réel et l'imaginaire"; and Naudeix 63: "une sorte de passerelle qu'empruntent les spectateurs afin de passer d'un monde à l'autre."

before presenting a play in which various characters present a threat to royal authority.[3]

Glorification of the king was of course common practice by 1673. By this time Louis, with the help of Colbert, Perrault, and the members of the various academies,[4] had accustomed his subjects to seeing his image everywhere, either in direct representation, in innumerable symbols and allegories, or in the splendors of his court and kingdom in general. To take but one example, the verses written for the various participants in the *ballet de cour* made explicit what the spectators could hardly help but notice. When the king danced the role of a shepherd in the *Ballet des Arts* (1663), his verses included:

> Voici la Gloire et la Fleur du Hameau.
> Nul n'a la Tête et plus belle et mieux faite,
> Nul ne fait mieux redouter sa Houlette,
> Nul ne sait mieux comme on garde un Troupeau,

Benserade hardly needed to add in the last stanza "Ce n'est pas tant un Berger qu'un héros."[5]

Just as one can see in the *ballet de cour* an early effort to combine poetry, music, and dance, one can see in its opening sequences a hint of what would become the full-fledged prologues of the *tragédie lyrique*. In two ballets of 1654, for example, Louis XIV appears as Apollo in the first entrée of the prologue of the *Ballet des Noces de Pélée et de Thétis* and is the subject of the opening *récit* in *Le Ballet du temps*, where Time and the four Seasons say "Nous n'égalons point la vitesse / Dont le plus grand des Rois / Va dans ses exploits" (1: 222). The verses Benserade wrote for Louis in the first of these ballets present him as "Plus brillant et mieux

---

[3] Among the many studies of the role of the theater in a monarchy, see Apostolidès, *Le Prince sacrifié* and Biet, *Œdipe en monarchie.*

[4] The Académie Française was founded in 1635, the Académie Royale de Peinture et de Sculpture in 1648, the Académie des Inscriptions et Belles-Lettres (Petite Académie) in 1663, the Académie Royale de Danse in 1661, the Académie des Sciences in 1666, the Académie Royale de Musique in 1669 (called the Académie d'Opéra from 1669 to 1672, when Lully took it over), and the Académie Royale d'Architecture in 1671. See Viala, *Naissance,* part 1, chapter 1. On the particularly important role of the Petite Académie, see Couvreur, *Lully* 43-52.

[5] Benserade 2: 605. On Quinault's role in this ballet, see Couvreur, "Collaboration."

fait que tous les Dieux ensemble" and as the conqueror of "ce Python qui désolait le monde (1: 181)."[6] As authors of court spectacles developed the art of royal praise to greater and greater heights, it must have become more and more difficult to find new vehicles to express the glory of the Sun King.

In his first opera, *Cadmus et Hermione,* Quinault followed the long tradition of using shepherds and pastoral divinities, but the high point of this prologue is the arrival of the Sun to destroy the monstrous serpent Python, send Envy back into her subterranean den, restore order and light, reassure the "danseurs rustiques," and set the stage for the celebration and *divertissement* that conclude the prologue. In the prologues to the rest of his operas, Quinault replaced the shepherds with a variety of gods, goddesses, and minor divinities, or with personifications such as Time, Peace, and Virtue. (The last three operas substitute for the gods of classical mythology the enchantresses and fairies of chivalric legend.) The prologue to *Cadmus et Hermione* represents at the same time an acknowledgment of the debt the new *tragédie lyrique* owed to the pastoral and a breaking away. The influence of the pastoral will remain, especially in the prologue to *Atys* and in the fourth act of *Roland,* but only as one element of a new whole.

The prologue to *Cadmus et Hermione* also differs from those of the following operas in that the character who personifies the king actually appears on stage:

> LE SOLEIL sur son char
> Ce n'est point par l'éclat d'un pompeux sacrifice
> Que je me plais à voir mes soins récompensés;
> Pour prix de mes travaux ce me doit être assez
> Que chacun en jouisse;
> Je fais les plus doux de mes vœux
> De rendre tout le monde heureux. (P.82-87)

---

[6] Canova-Green, in the introduction to her edition of Benserade's ballets, discusses these opening passages, pp. 14-15, and the evocation of royal power, pp. 28-25. Beaussant often compares the prologues of Quinault-Lully operas to the beginnings of court ballets (*Lully* 258, 307, 330, 343, 371, 524).

This is already one step removed from the ballets in which Louis actually performed the role of the mythological character that constituted a metaphorical representation of his glory. He had not danced in public since 1670, and one can already see by 1673 a tendency away from representations of the king as the Sun or as some other divinity. His image and his power were firmly established, and his encomiasts would rely more and more on representations of Louis in his various military, political, and social functions.[7]

Indeed, beginning with the prologue to *Alceste,* representations of Louis as a god will give way to allegorical references to "le Héros" or, less frequently, "le Maître,"[8] who incarnates virtue and wisdom and brings peace to France at the same time that he expands his kingdom through a series of glorious victories. It seems for a moment that Louis will appear in the form of Mars in the prologue to *Thésée,* but the god of war appears only to insure that "[...] rien ne trouble ici Vénus et les Amours" (P.42) and to announce that "Un nouveau Mars rendra la France triomphante" (P.69). Similarly, when Apollon appears in the prologue to *Isis,* it is to announce that "le Héros," though still away at war, will welcome "[...] [l]es Plaisirs et [l]es Jeux [...] Dans un asile heureux" (P.iii.60, 65). These representations of the king are indirect in the sense that he no longer appears as a character in the prologue, but in a way more direct and explicit in the sense that they refer clearly to a specific ruler in a specific time and place. When the Nymphe de la Seine opens the prologue to *Alceste* with "Le Héros que j'attends ne revienda-t-il pas?," she is thinking of the current ruler of the country through which the Seine flows, le "Maître de ces lieux" (*Thésée,* P.3), returning from an easily identifiable

---

[7] Hélène Himelfarb suggests that at Versailles in the 1680s the allegory of the Sun King is gradually replaced by "tantôt l'allégorie ouvertement politique [...] et tantôt la juxtaposition hédoniste de sujets de la fable sans programme systématique, dans le choix et le rapprochement desquels on soupçonne une influence croissante de l'opéra lullyste et postlullyste, forme dominante sans doute de la culture française à la charnière des deux siècles" ("Versailles, fonctions et légendes" 252). See also Néraudau, *Olympe* 229, where he comments on the new mode of royal representation and on the connection between opera and the paintings at Versailles. Néraudau discusses the prologue to *Cadmus et Hermione* and the appeal for peace on pages 154-56.

[8] The word "héros" appears 46 times in the 928 lines of the ten prologues that follow *Cadmus et Hermione.*

military campaign. His name is never given, but his exploits and virtues are more explicit than were those of the Sun in *Cadmus et Hermione.*

§ § §

As the above examples suggest, the prologues present more than one side of the king, more than one of his many qualities. Most obvious in the early prologues is his role as conqueror, specifically in the Dutch War that began in April 1672. There are no specific references to the war in the prologue to *Cadmus et Hermione,* only the obvious allegory of the Sun defeating the serpent Python. Beginning with *Alceste,* however, *Ludovicus trionfans* is everywhere:

> Le Héros que j'attends ne reviendra-t-il pas?
> Il ne te suit que trop dans l'horreur des combats;
> Laisse en paix un moment sa Valeur triomphante. (*Alceste,* P.19-21)

> Un nouveau Mars rendra la France triomphante,
> Le destin de la Guerre en ses mains est remis. (*Thésée,* P.69-70)

> Ses justes lois,
> Ses grands exploits
> Rendent sa mémoire éternelle. (*Atys,* P.7-9)

> Publions en tous lieux
> Du plus grand des Héros la valeur triomphante,
> [...]
> En vain, pour le troubler, tout s'unit, tout conspire,
> C'est en vain que l'Envie a ligué tant de Rois. (*Isis,* P.i.1-2, 7-8)

The king is ever faithful to his *gloire,* protecting his people and making France the ideal kingdom. Even Neptune sings his praises in the prologue to *Isis,* to celebrate the French naval victories in 1676.

Between *Isis* (1677) and *Proserpine* (1680), the treaties of Nimwegen brought the Dutch War to a triumphant conclusion and made Louis the "arbiter of Europe." The prologues now show him as peacemaker as well as conqueror: in the prologue to *Proserpine,* Victory frees Peace and puts Discord in chains in her place. Louis is still very much the conqueror, however, since "Il s'est servi de la Victoire / Pour faire triompher la Paix" (P.84-85).

After celebrating the joys of peace in the ballet *Le Triomphe de l'Amour* (1681), in which Venus "fait entendre que la paix est le temps destiné pour faire éclater la gloire de son fils" (opening stage directions), Quinault places more emphasis on a theme that will dominate the later libretti: the virtue and wisdom of Louis XIV. In the prologue to *Persée* (1682), he has not only brought peace to France, he orders La Fortune to be at peace with La Vertu (P.82-83). A "douce et charmante paix" is also an "heureuse intelligence" (P.138-39), that is, a felicitous harmony between rigorous Virtue and fickle Fortune. Even more flattering, perhaps, is the image of Louis in the prologue to *Phaéton* as the restorer of the Age of Gold. He assures justice as well as peace (P.76) and has retained little of his rather violent image from the earlier prologues:

> On a vu ce Héros terrible dans la guerre.
>
> Il fait, par sa vertu, le bonheur de la Terre.
>
> Sa victoire l'a désarmé;
>
> Il fait son bonheur d'être aimé. (P.82-85).

The prologue to *Amadis* also involves the restoration of happier, earlier times, since a "charme assoupissant" had overcome Urgande and Alquif "Jusqu'au temps fortuné que le destin du monde / Dépendrait d'un Héros encor plus glorieux" (P.38-39). The emphasis here is on "le grand art de régner" (P.48), since Amadis was thought to have been an exemplary king of Gaul.[9]

The last two prologues, in keeping with the emphasis in the last two operas on the dangers of love and the importance of duty, insist on the happiness and prosperity that "le Vainqueur" (*Roland*, P.44) has brought to his people. Peace is a time for innocent pleasures, but not specifically for love, as it had been in almost all the earlier prologues. Having expanded the boundaries of France (Peace of Ratisbonne, 1684) and

---

[9] Before the prologue to *Amadis* and after the introductory stage directions to *Cadmus et Hermione,* the only other mention of kings in the prologues is the "tant de Rois" allied against France in *Isis* (P.i.8).

vanquished the monster that represents the Protestant heresy (Revocation of the Edict of Nantes, 1685), Louis "se sert encor mieux / De la Paix que de la Victoire" (*Armide,* P.25-26), and this last Quinault prologue concludes that "C'est à lui qu'il est réservé / D'unir la Sagesse et la Gloire" (P.66-67).

§ § §

This combination of Wisdom and Glory is but one of many such pairs that provide a convenient structure for the representation of the various aspects of Louis XIV in these prologues. The most prevalent pair is that of war and peace, which is found in one form or another in all the prologues after that to *Cadmus et Hermione.* Like wisdom and glory, war and peace do not always coexist "peacefully," and it is only exceptional rulers such as Louis XIV who can use their military conquests to assure peace to their people. However, one could ask if such rulers are not so exceptional that they are unreal, if these panegyrics do not contain more than the usual dose of wishful thinking.

It is not just a question of whether France was really at peace, at a time when Louis's armies were in action every spring (and some winters, as Quinault points out in the dedicatory epistle to *Alceste,* E.13-14) and when it was inevitable that the periods of peace following Nimwegen and Ratisbonne could not last long. The question of the incompatibility of war abroad and peace at home is the first one Quinault raises in his libretti, beginning with the opening lines of the dedicatory epistle to *Cadmus et Hermione:*

> Grand Roi, dont la valeur étonne l'Univers,
> J'ai préparé pour Vous mes plus charmants concerts;
> Mais je viens vainement Vous en offrir les charmes;
> Vous ne tournez les yeux que du côté des armes.[10] (E.1-4)

---

[10] Quinault wrote dedicatory poems only for *Cadmus et Hermione* and for *Alceste.* Both have as their subject the absent king and neglected pleasures. Being addressed directly to the king, they are even more explicit than the prologues in their references to contemporary events. (The published scores for *Amadis* and *Roland* contain dedications by La Fontaine, though signed by Lully.)

Not only is peace necessary for domestic prosperity and for the arts to flourish, but royal support would be indispensable to the survival of the newly established Académie Royale de Musique. If Louis and the court were preoccupied with foreign affairs and absent each spring, at the moment when Quinault and Lully usually premiered the year's opera in Paris, the new *tragédie lyrique* would be lacking some of its strongest supporters.

Such questions of course represent a commonplace in works dedicated to the glory of a monarch. If Quinault portrayed himself and his libretti in the role of a neglected mistress, pining away while the king was at the front, it was little more than a not very subtle bit of royal flattery. However, such "complaints" about the wars of Louis XIV come precisely at the time when a few people were beginning to write—anonymous— criticisms of Louis's wars and of his expansionist policies (Ferrier-Caverivière 136-42). It is inconceivable that Quinault, especially in his first years as a librettist who depended on royal support and at a time when praise of Louis was almost unanimous, would write anything that could be considered criticism of the king. Yet, even if he suggests a period of peace only to "préparer des conquêtes nouvelles" (*Alceste* E.28), there is an undeniable element of criticism in the literal meaning of lines such as "Résistez quelque temps à Votre Impatience" (*Alceste* E.31) "Le Maître de ces lieux n'aime que la Victoire" (*Thésée* P.3).

This "criticism" is perhaps best understood in the context of the longstanding debate about the relative benefits of war and peace for a kingdom. Reservations about the excessive devotion of a king to war are common not only in sermons, but also in the harangues in the presence of the king by Quinault and other members of the Petite Académie.[11] They

---

[11] In his 1675 and 1677 harangues, Quinault asked Louis to spend more time on domestic concerns: "Demeurez au cœur de la France afin d'y pouvoir également animer tout ce qui doit agir pour vôtre gloire" (30 July 1675; *Recueil des haranges* 1: 379) and "La France n'a plus besoin que vous estendiez ses limites; sa veritable grandeur est d'avoir un si grand Maistre" (*Recueil des haranges* 1: 439; June 12, 1677). See Couvreur's discussion of the "appel à la paix," *Lully* 391-94, in particular the king's ambivalence about the contributions of peace to his *gloire,* and the quotation from Charpentier's *Panégyrique du roy sur la paix,* p. 393 (*Recueil des harangues* 1: 589; July 24, 1679). Criticism of Louis's wars is of course harsher later in the reign of Louis XIV. See, for example, book 5 of Fénelon's *Télémaque,* pp. 207-10, and his letter to Louis XIV (ca. 1694).

must have been so common that Louis would not take offense, but would rather consider them an important—if somewhat unpleasant—reminder of his duties and of the need for self-control. The latter is, of course, one of the most important themes of the tragedies themselves.

This hesitation between criticism and praise serves as a reminder of the dangers of taking everything in these prologues at face value. For example, when Quinault says, at the beginning of the prologue to *Cadmus et Hermione,*

> Le sens allégorique de ce sujet est si clair, qu'il est inutile de l'expliquer. Il suffit de dire que le Roi s'est mis au-dessus des louanges ordinaires, et que, pour former quelqu'idée de la grandeur et de l'éclat de sa gloire, il a fallu s'élever jusqu'à la divinité même de la lumière, qui est le corps de sa devise,

his comment doesn't really explain anything, and perhaps the allegory does require some elaboration. For Gros, "le sens allégorique du prologue [...] était facile à comprendre: ce Soleil [...] c'était Louis XIV terrassant la Hollande et ramenant partout la joie, les plaisirs, la tranquillité et la paix" (*Quinault* 529). Girdlestone finds the allegory equally transparent, but adds that "'Tu triomphes, Soleil, tout cède à ton pouvoir' n'est pour l'instant qu'un pieux souhait qui ne se réalisera qu'en 1678 avec la paix de Nimègue" (*Tragédie en musique* 60). Indeed, the Dutch resistance was strong, and Envy—in the form of other European countries who were forming an alliance against France—was hardly banished. Rather than see in the triumph of the Sun a specific military victory, the luster of which might be tarnished by future events, it makes more sense to see a general representation of Louis's power, be it military, political, or amorous. Why else would Quinault say that he needed to use the god of the sun, unless he meant his allegory to represent more than a military victory, no matter how exceptional this victory might have been?

- II -

In addition to creating much of the thematic complexity of the prologues, pairs such as wisdom-glory or war-peace provide their basic structure. From *Alceste* to *Armide*, most of the prologues begin with a complaint by one allegorical character that will soon be answered by a second allegorical character; the two characters usually form an obvious pair, often of two opposites. The two characters then reach a solution or compromise, and the prologue ends with a *divertissement* in which all the characters of the prologue sing the praises of love (or, in the cases of *Roland* and *Armide*, its dangers).

The prologue to *Alceste*, subtitled "Le Retour des Plaisirs," offers an excellent example of this structure. In front of the palace and gardens of the Tuileries, the Nymph of the Seine laments the absence of the king, who has left Paris for the battlefield, and the consequent absence of pleasure. Her "cruelle attente" (P.3) is emphasized by the seven repetitions of her opening line, "Le Héros que j'attends ne reviendra-t-il pas?," the last of which ends the first section (P.1-25). In the second section (P.26-46), she is reassured by la Gloire, who has appeared in a brilliant palace, accompanied by military music. Louis, who is of course almost inseparable from Glory ("Tu ne peux voir sans moi le Héros que tu sers," P.27) will soon return, after having forced the Rhine to submit to the Seine.[12] There will be no more cause for alarm, and the Nymph of the Seine, who had first seen la Gloire as her enemy, now joins with her to sing "Qu'il est doux d'accorder ensemble / La Gloire et les Plaisirs" (P.43-44).

A host of divinities arrive to celebrate this accord and the return of pleasure:

> La Nymphe des Tuileries s'avance avec une troupe de Nymphes qui
> dansent, les arbres s'ouvrent et font voir les Divinités Champêtres qui
> jouent de différents instruments, et les fontaines se changent en
> Naïades qui chantent. (P.47d)

---

[12] Lines P.31-32. This is one of a fairly small number of references to specific events; others include the naval victories mentioned in the prologue to *Isis* (P.ii.39-40) and the revocation of the Edict of Nantes in the prologue to *Armide* (P.27-29).

They sing the joys of love and of nature:

> L'Art d'accord avec la Nature
> Sert l'Amour dans ces lieux charmants;
> Ces eaux qui font rêver par un si doux murmure,
> Ces tapis où les fleurs forment tant d'ornements,
> Ces gazons, ces lits de verdure,
> Tout n'est fait que pour les amants. (P.49-54)

A "danse générale" concludes the prologue, and "les Plaisirs volent" to prepare even more *divertissements.*

This third and final section (P.47-88), of almost exactly the same length as the first two sections combined, completes a symmetrical AA'B structure in which two opening sections, of approximately equal length, are balanced by the third:

> A, 25 lines   Lament of the Nymph of the Seine.
> A', 21 lines   Reconciliation with La Gloire.
> B, 42 lines   *Divertissement,* love and nature.[13]

The general feeling at the end is definitely one of rejoicing, especially since the final chorus ("Que tout retentisse [...]," P.61) takes up approximately two-thirds of the final section. The opening opposition is not only resolved but almost forgotten, put aside by the exceptional qualities of a king who can go from one military conquest to another without neglecting pleasure and the arts. The spectator is now ready for a play in which glory and love, honor and pleasure, are reconciled (V.vi.944-45); in which the conflicts and dangers that appear in the first two acts are forgotten by the celebration at the end of the fifth; in which the exploits of Hercules guarantee the happiness of others.

The movement from conflict to resolution must therefore begin again. Before the first act begins, there is a repeat of the overture, a return to its predominantly sedate mood after the joyful and triumphant music

---

[13] In the 1992 Malgoire recording of *Alceste,* these three sections last six, three, and ten minutes, respectively.

that concludes the prologue.[14] Now that the prologue has prepared the spectator for the kind of play that is to follow, the repetition of the overture serves as a second beginning, the introduction of the main course. The spectator now has an idea of what is to come, and his/her appetite is whetted; the repeat of the overture comes to an end, and the play can begin.

This preparation of one of the main structural axes of the five acts of a *tragédie lyrique* by the basic structure of the prologue is an excellent example of how, as I said at the beginning of this chapter, these prologues are at the same time separate from and linked to the tragedy that follows—separate, since the five acts rarely contain allegorical characters such as la Gloire and la Paix, or references to specific exploits of Louis XIV; linked, since reconciliations such as those of glory and peace, or of glory and duty, will be important themes in many of the tragedies, and since gods and heroes in each of the tragedies will incarnate one or more of Louis's qualities.

§ § §

Before looking at some more examples of how the prologues prepare the tragedies that follow, it is important to insist on how different they are, no matter how tightly they are linked. Regardless of how many themes and structures they share, their orientation is radically different. The principal purpose of the prologues is an ideological one (to praise the king) whereas that of the tragedies themselves is esthetic (to evoke emotions and to move the spectator). The prologues are certainly not lacking in esthetic qualities—they are an integral part of the overall esthetic concept, they are beautiful to see and to hear, and they can be moving, especially when the opening opposition is resolved. Similarly, no one can deny the ideological aspects of the tragedies, even when they are considered in isolation from their prologues. However, to read them—or to

---

[14] In *Alceste,* the prologue ends in C major, while the beginning and end of the overture, as well as the beginning of act I, are in A minor. Although Lully does not always follow this key structure, the beginning of the overture is usually less celebratory than the end of the prologue.

watch them—as one would a prologue is to reduce art to propaganda.[15] Sévigné, La Fayette, and their contemporaries shed tears over basic human emotions, not over royal flattery.

Furthermore, one cannot approach the ideological content of the tragedies as one would that of the prologues, since the all-conquering and universally adored (except by his enemies) hero-king of the prologues is an allegorical construct, not a character in a tragedy. The closest thing to such a character is found in heroes such as Theseus and Perseus, but they are often in conflict with the king. It is not hard to see how one could flatter Louis by concentrating on the positive characteristics of these heroes, but one can neither read *Thésée* and *Persée* as examples of proper kingship nor identify the mature Louis XIV with these young adventurers.

It is even harder to find outstanding royal models in the other Quinault libretti. There are no real heroes in *Atys,* for example, and the king (Célénus) is preoccupied with his passion for Sangaride. Most of the other kings need help (see *Alceste, Thésée, Persée, Phaéton*), and the heroes of the later operas are overly ambitious (*Phaéton*) or subject to moments of madness and dissipation (*Roland, Armide*). Gods and goddesses such as Jupiter, Pluto, and Ceres (*Isis, Proserpine*) set equally bad examples, since they let their passions interfere with their duties. In short, perhaps the best one can do is to see this proliferation of potential royal models as an indication of Louis's exceptional nature, since it takes several characters to portray all his qualities. But this proliferation is also an indication of the exceptional nature of the new theatrical form that Lully and Quinault created, made up of so many different elements and open to so many different kinds of readings.

§ § §

---

[15] As Jean-Marie Apostolidès puts it, such readings "réduisent l'opéra à n'être que l'écho des événements contemporains et font de l'art un reflet, le ramènent au statut de l'idéologie" (*Le Prince sacrifié* 128). Even Apostolidès, however, relies almost exclusively on the prologues in his analysis of the "roi gestionnaire et triomphant" (181). For example, I could not agree more that the *tragédie lyrique,* in a sense, replaces Racinian tragedy, and that the prologue to *Alceste* represents, rather than a "univers sans médiation," a "mythe conciliateur, unificateur" under the control of a "roi gestionnaire et triomphant" (181). Yet the king in Quinault's tragedy (Admète) is neither *gestionnaire* nor *triomphant,* and Alcide, who is obviously meant to suggest many of Louis's qualities, remains a wanderer who in some ways represents a threat to royal authority.

The basic structure of the prologue to *Alceste*—a conflicting pair soon reconciled, preparing the way to a *divertissement* of general rejoicing—is found in most of the other prologues. It is a bit more complex in *Thésée:* the "Maître de ces lieux" has again abandoned "les Jeux et les Amours" for Victory, but Venus appears to recall them and announce Mars, who sends Bellone away. Mars sees no conflict, since Louis can pass, "au gré de ses désirs, / De la Gloire aux Plaisirs, / Des Plaisirs à la gloire" (P.82-84). A "magnifique divertissement" mixes songs of victory and love, war and peace.

In the prologue to *Proserpine,* Discord has put Peace in chains, but Victory descends to liberate Peace, punish Discord, and begin a joyous celebration of the peace that the "Vainqueur" has established; the only chains will be those of love. The prologue to *Persée* also concludes with a celebration of peace, with Virtue and Fortune in happy accord, but the only mention of love is a reference to Virtue as the "plus chères amours" of "le Héros qui calme l'Univers" (P.92, 85).

The prologue to *Persée* represents the beginning of a tendency to celebrate virtue more than love and to reduce the opening opposition. Fortune descends accompanied by a "bruit éclatant" and a "suite richement parée," only to announce the end of her conflict with Virtue: "Un auguste Héros ordonne à la Fortune / D'être en paix avec la Vertu" (P.83-84). In the next two prologues, the only oppositions are the replacement of a temporary, less than perfect condition by perfect happiness: in *Phaéton,* Saturn announces the return of the Golden Age, and in *Amadis* the enchantment of Alquif, Urgande, and their suite comes to an end as dawn gives way to the Sun. In both prologues, a final divertissement celebrates the joys of the new condition, emphasizing peace in *Phaéton* and love in *Amadis.*

The end of the prologue to *Amadis* represents the last positive mention of love in the prologues, unless one counts the unfulfilled expectation of the Chœur des Fées in *Roland* that peace will bring the return of "tendres amours" (P.25). In fact, the basic structure almost disappears in *Roland,* which is the shortest of the prologues.[16] Démogorgon

---

[16] The following chart gives the length, in lines, of each prologue and the number of characters that appear in it. In determining the number of characters, I have counted as a single character all those grouped in one line in the libretto, such as the "Chœur

announces the return of peace in line 5, and a *divertissement* celebrates
this news in lines 17-32. La Principale Fée then suggests a new *divertissement* in honor of the "[...] Héros glorieux / Qui prend soin du
bonheur du monde" (P.34-35), which the genies and fairies rehearse in
the concluding *divertissement*.

The prologue to *Armide* returns to the basic structure, as la Gloire
and la Sagesse finally decide that there is no need for rivalry between
them:

> Qu'un vain désir de préférence
> N'altère point l'intelligence
> Que ce Héros entre nous veut former:
> Disputons seulement à qui sait mieux l'aimer. (P.35-38)

The final *divertissement*, however, is not in praise of love and pleasure or
even of peace, but of Louis's glory.

The prologues to *Atys* and *Isis* are somewhat different from the
others, as are these operas in general—*Atys* is the most traditionally dramatic, the only one with a completely tragic conclusion, and *Isis* is the
least dramatic, the one with the largest number of scenes of pure *divertissement*. The prologue to *Atys* is also the first to mention the subject of
the tragedy to follow, which suggests that Quinault was trying to be inno-
vative, just as he was in not having a happy ending.

---

d'Amours, de Grâces, de Plaisirs, et de Jeux" in *Thésée* or "La Jalousie, la Haine, le Dépit, la Rage, le Désespoir, les Chagrins, etc." in *Proserpine*.

Prologue	Characters	Lines
Cadmus	16	135
Alceste	8	88
Thésée	18	128
Atys	19	68
Isis (3 scenes)	25	81
Proserpine	14	133
Persée	12	142
Phaéton	4	85
Amadis	4	73
Roland	3	63
Armide	4	67
Average	12	97

The prologue to *Atys* opens without any real conflict; indeed, lines 7-8 celebrate the same combination of Louis's justice and exploits that one finds toward the end of the prologues to *Amadis* (P.56-57) and *Armide* (P.62-63). Flora appears, in opposition to Time only in the sense that she is early,[17] hoping to find Louis before he leaves for the spring campaign; the songs and dances of the nymphs that accompany Flora make up the longest *divertissement* in the prologue (P.13-38). Then, instead of a reconciliation, Melpomène arrives to send Flore away and replace the pastoral with the tragic:

> Que l'agrément rustique
>
> De Flore et de ses Jeux
>
> Cède à l'appareil magnifique
>
> De la Muse tragique
>
> Et de ses spectacles pompeux. (P.46-50)

Combats between mythological heroes follow, which constitute another *divertissement*. Reconciliation finally arrives in the person of Cybèle, "pour accorder Melpomène et Flore" and to combine pure, natural beauty with that of the arts.

The prologue to *Isis* is unusual in several respects—though of less than average length, it has the largest number of characters (La Renommée, Neptune, Apollon, and their suites, including the nine muses and the seven liberal arts) and is the only one divided into scenes. It ends with a *divertissement* in which all the characters participate, but there is no opposition at the beginning. In the first scene, La Renommée and her suite sing the praises of "[le] plus grand des Héros," his exploits and his virtues. The next scene adds Neptune and his suite, to celebrate the naval victories of 1676 (Stromboli, Agosta, Palermo). The third and final scene brings Apollon, the muses, and the liberal arts to sing of "[l]es Plaisirs et [l]es Jeux" (P.iii.60), even though it is not yet time for peace. The mention of peace in a time of war is the only real opposition in this prologue, and it comes near the end.

---

[17] The personification of time operates on two levels here, that of the past (the prologue opens with "En vain j'ai respecté la célèbre mémoire / Des Héros des siècles passés") and that of a natural force that regulates the passage of the seasons.

- III -

These prologues, of course, do more than serve as a transition between the everyday world and that of the first act of a *tragédie lyrique,* more than remind the spectator of the political reality within which the heroes, gods, kings, and princes of tragedy will struggle with one another. In addition to introducing patterns of conflict and resolution, they introduce themes that will reoccur in the five acts that follow, and they sometimes make specific references to the subject of the tragedy that will unfold during these five acts. In the somewhat special case of *Cadmus et Hermione,* the serpent Python prefigures the dragon Cadmus must slay, and both monsters represent obstacles that must be overcome prior to the establishment of a new civilization. Furthermore, one can see in l'Envie the jealousy of Junon and Mars that will cause so many problems for Hermione.

One can even see the five acts of *Cadmus et Hermione* as "le reflet exact et agrandi de son prologue" (Couvreur, *Lully* 327). As Couvreur shows, both the prologue and the tragedy that follows have a ternary structure that can be described as a movement from peace to war and victory and then back to peace. Just as the Sun's victory over Python is framed by "divertissements champêtres," so Cadmus's victories over the dragon and the giant Draco are framed by "divertissements amoureux" in acts I, II, and V.

In a more typical prologue such as that to *Alceste,* the allegorical representations of pleasure and glory suggest the main lines of the tragedy in much the same way as do the mythological monsters and characters in *Cadmus et Hermione.* The prologue has as its title "Le Retour des plaisirs," and even spectators who did not read this title in the libretto could hardly help but notice the insistence on this idea at the end of the prologue:

> Nous allons voir les Plaisirs de retour;
> [...]
> Revenez, Plaisirs exilés; (P.84, 87)

and in the last act:

Alceste dans ces lieux ramène les plaisirs. (V.i.814)

[...]

Jouissez à jamais des plaisirs les plus doux. (V.vi.945)

Similarly, the reconciliation of the opposition between glory and pleasure that structures the prologue ("Qu'il est doux d'accorder ensemble / La Gloire et les Plaisirs," P.47-48) returns at the end of the tragedy. At the same time that part of the chorus rejoices in the love and pleasures that await Alceste and Admète, the other part sings of the glory and honor of Alcide:

Que {sans cesse l'Amour / toujours la Gloire} vous guide.

Jouissez à jamais des {plaisirs / honneurs} les plus doux. (V.vi.944-45)

Similar links between prologues and tragedies occur in all the Quinault-Lully operas, and I will mention many of them in the chapters devoted to each opera. In prologues with clear allegorical oppositions, such as *Proserpine*, it is fairly easy to see similar oppositions in the acts that follow—after a prologue which features la Paix, la Discorde and la Victoire, peace finally replaces the discord among Jupiter, Pluton, and Cérès, as the discord sown by the giants (Titans) is eventually overcome by Jupiter. In this case, the several mentions of the giants in the first two acts serve not only as a continuation of the theme of the prologue but also as a suggestion of various threats to the world order: jealous family members, the matriarchy, unbridled passion, or almost anything the status quo could consider infernal. To complete this cycle of references to the importance of order, the opera concludes with a specific allusion to the theme of the prologue:

Que l'on enchaîne pour jamais

La Discorde et la Guerre. (V.vi.1016-17)

In several of the later libretti, such as *Phaéton*, *Amadis*, and *Roland*, the absence of opposing allegorical characters sometimes makes the links between prologue and tragedy less clear. It is not obvious, for example, how the story of the fall of Phaéton is related to a new golden

age, or why a prologue that mentions the birth of the duc de Bourgogne should introduce a tragedy about an ambitious hero whose doubts about his birth lead him to his doom.[18] The link is perhaps more general and related to Ovid's treatment of creation myths in book I of the *Metamorphoses,* where the story of Phaéton follows those of Python and Io (the heroine of *Isis* and the mother of Phaéton's rival Épaphus). Furthermore, in this the last of Quinault's libretti based on classical mythology, it is tempting to see the end of a series of treatments of myths about threats to the world order, a series that began with *Cadmus et Hermione* and that features in particular *Proserpine.* In this context, the theme of "Le Retour de l'Age d'or" fits in very nicely.

In the other cases in which the connection between prologue and tragedy is less strong, the link is made explicit by a reference to the subject of the tragedy that is to follow; this is the case in *Atys* and in the last five libretti, except *Phaéton.* These references vary from simple statements of the subject of the tragedy, such as in *Atys* (the only one of the first six prologues to contain such a reference) and *Persée,* to considerable detail on how we should understand the story that is to follow, such as in *Armide:*

> Nous y verrons Renaud, malgré la volupté,
> Suivre un conseil fidèle et sage;
> Nous le verrons sortir du Palais enchanté,
> Où, par l'amour d'Armide, il était arrêté,
> Et voler où la Gloire appelle son courage. (P.52-56)

Except in *Atys,* which is different in so many ways from the other libretti, the hero mentioned in these explicit references is an obvious personification of Louis XIV, either in general, as in *Persée* ("Les Dieux, qui méditaient leur plus parfait ouvrage, / Autrefois dans Persée en tracèrent l'image," P.115-16) or *Amadis* (Louis is a "Héros encor plus glorieux," P.39), or because of a specific quality, as in *Roland* ("Montrons les erreurs où l'Amour / Peut engager un cœur qui néglige la Gloire," P.39-40).

---

[18] It could be, as Graves suggests, "an instructive fable [...], the moral being that fathers should not spoil their sons by listening to female advice" (42.d.2).

There are also more general references in several prologues to the tragedy that is to follow. In what seems to be an effort to create greater continuity between prologue and tragedy, the first four prologues after *Cadmus et Hermione* announce that a spectacle is to follow. This is presumably the tragedy we are about to see, though it is clear only in *Atys* and—especially—*Roland,* where the subject of the tragedy has already been announced. In *Alceste,* we find at the end of the prologue only "Les Plaisirs volent, et viennent préparer des divertissements," and *Thésée* and *Isis* contain similar statements in the stage directions about the "magnifique Divertissement qui va paraître" (*Thésée,* P.113d) or "la nouvelle fête" (*Isis,* end of the prologue). Even though these references remain somewhat vague, when one combines them with the more specific references to the subject of the tragedy in *Atys, Persée, Amadis, Roland,* and *Armide,* all but three of the eleven libretti (*Cadmus et Hermione, Proserpine, Phaéton*) contain explicit links between prologue and tragedy.

§ § §

These explicit links are really not all that helpful, however, since, like Quinault's comment about the allegory in the prologue to *Cadmus et Hermione,* they only underline the obvious. To take the example of *Armide,* which for many readers remains Quinault's finest libretto, there is so much more than just the moral lesson about how love can interfere with duty. If we were to follow the suggestion of the prologue to the letter, we would pay no attention to Armide, to the suffering and soul-searching that make her one of the most fascinating characters in any opera. Nor would we have any idea why spectators dared not breathe when she held her knife poised over Renaud (II.v), or why Rameau devoted so many pages to Lully's setting of this passage.[19]

The dangers of taking too much at face value are especially evident when one considers the ideological aspects of the prologues. The *tragédie lyrique* was created at what could be considered the high point of French civilization, a moment that saw not only the creation of its classical literature and the palace of Versailles, but also the beginning of many

----

[19] Lecerf 2: 329-30. Rameau's analysis is reproduced in Kintzler, *Musique raisonnée* 174-200.

of its modern structures. During the fifteen years of the collaboration between Lully and Quinault, from 1672 to 1687, a king who a few years before was fighting rebellious nobles and dancing in court ballets had established a monarchy and a bureaucracy that left him completely in charge, watching the nobility and his artists carry out his every wish. In the prologue to *Cadmus et Hermione* he is still the Sun, ushering in "jeux galants" and inspiring "les chants pleins d'appas" (P.88-90); in the prologue to *Armide*, he is called the "Auguste Héros" (P.2, 7, 12) and "le vainqueur" (P.16), but we know that he is aging, in bad health, and more devout than *galant*. He has followed "un conseil fidèle and sage" (P.53), avoided *volupté*, and revoked the Edict of Nantes, a decision that in many ways marks the beginning of the end. The prologues reflect all these changes, but only if one knows how to read between the lines, to keep in mind the complex political, social, and artistic context of the 1670s and 1680s.

Such a reading is beyond the scope of this book, which is concerned primarily with the esthetics of the *tragédie lyrique*. All I can hope to do here is to point out from time to time some of the ideological implications of Quinault's texts, such as his use of mythology, his choice of subjects and adaptation of sources, his portrayals of kings and heroes, or, more generally, how he presents the tensions and crises inherent in tragedy without offending his royal patron.[20] Quinault—like any writer in an age of absolute monarchy and institutional censorship—had to balance the esthetic and the ideological, artistic freedom and royal control (not to mention the balance between literary freedom and musical control). As an example of this balance, let me return briefly to an issue that is at the heart of these prologues: their links with the tragedies that follow and the implications of the one for the interpretation of the other.

A tragedy, even a *tragédie lyrique* about a glorious hero who overcomes all obstacles, is much more than a vehicle for royal praise. The playwright can bend his sources only so far, and he must establish characters and situations that form a satisfactory esthetic whole. His characters must remain within the logic of the play and within the bounds of verisimilitude, yet the prologue has made it very clear that we must not

---

[20] See, for example, the discussion above of the theme of the king who is so often away at war that he could be said to neglect the needs of his people, pp. 50-54.

forget the greater-than-life "plus grand des héros." Similarly, his characters can inspire in us a desire for a more humble version of their success and happiness, but the prologue has also made it very clear that our desires must remain secondary to those of the king. Just as it was difficult for Quinault to strike a just balance, it must have been difficult for a *vieux frondeur* such as La Rochefoucauld to watch a dramatization of the *gloire* that was once the privilege of his cast but now existed only in a royally approved representation by singers and dancers. Still, I would like to think that, like his good friend the countess of Lafayette, he was able to enjoy the beauty and the emotional power of the spectacle he was privileged to attend.

2

Cadmus et Hermione

A Recipe for Success

- I -

THE STORY OF THE BIRTH OF OPERA IN FRANCE is almost too good to be true. It seems inevitable and improbable at the same time, a logical development and a miraculous birth. Logical and inevitable because of a century-long tradition of combining theater, music, and dance in more and more well-integrated wholes; miraculous and improbable because of the increasing importance of an esthetic that privileged order, restraint, and unity of tone over individuality, exuberance, and the burlesque. In short, the debate over whether seventeenth-century France is classical or baroque is nowhere more appropriate than in the domain of musical theater—the period that literary historians call classical is known by historians of music as part of the French baroque.

It is not my intention to reopen this debate, which tends to resurface whenever one tries to compare two or more of the arts,[1] but to insist on the complexity and especially on the multigenericity of the *tragédie*

---

[1] Some of the earliest discussions of baroque style, such as Wölfflin's *Renaissance und Barock* (1888) involve the visual arts. The existence of baroque literature in France was hotly debated in the mid-twentieth century (Rousset). Today, one can be classified as "Kintzlérien" or "Beaussantiste," depending on whether one prefers to call the esthetic of the period of Louis XIV classical or baroque. To complicate matters even more, one can argue that the esthetic of the 1670s is more *galant* than *classique;* see chapter 3 (*Alceste*), section 2, and chapter 10 (*Amadis*), p. 300.

lyrique. To understand this new form fully, one needs to have studied not
only literature and music, but also dance, painting, architecture, costume
design, and mechanical engineering. So rich was this new art form, so
spectacular in every sense, that the story of its birth is far too complex to
present here in detail.[2] Still, in order to understand what Quinault and
Lully created in *Cadmus et Hermione*, some history is necessary.

When *Cadmus et Hermione* opened in the spring of 1673, the arts
in France were at a glorious peak. To mention but the most famous examples, Molière's brilliant career had just come to its premature end,
Corneille was working on *Suréna*, and Racine had just produced *Mithridate*. Boileau was about to publish the *Art poétique* and his translation of
the *Traité sur le sublime* (both 1674), and 1678 would bring the second
book of La Fontaine's *Fables*, Lafayette's *La Princesse de Clèves*, and
the definitive edition of La Rochefoucauld's *Maximes*. Le Vau had just
died, but Mansart, Le Nôtre, Le Brun, and Girardon were hard at work,
especially on the palace at Versailles.[3] The French language was beginning to take its modern form, and the written and spoken word was culti-
vated and appreciated in every domain, sacred as well as profane.

It is in this context that Quinault and Lully created a form that not
only combined the various arts but can be considered, without too much
teleological exaggeration, the culmination of a variety of experiments
with musical theater during the past century. At least as far back as 1570,
Antoine de Baïf and the other members of the Académie de Musique et
de Poésie were convinced that one could achieve the same miraculous
effects as those of ancient Greek theater by combining music, dance, and
"poésie mesurée à l'antique" in a dramatic spectacle. Attempts to realize

---

[2] In fact, the story has never been told in satisfactory detail, largely because of
lacking or contradictory sources. One of the earliest versions is Boscheron's biography
of Quinault, published in the eighteenth-century editions of his theater. La Gorce's
L'Opéra à Paris au temps de Louis XIV is a convenient overview of the early years of
opera in France, and Beaussant's *Lully* traces the early stages of the career of the most
prominent player in the story. See also the articles by Louvat, older works by Fajon, La
Laurencie, Nuitter and Thoinan, Parfaict, Pitou, Pougin, and Prunières, as well as the
works cited in note 2 of the introduction.

[3] The "Grande Commande" of 1674 marks a new era of royal construction and self-
glorification. See Néraudau, *Olympe*, especially pp. 225-28. The theme of cosmic unity
that is at the heart of Le Brun's plan has definite echoes in *Cadmus et Hermione*.

this dream can be divided, rather roughly, into the categories of ballet, spoken theater with musical interludes, and Italian opera.[4]

Dancing was so important in France during the Renaissance that it is hardly surprising that early efforts to develop a musical theater led to the *ballet de cour*, beginning with Beaujoyeulx's famous *Ballet comique de la Royne* in 1581. The key word is "comique," in the sense of theatrical, since these ballets were intended to tell a story, usually mythological.[5] A *livret* was distributed to the spectators, containing a plot summary, the text of the sung portions, and a few lines of verse (not to be performed) about each character and, later, also about the person dancing the role.

Lully's first involvement with music at court was as a dancer, and later composer, for these ballets. By this time, around 1653 (*Ballet de la Nuit*), the "ballet mélodramatique," which featured the unified dramatic action established by Beaujoyeulx, had given way to the "ballet à entrées," a series of episodes loosely related to a central theme and containing more and more sung *récits* to help explain the action. Less than ten years later, Lully would begin a collaboration with Molière that would include eleven comedy-ballets, moving toward—one can say with hindsight—a more complete integration of dance and music with comedy. *Le Bourgeois gentilhomme* (1670) is perhaps their greatest success and pushes the comedy-ballet close to the crucial step for the development of opera, that of having everything sung. In the realm of tragedy, an important step in this direction was taken with *Psyché* (1671), a "tragédie-ballet" by Molière, Pierre Corneille, and Quinault, who wrote the words to be set to music by Lully. This sumptuous spectacle, full of impressive machines and beautiful music, was also the best example, until this time, of "une interpénétration réussie entre musique et langue dramatique" (Louvat, "Le théâtre musical" 259).

Comedy-ballet is just one of several types of theater in the seventeenth century that included music. Although there was strong resistance

---

[4] La Gorce ("Les Débuts de l'opéra français" 140) includes a useful chart of how court ballet, tragedy, comedy, pastoral, and Italian opera can be seen as "leading" to *Cadmus et Hermione*.

[5] The narrative aspect was particularly strong in the "ballet de cour mélodramatique" between 1609 and 1621. See McGowan, *L'Art du ballet de cour*; Prunières, *Le Ballet de cour en France avant Benserade et Lully*; Yates.

on the part of writers such as Corneille and Saint-Evremond to "corrupt-ing" serious drama, including comedy, with music and dance,[6] it was not hard for playwrights and composers to satisfy the public's interest in these arts—and in the spectacular in general—by finding episodes in which it would be "natural" (given the conventions of the form) to intro-duce song and dance. The shepherds in pastorals, for example, which were popular early in the century and again from about 1660 to 1672, could be expected to sing and dance, as could participants in religious ceremonies.

An even more spectacular form, the machine play, enjoyed a tre-mendous vogue, beginning with Corneille's *Andromède* in 1650, and amazed spectators with gods and monsters that flew through the air or rose from the depths—accompanied, of course, by music. These works were so successful that, unlike pastorals and comedy-ballets, which dis-appeared rather suddenly in 1672-73, at the time when Perrin and then Lully founded the Académie Royale de Musique, they continued to enjoy success until about 1684 (the end of the run of a revival of *Andromède*, with new music by Charpentier). They would probably have continued longer without the numerous *ordonnances* of Lully limiting the number of performers, including one on July 27, 1682, eight days after the open-ing of this revival (Cessac, *Charpentier* 95-103).

It would seem, then, that by the 1660s all the elements for the creation of opera were in place—poetry, music, and dance of course, but also machines and spectacular sets. Still, the public and critics resisted having everything sung, even though the Italians had been doing it since the beginning of the century, in their efforts—like those of Baïf's Acad-emy and of the first *ballets de cour*—to recapture the emotional power of Greek tragedy. Mazarin had little success when he tried to introduce Ital-ian opera in 1645, though Torelli's sets and machines for Rossi and Buti's *Orfeo*, the first large-scale Italian opera staged in Paris (1647), were so popular the Mazarin and Anne d'Autriche commissioned Corneille's *An-dromède* so they could be reused. Somewhat more successful was Cavalli's *Ercole amante* (1662), again with a libretto by Buti, but the

---

[6] See Corneille's *argument* preceding *Andromède*, pp. 11-12 in Delmas's edition, and Saint-Evremond's Letter to the duke of Buckingham, "Sur les opéra."

public rebelled not only at its overly long and complex plot, but also at its "dry" recitative in a foreign language.

Efforts to combine poetry and music continued, however, especially in the poetic and theoretical works of Pierre Perrin,[7] the author of the words of M. Jourdain's beloved "Je croyais Jeanneton." His *Pastorale* of 1659, with music by Cambert, can rightly be considered what the libretto described as the "première Comédie Françoise en musique representée en France," and *Pomone*, which opened his Académie Royale des Opéra in 1671, was a huge success. Cambert was also the composer of the music of *Pomone*, as he would be for the next production of the new Academy, Gilbert's *Les Peines et plaisirs de l'amour* (February or March 1672). While these works were little more than a series of musical numbers, they showed that France—and the French language—were ready for theater in which all the words were sung. Lully and Quinault took the hint.

In 1672, with Perrin in financial difficulties, Lully purchased his privilege to operate the Académie Royale de Musique. At the risk of adding to the confusion that, for centuries, has surrounded this event and its consequences for French theater,[8] but that are relatively unimportant for an understanding of Lully and Quinault's artistic accomplishments, I feel obliged to point out that the standard histories of these events, in which Lully is always the key player, rarely mention how inconceivable it is that he would have decided to devote almost all of his considerable talent and energy to a yet unproven form if he had not been sure of the collaboration of a competent librettist. From a seventeenth-century point of view, there is no doubt that the *livret* is the key element in the success of an opera, and Lully must have consulted Quinault frequently before launching this complex and costly new venture.

Quinault was hardly an unknown in 1672. One of the most successful playwrights of the century, author of sixteen tragedies, comedies, and tragi-comedies between 1653 and 1671, he was a favorite of the *galant* society of the 1660s and 1670s, closely in touch with the sensibilities

---

[7] See Auld, *Lyric Art*, for a discussion of Perrin's career and for the text (in English) of his letter to Monseigneur della Rovera (1659) and the forward (in French and English) to his unpublished *Recueil de paroles de Musique* (ca. 1666). The French text of the letter is included in Pougin.

[8] La Gorce, *Opéra* 29-34, summarizes the question well and objectively.

of the potential audience of the new opera. If his contributions to most of the efforts to combine music and theater in the 1660s and early 1670s were not as extensive as those of Lully, who played a major role in almost every court ballet and comedy-ballet except *Le Malade imaginaire*, Quinault could write in 1684 that "il y a vingt-quatre ans que je travaille pour les divertissements de vostre Majesté" (Couvreur, "Collaboration" 9), and he stated in 1681 that he had known Lully well for twenty years (Campardon 2: 147). There is every reason to believe, as Couvreur suggests, that Quinault collaborated with Lully on several court ballets, before writing the libretto for the *Églogue de Versailles* (1668) and the passages of *Psyché* (1671) that were sung. We know also that the fifth act of his *Comédie sans comédie*, performed in 1655, contained a machine play on the subject of Armide and Renaud, and that he wrote a pastoral in 1660, *Les Amours de Lysis et d'Hespérie*, which is now lost. He thus had considerable experience with the predecessors of the *tragédie lyrique* (machine play, pastoral, comedy-ballet) and, between 1665 and 1672, was more involved with works involving music than with "straight" tragedy.[9]

It is therefore most probable that when, in 1672, Lully decided it was time to move from comedy-ballet to opera, the collaboration with Quinault was already a given.[10] With the two major elements in place, and the all-important royal support guaranteed, Lully and Quinault could turn to Beauchamps for choreography and to Vigarani to get a theater ready (La Gorce, *Opéra* 30-36). They knew that the public loved poetry, music, dance, spectacle, tragedy, and comedy; all they needed to do was put it all together.

That is more or less literally what Quinault and Lully did for the first work performed at the Académie Royale de Musique, *Les Fêtes de*

---

[9] On *Les Amours de Lysis et d'Hespérie*, see Gros, *Quinault* 62. Between the tremendous success of *La Mère coquette* in 1665 and *Les Fêtes de l'Amour et de Bacchus* in 1672, Quinault's contributions to the spoken theater are limited to *Pausanias* (1668) and *Bellérophon* (1671). During the same period, we know that his contributions to musical spectacles included not only the *Églogue de Versailles* and *Psyché*, but also the *Ballet royal des Muses* of 1666-67 and the *Carnaval* of 1668. See Ségalen's comments in Giraud, "Quinault et Lully" 208-09.

[10] Lully offered no explanation of his choice of collaborator when he wrote to Colbert on June 3, 1672, that he hoped to have "l'honneur de vous voir avec Monsr Quinault pour vous monstrer quelque projet pour le retour du Roy." See Charavay 112 and Nuitter and Thoinan 253-54.

l'Amour et de Bacchus, which opened in November 1672. Lacking time to create a new work, they created a pastoral by taking parts of works Lully had created with Molière, "ce qu'il y avoit de plus agréable dans les divertissements de Chambord, de Versailles et de Saint-Germain" (libretto, Avant-Propos). It includes parts of *Le Bourgeois gentilhomme*, *Les Amants magnifiques*, *George Dandin*, and *La Pastorale comique*, with dances by Lully and Des Brosses and machines by Vigarani. Quinault wrote several new scenes, as well as some material to link the borrowings together.[11] It is much more of a ballet than an opera, more closely related to the pastoral and to the machine play than to the *tragédie lyrique* that would be created a few months later.

When it came to creating their "premier grand Opéra,"[12] Quinault came up with something quite different, a tragedy (or rather, a tragicomedy, with noble characters and tragic situations but a happy ending) conceived to be sung from beginning to end and to incorporate dance, spectacle, and the supernatural. The form would certainly undergo development during the thirteen remaining years that Quinault and Lully would work together—in particular, Quinault would work the various elements of the *tragédie lyrique* into a more coherent whole—yet this first *tragédie lyrique* already has the basic form that Quinault, Lully, and their successors would follow for more than a century. This form, and especially the juxtaposition of the various elements, will be the subject of the second section of this chapter; however, the story of the creation of this first *tragédie lyrique* is not quite complete.

§ § §

The myth of Cadmus and Hermione was a brilliant choice. After years of wandering in search of his sister Europa, who had been carried off by Jupiter, Cadmus encounters an oracle that directs him to the site

---

[11] There was perhaps some help from Benserade, who for years had written the verses to be recited for participants in the court ballets. See Powell, "Pourquoi toujours des bergers" 194-96; Lecerf 2: 228; and Gros, *Quinault* 102-03 and 516-17; the latter two pages give details on Quinault's contribution.

[12] Lecerf 1: 164. La Vallière put it better: rather than being the first French opera, *Cadmus et Hermione* can be considered "comme l'ouvrage qui a fixé le goût de la Nation en ce genre et comme le modèle de celui que nous avons adopté" (Avertissement).

where he is to found the city of Thebes, teach men how to farm and mine, and introduce the alphabet. He must first kill a dragon, sow its teeth, and fight the armed men that spring up. The gods help him to accomplish these deeds and give him Hermione as his wife; their wedding is the first attended by all the gods. Once Quinault had adapted the myth so that Cadmus achieves his exploits for the love of Hermione, the story was perfect: a great hero through whom to praise the king, spectacular adventures, a tender love story, and a huge celebration at the end. Even better, this foundation myth suggests the creation of Lully's new Académie Royale de Musique, down to the detail of the hero-creator arriving from a foreign country. Quinault was not the first to combine Harmonie (Hermione), the daughter of Mars and Venus, with Harmonie, symbol of concord and harmony (Grimal 174).

As Quinault's emphasis on the love between Cadmus and Hermione suggests, he hardly followed the myth slavishly. He selected, rejected, and modified his sources as necessary, to satisfy the taste of the public and of the king as well as dramatic and musical needs.[13] For example, he conveniently neglects the continuation of the myth of Cadmus, especially Juno's hatred of his family and the long series of misfortunes that will fall on the royal family of Thebes, including Œdipus; it would hardly do to tarnish the image of Cadmus/Louis XIV as hero and benefactor of his people with a staging of his exile and metamorphosis into a serpent!

Quinault's primary source for *Cadmus et Hermione*, as it would be for *Thésée, Isis, Proserpine, Persée*, and *Phaéton*, was Ovid's *Metamorphoses*, a work immensely popular in the seventeenth century and the subject of numerous translations and commentaries. The story of Cadmus and his sister Europa occupies the end of book II and the beginning of book III, and it is perhaps more than coincidence that the story of Phaeton, the subject of Quinault's last libretto based on mythology, occupies a similar place in books I-II. Cadmus figures in a new beginning, after Phaeton had come close to destroying the universe, recently renewed after

---

[13] See Gros, *Quinault* 541-89 for a discussion of Quinault's sources and his use of them. In the case of *Cadmus et Hermione*, the cuts include almost all the details of Jupiter's rape of Cadmus's sister Europa and his wanderings in search of her. Additions include the giant Draco and the interventions of various divinities. Modifications include the timing of Cadmus's combat with the dragon and his sacrifices to Jupiter and Mars.

the deluge and Apollo's victory over Python, which is featured in the prologue to *Cadmus et Hermione*. Whether or not Quinault intended to write a "cycle," either in 1673 or in 1682 when he was writing *Phaéton*, the connection is striking, especially in light of the prominence of the theme of world order in so many of the libretti.[14]

The public, both at court and in Paris, certainly approved of the new spectacle: according to Du Tralage, it was a work that "tout Paris voulut voir et qui fit aisément oublier les operas de *Pomone* et des *Peines et Plaisirs de l'amour*" (72). *Cadmus et Hermione* was performed three or four times a week for at least six months in 1673, and revived in 1674-75, 1678, and 1679-80.[15] It is impossible to be sure of the date of the premiere—the *Gazette* suggests that the performance of April 27, 1673, was the first, but other sources give February or March as the date of the first performance. This is likely, since Lully and Vigarani's contract with the tailor François Bourgeois called for the dancers' costumes to be ready by March 9. There were performances in June and July, and they probably continued until November, when Vigarani had, according to the terms of the lease, restored the Jeu de Paume de Bel Air to its original state.[16]

Cadmus et Hermione remained popular enough to replace *Alceste* at the Académie Royale on October 31, 1674, and to continue until the Easter closing in 1675. It was included in the series of operas given before the court at Saint-Germain-en-Laye in January 1678 (but probably not at Fontainebleau in 1677), before a few more performances at the Palais-Royal. Lully revived it again at the Académie Royale in October or

---

[14] I will return briefly to the idea of the first eight libretti as a cycle at the end of chapter 9 (*Phaéton*).

[15] In this and other discussions of the history of performances of the various Quinault-Lully collaborations, I will give fewer details on the period after the death of Quinault in November 1688 (Lully died a year and a half earlier, in March 1687). A thorough account of later revivals, especially those after 1715, would require a discussion of eighteenth-century taste and of the changes—often considerable—to both words and music. See Rosow, "How Eighteenth-century Parisians Heard Lully's Operas."

[16] La Gorce, *Opéra* 41, 44-48. Several eighteenth- and nineteenth-century sources (see, for example, Parfaict, *Académie Royale* 92; Boscheron 35) say performances moved to the Palais-Royal in May or June 1673 (Louis XIV had granted Lully the rights to the theater on April 28), but the construction in November and December 1673 makes it more likely that the Palais-Royal was not ready until early 1674, for the premiere of *Alceste*. On the other hand, construction continued in 1674 (Gros, *Quinault* 107), so this argument is not conclusive.

November 1679, where it remained in repertory, in alternation with *Thésée* and *Bellérophon*, possibly until the following summer. After this remarkable success, it was not revived again until 1690 and 1691, after the deaths of Lully and Quinault. It had three more revivals during the eighteenth century, in 1703, 1711, and 1737.

The frequent revivals of *Cadmus et Hermione* during the 1670s are a good indication that *Cadmus et Hermione* held its own well against the later operas, including the immensely successful *Bellérophon* (1679). If it had been inferior to, or radically different from, popular Quinault libretti such as *Thésée* and *Atys*, it would certainly have died a quiet death.

- II -

Just as *Cadmus et Hermione* can be considered both a logical de-velopment—a culmination of various attempts to combine music and theater—and a miraculous birth, it can be seen both as a point of depar-ture for future *tragédies lyriques* and as a Minerva-like form, fully armed—if a bit awkward—from the beginning. It is quite true, as Beaussant says, that *Cadmus et Hermione* is best understood in relation to its antecedents:

> Tout est à inventer: il nous faut donc, si nous voulons la comprendre, mettre cette œuvre [*Cadmus et Hermione*] face à ce qui existe (l'opéra italien, la tragédie en machines, la comédie-ballet, la pastorale) en non à côté des opéras futurs, dont personne en 1673 ne sait ce qu'ils seront, ni même s'il y en aura. (*Lully* 504)

Yet, at the same time, there is no reason not to use hindsight in an effort to understand Quinault's libretti as a whole. The uniqueness of the *tragédie lyrique* is largely in its combination of various components,[17] and it is the means of combining these various components—and not the components themselves—that will change the most from one opera to the next. If I mention one libretto while discussing another, it is less to judge either than to reach a fuller understanding of them all. With all the differ-ent components that make up a *tragédie lyrique*, it is inevitable that one will receive more weight in one libretto that another, and this is only clear from the point of view of all eleven libretti.

Consider Quinault's task as he began to write the libretto for *Cadmus et Hermione*. He clearly felt that he had to work all of the

---

[17] See Robinet, June 3, 1673:
    Hé le moyen d'ici, déduire,
    Ce dont, à peine, peut instruire
    Un livre entier qu'exprez, l'on vend,
    Sur ce qu'on void, & qu'on entend
    Dessus cette Scéne admirable. (Brooks, *Théâtre et opéra* 143)
Among the elements that he cannot develop in detail ("déduire"), Robinet mentions the prologue, changes of scenery, machines, the tragedy by Quinault, ballets, and choral and orchestral music (*concerts* and *symphonies*). See also Romain Rolland's chapter "Éléments hétérogènes de l'opéra de Lully."

following combinations into his texts, forge some kind of unity out of considerable diversity:

1. poetry and music;
2. recitative, song, and dance;[18]
3. verisimilitude and the spectacular;
4. human emotions and the supernatural;
5. the serious and the comic, the noble and the burlesque.[19]

The first opposition, that of music and poetry, is obviously fundamental, but less relevant to a discussion of more general structural elements. For this reason, I will discuss Quinault's poetic styles in more detail in the next chapter and point out here only that Lully's music obviously required words that could express a variety of situations and emotions while remaining simple enough to be understood, that could be interesting in themselves without taking too much attention away from the music. There will be specific examples at every turn.[20]

In combining recitative, song, and dance, Quinault had the problem—or advantage—of combining three different means of expression;[21]

---

[18] In distinguishing between recitative—which is sung—and song, I mean to distinguish, in a very general way, between passages in which Lully set words written first by Quinault and passages in which Lully wrote dance tunes to which Quinault had to adapt his words. See the introduction, pp. 22, 27-30.

[19] All of these, in a way, can be grouped under the larger opposition of to please (music; singing and dancing; spectacular; supernatural; comic) and to instruct (poetry; recitative; verisimilitude; human; serious). Some of these contain the opposition between pleasure and instruction in themselves: poetry in particular, but also dance and comedy.

[20] For excellent discussions of stylistic elements in the words and music of *Cadmus et Hermione*, see Giraud and Rosow, "Articulations." My emphasis here is on the problem of combining different structural elements. I will look more closely at the organization of plot and at dramatic coherence in the chapters on *Thésée* and *Atys*, and at the structure of the *divertissements* in that on *Isis*.

[21] In the prologue to *Les Fêtes de l'Amour et de Bacchus*, Quinault gives special importance to the Muse Polymnia, in addition to Melpomene (tragedy) and Euterpe ("Harmonie pastorale"). The stage directions identify Polymnia as the Muse "qui preside aux Arts dépendants de la Géométrie, & qui a trouvé l'invention d'introduire sur le Theatre des Personnages qui expriment par les actions & par les danses ce que les autres expliquent par les paroles." The word *action* here refers to gesture and movement: "Se dit plus particulierement des gestes, du mouvement du corps, & de l'ardeur avec laquelle on prononce, on fait quelque chose" (Furetière). Among his examples, one finds "ce qui est le plus requis en un Orateur, c'est l'action." See Couvreur, *Lully* 287.

the solution in *Cadmus et Hermione* was to keep them mostly separate. Dancing is limited to the *divertissements*, where it can appear natural to find dancers entertaining or calming Hermione (I.iv; II.vi) or participating in a sacrifice (III.vi) or a marriage (V.iii). Quinault also had to make these scenes seem a natural part of the development of the plot, to integrate them into the action. He does so with considerable success, without relegating them to the end of each act, to a sort of *intermède*, as in a comedy-ballet. Only acts II and V end with a *divertissement*, though one could consider the interruption of the sacrifice in the last scene of act III as a continuation of the *divertissement* proper in the preceding scene, especially with the spectacular arrival of the furies and of Mars in his chariot.

The *divertissement* of Quinault's very first act is extremely well integrated into the action and even offers a solution to one of the main difficulties of writing a libretto, that of a lack of time to develop the motivations of the characters. Both Cadmus and Hermione look forward to the African dances, since it is their only means of expressing their love (they will not speak to each other until their *adieux* in II.iv). We do not know how their love began, but we do know that they have rarely been able to speak to each other of their passion. As Cadmus says,

> Ce divertissement, tel enfin qu'il puisse être,
> Me vaudra quelque temps le plaisir de la voir.
> S'il ne m'est pas permis de lui parler moi-même,
> Et d'oser dire que je l'aime,
> Du moins nos Africains, par leurs chants les plus doux,
> Pourront l'entretenir de mon amour extrême,
> En dépit d'un rival jaloux. (I.ii.70-76)

The *divertissement* thus becomes an opportunity for the spectators to witness one of their rare moments together and to feel that they know most of what there is to know about the love between Cadmus and Hermione. The African dances, indeed, do not even occupy the entire scene (iv), and we return immediately to the desperation of Hermione (I.iv.152-73) and to Cadmus's determination to save her (I.v).

The dancing is integrated even more thoroughly into act IV, since the action never stops. The *divertissement* in scene ii shows the struggle among the soldiers who spring up when Cadmus plants the dragon's teeth, a part of the myth that Quinault could not omit. There was a long tradition of representing combat in dance,[22] and this kind of pantomime fits in so well with the plot that the reader, if not the spectator, is hardly aware that there has been a *divertissement* at all. In fact, the stage directions do not mention dance, whereas those of the other four acts contain specific references to dancers.

The practice of limiting dance to the *divertissement* of each act is one that Quinault and his successors would continue to follow, with varying degrees of integration between the *divertissements* and the unfolding of the plot. On the other hand, the separation between recitative and song, rather extreme in *Cadmus et Hermione*, will become more flexible in future libretti, as early as *Alceste*, only one year after *Cadmus et Hermione*.[23] The first scene of *Alceste*, for example, combines the "Vivez, vivez, heureux époux," sung several times by the chorus, with the dialogue in recitative between Alcide and Lychas. The second scene consists of a short duet, and the third scene interrupts the recitative of Lychas and Straton with five brief airs. The first scene of *Cadmus et Hermione*, on the other hand, contains only recitative, as does the second scene, except for the two brief comic songs of Arbas (I.ii.56-59, 81-84). The act begins with eleven consecutive alexandrines, as if he were writing a spoken tragedy; this is an experiment—"mistake" would probably not be too harsh a term—he will never repeat.

The choice of the appropriate musical structure (air, monologue, duet, chorus, recitative, etc.) obviously lies to a great extent with Lully, but it also depends on the kind of poetry provided by Quinault. For example, by varying meter and line length he not only allows Lully to avoid monotony, but also to adapt his music to the dramatic situation. In such cases, Quinault's variety must also fit the dramatic situation, and his ability to create this appropriate variety is one of the keys to his success as a librettist.

To continue with the example of the first scene, the six-syllable line that finally interrupts the string of alexandrines is intended precisely

---

[22] For example, the *Ballet de Tancrède* in 1619 and the *Ballet de la prospérité des armes de France* in 1641.

[23] Beaussant (*Lully* 575) speaks of a "mosaïque discontinue" that is still found, though to a lesser degree, in *Alceste* and *Thésée*. See my introduction, pp. 25-27, for definitions of terms such as recitative, song, and monologue.

as an interruption, an objection: "Et cependant, seigneur, [...]" (I.i.12). Line 19 has a somewhat similar function, an octosyllable that breaks the rhythm of the three preceding alexandrines as Cadmus declares his intention to interrupt his search. The next speech (I.i.20-23) alternates lines of twelve and six syllables, offering Lully the chance to soften his music as the conversation turns to love on the softer sounds of "ce séjour" and "l'Amour."

It is the shorter lines, traditionally associated with lyric poetry and with song, that create the variety that allows Lully to avoid monotony in his recitatives and to introduce *petits airs* or *récits lyriques*, brief passages that, without being full-fledged airs or monologues, are more melodic than typical recitative. Lines 31-34 of this scene are a good example of the latter, as Cadmus describes the bearing and the beauty of his beloved Hermione. Even without looking at the score, this passage stands out, with its short lines and ABAB structure in which the alternating lines have the same syntactic structure and the same rhyme.

For moments that require greater emphasis, Quinault can provide a group of lines suitable for setting as a monologue, which one can usually recognize by their content and by their form. They offer the main characters an opportunity to express their emotions and are usually found in scenes in which the character is alone or with a confidant. More reflective in nature, they push recitative to the limits of song, but the words remain primary. They tend to contain more "singable" sounds, such as long vowels and soft consonants, and a variety of meters. Their most obvious characteristic, however, is the presence of at least one line—usually the first—that is repeated. In addition to emphasizing the state of mind of the character, these repetitions offer Lully a chance to create an easily recognizable musical structure, usually either a rondo (ABA or ABACA), by setting the lines to the same music each time they occur. There is really only one such passage in *Cadmus et Hermione*, Cadmus's "Belle Hermione, hélas! puis-je être heureux sans vous?" at the beginning of the last act, but they will be more frequent in subsequent libretti, especially in the role of Médée in *Thésée* (see chap. 4, 140, 142-44).

Cadmus et Hermione is hardly a string of identical recitatives, however, even if it is less varied than later collaborations between Quinault and Lully. Hermione opens the third scene of the first act with a passage that has the function of a monologue ("Cet aimable séjour, [...]")

but that has the form of a *petit air*.[24] It contains lines of six, eight, and twelve syllables, evoking her sadness with soft sounds such as those of "Offre du silence et de l'ombre" as well as her anxiety with harsher sounds such as "A qui veut éviter" (I.iii.87-88). Quinault offered Lully no repeated lines, but Lully took the hint offered by the interjection "Ah" after the only alexandrine in the passage to start a new section; both sections (I.iii.85-88 and 89-91) are repeated.

The famous *adieux* between Cadmus and Hermione (II.iv) also contain considerable variety. Hermione's first speech is almost a monologue, repeating the line "Ah! Cadmus! pourquoi m'aimez-vous?," but Lully does not dwell on the intervening lines (II.iv.321-25), treating them—as he had Cadmus's opening lines—as a *récit lyrique*. It is an effective beginning, as the lovers are somewhat restrained and formal at first (it is their first encounter in the opera) before becoming more passionate. And its effectiveness clearly has its point of departure in the dramatic rhythm of Quinault's text: the line-lengths of both speeches are fairly long at the beginning, then become gradually shorter in an exchange of octosyllables (II.iv.345-47), a divided alexandrine (349), six-syllable lines (355, 359), and fragments of three syllables (363, 366). It is an ideal form for a musical style that expresses moments of intense passion not with virtuosic, melodic arias but with declamation to which music gives great emotional force without losing contact with the normal rhythms and intonations of language, nor with comprehensibility.

The formal differences that separate these recitatives, *récits lyriques*, and monologues from each other are usually less marked than those that separate the scenes containing them from scenes consisting mainly of *divertissement*. In the latter, the lines are shorter and frequently *impairs*,[25] and there is more repetition, often of entire stanzas of a song. There is an appearance of greater metrical variety, since the line lengths vary considerably, but one does not always hear in Lully's music the rhythmic patterns that the words would suggest. Quinault was often following dance

---

[24] More specifically, it has the form of a *brunette*, AABB.

[25] Act II scene vi, for example, contains twelve 5-syllable lines as well as lines of 6, 8, 10, and 12 syllables. Lines with an uneven number of syllables are associated with lyric poetry and are rarely found in spoken theater, except in lyric passages such as choruses or *stances* or intercalated songs or letters, all of which began to appear less frequently after the 1630s (Hilgar 17).

tunes that Lully had already written and that contained their own rhythmic patterns, repeated numerous times, and he was sometimes obliged to force the natural spoken rhythms to fit the music.

For example, one would not expect the longest syllables of the first lines of the three songs in the *divertissement* of the first act (I.iv.127, 136, 144) to be the first and fourth, but the musical pattern imposes these accents.[26] An even more striking example is found in Charite's song in the last scene ("Amants, aimez vos chaînes," 726-33), in which fifteen of the twenty-four measures (not counting repeats) consist of a half note followed by a quarter note. Quinault does a remarkable job of fitting his verse to what is basically a string of iambs (there is an upbeat on the first syllable of "Amants"), but, in the last line, the *les* of *tous les maux* is twice as long as *tous* and *maux*. Misunderstanding between Quinault and Lully, or a conscious effort to insist on the independence of the music? One might even suspect an ironic pun on *maux* and *mots!*

§ § §

Several other juxtapositions that characterize *Cadmus et Hermione* and other *tragédies lyriques* involve the *divertissements*, which differ from other scenes not only by their formal characteristics and by the presence of dance, but also by the presence of the spectacular and the supernatural. Elaborate machinery had been popular at least since the Italian operas of the late 1640s and Pierre Corneille's *Andromède* of 1650, and Quinault could hardly omit it. The spectacular aspects of the *tragédie lyrique* go beyond the machines, however, to include the elaborate costumes and scenery that changed frequently and were constantly before the eyes of the spectators. If Quinault certainly felt obliged to include all this spectacle, in order to please both his wide-eyed public and his magnificent monarch, he was, at the same time, able to make it contribute to the overall effect of the opera, that is, to the evocation of various emotions in the public. I will look more closely at the role of the spectacular in the overall esthetic of Quinault's libretti in chapter 6 (*Isis*)

---

[26] The first two measures of each of these songs, as well as numerous other measures, have a rhythm of a quarter note followed by a dotted quarter note and an eighth note. The first and fourth syllables of each song fall on the dotted quarter note.

and thus limit the discussion here to how he worked the spectacular into *Cadmus et Hermione*.

He introduces it slowly, presenting all the main characters in the first three scenes and limiting the *divertissement* of the fourth scene to the Africans and giants that accompany, respectively, Cadmus and Draco. The decor of the garden is obviously magnificent, as are the costumes of the characters and of the dancers, but it is only in the last scene of the act, when Cadmus has decided to try to save Hermione, that machines are used to bring down Juno and Pallas in their chariots. The machines are almost relegated to a sort of *intermède*, without having a direct impact on the action.

The second act is organized in much the same way. The down-to-earth humor of the first three scenes has no more need of spectacular effects than do the poignant *adieux* of the fourth and Hermione's despair in the fifth. It is as if there is a conscious effort to reject the spectacular, since she has no interest in the *divertissement* that closes the act. Again, the only use of machinery is at the very end, as Amour flies off.

The spectacular plays a greater role in the last three acts. The third includes the dragon, a pompous sacrifice, and the appearance of Mars and the furies, all of which would require impressive special effects. The fourth act features not only impressive battle scenes (ii, v) but spectacular descents of Amour (ii), Pallas (v), and Juno and her peacock (vii). The last act could hardly be more spectacular, since it includes all of the gods of Parnassus who bring presents to Cadmus and Hermione during their famous wedding, which features Comus, "dieu des festins."[27]

This gradual increase in spectacular effects serves not only to build to an impressive conclusion, but to maintain a maximum of verisimilitude during the opening acts.[28] Much the same can be said about the use of the supernatural, since it is usually the arrival of gods and monsters

---

[27] Comus is a substitute here for Bacchus who, as the grandson of Cadmus and Hermione, could hardly attend their wedding. The entry in the *Encyclopédie* for Comus says that "Il y a tout lieu de croire que c'étoit le même que le chamos des Moabites, un beelphegor ou baalpeor, Priape & Bacchus." The editions of *Cadmus et Hermione* of 1673 and 1674 have Bacchus instead of Comus in the stage direction that precedes the final four lines, though it is Comus who arrives for the final celebration (preceding line 712).

[28] The supernatural, of course, has its own verisimilitude, what Kintzler calls "la vraisemblance du merveilleux." See my introduction, p. 21.

that offers a justification for the use of machinery and other special effects. In order to concentrate the spectators' attention on the human elements, Quinault downplays the role of the gods, in particular the hatred of Juno for the family of Cadmus and Hermione, for which he offers little explanation, and then only near the end of the opera.[29] There are no gods in the *divertissement* of the first act, and only Amour in that of the second. When Juno and Pallas appear at the end of the first act, it is less to show their quarrel than to call attention to the dangers Cadmus will face and to offer the most succinct statement in all eleven libretti of one of their main themes:

> Qui peut être contre l'Amour,
> Quand il s'accorde avec la Gloire? (I.vi.202-03)

By the end of the scene, Juno and Pallas are relegated to the background:

> Entre deux Déités qui suspendent mes vœux,
> Je n'ose résister à pas une des deux,
> Mais je suis l'Amour qui m'appelle. (I.vi.208-10)

The gods begin to play a more important role as the tasks of Cadmus become more difficult.[30] He slays the dragon without any evident divine help (III.iii) but, since Mars is not satisfied (III.vii), needs Amour to help him overcome the soldiers that spring from the earth when he sews the teeth of the dragon (IV.ii) and Pallas to help him defeat Draco and the other giants (IV.iv-v). Finally, Jupiter himself must put an end to his quarrel with Juno and ensure the happiness of Cadmus and Hermione (V.ii).

---

[29] Quinault mentions only Juno's jealousy of Cadmus's sister Europa and her quarrel with Jupiter for helping Cadmus:
> Le soin que prend pour toi mon infidèle époux
> Attire sur tes feux l'éclat de ma vengeance. (IV.vi.653-54)
He does not mention her preference for her son Mars, nor Vulcan's hatred of Hermione, the fruit of his wife Venus's affair with Mars.

[30] One could certainly see here a comment on the importance of religion and on the limits of royal power. Even if Quinault was consciously trying to make political statements, I prefer to concentrate here on the esthetics of the presence of the gods in opera.

In short, Quinault wants to have his cake and eat it too. He begins
Cadmus et Hermione very much like he would a spoken tragedy, with the
gods relegated to the background as a cause of human problems, but fills
the last two acts with divine interventions and spectacular effects. His
goal was to write a noble tragedy that could accommodate music, dance,
spectacle, and the supernatural, and one can hardly say that he failed. All
the elements are there, even if their combined presence at the end seems a
bit overwhelming.

§ § §

Of all the juxtapositions that one finds in *Cadmus et Hermione*,
the mixture of the serious and the comic, of the noble and the burlesque,
is certainly the most striking. It met with considerable opposition from
the beginning, though not enough for Quinault to eliminate the comic
immediately. He included several comic scenes in *Alceste* and *Thésée*,
though not quite so burlesque, and even added a delightful, gracious
comic scene to *Isis* (I.iv, between Mercury and Iris).

Robinet did not complain about the "Balets / Demi sérieux & fo-
lets" in *Cadmus et Hermione* (143), but the critics of *Alceste* include
among its defects "des Episodes ridicules, mal liez et mal assortis au
sujet" (Perrault, *Critique d'Alceste* 81). It is especially the eighteenth-
century critics who praised Quinault for eliminating these comic scenes,
an unfortunate leftover from Italian libretti, such as those of the Abbé
Buti for *Orfeo* and *Ercole amante*. To take but one example, Du Bos
wrote in 1719,

> Nos premiers faiseurs d'Opera se sont égarés, ainsi que nos Poëtes
> Comiques, pour avoir imité trop servilement les Opera des Italiens de
> qui nous empruntions ce genre de spectacle, sans faire attention que le
> goût des François ayant été élevé par les Tragédies de Corneille & et
> de Racine, ainsi que par les Comédies de Moliere, il exigeoit plus de
> vrai-semblance, qu'il demandoit plus de regularité & plus de dignité
> dans les Poëmes dramatiques, qu'on n'en exige au-delà des Alpes.
> Aussi nous ne sçaurions plus lire aujourd'hui sans dedain l'Opera de
> Gilbert & la Pomone de l'Abbé Perrin. Ces pieces écrites depuis
> soixante-huit ans nous paroissent des Poëmes gothiques composés

cinq ou six générations avant nous. Monsieur Quinault, qui travailla pour notre Théâtre Lyrique après les Auteurs qui j'ai cités, n'eut pas fait deux Opera, qu'il comprit bien que les personnages de bouffons, tellement essentiels dans les Opera d'Italie, ne convenoient pas dans des Opera faits pour des François. Thesée est le dernier Opera où Monsieur Quinault ait introduit des bouffons; & le soin qu'il a pris d'annoblir leur caractère, montre qu'il avoit déja senti que ces rôles étoient hors de leur place dans des Tragédies faites pour être chantées, autant que dans des Tragédies faites pour être déclamées. (1: 176-77)[31]

The comedy in *Cadmus et Hermione* is indeed rather low, and it is probable that most of the criticism was directed more at the nature of this comedy than at the inclusion of comedy in this new theatrical form. The principal comic characters are inherited from Italian comedy—the cowardly servant Arbas and the old nurse (sung by a male *haute-contre*). While definitely funny, they are neither subtle nor original, either compared to Molière's characters or to Céphise, Lychas, and Straton in *Alceste*, who at least have some personality and serve as an effective counterbalance to Alceste, Alcide, and Lycomède.

The nurse presents little interest beyond that of the standard aging woman in love, rejected by Arbas and ridiculed by her rival Charite.[32]

---

[31] See also Lecerf's Chevalier who, as he begins his attack on Raguenet's *Parallèle*, cannot understand why Raguenet would want to compare "le burlesque de *Thesée* et d'*Alceste*" to Molière's comedies. "[B]ien loin que Quinault puisse tirer de fort grandes loüanges de ses paroles plaisantes & boufonnes: la plus grande loüange qu'il ait peut-être méritée est d'avoir û enfin le bon sens de purger de ces fades boufonneries nos Opera, où nous les avions introduites à l'imitation des Italiens" (1: 8-9). Couvreur (292) points out that the Petite Académie, which Quinault joined in 1674 and which was probably the group mentioned by Lecerf and other sources as a testing ground for new libretti, could have had a role in convincing Quinault to eliminate these comic scenes all together.

It is important to note that this mixture of comedy and tragedy is not just a carryover from Italian opera; the combination of the serious and the light was an important feature of the "esthétique galante" with which the *tragédie lyrique* shares so many features; see Viala, *L'Esthétique galante* 33-34.

[32] Quinault will present an aging, rejected man in love in Égée (*Thésée*). He is less ridiculous than the nurse in *Cadmus et Hermione*, though it is hard to tell if he is less ridiculous because he is a male or because he is a king with several good qualities, while we know almost nothing about the nurse.

Her speech at the beginning of the third scene of act II is nonetheless successful, a clever parody of tragic style until the concluding line of contrasting familiarity:

> Il me quitte, l'ingrat, il me fuit, l'infidèle!
> Ne crains pas que je te rappelle;
> Va, cours, je te laisse partir;
> Va, je n'ai plus pour toi qu'une haine mortelle:
> Puisses-tu rencontrer la mort la plus cruelle,
> Puisse le Dragon t'engloutir. (II.iii.283-88)

Arbas has a more interesting, and considerably larger, role. He is almost always on stage with Cadmus, though his cowardliness is hardly necessary to highlight his master's courage. His first scene (I.ii) is especially effective and reminds us that Quinault had several successful comedies behind him, especially *La Mère coquette* (1665). Arbas's account of Draco's insistence that his giants dance alongside Cadmus's Africans introduces a touch of social criticism that remains relevant today, about high-ranking people who think that "la raison doit être au-dessus d'eux" (I.ii.56-59). Like Cadmus, we almost believe, in spite of the exaggeration, that he had been brave enough to react with "mille injures" and to call Draco a tyrant a hundred times until, twenty lines later, Arbas admits that all his comments were inaudible.

This delayed punch line is extremely effective and creates a striking contrast with Hermione's grief in the following scene, with her desire for peace and solitude. It was probably this kind of contrast that Quinault's contemporaries refused to accept in a tragedy, just as they could not appreciate the "irregularity" of Shakespeare.

Arbas has many more comic scenes, punctuating the action regularly from the second scene of act I to the first of act IV (where he "reluctantly" allows his master to sow the teeth of the dragon alone). He then disappears, except to sing, with the nurse, in the final *divertissement*. He disappears at the precise moment that the presence of the gods begins to increase, which suggests an interesting parallel between the use of the comic and of the divine to set off the heroism and love of Cadmus. The latter is of course far more valiant than his servant, but requires considerable help from the gods. In between the everyday and the supernatural, his heroism represents an ideal that was almost impossible to attain in the France of Louis XIV, where courtly ideals were fast giving way to absolutism and to bourgeois commercialism. His love is perhaps equally idealized, free of the quarrels that characterize the relations between servants and gods alike.

§ § §

Before leaving this series of juxtapositions, and in particular the mixture of comic and serious scenes, it is important to recall the intimidating presence of classical tragedy, as perfected by Corneille and Racine. I of course did not include it in the discussion above of the contributions of various combinations of music and theater to the development of the *tragédie lyrique* (pastoral, machine plays, Italian opera, ballet, and comedy), but spoken tragedy can nonetheless be considered the most important influence of all on the new art form. Quinault and Lully's operas aspired first of all to be *tragédies*, and one finds the word on the title page of all of the libretti considered here, and not always followed by "en musique" (*Cadmus et Hermione, Alceste, Persée*). To take advantage of hindsight again, in part that of eighteenth-century critics such as Du Bos, in order to acquire its *titres de noblesse*, opera had to emulate tragedy as much as possible, "le goût des François ayant été élevé par les Tragédies de Corneille & de Racine."[33] There was no question of eliminating music and dance from the new dramatic form, but other genres whose presence was quite noticeable in Quinault and Lully's first collaborations would be put more or less aside. This is particularly true of pastoral, though it would return periodically, as early as 1686 in Lully and Campistron's *Acis et Galathée*. Opera would remain a composite form, but, at least during the high tide of classicism that corresponds to

---

[33] *Réflexions critiques* 1: 176; the complete passage is quoted above, pp. 88-99. Beaussant says that a "velléité de tragédie [...] est toujours le but poursuivi" (498). Note, however, that performances of tragedies were often followed by performances of a brief farce and that, at court at least, music, dance, and even acrobatics were performed before or after a tragedy. In November 1684, for example, the *Mercure* reported that the chaconne from *Amadis* was performed before Racine's *Mithridate* (228-29), and Madame (Elisabeth Charlotte, duchesse d'Orléans) reported that on Nov. 3, 1700, acrobatics were featured between performances of Corneille's *Rodogune* and Molière's *Le Mariage forcé*. See Brooks, "From Lazzi to Acrobats," and Brooks and Yarrow 104, 187.

the years of the Quinault-Lully *tragédies lyriques*, it would never escape from the gravitational pull of Racinian tragedy, nor from the inevitable comparison with it.

3

Alceste

The Creation of a Style

- I -

THE SUCCESS OF *CADMUS ET HERMIONE* was a sure guarantee of a hostile reception for the next collaboration between Quinault and Lully, *Alceste*. The list that Beaussant gives of their potential enemies—elaborating on Perrault's list at the beginning of the *Critique d'Alceste*—is impressive:

> Depuis deux ans, depuis *Psyché,* et plus encore depuis *Cadmus,* Lully avait lésé et blessé trop de monde. Tous les auteurs de pièces à machines—Donneau de Visé, Guichard, Sablières, Sourdéac; tous les comédiens—ceux de Molière, ceux de l'hôtel de Bourgogne, ceux du Marais surtout, touchés de plein fouet; tous les musiciens lésés, tous les envieux, tous les anciens amis et leurs amis, tous ceux qui gravitaient autour de Guichard et de Sourdéac en particulier; et les ennemis de Quinault, c'est-à-dire toute la tragédie, non seulement Racine et Boileau, mais les Chapelain, les Pelletier, les Pradon; et autour de Racine les protecteurs de Racine, c'est-à-dire Madame de Montespan et Madame de Thiange, et parmi elles Madame de Sévigné [...] étaient liguées contre *Alceste*. (515)[1]

---

[1] Molière's troupe was forced to leave the Palais-Royal theater after Louis XIV gave Lully the rights to it on April 28, 1673, the day after he saw *Cadmus et Hermione*. In May, Molière's troupe negotiated with Sourdéac and the other successors of Perrin

It is hardly any wonder, then, that Claude Perrault could write on January 27, 1674,

> Nous allasmes hier, M^r. le Brun mes freres et moy, voir l'opera d'où nous sortismes tres satisfaits [...]; mais rien ne nous a tant estonné [sic] que la prevention et l'obstination à trouver tout cela miserable, que l'on voit dans la plus grande part des spectateurs. (*Alceste,* ed. Brooks et al., x)

It may well be that the Perrault brothers were equally determined to find the new opera admirable, but there is plenty of other evidence of a serious cabal organized against *Alceste.*

The new work had been awaited eagerly, however, and rehearsals very well received. In fact, Charles Perrault mentions the success of the rehearsals at court as one reason for the negative reception in Paris (*Critique d'Alceste* 80). One can follow this shift in the letters of Sévigné, who mentions the rehearsals as early as November 1673:

> M. de La Rochefoucauld ne bouge plus de Versailles. Le roi le fait entrer et asseoir chez Mme de Montespan pour entendre les répétitions d'un opéra qui passe tous les autres. (1: 627; Nov. 20, 1673)
>
> On répète une musique d'un opéra qui effacera *Venise.* (1: 627; Nov. 24, 1673)
>
> On répète souvent la symphonie de l'opéra; c'est une chose qui passe tout ce qu'on a jamais ouï. Le Roi disoit l'autre jour que s'il étoit à Paris quand on jouera l'opéra, il iroit tous les jours. Ce mot vaudra cent mille francs à Baptiste [Lully]. (1: 630-31; Dec. 1, 1673)

She added later, just before the first performances, that

---

and moved into the Jeu de Paume du Béquet (La Gorce, *Opéra* 48). The Marais theater specialized in machine plays.

Il y a déjà des endroits de la musique qui ont mérité mes larmes. Je ne
suis pas seule à ne pouvoir les soutenir; l'âme de Mme de La Fayette
en est tout alarmée. (1: 661; Jan. 8, 1674)

On January 29, however, she had changed her mind:

On va fort à l'Opéra, on trouve pourtant que l'autre [*Cadmus et Hermione*] étoit plus agréable; Baptiste croyoit l'avoir surpassé; le plus
juste s'abuse. Ceux qui ayment la symphonie y trouvent des charmes
nouveaux. (1: 686)

In short, the enemies of Quinault and Lully seem to have taken the
upper hand as soon as the rehearsals at court gave way to public performances in Paris at the newly renovated theater of the Palais-Royal, the new
home of the Académie Royale de Musique.[2] *Alceste* was hardly a flop,
however, since, as Sévigné says, "on va fort à l'Opéra." Performances
probably continued uninterrupted (except for the usual three weeks at
Easter) until the reprise of *Cadmus et Hermione* on October 30, 1674. It
returned to the stage of the Palais-Royal in early 1678, following a series
of performances at court (Fontainebleau, August-September 1677; Saint-
Germain-en-Laye, January 1678) and again in August 1682, continuing
until the traditional break before Easter, in late March or early April
1683. *Alceste* remained popular throughout much of the eighteenth century, with revivals at the Académie Royale in 1706-07, 1716, 1728, 1739,
and 1757, as well as at court in 1700, 1703, and 1754. It was finally replaced in the public favor by Le Blanc du Roullet's adaptation of Cal-
zabigi's libretto for the Paris version of Gluck's *Alceste* of 1776.

The most famous performance of Quinault's *Alceste*, however,
was at the lavish "Divertissements de Versailles," given from July 4 to
August 31, 1674, to celebrate Louis's return from the conquest of the
province of Franche-Comté. Just before the "medianoche" supper that
concluded the first day,

---

[2] These performances could have been as early as January 11, since Sévigné wrote
on Monday the 8th that "on joue jeudi l'opéra [...]." Other sources give the 18th or 19th
as the date of the first performance, however; the *Gazette* of January 20 records that
Monsieur, Madame, and Mademoiselle came to Paris on the 18th for a performance.

> Le Roy étant placé, les musiciens et les autres acteurs de l'Académie royale de musique représentèrent la tragédie d'*Alceste,* dernier ouvrage de sieur Quinault, qui reçut de toute la cour la même approbation que cette excellente pièce en a toujours eue; et la musique reçut les mêmes applaudissements qu'on donne toujours aux productions du sieur de Lulli. (Félibien 115)

Félibien's wording is interesting. First, as is frequently the case in the seventeenth century, the primary authorship of the opera—called simply a *tragédie*—is given to Quinault. Second, Félibien's comment that the *court* has always appreciated *Alceste* seems to be a specific reference to the cabal in town. Finally, one could infer that, for Félibien, the objections to *Alceste* were more to the libretto than to the music, which is mentioned after Quinault and after the suggestion that the court's appreciation was not universally shared.

This last inference is in fact quite probable, since the considerable "querelle d'*Alceste*" that broke out immediately after the first performances is basically a literary quarrel, largely because Quinault had chosen as his subject a myth that had already inspired one of Euripides's great tragedies, a subject that Racine had considered treating himself.[3] Since this quarrel is so important, not just for opera but also for literature and for the cultural climate of late seventeenth-century France in general, it is useful to look fairly closely at the two treatments of the myth and at Charles Perrault's dialogue *Critique de l'Opera, ou Examen de la tragedie intitulée Alceste, ou le triomphe d'Alcide,*[4] one of the first salvos in what would become known as the Querelle des Anciens et des Modernes.

---

[3] See Couvreur, *Lully* 294-96. Other indications of the extent of the quarrel can be found in chapter XXIII of the 1674 version of Rapin's *Réflexions sur la Poétique d'Aristote,* where he complains about the growing influence of opera (Dubois ed., p. 113), and Brébeuf's *Ombre de Molière,* where in scene ii he makes fun of the first scene of act IV of *Alceste.* An interesting indication of the extent of this quarrel is the publication of the libretto of *Alceste* in 1675; this is the only example I have found of a libretto published in a year in which there were no known performances. Even though it differs from what is probably the last edition of 1674 (Al_1674d in my edition) only in its title page, it reveals a continuing interest in the opera, and especially in its *poème.*

[4] Published in 1674 in two identical editions, except for the title pages, by Claude Barbin and Louis Billaine. I will refer to it below by its traditional short title, *Critique d'Alceste.* References will be to the edition of *Alceste* by Brooks, Norman, and Zarucchi,

Alcestis was the daughter of Pelias, the uncle of Jason who sent him in quest of the golden fleece. She married Admetus, one of the Argonauts and king of the city of Pheres, in Thessaly, and son of king Pheres, who gave his name to the city. When Apollo was sentenced to tend the flocks of a mortal (as punishment for having killed the Cyclops, forger of the thunderbolt that killed his son Escalapius), Admetus was chosen, because of his virtue.

Euripides's tragedy, which contains magnificent speeches and choruses, opens with a dialogue between Apollo and Death, in which the basic outline of the plot is given. Admetus is dying, but Apollo has an understanding with the Parcae that Admedus's death can be postponed if someone is willing to die in his place. Alcestis is the only person willing to make the sacrifice, and in the first act she is preparing to die. She says prayers to several gods, recommends her children to the gods, then breaks into a loud lament at the sight of her wedding bed, where she fears another will soon lie. The second act consists mostly of the farewell scene between Alcestis and Admetus, in which he promises, among other things, not to remarry and to abandon all pleasures.

In the third act, Hercules arrives during Alcestis's funeral, on the way to one of his twelve labors, and requests hospitality. Admetus tells Hercules that it is the funeral of a servant, and lodges him in a part of the palace where he will not be disturbed. When Admetus's father arrives to console him, there is a heated argument between the two, in which the son and father accuse each other of cowardice; Admetus goes so far as to deny that Pheres is his father.

In the fourth act, Hercules, after having gotten drunk and annoyed the servants with his loud singing, learns the truth about Alcestis's death. Touched by Admetus's efforts to offer him hospitality in spite of his grief, he offers to snatch Alcestis from the arms of Death or, if necessary, descend to Hades and bring her back. He in fact appears in the last act (he did not have to descend to Hades) with a veiled Alcestis whom he offers to Admetus, who is not interested in any woman but Alcestis. At this point Hercules removes Alcestis's veil, and the play ends happily.

---

the introduction to which contains an overview of this stage of the Querelle. See page 9, note 9 in my introduction for additional references.

Quinault's *Alceste* is quite different. It begins with the wedding of Alceste and Admète, with a jealous but resigned Alcide (Hercules) in attendance. Lycomède, king of the island of Scyros, invites the guests to a feast on his ship, but removes the gangplank once he, his followers, and Alceste are aboard. Admète and Alcide pursue the abductors, after Jupiter sends Éole to subdue the storm stirred up by Thétis, who is described as the sister of Lycomède.[5] In the second act, Alcide helps Admète and his soldiers defeat Lycomède and win Alceste back; a dying Lycomède, however, deals Admète a fatal blow. After a touching duet with Alceste, Admète learns from Apollon that he can be saved if someone dies in his place. Apollon even offers to construct a monument to the eternal glory of the person who dies in Admète's place.

In the third act, after Admète's aging father and Alceste's young servant explain why they are unwilling to die, we learn that someone has made the sacrifice, only to learn almost immediately that it is Alceste. After a moving funeral ceremony, Alcide offers to descend to Hades to bring back Alceste if Admète will yield her to him. Admète agrees, and Diane and Mercure help Alcide find a passage to Hades. There, after the famous scene in which Charon ferries Alcide across the Acheron, Alcide forces his way into Pluton's court and reveals his love to Pluton and Proserpine, who agree quickly that love is stronger than death.

In the last act, then, Alcide returns with Alceste, who is still very much in love with Admète. Alcide insists briefly on his rights, then decides that he can triumph over love as well as over Hades and Death, and the final chorus praises the "généreux Alcide" and "heureux époux."

The differences in the two versions are striking, even without mentioning the comic scenes that Quinault added involving the servants Céphise, Straton, and Lychas, as well as Charon and the shades who do not have enough money to pay for their passage. Quinault's first two acts are of his own invention, except for the appearance of Apollon in the last scene of the second act, which can be understood as the equivalent of Euripides's prologue. Indeed, the last three acts follow the main lines of the Greek tragedy and incorporate its main scenes: laments by Alceste and

---

[5] I know of no classical source that makes Lycomedes the brother of Thetis, though it was to him that she sent her son Achilles, disguised as a girl so he would not have to meet an early death in the Trojan War.

Admète, the funeral of Alceste, Alcide's decision and victory, and the happy ending.

Why all these changes? Before looking at them from the more particular point of view of the new *tragédie lyrique,* we can find a more general answer in Perrault's *Critique d'Alceste.*[6] Perrault too begins with plot summaries—in considerable detail but not without a bit of editorializing—of the two plays, followed by a discussion of scenes Quinault omitted and added. He justifies each omission and addition, arguing that Quinault was right to adapt the myth to modern taste, even if it meant leaving out some of the most effective passages in Euripides's play:

> Ce n'a pas esté parce que je trouve ces endroits-là absolument mauvais; mais parce qu'ils ne sont pas conformes aux mœurs de nostre Siecle. [...] il ne suffit pas que les choses soient bonnes en elles-mesmes; il faut qu'elles conviennent aux lieux, aux temps, et aux personnes. (97)

It is easy to see why, in almost any century, Perrault would defend Quinault for leaving out almost all of the scene between Admète and his father,[7] the vehemence of which has shocked more than one reader. His judgment of the Servant's account of Alceste's lament is more closely tied to seventeenth-century taste:

> Je croy bien qu'en Grece, on pouvoit prendre plaisir à voir une Princesse déja sur l'âge, et ayant des enfans à marier, qui pleure sur son lict dans le souvenir de sa virginité qu'elle y a perduë. Car les mœurs de ce temps-là le pouvoient permettre; mais je suis asseuré que cela n'est point du tout au goust de nostre Siecle, qui estant accoûtumé à ne voir sur le Theâtre que des Amans jeunes, galans, et qui ne sont point

---

[6] For a more thorough discussion, see my "Ancients and Moderns, Tragedy and Opera: the Quarrel over *Alceste*" and the introduction to *Alceste,* ed. Brooks, Norman, and Zarucchi.

[7] All that remains is Phérès's speech in act III scene i (508-12):
J'aime mon fils, je l'ai fait Roi;
Pour prolonger son sort je mourrais sans effroi,
Si je pouvais offrir des jours dignes d'envie.
Je n'ai plus qu'un reste de vie;
Ce n'est rien pour Admète, et c'est beaucoup pour moi.

mariez, auroit eu bien du mépris pour les tendresses de cette Epouse
surannée. (88-89)

Racine apparently agreed, in spite of his dislike of much of what
Perrault wrote in the *Critique d'Alceste*. In the preface to his *Iphigénie*
(1674; printed early 1675), he took Perrault to task about the age of Alcestis and her children, but not about the appropriateness of the scene. He
could hardly question the principle of adapting a myth to contemporary
taste, having written earlier in the same preface,

> Et quelle apparence encore de dénouer ma Tragédie par le secours
> d'une Déesse et d'une machine, et par une métamorphose qui pouvait
> bien trouver quelque créance du temps d'Euripide, mais qui serait trop
> absurde et trop incroyable parmi nous?[8]

On the subject of the need to adapt ancient myth or history to the taste of
the public, Racine and Perrault are obviously in basic agreement, and
Quinault was not the only one to infuse some seventeenth-century *galanterie* into his plays. As we will see in section 2, his contemporaries referred to the "tendre Racine," whose Alexandre and Achille are no less
galant than Quinault's Alcide.

The real quarrel between Racine and Perrault, or between Racine
and Quinault, was much more complex, more complex even than the oft-
debated issue of the superiority of the Moderns over the Ancients, a superiority that Perrault posits thirteen years before his famous "Siècle de
Louis Quatorze" would officially launch the Querelle des Anciens et des
Modernes: "[...] nostre Autheur a mieux fait qu'Euripide; Et il se trouvera
que non seulement on égale aujourd'huy les Anciens, mais que l'on les
surpasse" (97).[9] Racine does not deny this superiority of seventeenth-

---

[8] P. 698; see also the edition of *Alceste* by Brooks, Norman, and Zarucchi, p. 106.
This edition also contains Perrault's response ("Lettre à Monsieur Charpentier [...]"), in
which he defends his estimates of the ages of Alcestis and her children, but falls back on
the more general issue of the acceptability of Admetus's acceptance of her sacrifice
(118).

[9] I cannot agree with DeJean (*Ancients against Moderns* 161, n. 14) that Racine, in
his preface to Iphigénie, is not referring to a faction in the Querelle when he writes of
"des Modernes" (699). Perrault, in the *Critique d'Alceste* to which Racine is responding,
had clearly established the opposition between the two terms: "Parce que si d'un costé le

century authors (of which he was, of course, one of the most famous), though he does warn Perrault against being overly critical of the Ancients (preface to *Iphigénie*, last paragraph).

A more important issue—especially for an understanding of *Alceste* and of the *tragédie lyrique*—is that of the nature and form of tragedy. If Racine responded so quickly and so strongly to *Alceste*, but not to *Cadmus et Hermione*, it is largely because, by adapting Euripides, Quinault clearly meant to show that the new opera was much more than a pastoral with music or a ballet with dramatic text; it was *tragedy*, like that of the ancient Greeks. By giving their operas this noble label, Quinault and Lully could not only lend immediate respectability to the new form (Gros, *Quinault* 555-56; Girdlestone, *Tragédie en musique* 60), but also ensure royal favor by associating Louis XIV's exploits and patronage with the greatest works of classical Greece.

They also invited comparison to Racine's tragedies, perhaps the greatest works of classical France. The comparison has not worked to their advantage, partly because the most influential French writers, from the seventeenth century to the present, have shared what has been called the "Racinocentric" view of French classicism (Brody, Nelson). Quinault and Lully had reasons for entering into this rivalry, however, for the *tragédie lyrique* could be said to be more like ancient tragedy than Racine's own works were since, like Greek tragedy, it included a chorus, music, and dance. Furthermore, while one could view opera as an exception to classical rules and restraint, it makes more sense, as I suggested in the introduction (4), to see classicism as a temporary narrowing and focusing that occurs within a broader, more widespread esthetic framework that privileges heroism, spectacle, and pleasure. At the risk of oversimplifying a complex situation, one could say that heroism, spectacle, and pleasure were in vogue during the baroque period in the first half of the seventeenth century and during the Fronde, when the aristocracy was not yet under the thumb of Louis XIV, and in vogue again during the rococo period at the beginning of the eighteenth, after Louis XIV. In the middle of the seventeenth century the *esthétique galante,* which I will discuss in

---

mépris des Anciens est une disposition tres-mauvaise pour ceux qui estudient; d'un autre costé le mépris qu'on fait des Modernes, est aussi d'une fâcheuse consequence [...]" (98).

more detail in section 2, is a somewhat tempered example of this more widespread framework, as is the *tragédie lyrique* of the 1670s and 1680s. From this point of view, classicism (often dated roughly from 1660 to 1685) is very much what Paul Hazard called "un arrêt provisoire; un paradoxal équilibre qui se réalise entre des éléments opposés" (2: 300). And what does Hazard cite as an example of the weakening of classical reason and restraint in the 1680s (I would cite it as an example of the tenuous hold of classicism in the 1670s)? "Précisément: l'opéra était déraisonnable, et l'opéra plaisait!" (2: 212).

If posterity has been kinder to Racine than it has to Quinault, he and Lully were in a way right to invite a comparison with Racine. They knew their public, and their tragedies were more successful than those of Racine, who had complained about the public's taste for the heroic and the pastoral in the first preface to *Andromaque* (1667) by reminding his readers that "tous les héros ne sont pas faits pour être des Céladons."[10] By the time Quinault was writing his first libretti, Racine's *Mithridate* (1673) and *Iphigénie* (1674), with their quite modern young lovers united at the end, can be seen as moving in much the same direction.[11] Racine was as eager to please his public as he was to defend the ideals of the Ancients (Picard, *Carrière*; Viala, *Racine*), and this public would flock to the Académie Royale to see the same work for as many as twelve consecutive months, whereas Racine's greatest successes ran for no more than three (Picard, *Carrière* 91). Many reasons have been given for Racine's withdrawal from the stage in 1677 after *Phèdre*, his only profane tragedy after *Iphigénie*, but one of the most convincing—which does not have to be the only reason—is that he realized that the public was more interested in Quinault's *tragédies lyriques* than in his own tragedies. Indeed, if he had gone much further in the direction suggested by *Iphigénie*—with a noble, sacrificial title character[12] and a bold, brash Achilles who are strikingly similar to Alceste and Alcide, with a denouement not unlike

---

[10] Céladon is the "perfect lover" in d'Urfé's pastoral novel *L'Astrée* (1607-27). Corneille's *Agésilas*, written in 1666, can also be considered a concession to the reigning *galant* esthetic; see Girdlestone 67, n. 9.

[11] See my "Trailing Clouds of Glory [...]" and Niderst, "*Mithridate* opera?"

[12] Couvreur suggests that the Petite Académie "invited" various artists to treat the subject of the "sacrifice glorieux" (296). I will return to the role of the Petite Académie in chapter 4 (*Thésée*), 132.

that of *Thésée,* in which the sudden revelation of true identity and the downfall of a jealous rival guarantee the happiness of the young lovers— he would have been ready to write a libretto for Lully. And, as we will see in the next chapter, he quite possibly was.

Putting such speculation aside, the fact remains that, for Racine, Quinault was a serious rival, that *Phèdre* can be seen as a "lesson" to Quinault and Lully in the proper adaptation of Greek tragedy, and that he made considerable use of music in the two remaining plays he would write. It is disappointing that the "Querelle d'*Alceste*"—at least the written record that we have of it—does not go more deeply into the nature of tragedy and the most appropriate use of music, dance, and the *merveilleux* for, if it had, our knowledge of this key period in French literature would be much more complete. Instead, Racine's preface to *Iphigénie* deals mostly with the accuracy of Perrault's criticisms of Euripides in the *Critique d'Alceste,* and the latter, while promising to "parler des vers et des chansons," never really gets beyond "la conduite du sujet" (81). Fortunately, however, we have *Iphigénie* and *Alceste.*

§ § §

One can easily understand the choice of the myth of Alcestis for a new opera, even though Quinault felt obliged to make the numerous changes I outlined above. Like *Cadmus et Hermione,* it contains a touching love story, involving a famous hero and a noble princess, and a conflict between love and duty. It has a happy ending, in spite of several tragic moments, and ample opportunities for divine intervention (Apollo in particular, but also all the divinities of the underworld).[13] Perhaps even more important, it contains scenes appropriate for considerable musical development without interrupting the action: the wedding of Alceste and Admète, the battle with Lycomède, Alceste's death and funeral, and the final celebration.

It is important to remember the importance and the theatricality of these large-scale public spectacles during the early years of the reign of

---

[13] Scenes set in the underworld had been extremely popular since Buti and Rossi's *Orfeo* in 1647; the sets for that production were reused for Corneille's *Andromède.* A more recent example would be the fourth *intermède* of Molière, Corneille, and Quinault's *Psyché* (1671).

Louis XIV (Félibien; Moine; Néraudau, *Olympe*). Beaussant cites the example of the funeral of Chancellier Séguier in May 1672, described by
Sévigné in her letter of May 6, 1672 "[...] en termes de théâtre. Et ce fut
du bon théâtre, puisqu'elle y pleura" (*Lully* 773). He also points out that
the Arc de Triomphe of the fifth act could not help but recall the recent
construction of the Arc at the Porte Saint-Denis (*Lully* 527), and Girdlestone notes the recent installation of a "fleet" on the Grand Canal at Versailles (61), the location of numerous nautical *fêtes* similar to the one in
the first act, such as the one August 18, 1674, the day of the performance
of Racine's *Iphigénie* during the same "Divertissements de Versailles"
that had begun with a performance of *Alceste* on July 4.

It is one thing to choose scenes that are sure to please the public,
and quite another to put them together into a successful whole. There has
been more than enough emphasis in the relatively few works devoted to
the *tragédie lyrique* on a small number of spectacular scenes, more than
enough accusations of lack of coherence due to the necessity of including
music, dance, and machinery as well as poetry. Yet if one is willing to
remember that the pomp and ceremony of Louis XIV's glory years were
not incompatible with rigorous control, that everything in the palace and
gardens of Versailles was organized around a central concept, that the
animals of La Fontaine and the servants "forte[s] en gueule" of Molière
(*Tartuffe* I.i.14) could offer advice as moral and useful as that of Pascal
and Bossuet, it is not hard to notice the carefully worked out structure of
Alceste. The first two acts, of Quinault's invention, do more than bring
the story of Alcestis into conformity with contemporary taste; they combine with the remaining three acts to provide the symmetrical and circular
form that can be considered "classic" not only because it appealed to the
age of Louis XIV but also because it is universally recognizable (see
Couvreur, *Lully* 339-40).

The sacrifice and funeral of Alceste in act III are framed, in acts II
and IV, by the battle that caused her death and Alcide's combats in Hades
that bring her back to life and, in acts I and V, by her abduction and return, the first by a jealous Lycomède and second by a no-longer-jealous
Alcide. This symmetry is emphasized by the remarkable similarity between the opening and closing lines of the text: "Vivez, vivez, heureux
Époux" in the first line and "Aimez en paix, heureux Époux" in the last.
Much has happened in between however—the devotion of Alceste and

Admète to each other is no longer threatened by jealous rivals, since one has been punished and the other has learned an important moral lesson. Heroism and divine intervention have saved the day, and all is well in Yolcos and in Versailles.

One could cite many other examples of the admirable structure of *Alceste,* but it is more interesting to see how this structure, even at its most basic level, provides the necessary framework for a considerable diversity of characters and points of view, a series of doublings that would indeed get out of control without a rigorous structure. The plot of *Alceste* differs slightly from that of most of Quinault's other libretti based on classical mythology, in which the hero overcomes a rival and numerous obstacles to marry the woman he loves (Cadmus, Thésée, Persée, for example). There is obviously a marriage at the end, but one can hardly say that Admète is the hero. He is a noble king, generous and hospitable, but pales in comparison to Alcide, who not only becomes one of the handful of mortals to have returned from Hades, but also turns the tide of the battle for Admète:

> C'est trop disputer l'avantage,
> Je vais vous ouvrir un passage,
> Suivez-moi tous, suivez-moi tous. (II.iv.389-91)

This inclusion of a hero as well as of a king can be interpreted in several, and not necessarily absolutely contradictory, ways, such as:

Louis is such a great monarch that it takes more than one character to suggest all his strengths;
the king is helpless without the support of the army;
the king needs the assistance of a warrior/hero, but the latter must not trouble the status quo;
the time when the hero naturally assumed the throne remains only in chivalric novels and epics—Louis is in charge.

It is true that Quinault inherited this plot that contained both hero and king, that he could hardly treat the myth without Alcide and Admète in their traditional roles. The fact remains that *Alceste* raises questions about the nature of kingship, presents a much more complex situation than one finds in the prologues.[14] In this way it is not unlike the numerous trage-dies of Corneille and Racine that act out situations that put the legitimacy, or at least the nature, of monarchy in question.

Just as there are two heroes, there are two rivals to threaten the happiness of the loving couple. One, Alcide, is noble enough to hide his passion, which he will eventually overcome, and he will only use his su-perhuman force with the consent of his rival; the other, Lycomède, will turn to force when persuasion fails, only to be defeated by force. We have two examples of frustrated desire, and, of course, the more honorable one is not only praised but shown to lead to happiness.

§ § §

The expansion of standard roles to include two heroes and two ri-vals is one kind of doubling; another consists of pairing Alceste and her three suitors with four secondary characters, each of which represents a negative ethical standard. In the case of the characters with the most positive moral traits, Alceste's virtue and sacrifice find their counterpart in Céphise's fickleness and hedonism, as does Alcide's self-control in Lychas's efforts to displant Straton in the affections of Céphise. On the other hand, Straton is much like his master Lycomède: faithful while he has hope, he turns to force when his affections are rejected, but will soon be defeated by Lychas (II.iv), as Lycomède will be by Alcide and Ad-mète. In a somewhat different way, Admète's weaknesses are reflected in those of his father Phérès, both of whom are less than effective warriors (Admète needs the help of Alcide, Phérès arrives too late; II.iv and II.v) and who could be said to be overly afraid of death (Admète allows some-one to die in his place, Phérès is unwilling to save his son).

These numerous examples of positive and negative moral traits serve as a reminder that *Alceste,* in spite of comments by Céphise and Straton such as

---

[14] *Alceste* is hardly alone in this regard. *Cadmus et Hermione* had already shown the overthrow of a tyrant, and *Thésée*—like *Persée* and *Phaéton*—would deal with ques-tions of succession. In fact, all of Quinault's libretti, except *Isis,* deal in one way or an-other with the nature of kingship, even if it is only the choice of a consort (*Roland*) or the presentation of the virtues of a hero who was an exemplary king (*Amadis;* see lines 44-51 of the prologue). I discuss the representation of kingship in the introduction, pp. 33-36.

Si je change d'amant
Qu'y trouves-tu d'étrange?
Est-ce un sujet d'étonnement
De voir une fille qui change? (I.iv.114-17)

and

A quoi bon
Tant de raison
Dans le bel âge? (V.vi.909-11)

remains quite moral; after all, its subtitle is "Le Triomphe d'Alcide." The three principal characters (Alceste, Admète, Alcide) are extremely noble and virtuous, ready to sacrifice their own happiness for that of others. Alceste is of course the best example, willing to die for Admète and then, in the last act, to honor the agreement with Alcide and give him up. Admète is willing to give up Alceste if doing so will bring her back to life, even if it is largely in order to gaze once again at her beauty (III.vi.641). Alcide struggles to repress his desire from the first scene and only reveals his love after Alceste's death. It is true that he could have offered to bring her back without demanding her for himself (III.vii), but this moment of weakness only makes his final triumph all the more impressive (V.iv).[15]

All of these praiseworthy moral examples hardly suggest, of course, that virtue is its own reward. The opera ends in an atmosphere of pleasure and happiness, expressed both in the "heureux époux" of the last line and in the words of the two songs that dominate the final *divertissement:* "Tout rit aux amants" and "C'est la saison d'aimer / Quand on sait plaire" (V.vi.918 and 924-25). There is no use pretending that the *tragédie lyrique* was not intended to afford considerable pleasure as well as instruction. Or, to replace this classic pair with a more modern one, to

---

[15] La Fontaine characterizes Hercules as "maître à surmonter les vices, / A dompter les transports, monstres empoisonneurs" ("Pour Monseigneur le duc de Maine," *Fables,* XI.2). While Hercules here is offering to instruct Louis XIV's son, the king himself was often compared to Hercules, such as in the royal almanac for 1658, "Ou l'on voit Nostre Auguste Monarque triomphant de soi mesme et de ses ennemis puis qu'il met ses passions au nombre de ses Trophées"; see Zanger.

offer the illusion of pleasure that occults the ever-present threat of abso-
lutist power, "to bask in the pleasure one thinks is there" (Hoffmann 5).

One can object, of course, as did many of Quinault and Lully's
contemporaries, that the comic, hedonistic trio of Céphise, Lychas, and
Straton is on such a different plane from that of Alceste, Alcide, and Admète that their scenes not only place too much emphasis on pleasure but
detract from the more "noble" and "pure" pleasure of the more tragic, or
at least more serious, scenes. The comedy in *Alceste* is considerably more
refined than in *Cadmus et Hermione,* but criteria of unity of tone and action in spoken tragedy made it hard for many critics to accept any break
in the unfolding of the main intrigue, whether the denouement was happy
or sad.

Indeed, it seems clear that the strongest arguments against these
lighter scenes involving secondary characters was not an ethical one
against their immorality, but an esthetic one against the change in tone.
Perrault's argument about the effectiveness of their role as moral counterparts, as "contremasques" (Couvreur, *Lully* 384) is more convincing
than his defense of the variety that inevitably came with such scenes:

> De sorte que bien loin de blâmer l'Episode enjoüé des Amours et de
> l'Inconstance de Cephise, je le loüe extremement, parce que les choses
> agreables de cette Scene sont dites par des personnes du commun, une
> Suivante et des Confidents, et que ces mesmes choses font une tres-
> belle varieté. De plus, rien n'est de mieux lié ny de plus naturel au
> sujet. On sçait que c'est une des regles principales de la Rethorique, de
> relever le merite des vertus par l'opposition des vices qui leur sont
> contraires. Estant donc question de mettre en son jour la beauté de la
> constance et de la fidelité conjugale, il estoit de l'industrie du Poëte de
> donner un exemple d'inconstance et d'infidelité qui inspirast de la
> haine et du mépris pour cette foiblesse de l'esprit humain. (*Critique*
> 93)

It is as unreasonable to criticize the "morale lubrique" of *Alceste* as it
would be to complain of the immorality of *Le Misanthrope.* Célimène is
no less fickle than Céphise, and no more clearly contrasted to highly
moral characters such as Éliante. Perhaps Célimène brought less criticism
to Molière than Céphise did to Quinault because, during most of the play,

she tries to maintain a facade of adherence to reigning social norms, whereas Céphise is alarmingly frank. Still, there is no more reason to make the leap from Céphise's hedonism to a "morale lubrique" of the *tragédie lyrique* in general than there is to accuse Molière of immorality because of his numerous characters who put the end before the means or who are blind to their monomania. We have been conditioned to believe that Molière and La Fontaine, for example, believed strongly in every moral statement in their *œuvres;* why not accord the same grace to Quinault?

In the libretti that follow *Alceste,* from *Thésée* to *Amadis,* it is the changes in tone, in register, that tend to disappear, not the praise of love and pleasure. There are no comic scenes in *Persée,* for example, but the celebration of Persée's freeing of Andromède includes:

> Que n'aimez-vous,
> Cœurs insensibles?
> Que n'aimez-vous?
> Rien n'est si doux. (IV.vii.766-69)

The presence of the comic and the variety of tone can be seen as continuations of the esthetic of the *ballet de cour* and of Italian opera, an esthetic that was fast losing favor at the expense of "regular" tragedy and comedy, as defended by Boileau in the *Art poétique,* published the same year as *Alceste* (see Lecerf 1: 9). The taste for variety and lighter entertainment would hardly disappear, but Quinault and Lully obviously decided that the *tragédie lyrique* contained enough variety as it was, that the public would be satisfied with poetry, music, dance, and spectacle and could satisfy its taste for comedy elsewhere.

- II -

This variety of *Alceste,* perhaps the most extensive of any of the Quinault-Lully operas, makes it an ideal text in which to study the different styles Quinault employed to provide words that were appropriate both to the situation and to the kind of music Lully would use. In emphasizing a variety of styles, I am using a notion of style that refers not to the expression of a writer's personality in his or her writing, but to what Barthes called "le choix général d'un ton, d'un éthos," "la réflexion de l'écrivain sur l'usage social de sa forme" (*Degré zéro* 23, 25-26). Quinault was working within a *galant* esthetic in which writers sought to please "le beau monde et les honnêtes gens" (Perrault, *Parallèle* 3: 286), in which it was important to use a style that reflected less the subjectivity of the writer than the nature of the subject about which he or she was writing, that reflected the taste of the public more than that of the writer.[16] Indeed, as Viala points out, *galanterie* is itself a style, "une manière de concilier la science et la plaisir de jouer, la gaieté" (*L'Esthétique galante* 33).

As the quarrel over *Alceste,* which I discussed in section 1, shows, the taste of the public was in a period of transition in 1674. Boileau's *Art poétique,* while traditionally read as just that, a statement of accepted doctrine, is more of a reaction, a manifesto for an emerging esthetic that we have come to call "classical" (Viala, *L'Esthétique galante;* Zebouni). If Racinian tragedy and the *tragédie lyrique* existed side by side, enthralling the same audiences, if Boileau felt so obliged to teach his contemporaries a lesson, it was because the classical had by no means replaced the *galant* esthetic that had dominated the literary scene in Paris in the 1650s and 1660s. This was a time when new theatrical productions included not only Italian operas, comedy-ballets by Molière and Lully, court ballets, and the first "musical comedies" by Perrin and Cambert, but tragedies by Racine and Quinault, both of whom were known for their *tendresse.* Boursault said of Quinault:

---

[16] See Pelous 475: "La littérature galante et plus encore l'esprit galant sont devenus inséparables d'une forme de rapports sociaux," and Cuénin, *Roman et société* 330: "la galanterie fut d'abord un fait de civilisation." The variety that characterizes the *galant,* its insistence on conciliation and adaptability, help explain how one can speak both of Quinault's style and of his styles in Alceste and his other libretti.

C'est un auteur doux, agréable,

A qui la scène est redevable;

Il écrit toujours tendrement,

Il conjugue amo galamment. (Rothschild 1: 120; July 19, 1665)

It is true that love is rarely far away in Quinault's tragedies and tragi-comedies; Astrate, for example, who has forgotten his duty and dared to love the queen, is not ashamed of his "crime"; "alarmer" rhymes with "aimer" and "coupable" with "cœur insatiable":

Mais quelqu'affreux péril qui me dût alarmer,

J'aurois bien du regret d'avoir pu moins aimer.

D'un crime si charmant mon cœur insatiable,

En voudrait, s'il pouvait, être encor plus coupable.

(Astrate II.iv.655-59)

Note, however, that this scene comes before Astrate learns his true identity and realizes that the woman he loves has caused the deaths of his father and two brothers.

Note also that love is rarely far away in the works of "le tendre Racine," whose early tragedies were, in many ways, not unlike those of Quinault. Racine's *Alexandre,* written in 1665, the same year as *Astrate,* presents a conqueror as concerned with the power of those "aimables tyrans," the "beaux yeux" of Cléofile, as with military power and political tyrants (III.iv.893-901). Could one be more *galant* (and less what we think of as Racinian) than Alexandre at the end of the play, "Souffrez que jusqu'au bout achevant ma carrière, / J'apporte à vos beaux yeux ma Vertu tout entière" (V.iii.1517-18).[17] And lest one think that Racine made a complete change while Quinault remained much the same, the comparison between Quinault's Alcide and Racine's Achille that I mentioned in section 1 (p. 100) is quite revealing.

The *galant* esthetic featured much more than love; in fact, it encouraged diversity, embracing a tremendous variety of literary forms

---

[17] Gros says that at the end of the seventeenth century, "on mettait encore Racine sur le même plan que Quinault" (*Quinault* 444). See also Pelous 128, 404 and the reference to the "tendre Racine" in Picard, *Carrière* 230 (concerning *Bérénice*).

between the sustained, "high" noble style of tragedy, epic, and formal eloquence on the one hand and the low comedy and burlesque on the other. According to Viala, Quinault and other *galant* writers forged a "polymorphic" style which is not "une rupture avec le registre élevé ni avec le 'bas': au contraire, il joint l'ensemble et parcourt toute la gamme des tons littéraires" (*Naissance* 172). *Galant* works are light and agreeable, yet their writers knew how to combine the *galant* and the *enjoué* with the serious (Viala, *Esthétique galante* 33-34).

 Alceste, with all the variety that I discussed at the end of section 1, offers excellent examples of this "scale of literary tones" that is so characteristic of the *galant*. Quinault used not only two registers, the serious and the light, but four styles within each register—the heroic, the tender, the menacing, and the energetic.[18] Before looking at these styles in detail, a brief example of each would be useful. One can find in the character of Alcide an example of the four serious styles, since he is heroic when he returns from Hades, tender when he expresses his love for Alceste, menacing when he stands firm before Pluton, and energetic when he leads the assault against Lycomède. In the light register, the would-be combatant Phérès offers an example of the heroic, the love and jealousy of Straton are tender and menacing in their way, and the coquettish badinage of Céphise is the very model of the energetic, or *enjoué*.

 While it may seem inconsistent at first to see the warlike Alcide and the flirtatious Céphise as using a similar style, I hope to show that his exhortations and her taunts, as well as expressions of rejoicing in the *divertissements,* share common characteristics. Equally important, having a serious and a light register within each style not only offers a more manageable classification; it remains within the spirit of *galanterie,* with its combination of the *enjoué* and the *sérieux*.

§ § §

---

[18] Pelous also uses this term, speaking of an "énergique refus" (403) by the *galant* of the "langueurs précieuses." This style could also be called *enjoué;* see Cowart's "Lully enjoué" for an excellent discussion of the *galant* and the *tragédie lyrique* with its "amalgam of different styles" (35). See also the 1811 edition of Quinault's *Œuvres:* "[Quinault] sait être tour-à-tour tendre, énergique, et même passionné, selon que la situation le demande" (ix).

To begin with the serious register, it is in the words of the gods that one finds the heroic style in its most basic form. At the end of act II—divinities have the last word at the end of the first four acts and in the next-to-last scene of the last—Apollon announces that someone who loves Admète "parfaitement" can take his place in the underworld:

> La lumière aujourd'hui te doit être ravie;
> Il n'est qu'un seul moyen de prolonger ton sort:
> Le Destin me promet de te rendre à la vie,
> Si quelqu'autre pour toi veut s'offrir à la mort.
> Reconnais si quelqu'un t'aime parfaitement;
> Sa mort aura pour prix une immortelle gloire.
> Pour en conserver la mémoire,
> Les Arts vont élever un pompeux Monument. (II.ix.475-82)

The vocabulary is noble, the tone is serious, but the key characteristics of this style, as is fitting for a text to be set to music, are its rhythms and sounds. Seven of the eight lines are alexandrines, with eight of the fourteen hemistichs divided into two groups (*coupes*) of three syllables (3-3/3-3), suggesting equilibrium and nobility. Of the six hemistichs that are not divided into two groups of three syllables, four are in lines with a structure of 2-4/4-2 that creates a balance almost as obvious as that of lines with a 3-3/3-3 structure. The one hemistich that does not fall into one of these two patterns is "t'aime parfaitement," which not only emphasizes the essential notion of love but the idea of perfection associated with the "amitié parfaite" of Alceste (III.iii.544), who is the perfect model of a faithful spouse and of true love (III.v.596-99). Hemistichs of this type, with a *coupe* after the first syllable, are not frequent in Quinault's libretti, and his alexandrines are generally more balanced than those of Racine.[19] This tendency toward regularity is especially noticeable in heroic passages; for example, lines 477-79 contain five consecutive hemistichs divided into two groups of three syllables, something I have never noticed in Racine's tragedies. This steady rhythm is hardly an indication

---

[19] For two examples in Racine's *Iphigénie*, see how *loin* and *seule* are emphasized in "Loin de ces lieux cruels précipitez ses pas" (IV.x.1467) and "Que je la retiens seule, et que je vous renvoie" (IV.x.1474).

of poor writing, however, since it reflects the "décorum de la divinité" (Molière, *Amphitryon* P.14) and prepares the departure from the norm in "t'aime parfaitement."

If the tone of this passage is serious, it is largely because the sounds are. The return to the regularity of a symmetrical hemistich at the end of the last line ("un pompeux Monument") is a good example. Three of the six vowels are nasal, a fourth is a nicely rounded /eux/, and the other two vowels fall on unaccented syllables. Posterior and median vowels, frequently nasal and rounded, dominate this passage, and the consonants are not especially hard. The main exception is at the end of the first line, "te doit être ravie," where harsher sounds are not out of place, suggesting the seriousness of what is to follow. As in the case of the rhythmic "irregularity" of "t'aime parfaitement," the presence in this first line of sounds that are harsher than most of the others is the exception that confirms the rule, evidence that Quinault knew how to vary his styles and that, pace Boileau, everything in his works is not expressed "tendrement."

When Alcide is more the hero than the lover, he knows how to speak like Apollon:

> Non, vous ne devez pas croire
> Qu'un vainqueur des tyrans soit tyran à son tour.
> Sur l'enfer, sur la Mort j'emporte la victoire;
> Il ne manque plus à ma gloire
> Que de triompher de l'Amour. (V.iv.891-95)

After a line of seven syllables, which echoes the rhyme of the preceding lines and assures the transition between Alcide's victory over death and his victory over love and selfishness, three equally balanced hemistichs prepare the announcement of this second victory, "j'emporte la victoire," which will be followed by two isorhythmic octosyllables explaining the nature of this victory. Nasal, rounded vowels are still present, along with an excellent example of antithesis which, for Pelous (173), characterizes the *galant* style: "Qu'un vainqueur des tyrans soit tyran à son tour."

There is also a large number of syllables ending in a liquid consonant, such as *vainqueur, enfer, mort,* and *amour.* While these syllables with their long vowels suggest heroism and grandeur, the presence of /l/ and /r/ is also characteristic of the tender style, where words such as

amour, charme, cœur, larmes, douceur, plaisir, and *fidèle* are common.
(The four most frequent nouns in *Alceste* are *amour, cœur, jour,* and
mort.) These words—or more specifically, their final syllables—often
stand out because of their place at the end of lines or before the pause in
lines with a less regular rhythm than in the heroic style. The fact that
these sounds can be characteristics of two different styles is not an indication that there is little difference between the two styles, nor that Quinault is incapable of distinguishing between them. Indeed, what could be
more appropriate in a *tragédie lyrique* than the juxtaposition of glory and
love (Newman 67; Pelous 49, 129), of the heroic and the tender? After
all, at the beginning of the first act of *Alceste,* one reads "Le Théâtre
représente un port de mer, où l'on voit un grand vaisseau, orné & préparé
pour une fête galante, au milieu de plusieurs vaisseaux de guerre." Such a
setting helps explain why Alceste says, in two lines that one could consider a classic example of the heroic-galant style, "C'est votre valeur triomphante / Qui fait le sort charmant que nous allons goûter" (II.vi.426-
27). *Charmant* at the end of the first hemistich of the second of these two
lines contains some of the heroic sounds of "triomphante," but the nasal
/an/ is tempered by the /arm/ that precedes it as well as by the meaning of
the word. Furthermore, after the mounting energy (and pitch) of "C'est
votre valeur triomphante," "que nous allons goûter" ushers in a state of
peaceful expectation.[20]

True happiness in love is rather rare in *Alceste;* even at the end,
after all the obstacles have been overcome, the private happiness of Alceste and Admète figures less prominently than the heroism of Alcide and
the public rejoicing. The most direct expression of happiness is perhaps
that of Admète when he learns that someone has agreed to die in his place
but before he learns that this person is Alceste:

> Alceste n'aura plus d'alarmes;
> Je reverrai ses yeux charmants,
> A qui j'ai coûté tant de larmes.

---

[20] In Lully's music, Alceste's voice climbs an octave on "c'est votre valeur triomphante," from G to G, then falls to D before tracing two gentle curves on "Qui fait le sort
charmant" and "que nous allons goûter." The final note is in the key of the dominant
(D), suggesting a wait before this charming fate is realized.

Que la vie a de charmes
Pour les heureux amants! (III.iii.554-58)

The sounds are tender and soft: /l/ and /r/ abound, and the only really hard consonants are the two /t/ that one hears when Admète remembers the suffering Alceste went through because of his impending death "A qui j'ai coûté tant de larmes." The lines are shorter—less heroic, more direct, easier to understand—and each has a different rhythm (2-6, 4-4, 5-3, 3-3, 4-2). The more tender, and important, words are at the ends of the lines, a location that receives even more emphasis in these shorter lines with fewer accented syllables.

The tender style is not limited to happy moments; with similar sounds and rhythms but with a different vocabulary, it can express pain and despair, be they from amorous, military, or family difficulties. The best-known example in *Alceste* would be the famous lamentations "Admète vous mourez—Alceste vous pleurez" (II.viii) and "Alceste est morte" (III.iv), where the death of a loved one creates a situation of intense grief. The joys of love are not forgotten, however, and in fact, a subject such as that of *Alceste* makes juxtapositions of sadness and happiness almost inevitable:

Je meurs, charmante Alceste.
Mon sort est assez doux,
Puisque je meurs pour vous. (II.viii.448-50)

The menacing style contains the frequently strident sounds of the posterior and median vowels of the heroic style and the less regular rhythms of the tender style, but its sounds are usually harder and the rhythmic irregularities more accentuated. These irregularities are often caused by interjections and questions, or by repetition. For example, when Lycomède is speaking of love to Alceste, he tries to be noble and tender, but the rhythm of his alexandrines calls attention to words such as *funeste* and *cruelle*, which would be out of place in passages characterized by the tender style. He soon begins to use shorter lines that are more and more menacing:

Que ne m'ont point coûté vos funestes attraits!
Ils ont mis dans mon cœur une cruelle flamme;
Ils ont arraché de mon âme
L'innocence et la paix.
Non, ingrate! non, inhumaine!
Non, quelle que soit votre peine,
Non, je ne vous rendrai jamais
Tous les maux que vous m'avez faits. (II.ii.336-43)

The rhyme *flamme-âme,* common in the tender style, is marred by the
/ach/ of *arraché,* a harsh sound frequently used by poets to create a harsh
effect; "Et l'avare Achéron ne lâche point sa proie" (*Phèdre* II.v.626) is a
classic example. The word *ingrate* is equally harsh, and the *e muet,* rather
than add the rhythmic lilt that it can contribute to lyric poetry, closes the
syllable and brings out the explosive /t/. The repetition of *non* is striking
but, apparently, so obvious that Lully did not feel the need to call attention to it. He accented *ingrate, inhumaine, peine,* and *jamais,* with the
three *non* falling on the second beat of three- or four-beat measures.

One finds a similar style when Alcide comes before Pluton:

Son bras abat tout ce qu'il frappe;
Tout cède à ses horribles coups;
Rien ne résiste, rien n'échappe. (IV.iv.756-58)

The /a/ and the hard consonants combine with the threatening /s/, and the
strength of Alcide can be heard in the repetitions of *rien.*

When one moves from threats to action, the lines become even
shorter and words, or groups of words such as "Aux armes," are often repeated. The imperative replaces interjections and the rhythm is often iam-
bic. In the serious register, one finds the energetic style mostly in scenes
of war or celebration:

ADMETE, ALCIDE
A l'assaut, à l'assaut.
LYCOMEDE, STRATON
Aux armes, aux armes.

ASSIÉGEANTS

A l'assaut, à l'assaut.

ASSIÉGÉS

Aux armes, aux armes.

ADMETE, ALCIDE, LYCOMEDE

A moi, compagnons, à moi.

ADMETE, LYCOMEDE

A moi; suivez votre Roi.

ALCIDE

C'est Alcide

Qui vous guide.

ADMETE, ALCIDE, LYCOMEDE

A moi, Compagnons, à moi.

TOUS ENSEMBLE

Donnons, donnons, de toutes parts. (II.vi.369-78)

In the case of celebrations, the sounds are somewhat softer and the lines are somewhat longer. Repetition of words or of short groups of words is less frequent, but complete lines are often repeated:

> Alcide est vainqueur du trépas;
> L'enfer ne lui résiste pas:
> Il ramène Alceste vivante.
> Que chacun chante,
> Alcide est vainqueur du trépas,
> L'enfer ne lui résiste pas. (V.i.798-803)

One often hears the same line sung by two characters, or two choruses, with a few words changed. This type of repetition is of course not limited to scenes of rejoicing, but they are more frequent here:

> Triomphez, généreux Alcide;
> Aimez en paix, heureux époux:
> Que {toujours la Gloire / sans cesse l'Amour} vous guide.
> Jouissez à jamais des {honneurs / plaisirs} les plus doux.
> Triomphez, généreux Alcide,
> Aimez en paix heureux époux. (V.vi.942-47)

This last line of course recalls the first line, "Vivez, vivez, heureux époux," completing the symmetrical structure described earlier (p. 104).

The iambs that one finds in lines such as "L'enfer ne lui résiste pas" et "Vivez en paix heureux époux" are normally much less frequent in French poetry than are anapests, which Lully has often been accused of using abusively. The number of alexandrines which I have already quoted that contain a 3-3/3-3 rhythm shows that anapests are certainly frequent, but it is important to remember that alexandrines represent only about 25 percent of the lines in *Alceste* (251 of 1038, or 225 of 947 not counting the prologue). One can of course find groups of three syllables in octo-syllables and other types of lines, but there remains a large number of groups of two or four syllables (see Giraud, "Quinault et Lully" 200). In such situations, one often finds series of alternating short and long, non-accented and accented syllables which, according to Bacilly, all good singers should favor (329 sq.).

§ § §

To move toward the light register, it is not rare to find the light energetic style in the same scene with the serious energetic style, since the scenes of celebration, in which one often finds the latter, are usually found in the *divertissements*, where a celebration of victory normally leads to a celebration of peace, which leads inevitably to love. It is these glorifications of the pleasures of love (rather than of its strong emotions) that offer the best examples of the light energetic, or *enjoué*, style, "un certain badinage dans les paroles qui cache cette passion sous des ap-parences de raillerie" (Perrault, *Parallèle* 3: 286), which characterizes *galanterie* in its sense of lightheartedness and of sexual dalliance. It is also in these passages that one finds the most obvious musical equivalent of the *galant*: light, charming, graceful, and based on dance rhythms, in particular the minuet (Cowart, "Lully enjoué" 43).

For example, between the end of the scene discussed above (V.vi), which is dominated by the serious energetic style of "Aimez en paix heureux époux," and the beginning of the scene, with "Chantons, chan-tons, faisons entendre / Nos chansons jusques dans les cieux" in a similar style, one finds the short lines, repetition, and alternation of nonaccented and accented syllables of the energetic style but a different subject matter:

> A quoi bon
> Tant de raison
> Dans le bel âge?[21]
> [...]
> C'est la saison d'aimer.
> Quand on sait plaire;
> C'est la saison d'aimer,
> Quand on sait charmer. (V.vi.909-11, 938-41)

It is completely normal, in the *tragédie lyrique* at least, to juxtapose these two styles, to associate love and war, the two preferred activities of the heroes of these libretti (though opposed in the prologues). It is true that comic scenes begin to disappear after *Thésée* (1675), but one continues to find *airs gais* such as those of Céphise; see, for example, act V scene iv of *Phaéton* and act IV scene vii of *Persée*.

In the energetic style, be it serious or light, the content and the tone are different but the sounds and rhythms remain similar. The same is true for the other styles; a character such as Straton threatens menacingly and purrs tenderly, in much the same way that Alcide and his master Lycomède do, yet it is hard to take his threats seriously, such as in the case of:

> Le mépris d'une volage
> Doit être un assez grand mal,
> Et c'est un nouvel outrage
> Que la pitié d'un rival. (I.iii.85-88)

It is far from tender, but less harsh that the *arraché* and *ingrate* of Lycomède (II.ii.338, 340). Similarly, in spite of the change in punctuation in the 1778 edition, which replaced the exclamation point after "vrai" with a question mark and the question marks at the end of each line with exclamation marks, Straton questions as much as he accuses:

---

[21] One finds the alternation of nonaccented and accented syllables even when the music goes against the normal rhythms of the spoken language, as in "Tant de raison / Dans le bel âge." In passages such as this one, Lully wrote the music first, and Quinault had to adapt his words to Lully's rhythms. See also Lecerf's comments on these "petits vers," 2: 83.

Comment! il est donc vrai! tu n'en fais point d'excuse?
Tu me trahis ainsi sans en être confuse? (I.iv.108-09)

His "Tu me trahis ainsi" sounds menacing, but by ending the line with
"confuse" he reveals that he is talking more about a lovers' spat than
about betrayal in more heroic circumstances.[22]

Straton is somewhat more successful when he speaks as a rejected
lover; as in the examples of happy and unhappy love discussed above,
one finds the posterior and median vowels, /l/ and /r/, and rhythmic
variety:

Par un espoir doux et trompeur,
Pourquoi m'engageais-tu dans un amour si tendre?
Fallait-il me donner ton cœur
Puisque tu voulais le reprendre? (I.iv.122-25)

The two balanced halves of the first line suggest his desire for a faithful
lover, but this rhythmic constancy, along with his hope, soon disappears
beneath the variety created by three lines in which one hears neither the
rhythm of the first line (4-4) nor a repetition of any other pattern (2-4, 4-
2, 3-5, 5-3). He will soon move on to the light menacing style, which often expresses jealousy, before trying in vain, in an energetic, *enjoué* style,
to replace the *changer* and *nouvelles* of Céphise by *aimer* and *fidèles:*

Ingrate! est-ce le prix de ma persévérance?
[...]
Il faut {aimer / changer} toujours.
Les plus douces amours
Sont les amours {fidèles / nouvelles}. (I.iv.130, 135-37)

Whatever style he chooses, his words are rarely convincing.

In the light register, the words of heroic style obviously do not
evoke heroic sentiments, and the word "heroic" is used here to suggest a
form, and not a content. The light heroic style is often characterized by

---

[22] Lully underscores this confusion by setting "sans en être confuse" to a descending
melodic line, whereas normally exclamation marks and question marks suggest rising
intonation.

irony, which Pelous has identified as one of the most striking characteristics of "la rhétorique galante" (173-81). In the case of Phérès, it is a matter of his truly unheroic fear of dying revealing itself in spite of his noble words:

> J'aime mon fils, je l'ai fait Roi;
> Pour prolonger son sort, je mourrais sans effroi,
> Si je pouvais offrir des jours dignes d'envie.
> Je n'ai plus qu'un reste de vie;
> Ce n'est rien pour Admète, et c'est beaucoup pour moi. (III.i.508-12)

The second line (509), with its nasal vowels and its syllables lengthened by /r/, seems heroic enough, but Phérès is as incapable of maintaining this tone as he is of fighting or of sacrificing himself for his son.

Charon is another not quite heroic character, following a line worthy of Apollon with one worthy of Lycas or Straton:

> Il faut auparavant que l'on me satisfasse;
> On doit payer les soins d'un si pénible emploi. (IV.i.672-73)

The alexandrines are well balanced and the sounds are noble, until one reaches *pénible*, where the front vowels, as well as his meaning, destroy all the nobility of the line.

§ § §

What I have described as the *galant* style of *Alceste* is thus really four different styles, each of which has its role in the *tragédie lyrique*. There is a place for the two omnipresent themes of glory and love (heroic, tender styles), but also for bemoaning the problems and obstacles that the heroes and lovers must overcome. And, when one has talked enough about happiness and unhappiness, threatened and been threatened by human and divine enemies (menacing style), and is ready to move on to action, celebrate success, or enjoy the pleasures one has earned, the style can become more energetic. Rather than create excessive diversity, these four styles, each of which shares some characteristics with some of the others, facilitate the transitions from one scene to another and, particularly in *Alceste*, remind us of the links between heroism and love, love and death, mourning and rejoicing.

If the presence of different styles within a single work seems to violate what La Fontaine called "la règle la plus étroite que nous ayons" (preface to *Psyché*), that of uniformity of style, it is because our concept of uniformity of style in the classical period is too narrow. Not only is it impossible, as Brody has pointed out (52) to describe a classical style that would embrace the styles of Pascal, La Fontaine, Bossuet, Sévigné, and La Bruyère; La Fontaine, that expert in "the recuperation of coherence by subtleties of technique and of style" (Rubin 107), combined the *galant* and the heroic, along with poetry and prose, in *Psyché* (not to mention the different styles and tones in his fables), and Boileau mixed in his *Satires* "seemingly incompatible moods and elements, [...] farce and seriousness, morality and pleasure, the lofty and the undignified" (Pocock 175). As I suggested at the beginning of this section, there is no overall "Quinault style" in the libretti, no one *galant* style, but rather an uncanny ability on the part of Quinault to create lines that were appropriate for his characters and for Lully's music and to please his public. To quote La Fontaine's preface to *Psyché* again, "Mon principal but est toujours de plaire: pour en venir là, je considère le goût du siècle."

ACTE SECOND.

Le Theatre change & represente le
Palais d'Ægée Roy d'Athenes.

SCENE PREMIERE.

MEDE'E, DORINE.

MEDE'E.

 Oux repos, innocente paix,
Heureux, heureux un Cœur qui
ne vous pert jamais !
L'impitoiable Amour m'a toûjours
poursuivie ;   [*faits !*
N'estoit-ce point assez des maux qu'il m'avoit
Pourquoy ce Dieu cruel avec de nouveaux Traits
Vient-il encor troubler le reste de ma vie ?
Doux repos, innocente paix,   [*mais !*
Heureux, heureux un Cœur qui ne vous pert ja-

C ij

4

Thésée

omnia vincunt amor ... gloriaque

- I -

IT IS ALMOST CERTAINLY NOT A COINCIDENCE that the opera which followed the quarrel over *Alceste* turned out to be the one that would have
the greatest number of revivals during the Ancien Régime, as well as the
last one performed (1779) without major modifications to the libretto
and/or new music (see appendix 1). Quinault and Lully must have been
especially anxious to satisfy their critics, even though they would not
cease to experiment with different ways of approaching the *tragédie lyrique*. *Thésée* represents a move toward the regularity that we have come to
associate with classical tragedy and it features, in comparison to *Alceste*,
more unity of tone, fewer secondary plots and comic characters, and less
divine intervention. While these features were certainly not universally
preferred in 1675, they were becoming more characteristic of the taste of
the theater-going public and would continue to be throughout most of the
eighteenth century. For example, the largest number of criticisms of Quinault for introducing the comic characters into *Cadmus et Hermione* and
Alceste (or of praise for eliminating them from later libretti) are from
eighteenth-century writers such as Du Bos and Cahusac, who were writing at a time when the norms for tragedy favored by Boileau and Racine
had become generally accepted.

The success of *Thésée* was indeed prodigious. After the "opéra tout neuf qui est fort beau"[1] opened at court at Saint-Germain on January 11, 1675, it ran for almost a year, perhaps as many as 150 performances from the reopening of the Palais-Royal theater after Easter in late April 1675 to the Easter closing in late March 1676.[2] This was obviously not enough for the public, since Lully revived *Thésée* in April 1677, as a replacement for *Isis,* which had not met with much success at court; it was revived again in January 1678, after the performances at Fontainebleau in 1677 and at Saint-Germain in early January 1678, and in October 1679. There would be at least ten revivals after Lully's death: 1688, 1698, 1707, 1720, 1729-30, 1744, 1754, 1765, 1767, and 1779. Two other composers would set revised versions of this amazingly popular libretto: Mondonville in 1767, Gossec in 1782 (see appendix 1), and Handel set a remarkably faithful Italian adaptation in 1713 (*Teseo*).

Before looking at just what made this libretto so successful, it is important to consider two important consequences of the polemics that followed *Alceste:* the efforts to replace Quinault as Lully's librettist and the official approval of libretti. The enthusiastic reception of *Alceste,* in spite of the serious cabal that opposed it, made it clear that the success of *Cadmus et Hermione* was not a fluke, that the *tragédie lyrique* had become a prominent feature on the theatrical and musical landscape. Yet, precisely, *Alceste* almost failed; as Lully's son put it in the dedication of the first printing of the score of *Alceste,* in 1708,

> Le public peu accoutumé encore à la Musique de Théâtre, hésita sur le jugement qu'il devait porter de celle-ci; mais le goût de Votre Majesté fut sa Loi, et le détermina aux applaudissements, que cet ouvrage a toujours reçus dans la suite. Peut-être sans cela, n'en serait-il plus parti aucun de la main d'un auteur découragé.

---

[1] Sévigné 1: 704; Jan. 20, 1675. Later, she sent some airs (1: 751, July 3; 2: 23, July 26) and "les premiers actes de l'opéra" (2: 42, Aug. 7); she probably means the score of the opening acts, since it would have been easy for the Grignan to find a copy of the libretto and odd to send only part of what was normally printed as a whole. Bayle's letter of March 28, 1677 (f. 130ᵛ), refers to the wide availability of the libretto of *Atys* and of the need to make special arrangements to obtain a copy of the score, which, like that of *Thésée,* had not been printed.

[2] There were probably a few performances of *Le Carnaval* at the Palais-Royal in October 1675.

If Lully was temporarily discouraged, Quinault must have been even more worried, since the numerous criticisms of his libretto meant that he was in danger of losing his post as official librettist.

The position as librettist had become a lucrative one.[3] We know that a host of potential librettists offered their services to Lully and/or to Louis XIV, but we are not sure that all of these offers came at this time, between *Alceste* and *Thésée*. It seems probable that they did, however, and I have chosen to discuss them here as a group, while explaining in notes which events could have taken place at other times.

Perrault's accounts of the efforts to convince Lully to replace Quinault seem to refer to the quarrels after *Alceste,* since he mentions the early success of their operas and the concerted criticism—unfounded according to him—of Quinault's texts:

> Quand il vint à faire des Opera, un certain nombre de personnes de beaucoup d'esprit, & d'un merite distingué, se mirent en fantaisie de les trouver mauvais, & de les faire trouver tels par tout le monde. Un jour qu'ils souppoient ensemble ils s'en vinrent sur la fin du repas vers Monsieur de Lulli, qui étoit du soûper, chacun le verre à la main, & lui appuyant le verre sur la gorge, se mirent à crier, renonce à Quinault ou tu es mort. Cette plaisanterie ayant beaucoup fait rire, on vint à parler sérieusement, & l'on n'obmit rien pour dégouster Lulli de la Poësie de Monsieur Quinault. (*Parallèle* 3: 238)[4]

---

[3] According to recent research by La Gorce ("Un proche collaborateur" 366), Quinault received 3,000 livres from Lully for each libretto and a royal pension of 3,000-4,000 livres per year. By comparison, Racine had a pension of 1,500-2,000 livres and rarely received more than 1,500 livres for the publication of his plays (Picard, *Carrière* 198-204). These figures are of course only estimates, and sources do not always agree. For example, the *Comptes et Bâtiments du roi* published by Guiffrey, which lists Racine's pension at 1,500 livres from 1670 to 1678 and 2,000 from 1679 to 1684, lists Quinault's at 800 in 1670 and 1671, 1,200 in 1672 and 1673, and 1,500 from 1674 to 1687. La Gorce uses information in manuscripts in the Mélanges Colbert at the Bibliothèque Nationale (see Clément's fairly complete edition), which are also cited by Picard.

[4] See also p. 242, "[E]n ce temps-là, j'estois presque le seul à Paris qui osast se declarer pour Monsieur Quinault, tant la jalousie de divers Autheurs s'estoit eslevée contre luy, & avoit corrompu tous les suffrages & de la Cour & de la Ville." Both these passages are given, in slightly different wording, in Boscheron's biography of Quinault, pp. 38 and 40. Forestier suggests this period after *Alceste,* "au moment de la plus forte tension entre les partisans de la tragédie et ceux de l'opéra," as the most probable date

> Les Opera estant venus à la mode en France, Monsieur Quinault en fit de trés excellens, mais qui n'eurent pas d'abord les applaudissemens sans bornes qu'ils ont receus depuis. On tascha mesme d'en dégouster M. de Lully, mais cet excellent Homme avoit trop de goust & trop de sens, pour ne pas voir qu'il estoit impossible de faire des Vers plus beaux, plus doux & plus propres à faire paroistre sa Musique. (*Hommes illustres* 81)

Among the candidates to replace Quinault was Henri Guichard, who had hoped, along with the composer Sablières, to build on the success of the *Pomone* of Perrin and Cambert (1671). In collaboration with Mme de Villedieu, he proposed two libretti to Lully in 1674, *Céphale et Procris* and *Circé et Ulysse*.[5] It is hardly surprising that Lully refused to collaborate with one of his principal rivals.

On the other hand, it was quite natural for him to think of La Fontaine, known for his harmonious and varied verse, as a potential librettist. It is impossible to know for sure whether Lully really wanted to collaborate with him, or if La Fontaine (who was perhaps one of the dinner guests who put his glass to Lully's throat) and Mme de Thiange pressured him, but La Fontaine allowed himself to be "enquinaudé" and wrote a libretto, *Daphné,* between May and September, 1674, perhaps as early as June.[6] As he recounts so well in "Le Florentin" and in "A Madame de Thiange," Lully refused to set his text, ostensibly—and reasonably—

---

for the rather vulgar epigram by Racine, attacking both Quinault and Lully (*O.C.* 1: 693 and n. 1, p. 1554).

[5] La Gorce, *L'Opéra* 24-26 and 57-59. For a fuller account of Guichard's attempts, in 1675, to poison Lully and the trial that followed, see Beaussant, *Lully* 568-70.

[6] Clarac dates the "Lettre à Monsieur de Turenne," in which La Fontaine mentions working on a opera (line 23), in June 1674 (*O.D.* 924). A letter to the prince de Condé, probably by Jean Perrault, Président des Comptes, dated Sept. 13, 1674, says "La Fontaine s'est rebutté; il a quitté son entreprise et laissé le champ de bataille à Quinault" (Henriet 235; also in Mongrédien and La Fontaine, *O.D.* xxxiv and 957). See Orcibal 248-29; Duchêne, chapter 43; Prunières, "La Fontaine et Lully"; Néraudau, *Olympe* 158-60; Beaussant, *Lully* 549-52; Giraud, *La Fable de Daphné* 466-80. This episode in La Fontaine's life is often placed erroneously in 1679, possibly because of the error in the life of Quinault by Boscheron first published in the 1715 edition of his *Théâtre* (p. 42).

Mme de Thiange and her sister, Mme de Montespan, supported Racine and Boileau as well as La Fontaine, and worked against Quinault. They were also fond of Lully's music and had helped him establish himself at court.

because the public was no longer interested in pastorals. Perhaps, as La Fontaine's poem suggests, Lully never intended to go through with the deal, either out of avarice or because he had no intention of abandoning Quinault. La Fontaine never lost interest in the opera, however. He wrote two acts of another pastoral, *Galatée,* in 1674 or 1675, and had yet another pastoral, *Astrée,* performed by the Académie Royale in 1691, with music by Colasse.

La Fontaine's case is quite different from that of Racine and Boileau, who attributed their collaboration on a *Chute de Phaéton* to the insistence of Mme de Montespan and her sister Mme de Thiange, who was also involved in La Fontaine's first efforts as a librettist. According to Boileau's account in the *avertissement* to his fragment of a "Prologue d'Opéra," Racine made his decision to write a libretto "assez légèrement" and soon regretted it. He begged Boileau to help him by writing a prologue:

> Madame de M[ontespan] et Madame de T[hiange] sa sœur, lasses des
> Opera de Monsieur Quinaut, proposerent au Roy d'en faire faire un
> par Monsieur Racine [...]. Mais comme Monsieur Racine n'entre-
> prenoit cet Ouvrage qu'à regret, il me temoigna resolument qu'il ne
> l'acheveroit point que je n'y travaillasse avec lui, et me declara avant
> tout, qu'il falloit que j'en composasse le Prologue.

Boileau obliged, and after three or four days of work "avec un assez grand dégoût," finished the first scene, which he published in the 1713 edition of his *Œuvres.* Quinault finally saved them from any further work by convincing the king not to replace him.

Various efforts have been made to date this event and to relate it to the *Alceste* that Racine was supposed to have considered writing.[7]

---

[7] Both Racine's son Louis and La Grange-Castel affirm that Racine had written at least part of an *Alceste;* see Mesnard's edition of Racine, 1: 96. It is impossible to date Racine's work on this *Alceste,* but the growing popularity of the *tragédie lyrique* seems to have influenced his unusually long absence from the stage between *Iphigénie* (1674) and *Phèdre* (1677), as well as his retirement from the profane theater after *Phèdre.* Since some critics see in *Phèdre* a lesson to Quinault in how to treat Greek myths, it is reasonable to assume that he considered writing a rival *Alceste,* just as his own rivals had done for *Bérénice, Iphigénie,* and *Phèdre.* Among the immense bibliography on this subject, see Gros, *Quinault* 730-41; Knight, 31-39; Picard, *Carrière* 256-57 and 302-03;

Boileau's wording makes me think it was literally a matter of Quinault's not being replaced at a time when he was the titular librettist, which would make more sense in 1674 than at the end of his two years of disgrace following *Isis* (1678-79; see chap. 6).

> Monsieur Quinault s'estant presenté au Roy les larmes aux yeux, et lui ayant remonstré l'affront qu'il alloit recevoir s'il ne travailloit plus aux divertissemens de Sa Majesté, le Roy touché de compassion declara franchement aux deux Dames [Montespan, Thiange] dont j'ay parlé, qu'il ne pouvoit se resoudre à lui donner ce deplaisir.

If this was in 1678 or 1679, Quinault would have already spent one or two years without writing a libretto, and had thus already received the "affront" which, according to Boileau, he hoped to avoid.[8]

In the long run, the precise dates are less important than the undeniable interest on the part of some of the greatest writers of the time in writing the same kind of texts they so often criticized. Perhaps they thought they could do better? Perhaps they realized the importance of collaborating with a composer who was in such favor with the king? In any case, Quinault was not replaced and would continue to furnish Lully

---

Pommier, "Le Silence de Racine"; Brunetière, *Époques* 168-81 and *Manuel* 218-20; Vanuxem, "Racine et le baroque"; Viala, *Racine* 154-57.

On Racine and Boileau's proposed *Chute de Phaéton,* see Orcibal; Couvreur, *Lully* 56-60; Gros, *Quinault* 115-16; Beaussant, *Lully* 553-54; Néraudau, *Olympe* 160-61; Vanuxem, "Sur Racine et Boileau librettistes"; Picard, *Carrière* 354-55. Vanuxem and Picard date this episode in 1682, the year of Quinault's *Phaéton;* this seems unlikely, especially since Mme de Montespan was out of favor by then. There remains, however, the mystery of the 10,000 livres that Boileau and Racine each received in March 1683 "pour les récompenser d'un petit opéra qu'ils ont fait en trois jours et qui a été un des divertissements de la Cour à ce Carnaval"; Quinault received 20,000 livres at the same time (Picard, *Carrière* 255 and *Nouveau Corpus* 151). Boileau's account suggests a collaboration that lasted much more than three days.

It is conceivable that the whole episode is fictitious, that Boileau's prologue was meant to be considered satirical. See the Boudhors edition of Boileau's *Odes et Poésies diverses*, p. 216.

[8] There is a similar argument in Couvreur, *Lully* 58. I also agree with Couvreur that there is nothing in Boileau's text that refers explicitly to the Treaty of Nimwegen in 1678. In fact, the fear Boileau mentions in the Avertissement "que quelque audacieux ne vint troubler, en s'élevant contre un si grand Prince, la gloire dont elle [l'Harmonie] jouïssoit avec lui" suggests a continuing war much more than the end of a war.

with a libretto each year until 1686, except for the two years after *Isis*. This success is a remarkable confirmation of his talent—how many writers can claim to have been preferred to La Fontaine, Racine, and Boileau?

§ § §

With all these candidates for writing libretti, it is only natural that Louis XIV and Colbert would try to impose some kind of order. Perrault wrote in 1690 that "Le Roy, ayant voulu donner à la Cour le divertissement des Opera, ne voulut point prendre d'autre Auteur que M. Quinault" (*Hommes illustres* 81-82). As in the case of the various efforts to replace Quinault, the dates of official royal control are far from clear, and contemporary accounts are often contradictory. We know that Lully and Quinault proposed a project, probably *Cadmus et Hermione*, to Colbert in 1672,[9] and that Sévigné mentions official approval of *Proserpine* in 1680: "Il faut qu'on l'ait approuvée puisqu'on la chante" (2: 833; Feb. 9, 1680). In between, some kind of standard process of revision and approval was probably established; the best known account is that of Lecerf:

> Quinaut cherchoit & dressoit plusieurs sujets d'Opera. Il les portoient
> au Roi, qui en choisissoit un. Alors Quinaut écrivoit un plan du
> dessein & de la suite de sa Piéce. Il donnoit une copie de ce plan à
> Lulli [...]. Quinaut composoit ses Scenes: aussi-tôt qu'il en avoit
> achevé quelques-unes, il les montroit à l'Académie Françoise, dont
> vous sçavez qu'il étoit. (2: 212-13)

At this point in Lecerf's dialogue, the Chevalier interrupts the Marquis to mention the different accounts in the *Ménagiana*—confusion was already rampant in 1705! The first edition of the *Ménagiana* (1693; p. 434) attributes an important role to Mademoiselle Serment, but Boscheron, in his biography of Quinault, claimed that she worked with Quinault only on *Armide* (35). The passage about Serment disappears from subsequent editions of the *Ménagiana* and is replaced by another version of the revision process: "M. Quinault n'a rien publié depuis l'Alceste qu'il n'ait consulté Messieurs B*** et Pérrault qui avoient soin de revoir ses

---

[9] Letter to Colbert, June 3, 1672. In Charavay, p. 112; cited by Couvreur, *Lully* 54.

Ouvrages par ordre de M. Colbert" (1694; 1: 339). Lecerf identifies "B***" as Boileau, whereas Boscheron identifies him as Boyer (34; Couvreur, *Lully* 56).

This latter version corresponds to accounts of the role of the Petite Académie,[10] of which Quinault became a member in 1674, as a replacement for the recently deceased Chapelain:

> Ce fut environ en l'année 1676 que Le Roy commençâ d'aimer les Tragédies en musique, ou Monsr Quinault qui avoit un talent particulier pour le Lyrique, et qui avoit desja composé Cadmus et Alceste, fut choisy par sa Majesté pour travailler à ces sortes d'ouvrages, mais à condition de les consulter dans la Petite Academie. Il commençâ par Thesée; on examinoit d'abord le sujet, on en regloit les Actes, les Scenes, les Divertissemens, et Monsr QUINAULT à mesure que la Piece avançoit, monstroit tout au Roy qui luy demandoit toujours si cela avoit esté veu à la Petite Academie.[11]

Perhaps Lecerf confused the Académie Française and the Petite Académie, or perhaps members of both bodies participated in the revision (for example, Perrault from the Petite Académie and Boileau from the Académie Françoise; the latter did not become a member of the Petite Académie until 1683). We will probably never know for sure, but most of the sources agree on the essential: beginning with *Thésée,* and almost certainly as a consequence of the "Querelle d'*Alceste,*" Quinault was obliged to consult at least two of his colleagues at almost every step in the composition of his libretti. And even then, as Lecerf tells us, Lully often demanded frequent revisions.

§ § §

---

[10] Founded in 1673, its official existence dates from 1701, when it became the Académie Royale des Inscriptions et des Médailles. Devoted to the *gloire* of Louis XIV, it composed the texts for medals, monuments, and other types of panegyric and approved a variety of projects, such as Félibien's account of the Versailles *fêtes* of 1674, the tapestries relating the *Histoire du roi,* and the decoration of the apartments and gardens of Versailles. See Couvreur, *Lully* 43-52.

[11] Extract from the Register of the Academy, in Jacquiot, *Médailles et jetons* 1: xcii. Gros de Boze gives a similar account; he mentions no year, but says that *Alceste* was one of the operas to have been "le fruit de cette attention" (1: 3-4). The date in the first sentence clearly should be 1675, or late 1674.

As I suggested at the beginning of this chapter, the prodigious success of *Thésée* is probably due to a large extent to Quinault's reflections on the issues raised during the polemics following *Alceste*. Along with the beginnings of more consistent royal control over the contents of the libretti, these reflections would tend to make his next libretto more in tune with the taste of the public and with the developing literary orthodoxy of the 1670s than was *Alceste* (Beaussant, *Lully* 562).

It is clear, however, that Quinault and Lully were at the same time trying to please a part of their public that still enjoyed the more heterogeneous entertainment of court ballets and mascarades. In the days before the beginning of Lent in 1675, while the success of *Thésée* at court was making the Parisian public eager to see the new work, Lully prepared a revised version of the mascarade *Le Carnaval,* which he had first produced in 1668. Like *Les Fêtes de l'Amour et de Bacchus,* it consisted mostly of excerpts from earlier comedy-ballets, such as *Monsieur de Pourceaugnac* and *Le Bourgeois gentilhomme.* Quinault's role is not clear, but Bacilly's *Recueil des plus beaux vers* of 1668 attributes two of the songs to him; one of these, "Soyez fidèle / Le soin d'un amant," also appeared in the 1675 version. He may also have helped Lully put the excerpts together (in 1668 and in 1675) and written the introductory "Récit du Carnaval" (see Couvreur, "Collaboration" 28-29). Whatever his role may have been, this work obviously catered to the public's taste for comedy and burlesque and for sung and danced *entrées* with no plot to tie them together. That they would stage such a work immediately before *Thésée* is one of the most obvious indications that the classical esthetic proposed by Boileau in the *Art poétique* of 1674 was far from having replaced the taste for the *galant.*

It is also clear that *Thésée* is a much more important work than *Le Carnaval* and that it represents an effort to placate some of the critics of *Alceste.* The most obvious difference between *Thésée* and *Alceste* is that in the former our attention is focused more on the actions and motivations of the primary characters, since the role of gods and of the secondary characters—and thus of spectacle and of humor—is reduced. Du Bos, in the passage quoted in full in chapter 2 (pp. 88-89), definitely saw the changes in the roles of the comic characters as a concession to the new esthetic, under the influence of spoken tragedy:

le soin qu'il a pris d'annoblir leur caractere, montre qu'il avoit déja
senti que ces rôles étoient hors de leur place dans des Tragédies faites
pour être chantées, autant que dans des Tragédies faites pour être
déclamées (1: 177).

    The secondary characters are still present, especially in the first
two acts, but their actions are less burlesque and better integrated into the
action than in the first two operas. One way Quinault does this is to place
the scenes with secondary characters in the middle of each of the first
three acts, thereby linking their roles to the preceding and following action. In scenes four and five of the first act, for example, Arcas has been
sent with a message from the king to Églé who, unable to conceal her
concern for Thésée, must rely on her confidant, Cléone, to find out if
anything has happened to him (I.iv.61-62). Cléone must in turn rely on
Arcas, which naturally arouses his suspicions as to why Cléone is so concerned about Thésée (I.v.79). The malentendu affords Lully the occasion
for several of his ever-popular airs, but neither scene takes us far from the
main action nor from its serious, heroic tone.

    Scenes four and five of the second act are more like the comic
lovers' quarrels in *Cadmus et Hermione* and *Alceste,* but the songs of Arcas and Dorine in scenes four and five of the third act are more desperate
than comic and more closely related to the primary action, as they try to
convince Dorine that Arcas still loves her and that she should protect
them from Médée's wrath. They escape danger more because they present
a nuisance to Médée (III.v.643-45) than because their plea to Dorine has
been effective and, as in *Cadmus et Hermione* and *Alceste,* they play almost no role from the middle of the third act until the final *divertissement.* It is in this latter half of the opera that the main emotional battles
will be played out.

    If the gradual elimination of what Du Bos called the "bouffons"
can be considered a step forward from the point of view of unity of tone
(and "progress" is a dangerous concept in the comparison of works of
art), it might be considered a step in the opposite direction from the point
of view of moral content. In *Alceste,* only the minor characters expressed
sentiments of dubious moral value (Lycomède's spite, Céphise's fickleness for examples), whereas in *Thésée* we find Égée and Médée singing a
duet to words that would seem more appropriate to Céphise:

Ne nous piquons point de constance;
Consentons à nous dégager.
Goûtons d'intelligence
La douceur de changer. (II.ii.362-65)

We also find Dorine giving advice to Médée that would seem more appropriate for Céphise to give to Straton: "On n'est pas volage / Pour ne changer qu'une fois" (II.i.310-11).[12]

The reduction of the comic elements has little effect on expression of pleasure in the *divertissements*. This is especially true in the fourth act, where the inhabitants of the Enchanted Ile celebrate the happiness that Thésée and Églé think will be theirs:

Sans Amour, tout est sans âme,
L'Amour seul nous rend contents. (IV.vii.985-86)

and in the last act, where Cléone and Arbas celebrate what seems to be definitive happiness:

Le plus sage
S'enflamme, et s'engage.
[...]
Qui n'est point dans l'empire amoureux
N'aura pour partage
Que des soins fâcheux. (V.ix.1132-33, 1158-60)[13]

As in the case of the rather dubious moral advice quoted above, the absence of comedy does not mean the dominance of seriousness. An atmosphere of pleasure is quite possible and can be considered an appropriate

---

[12] One could compare either of these quotations to Céphise's air in *Alceste* I.iv.131-34:

Essaie un peu de l'inconstance.
C'est toi qui le premier m'appris à m'engager;
Pour récompense
Je te veux apprendre à changer.

[13] Lines 1004-1163 are numbered incorrectly as 1005-1164 in my edition; I use the correct line numbers here.

reward for the courage and constancy of the hero and heroine. It was obviously considered a greater violation of the unity of tone to mix tragedy and comedy than to mix tragic situations with extremely happy ones.

The considerably reduced role of the gods in *Thésée* is another example of an apparent concession to criticisms of *Alceste* and of *Cadmus et Hermione*. Although Perrault defended the presence of "ces Divinitez qui viennent à tous momens se presenter sur le Theatre, sans qu'il en soit aucun besoin" as appropriate in opera and machine plays (*Critique d'Alceste* 98-99), Quinault must have decided to take some of the criticisms to heart. In *Thésée*, Minerva is the only visitor from Olympus and, though she is invoked frequently in the first act and helps the Athenians achieve victory, she appears only at the end of the last act. Even then she has only four lines (1120-23), plus seven with the chorus (1124, 1126-31).[14] Her powers are greater than those of Médée, and it is fitting that her presence—real or imagined—frames the five acts of the tragedy. It is only with her divine help that Médée's plans are thwarted, just as it was only with her help that Thésée and the Athenians defeated their enemies in the first act. At the same time, however, her intervention in the last act leaves the Athenians free to work out their own future—Médée and her magic are gone, and Minerve remains "dans la gloire," that is, suspended above the humans in a representation of celestial glory. (Furetière defines *gloire* as "Un lieu fort éclairé, une représentation imparfaite de la Gloire Céleste.") She is more a personification of wisdom and valor than a participant, quite different from a goddess such as Juno, whose very human feelings often bring her to cause unhappiness on earth. There is no indication that she is present in the last scene of the act, which represents a considerable departure from *Cadmus et Hermione*, in which all the gods were present, as well as from *Alceste*, which featured Apollo and the muses in the final scene.

This conclusion, in which the mortal characters are in relative control of their fate, emphasizes the theme of self-control, which dominates the end of *Alceste* and will return in almost all of Quinault's libretti:

---

[14] In comparison, *Cadmus et Hermione* contains speaking roles for Junon, Pallas, l'Amour, Mars, Jupiter, Venus, and l'Hymen, as well as a solo dance for Comus. *Alceste* contains speaking roles for Thétis, Éole, Apollon, Diane, Charon, Pluton, Proserpine, and Alecton, as well as a winged Mercure.

Jupiter must learn his lesson in *Isis,* Phinée and Phaéton meet their doom
in *Persée* and *Phaéton,* and Roland and Renaud stray dangerously far
from duty in *Roland* and *Armide.* It was definitely a popular theme, and
the aging Égée's willingness to control his passions and give up the
woman he loves to his son[15] must have contributed to the success of
Thésée. It is the kind of act that was in accord with the moral code of the
older feudal nobility, with the more modern *galanterie,* and with the strict
morality of Jansenism; in short, it was sure to please.

The recognition scene (V.iv), in which Égée recognizes his son
just before the latter drinks the poison Médée and Égée had prepared for
him, is another example of a scene that was sure to please the spectators.
We learn Thésée's true identity in act IV, scene v, and suspense builds as
we wonder when and how he will reveal himself to his father. Gros criticizes this scene (*Quinault* 599), but it was successful enough to generate
parodies, such as that of Favart, in which we find this dialogue:

THÉSÉE

Du Roi je crains peu la colère;

Apprends enfin qu'il est mon père.

ÉGLÉ

Quoi?...

THÉSÉE

       Oui, sans qu'il en sache rien.

Je suis ce fils qu'il idolâtre....

ÉGLÉ

Pourquoi te taire?...

THÉSÉE

          Il le faut bien:

Je ménage un coup de théâtre. (scene xiv, p. 39).

[...]

LE ROI

Qu'allois-je faire!

---

[15] Trop aimable Églé, je vous aime;
    Mais je veux être heureux dans un autre moi-même. (V.v.1086-87)
Égée is of course less heroic than Alcide, and his "triomphe" is less noble. He is old,
somewhat ridiculous as a lover, and willing to sacrifice Thésée to his own political and
amorous goals (V.iii).

> Dieux! je suis son pere
> Je le vois à ce sabre là;
> Viens embrasser ton papa. (scene 18, p. 49)

On a somewhat more serious level, this recognition scene provides not only a bit of melodrama but a suggestion of divine providence that protects Thésée so that he may inherit the throne of his ancestors. Until the fourth act, he had relied on his own merits, both to prove his prowess and to be sure Églé loved him for himself:

> Je n'ai montré d'abord que ma seule valeur;
> C'était à mon propre mérite
> Que je voulais devoir ma gloire et votre cœur. (IV.v.832-34).

It is hard to say whether he raises his sword in the fourth scene of the last act to give his father a chance to recognize him, or simply to highlight his oath, but the overall effect is that of a near-miraculous escape from death. To his royal blood, almost literally superhuman valor,[16] and his faithful love, there is now added a hint of divinity, a confirmation of the divine right claimed by monarchs in the seventeenth century.

It is one of the functions of tragedy and of tragi-comedy, at least in a monarchic society, to play out various political situations, and especially questions of succession. By presenting father and son as potential candidates for the same marriage and the same throne, Quinault gives to *Thésée* a plot that is both tightly knit and rich in episodes that will guarantee its success: a tender love story, the danger of popular insurrection, the choice of a ruler, a long-awaited reunion between father and son, and much more. However, before looking at this plot in more detail in the second section of this chapter, one should consider the role of Médée,

---

[16] In addition to fairly typical characterizations of heroes such as "Tout cède à sa valeur extrême" (I.iii.39) and "On l'a vu triompher dès qu'il a combattu" (II.i.304), Thésée is literally described as a god: "Thésée est le Dieu tutélaire / Qui me donne en ce temple un refuge assuré" (I.iii.22-23). See Couvreur, *Lully* 355-57 for a more detailed discussion of *Thésée* in the context of the representation of kingship, and, on the topic in general, the introduction, 32-35.

which is perhaps the most important ingredient of all in the recipe for the continuing success of *Thésée*.[17]

§ § §

Médée is Quinault's first character with magical powers, and the first of a very long series of magicians who will appear in the *tragédie lyrique* of the seventeenth and eighteenth centuries (Gethner, "La Magicienne à l'opéra"). In fact, it is a commonplace that magicians are perfect for opera, since they provide an excuse for special effects such as demons, monsters, and flying chariots. Even the vocabulary of the period made it seem natural to place magicians in operas, since *charme* and its related words, so popular with *galant* authors and so often used by operatic lovers, retained the earlier, stronger meaning of magical powers.[18] Characters with magical powers figured frequently in court ballets, Italian operas, and machine plays (including Armide in his own *Comédie sans comédie*, 1655), and Quinault must have been aware that a character such as Médée could assure the success of his next libretto. Still, he took care to integrate her skillfully into the story of Thésée, Égée, and Églé, to the point of adding considerably to the role of the latter in order to provide Médée with a rival and an obvious motive for vengeance.[19]

The role of Médée also provides another angle on the futility of trying to use power to win love. In these operas, in which love is almost inseparable from glory and/or merit, neither political nor magical powers can guarantee love, though both types of power are presented as desirable

---

[17] Médée of course figures frequently in seventeenth-century tragedy and opera. Two of the best known examples are Corneille's machine play *La Conquête de la toison d'or* (1662) and the opera *Giasone* by Cavalli, whose *Ercole amante* played such an important role in the introduction of opera into France (see chap. 2, *Cadmus et Hermione*, 72).

[18] For example, Dorine tells Médée that "Thésée est un Héros charmant" (II.i.296), but the latter replies shortly thereafter that "[...] on ne force point un cœur à s'enflammer; / Mes charmes les plus forts ne sauraient l'y contraindre" (II.i.337-38). The best-known example in Quinault's libretti of a woman with both physical and magical charms is of course Armide.

[19] In Ovid's *Métamorphoses*, Medea has married Ægeus and tries to kill Theseus; her motive is not stated explicitly. I will discuss Églé in more detail near the end of section 2.

and important.[20] Draco (*Cadmus et Hermione*), Lycomède, Straton, and
Alcide (*Alceste*) had already tried to force themselves on the women they
loved and failed, and now both Égée and Médée will be equally unsuccessful, as will numerous others after them.

Ovid's story of Medea offers an especially rich source for this
theme: at the beginning of book VII, Medea tries to resist her violent passion for Jason, though she knows she has the powers to help him and
thus, she hopes, to win his affections. She can of course not resist when
he asks for her help and offers to marry her, and the tragic conclusion of
their marriage is well known. Quinault summarizes Médée's hesitations
briefly in what is the first of her several monologues, though here it is her
love for Thésée that she is trying to resist:

> Doux repos, innocente paix,
> Heureux, heureux un cœur qui ne vous perd jamais!
> L'impitoyable Amour m'a toujours poursuivie;
> N'était-ce point assez des maux qu'il m'avait faits?
> Pourquoi ce Dieu cruel, avec de nouveaux traits,
> Vient-il encor troubler le reste de ma vie? (II.i.287-92)

The combination of a yearning for virtue with uncontrollable passion and
a capacity for cruel violence offers the potential for an extremely complex
character, rich in irony, a potential that Quinault exploits to the maximum
allowed by the brevity imposed on librettists and that Lully expresses
with some remarkable music.[21]

---

[20] Égée's angry oaths (I.viii.200-02) will be of no avail, and Médée's plans will be
thwarted by chance (the recognition of Thésée as the son of Égée) and by Minerva. Célénus and Cybèle, in *Atys*, will also find that their power, royal in the first case and divine in the second, is unable to win the love of Sangaride and Atys. See Couvreur, *Lully*
366, on power as the Achilles heel of Draco, Lycomède, Straton, Égée, Médée, and
Phinée.

[21] It is true that Médée is not alone here, that her confidant Dorine is listening and
will react to what Médée has said. Still, the passage is not addressed to anyone, and it
has the function and form of a monologue. See the introduction, pp. 26-27. For an example of the violent side of Médée's character, see II.i.330-33: "Mon dépit, tu le sais,
dédaigne de se plaindre: / Il est difficile à calmer, / S'il venait à se rallumer, / Il faudrait
du sang pour l'éteindre." I will return to Quinault's use of irony in the discussion of
Médée's monologues, toward the end of section 1 of this chapter.

In fact, Quinault's Médée is not unlike much better-known characters such as Racine's Phèdre, who would appear two years after *Thésée.* Both were attracted by virtue, before giving in—with encouragement from their confidant—to their passion. Both love the son of their husband or fiancé, both try to have the son killed by the father, after they find out that the son loves someone else (in both cases, a woman forbidden by the father). It is probably only coincidence that Thésée figures in both plays (at quite different periods in his life), and it is as problematic to speak of influence in such cases as it is of progress (see p. 134, above), but the similarities are striking. In any case, what dramatist would not be tempted by such a heroine?[22]

§ § §

In addition to several rather tangible features of *Thésée*—unity of action, reduced and refined comedy, limited presence of divinities, the recognition scene, the question of royal succession, the fascinating sorceress-heroine—that make it different from *Cadmus et Hermione* and *Alceste,* there is the more subjective question of the general quality of the writing. Several critics have felt that Quinault's writing is more "mature" in *Thésée,* that he avoids some weaknesses that they have noticed in the first two libretti. Gros, for example, wrote that

> Malgré quelques maladresses dans la conduite de l'action, le livret de *Thésée* marque un progrès évident sur *Cadmus* et sur *Alceste;* on y devine que le poète prend de plus en plus conscience des besoins de son art. Les scènes épisodiques ont pour ainsi dire disparu, l'élément comique est à peu près éliminé et l'unité de ton partiellement atteinte. Si l'on ajoute que la peinture des sentiments est moins superficielle, le vers aussi coulant, mais plus ferme que dans les opéras précédents, on

---

[22] It is of course almost inevitable that Racine and Quinault, the two most successful playwrights of the 1670s, would use similar characters and situations in their plays. To take but one additional example, one could compare Médée's observation of Thésée and Églé in IV.v, where she has forced the latter to hide her love from her beloved and to pretend that she loves Égée, to II.vi of *Britannicus,* in which Néron watches while Junie is forced to feign "froideurs" (II.iii.673) to cause her beloved Britannicus to believe that she cannot be his.

comprendra que *Thésée* mérite une place à part dans cette première période de l'activité lyrique de Quinault. (*Quinault* 602-03)

Each reader will have to decide for him or herself what it means for poetry to be "firm." Perhaps the characters seem to express themselves more
forcefully in *Thésée* than in *Cadmus et Hermione,* with more passion, but
it would be difficult to improve on the passion of the *adieux* of Cadmus
and Hermione (II.iv); or perhaps the first six scenes of *Thésée* constitute a
more gripping climate of war than the second act of *Alceste,* though Alcide's crossing of the Acheron and entry into Hades in the fourth act of
Alceste are striking. And it would seem to be impossible to go beyond the
moving simplicity of "Alceste, vous pleurez / Admète, vous mourez"
(II.viii) or of "Alceste est morte" (III.iv). On the other hand, as Girdlestone suggests (71), these scenes of farewell and death are more elegiac,
more "poétiques et chantants" than forceful and firm, and there are fewer
of them in *Thésée.*

There is at least one quite tangible aspect of the writing in
Thésée—Médée has several powerful monologues that offer Quinault
more opportunities to dwell on the feelings of a character than he had had
in *Cadmus et Hermione* or in *Alceste.* One can imagine how he felt as he
began to compose Médée's first monologue, at the beginning of act II
(quoted above, p. 140), remembering the marvelous pages with which
Ovid began his account of the adventures of the famous sorceress (book
VII, lines 9-74). This first monologue introduces Médée, and the other
two (II.ix and V.i) frame the central section of the opera, centered on her
vengeance (see below, section 2). Médée expresses not just her passion
and her notorious tendency toward bloodshed, but also her doubts and
hesitations, thus making her a multidimensional character, a reluctant
criminal instead of simply a vengeful villain. Like Ovid's Medea, she has
known a period of calm, undisturbed by passion, and Quinault makes her
somewhat innocent of the fury she will soon unleash. She is all fury in her
second monologue, at the end of act II, when she learns of Thésée's love
for Églé, but her moment of pity and admiration for Thésée in IV.vi.861-
67 seems sincere, as does her love for him, which makes her hesitations
in her last monologue so moving.

Quinault introduces his Médée with two lines that suggest the *tendresse* for which he is so famous, but changes the mood quickly with the harsh sounds of *impitoyable* and especially of *N'était-ce point assez*. These sounds create a remarkable counterpoint to *Doux repos, innocente paix:* the /é/, /t/, /è/, and /s/ at the beginning of line 290 are far from the /ou/, /r/, and /o/ at the beginning of line 287, yet the /p/, /in/, /t/, /s/, /é/ of *N'était-ce point assez* are just close enough to the /s/, /an/ /t/, /p/, /è/ of *innocente paix* to recall these opening words (Lully uses almost the same melody to set the two phrases). Quinault thus underlines the duality of Médée's character before ending the monologue with the loss of peace that will be definite by the end of the act, which closes with another monologue by Médée. Here there is no hesitation, and we hear Médée's fury in *dépit* before we learn from the next line that she has abandoned herself to it. *Tendresse* has become "fatale," and it must disappear, as had her *repos* at the beginning of the act:

> Dépit mortel, Transport jaloux,
> Je m'abandonne à vous.
> Et toi, meurs pour jamais, tendresse trop fatale;
> Que le barbare Amour, que j'avais cru si doux,
> Se change dans mon cœur en Furie infernale. (II.ix.491-95)

The similarities of sound between *vous perd jamais* (II.i.288) and *meurs pour jamais* are striking.

Médée's last monologue (V.i) returns to the duality of the beginning of the second act but moves quickly to a terrifying conclusion by means of a rhetorical device similar to that in Rodrigue's famous *stances* in *Le Cid* (I.vi), in which slight changes in a repeated passage reveal that the speaker has made a difficult decision. In the present case, the change from "faut-il" (998) to "il faut" (1004) tells us that Médée is ready to commit murder:

> Que fais-tu ma fureur, où vas-tu m'engager?
> Punir ce cœur ingrat, c'est me punir moi-même,
> J'en mourrai de douleur, je tremble d'y songer,
> Ah, faut-il me venger

> En perdant ce que j'aime?
> Ma rivale triomphe, et me voit outrager!
> Quoi, laisser son amour sans peine et sans danger?
> Voir le spectacle affreux de son bonheur extrême?
> Non, il faut me venger
> En perdant ce que j'aime.[23] (V.i.995-1004)

It is safe to say that Médée is "firm" here at the end; not only has she made up her mind, but she uses short lines with straightforward syntax and hard vowels (/f/, /p/, /d/, /k/).

At the same time that these hesitations and doubts make Médée an interesting character, "ni tout à fait coupable ni tout à fait innocente" (preface to *Phèdre*), her expression of her innermost feelings to the spectators—but not to the other characters—provides several opportunities for effective tragic irony. For example, when Médée pretends to help Thésée or Églé, the spectator knows that she is insincere, though it is possible that some part of Médée believes in some way that she is sincere, the same part that regrets her lost peace and will hesitate before deciding to try to murder Thésée:

> Laissez-moi voir Églé, laissez-moi voir le Roi,
> Vous connaîtrez bientôt les soins que je vais prendre: (II.viii.487-88)
> [...]
> Vous aimez donc Thésée? ah! n'en rougissez pas,
> Il n'est que trop digne qu'on l'aime.
> Je m'intéresse en votre amour;
> Parlez, vous connaîtrez mon cœur à votre tour. (III.iii.565-698)

---

[23] Two words here require some explanation. Line 1000 contains the only occurrence in these libretti of the verb *outrager* without an object, an unusual usage that should probably be taken to refer to Médée's unusually cruel efforts to separate Églé and Thésée in the fourth act. *Perdre,* in lines 999 and 1004, means to cause someone to die.

In *Le Cid,* Rodrigue ends his first *stance* with:

> O Dieu, l'étrange peine!
> En cet affront mon père est l'offensé,
> Et l'offenseur le père de Chimène!

and the last with:

> Ne soyons plus en peine,
> Puisqu'aujourd'hui mon père est l'offensé,
> Si l'offenseur est père de Chimène.

Such ironic moments also create a certain kind of suspense, since the spectator knows that this moment of accord cannot last but does not know just when it will end. This suspense is especially strong in the last act, when what we have learned about Médée from her monologues is combined with our knowledge that Thésée is the son of Égée and that Médée and Égée plan to murder him. When these last two say to Thésée and Églé, "Ne craignez rien, parfaits amants; / Les plaisirs suivront vos tourments" (V.iv.1049-50), the spectator cannot help but fear that the horrible fate hidden beneath their irony will indeed come to pass. Once again, as in *Alceste,* the opposition between moral and immoral, between peace and war, underlies the action.

- II -

The continued success of *Thésée* can be attributed in part to the presence of themes and to a structure that are typical of the *tragédie lyrique* in general yet handled in an especially successful way. Works that stray too far from the mold are soon forgotten, as Quinault and Lully would learn from the criticisms of *Isis,* yet works that repeat a consecrated formula are equally forgotten.

Thésée is a perfect example of an opera with a theme that is at the heart of the *tragédie lyrique,* the effort to reconcile love and glory. As I pointed out in the introduction (20), the most typical plot (*Roland* and *Armide* are the main exceptions) involves a hero who overcomes many obstacles, often with supernatural help, and marries his beloved. He covers himself with glory as he overcomes the obstacles, for without glory he would be unworthy of his beloved. Glory often takes him away from the pleasures of love—and one finds tender farewell scenes from *Cadmus et Hermione* (II.iv) to *Amadis* (I.ii)—but the true hero manages to effect a happy combination of the two; as Alcide said in *Alceste,* "Ah! qu'il est doux de courir à la gloire / Lorsque l'Amour en doit donner le prix!" (V.iv.866-67). In *Thésée,* at the beginning of act III, Églé still has not seen Thésée, and is of course worried that his glory has caused him to forget his love for her:

ÉGLÉ
Ne verrai-je point paraître
Un si glorieux vainqueur?
Il négligera peut-être
La conquête de mon cœur.
CLÉONE
On n'est pas inconstant pour aimer la Victoire.
Si le passage est beau de l'Amour à la Gloire,
Rien n'est si doux que le retour
De la Gloire à l'Amour.
ÉGLÉ
Non, son amour n'est point extrême:
Faut-il qu'il trouve ailleurs tant de soins importants?
Il n'ignore pas que je l'aime,

Il doit songer que je l'attends.

ÉGLÉ et CLÉONE

La Gloire n'est que trop pressante,

Un Héros doit la suivre avec empressement,

Mais dès que la Gloire est contente,

L'Amour doit promptement

Ramener un amant. (III.i.512-28)

Could one sum up better the dilemma that confronts these heroic couples? Love is impossible without glory, yet glory demands long separations. It is a situation that is emminently dramatic, with tender love scenes followed by farewells, perilous adventures for the hero and anxiety for the heroine, and then either a sad or a happy conclusion. If what seems to be a conclusion comes before the end, we can be sure that one more reversal of fortune is still to come, such as the abduction and return of Hermione or the destruction and reconstruction of the palace in *Thésée.*

The love-glory dilemma also presents numerous opportunities for discussion of the pros and cons of both sides, a favorite activity of *galant* society. The passage I just quoted (III.i.512-528) is a rather extended example, similar to the "questions d'amour" in which the young Quinault excelled.[24] Though it may seem extraneous to the action, it contributes to one of the peculiarities of the structure of this libretto: the delayed arrival of Thésée on stage. Before looking at this structure in more detail, however, it is important to consider some of the variations on the themes of love and glory that one finds in *Thésée.*

Thésée is especially rich in these variations, thanks in large part to the semantic flexibility of the verb *charmer,* which can refer to the charms of a lover, of a ruler, or of a magician (see p. 139 and n. 18). The "beaux yeux" of Églé (IV.v.818) charm both father and son, but she loves only the latter, largely because of his glory:

---

[24] This parlor game was in vogue in the 1660s, when Quinault was a popular author who frequented the court as well as *galant* salons. People were invited to respond to questions such as "Si l'on doit haïr quelqu'un de ce qu'il nous plaît trop, quand nous ne pouvons lui plaire." This is one of five questions proposed by Mme de Brégy around 1665, to which Louis XIV asked Quinault to respond. The questions and Quinault's responses are published in *Les Œuvres galantes de Madame la Comtesse de B;* see Gros, *Quinault* 66-70.

> Ah! qu'un jeune Héros, dans l'horreur des combats,
> Couvert de sang et de poussière,
> Aux yeux d'une Princesse fière
> A de charmants appas! (I.iii.34-37)

Médée herself falls under the charm of Thésée ("La Gloire de Thésée à mes yeux paraît belle," II.i.303), but must rely on a different kind of charm to try—unsuccessfully—to win his love. Finally, Thésée's glory charms the lower classes ("Ses glorieux exploits charment la populace," II.iii.376), and he tries to keep their favor while keeping them at a distance (II.vii). In short:

> Églé's beauty charms Thésée and Égée, who want to marry her.
> Thésée's glory charms Églé and Médée, who want to marry him.
> Thésée's glory charms the people, who want him as king.

Beauty and glory—the point of view is of course rather masculine—are at the origin of a variety of attractions, some of which are mutual, while others generate conflicts that structure the action at several levels. Égée uses persuasion and power to try to influence Églé, Médée uses magic charms to try to separate Thésée and Églé, and the people are tempted to replace Égée with Thésée.

§ § §

Like many of the Quinault-Lully *tragédies lyriques,* these conflicts constitute a series of variations on the general theme of war and peace, which provides a high-level structure for the prologue as well as for the five acts. In one version of the prologue, probably the first,[25] Pleasure, Games, and the Graces flee the horrors of war:

---

[25] In most editions of the prologue, one finds:
    Les Jeux et les Amours
    Ne règnent pas toujours.
This change was perhaps made because Turenne's victory on Jan. 5, 1675, had removed the threat of war and/or to remove the idea of headlong flight—the Jeux are only going to go a slight distance, into nearby woods—in order better to prepare the coexistence of

Fuyons, la guerre est de retour.
Fuyons ses fureurs inhumaines. (P.1-2)

while in the other they are leaving because Louis has neglected them for Victory and Glory. In both versions, Mars arrives, not to replace war with peace, but to establish a climate in which the people can enjoy the pleasures of peace even during a time of war:

Au milieu de la guerre
Goûtons les plaisirs de la paix. (P.94-95)

The prologue concludes with a repetition of these lines, a moment of joy in the midst of conflict. The first act continues this opposition, with Églé having fled the battleground and hoping for victory in order to be able to concentrate on love. By the end of the last act, war has given way to peace, in the literal sense that the battle is over, but also in the sense that the various conflicts are resolved—Médée's vengeance is thwarted and Thésée is no longer a political or amorous rival to Égée.

The various movements from war to peace, or from conflict to resolution, provide several structures through which the spectator can understand and order the action. There is no one obvious structure, except for the movement from opening conflict to closing resolution that one finds in almost any play. Couvreur (*Lully* 328) suggests a modified binary structure, with an opening opposition between war and victory resolved by the establishment of peace (marriage and the agreement on a successor to Égée):

Themes:	War	Victory	Peace
Prologue:	Plaisirs dispersed by war	Arrival of Mars and Bellone	Restoration of peace
Politics:	Rebellion against Égée (act I)	Victory of Thésée (acts I et II)	Recognition of Thésée by Égée (act V)
Tragedy, Love:	Jealousy of Médée (act II)	Elimination of Médée (act V)	Marriage of Thésée and Églé (act V)

---

war and peace; see Denécheau, "*Thésée* de Lully et Quinault: histoire d'un opéra (1675-1779)" 36.

While this structure provides a useful means to see war, politics, and love from a similar point of view, it does not—nor did Couvreur intend for it to—take into account the peculiarities of the sequence of events in *Thésée:*

> Thésée does not appear until near the end of act II (II.vii.450), and then he disappears again until IV.ii. Even there he is asleep for two scenes; in all, he appears in ten of forty-three scenes.[26]
>
> Médée dominates acts II-IV, but is absent from the beginning and end.
>
> The secondary characters Arcas, Cléone, and Doris play an important role in key places, especially in the middle of the libretto (III.v-vi). In fact, Arcas is the only male present in act III.
>
> There are five changes of scenery, as opposed to the usual four, and only two of them come at the ends of acts. Acts III and IV of *Thésée* are the only examples in Quinault's libretti of acts that do not begin with a new decor.
>
> The action is set in public buildings, especially palaces, in acts I, II, and V, as it is in the prologue, but in supernatural settings in acts III and IV.
>
> The conflict in the central scenes (III.iii-IV.iii) involves Médée and Églé, although what would seem to be the principal conflicts involve Thésée and Égée.

All of these peculiarities involve the middle acts, which constitute both a new beginning and a central panel around which the exterior acts form a ABCB'A' frame.

From this point of view, the main love story begins after the resolution of the military conflict, rather than being superimposed on it, as in Couvreur's binary diagram. What one could call the military section comes to a close with the *divertissement* of act II (scenes vi-vii), which celebrates the victory of the Athenians. The act does not stop here, however, and Thésée's arrival brings the beginning of the second main

---

[26] Églé is present the most often, in twenty-five scenes. Médée figures in eighteen, Égée in twelve, and Thésée in ten (plus the two in which he is asleep).

section (II.viii), Médée's desire for vengeance. It features a monologue by Médée in its second and next-to-last scenes (II.ix; V.i), and in between all the characters except Égée and the Grande Prêtresse reenter in the same order as in the first section, including the servants. This section actually has its own five "acts," the first and third concluded by a change of scenery (these are the only acts in Quinault's libretti where the change does not occur at the beginning), the second and fourth by a *divertissement*.

1. Thésée's arrival, Médée's plans for vengeance and her confrontation with Églé (II.viii-III.iii).
2. Églé's suffering at the hands of Médée and her demons (III.iv-III.viii).
3. Médée and Églé; Thésée asleep (IV.i-IV.iii).
4. Églé tries to give up Thésée; Médée has pity on them and promises them happiness (IV.iv-IV.vii).
5. Médée changes her mind and swears vengeance (V.i-V.ii).

The third and final section, in this view, is made up of the last seven scenes, beginning with Égée's return in V.iii (V.ii can be seen as the end of the second section or as an introduction to the third). Though the question of Médée's vengeance is of course not resolved, it appears to be at the end of act IV, and the setting is now quite different—Médée is back in a public place, after having been isolated with Thésée and Églé in a desert and on an enchanted isle. All the main characters are together, for the first time (V.iv), and Médée has tried to make Égée the instrument of her vengeance. Even this brief section could be said to have five acts:

1. The agreement between Égée and Médée (iii).
2. The recognition scene (iv).
3. Médée's flight and the apparent happy ending (v).
4. The destruction of the enchanted palace (vi-vii).
5. Minerva provides a new palace; celebration (viii-ix).

This final section ends—appropriately—quite conclusively: the lovers are reunited, as are father and son; the future of the Athenian monarchy is secure; Médée is gone, "replaced" by Minerva; Égée and his court have a secure palace. There is nothing left but a final celebration of love, sung by Arcas and Cléone.

The conclusion is all the more satisfactory in that it brings back several elements that were prominent at the beginning—the décor of a palace, the presence of a chorus and of Arcas and Cléone (absent from act IV), and Égée. All of this suggests a structure around a central panel, the section from II.viii to V.ii where the main love story begins. The first section also has a five-part structure:

1. Églé in the temple (I.i-vi).
2. Égée and Églé; the sacrifice (I.vii-x).
3. Médée and Égée (II.i-iii).
4. Arcas and Doris (II.iv-v).
5. Celebration (II.vi-ix).[27]

After the first six scenes, in which we learn the basic situation (but nothing about Médée) from Églé, Arcas, and Cléone, the king enters and expresses his love for Églé. After the sacrifice, which constitutes the *divertissement* of the first act (ix-x), Égée and Médée decide to break their engagement so he can be free to love Églé while Médée pursues Thésée. The rest of the act is devoted to the secondary characters Arcas (who is also eager to break a previous engagement) and Doris and to the celebration of victory.

This structure around a central panel is reinforced by similarities between parts of the first section and parts of the third. Scenes vii-viii of act I, in which Égée declares his love for Églé, find an echo in V.v, when he decides to yield her to Thésée. Similarly, scenes ii-iii of act II, in which Égée and Médée change their previous plans, has its counterpart in V.iii, when they make new plans. In short, one finds the king interacting with Églé and Médée at the beginning and end, providing a frame which adds a sense of closure, although not a very neat symmetry. First of all, the third section consists of only seven scenes, whereas the first two sections occupy seventeen and nineteen, respectively. Furthermore, the first

---

[27] There is also a slightly different way of looking at this first section:
    1. Églé in the temple (I.i-vi).
    2. Égée and Églé (I.vii-viii).
    3. Sacrifice (I.ix-x).
    4. Médée and Égée (II.i-iii).
    5. Arcas and Doris; the celebration (II.iv-ix).

section is interrupted by Médée's monologue in II.i, and there is no strong relationship between the first six scenes of act I and the last four scenes of act V, except that both sequences involve participants who are helpless to stop a struggle (the battle outside the Temple and Médée's destruction of the palace followed by Minerva's revelation of a new one).[28]

The two previous libretti had a much more obvious ABCB'A' structure. As Couvreur points out in the case of *Cadmus et Hermione* (*Lully* 339), each act is dominated by one of the following subjects:

1. A: Declaration by Cadmus of his love for Hermione (I.iv).
2. B: Separation of Cadmus and Hermione (II.iv).
3. C: Combat of Cadmus against dragon, soldiers, and Draco (III.iii; IV.iii-v).
4. B': Reunion of Cadmus and Hermione (IV.vi).
5. A': Marriage of Cadmus and Hermione (V.iii).

There is a similar structure in *Alceste,* in which a central act, dominated by the death of Alceste, is flanked by two acts in a different location and characterized by a battle or struggle (the siege of Scyros in act II, Alcide's entry into Hades in act IV) and by two acts that feature the wedding of Alceste and Admète (interrupted in act I, completed in act V).

I think it is precisely this absence of such a neat, symmetrical structure that helped make *Thésée* such a success in the seventeenth and eighteenth centuries. Quinault has moved away from the model of

---

[28] Lully's choice of keys also suggests a circular structure, organized around a central panel. The key of C major opens and closes the opera, and the second and fourth acts also end in C. Médée's first and third monologues come in the only two scenes (II.i, V.i) that feature E minor prominently. The third act has its own tonal center of F major, related to C major, but combined here with B flat major and D minor, whereas in the other acts C major is most often used in combination with G major and A minor. The result— to simplify considerably—is that one finds the same groupings I just described in an ABCB'A' structure: a separation of the first two acts from the third; a feeling that Médée's first and third monologues define a central section; a fifth act that, after the two opening scenes, returns to keys used in the first two acts.

This book is not the place for a detailed discussion of Lully's use of keys, an important and often unrecognized aspect of his musical style. For a more complete treatment, see Duron's analysis of *Atys,* to which I will refer often in the next chapter, and his "L'Instinct de M. de Lully," pp. 81-84. Note also the comment by Lecerf, "Quand je vois ces belles scènes d'*Armide* ou de *Thésée,* rouler toujours sur le même ton, je ne puis m'empêcher de m'écrier: y avait-il tant de belles choses dans ce ton seul?" (2: 136).

Cadmus et Hermione and *Alceste,* in which the presence of a hero (Cadmus, Alcide) from beginning to end provides a convenient way to conceptualize the unfolding of the plot, in spite of episodes that involve other characters. This move away from a single hero is already nascent in *Alceste,* where Alcide is temporarily forgotten during the agony of Admète and the death of Alceste, but taken much farther in *Thésée,* in which no character appears in every act and in which the title character does not play an important part in the action until the fourth act. Our interest moves from Égée and Églé as a potential couple (I.viii) to Médée (II.i) to the clash between Médée and Églé (III.iii-IV.iii) to the love between Églé and Thésée (IV.iv-v) to their confrontation with Médée (IV.vi) and finally to all four of these characters together (V.iv-V.viii).

Thésée is certainly not without structure, nor without similarities to the two preceding Quinault-Lully operas. In addition to the three-part structure I have discussed, the libretto contains other features that create overall unity, such as the concentration of scenes with the chorus at the beginning of the first act and at the end of the last. Like *Cadmus et Hermione* and *Alceste,* there are five acts, each with its *divertissement,* and much of the action revolves around exploits or the love of a hero. Within the acts, formal elements such as the alternation between air and recitative and the use of a variety of verse forms and of styles create unity for smaller units while making each scene distinct from its neighbors. In short, Quinault's contemporaries must have recognized in *Thésée* a new opera in a now-familiar mold, but also something quite new.

One reason for the newness and complexity of *Thésée* is the expansion of the "love triangle," in which one member of a couple has a rival (or two, as in *Alceste*), to a four-part scheme in which each member of a couple is loved by someone else. That is, $\rightarrow \leftrightarrow$ becomes $\rightarrow \leftrightarrow \leftarrow$, as the happiness of the couple Thésée-Églé is threatened on the one hand by Égée and on the other by Médée. Quinault thus has to present four principal characters and four couples or potential couples (Égée-Églé, Églé-Thésée, Thésée-Médée, Médée-Égée), which obviously makes for considerable complexity. It is as if he were moving gradually toward this structure, beginning with *Cadmus et Hermione* in which there are really only two principal characters (Cadmus, Hermione), who are threatened by a rather stereotypical giant. *Alceste* has three main characters (Alceste, Admète, Alcide) plus a second rival (Lycomède) who, if not as complex as Alcide, is more interesting than Draco. Then comes *Thésée* with four principal characters and two important rivals, both of whom are interesting in their own right and wield enough power (political or magical) to present a serious threat. Quinault will use a similar set of characters in *Atys,* where a king and a goddess threaten the happiness of the couple, but will return to a simpler arrangement in the remaining libretti.[29]

      Quinault went to considerable trouble to develop the character of Églé and complete this two-couple structure. She does not figure in most versions of this part of the myth of Medea, including that of Ovid, who is Quinault's main source. He apparently found her in Plutarch's account of the life of Thésée (12-13), in which she is identified as the daughter of Panopeus (and thus the great-granddaughter of Æacus, whose story follows immediately that of Medea and Theseus in the *Metamorphoses*) and the woman for whom, in some versions of the myth, Theseus abandoned Ariadne on Naxos. Quinault moves her from Naxos to Athens and involves her with each aspect of the plot of *Thésée:* she resists the advances of Égée, tries hard to stand up to Médée, and does her best to save Thésée's life. She plays a more passive role at the end (V.iv-viii), but her presence there completes one of the most important structural elements that hold the work together. It was with her that the opera began, and her marriage to Thésée ends the last act as her resistance to a marriage with Égée did the first. In fact, as I pointed out earlier, she is present in far more scenes than any other character, and it is she who provides the most continuous strand in this texture of coexisting structures.[30]

§ § §

---

[29] *Persée* and *Phaéton* contain four principal characters in similar relationships to those in *Thésée* and *Atys,* but Mérope (*Persée*) and Théone (*Phaéton*) are so much more passive than Médée and Cybèle (*Atys*) that the situation in these two operas is quite different.

[30] Lully gives her special treatment by reserving the key of D minor for the key moments in her story: her resistance to Égée (I.viii), her avowal to Médée of her love for Thésée (III.iii), and her willingness to die for Thésée (IV.vi).

A final similarity between *Thésée* and the two preceding libretti is its happy conclusion and joyous final *divertissement*. Médée has fled, and Minerva has, in addition to saving the Athenians and providing a new palace, swept away the infernal charms of Médée and the décors for which she was responsible (III.iv; IV.iv; V.i). We are left with the same situation as at the end of *Alceste,* in which the rival has agreed to the happiness of the original couple and in which the reigning king is not the most heroic or the most virtuous hero on stage. The line "Un roi digne de l'être," two lines before the end of the next to last scene literally refers to Égée, who has yielded Églé but not yet the throne to his son, but it also suggests Thésée, the glorious hero. Is this a convenient ambiguity, allowing the people to praise both princes with one statement, or a sign of trouble, in which the people express their desire for a king (Thésée) who is truly worthy? There is not much time, during the performance, at least, to ponder this question, for the celebration is soon over and Arcas and Cléone step forward again to celebrate the joys of *galant* love. We are firmly within the traditional bounds of the *tragédie lyrique,* but this new form has undergone a considerable enrichment.

5

Atys

The Tragic Chord on the Lyre

> [*Atys*] équivaut, dans le genre opéra, à ce
> qu'était une œuvre de Racine dans le domaine
> de la tragédie.
>
> Gros, *Quinault* 607

- I -

ONE COULD SAY, for several reasons, that a book begun in the late twentieth century about Quinault's libretti should begin with *Atys*. First of all,
without the remarkable success of the 1986-87 production by Jean-Marie
Villégier, William Christie, and the Arts Florissants, it is possible that the
Quinault-Lully operas would still be the museum pieces they had been for
200 years, a part of what even enlightened critics call the "dark ages" of
opera:[1]

---

[1] The reference to the "dark ages" is from Kerman's *Opera and Drama* (chap. 3),
discussed in the introduction, p. 18, n. 21.

As a result of the success of *Atys,* the amount of critical literature devoted to it—including an issue of *L'Avant-Scène Opéra* and modern editions by Bassinet, Truchet, and
myself—is vastly greater than that devoted to any of the other Quinault-Lully operas. In
my discussion of the other libretti included in this book, I have been able to synthesize
much of what has been written about them, but that is obviously impossible in the case
of *Atys*.

> Avant *Atys*, personne n'aurait imaginé qu'un opéra de Lully, au cœur
> d'une saison parisienne, pût être donné une quinzaine de représenta-
> tions à guichets fermés. Créé en 1676, oublié un siècle plus tard, re-
> créé en 1986-1987, repris en 1988-1989 et repris une deuxième fois en
> 1992, spectacle emblématique promené à travers l'Europe et les deux
> Amériques, *Atys* constitue une référence dans les histoires (croisées)
> du spectacle et de l'évolution des goûts musicaux. (Deshoulières 37)

Indeed, who would have dared suggest, as late as 1985, that by 1994 Paris
would have seen four Quinault-Lully operas fully staged, much less that
they would play to full houses with people outside begging for tickets, or
that *Phaéton* would be staged to inaugurate the new opera house in Lyon?
Or, better still, that *Atys* would be described by *Newsweek* in 1989 as the
hottest ticket of the New York season?

All this, and more, has come to pass, and of all the surprises that
Atys held for audiences in the late 1980s, one of the greatest—though one
that would not have been a surprise at all for their ancestors three centuries earlier—was the strength of Quinault's libretto and its contribution to
the overall success of the production. Christie has said that he chose *Atys*
because of the dramatic qualities of the libretto ("Lully réévalué" 115),
and many reviews of the performances singled out Quinault for special
praise. Here was a work worthy of comparison to Racinian tragedy, a
gripping drama that—with no small thanks to Villégier—met our expectations of what seventeenth-century theater should be. Indeed, *Atys* has
come to be considered Quinault's best libretto, a correction of earlier
faults and a model to follow.[2] The fact remains, however, that Quinault
did not follow the model of *Atys*, and that it remains a unique work, neither the culmination of an evolution nor a new direction. It is in many
ways a brilliant work, yet the judgment of the seventeenth century was
not always favorable. In the pages that follow I would like to look more
closely at some of its strengths (in particular those of act I, to which I will
devote section 2) and weaknesses, along with some of the reactions of

---

[2] See, for example, Rosow's entry in the *New Grove Opera:* "Twentieth-century
scholars have often cited *Atys* as marking the start of a style period, particularly for its
avoidance of subplots and dramatic interludes in the Venetian manner, along with its
'Racinian severity'" (242); she is referring in part to the work of La Laurencie and of
Gros (*Quinault* 603).

spectators to *Atys* from 1676 to 1992, reactions that are rich in suggestions about the nature of the *tragédie lyrique* and about what it means for
an opera to be dramatic.

§ § §

Following the pattern established with *Thésée, Atys* was created
for the court at Saint-Germain-en-Laye on January 10, 1676, and opened
in Paris in April or May, perhaps for the reopening of the Académie Royale after Easter (probably Tuesday, April 14). It had a remarkable first
run, continuing until the Easter closing the following year, which probably took place in 1677 on February 20, the beginning of the Jubilee. It
would be back less than a year later, first as one of the operas given at
Fontainebleau in August and September of 1677 and at Saint-Germain-
en-Laye in January and February of 1678, then at the Palais-Royal, first
in January-February and again in August 1678, this time for a run of
about five months. It would not be seen again in Paris during the lifetimes
of Quinault and Lully, though it would have a revival at court in January
1682. Later revivals in Paris took place in 1689-90, 1699-1700, 1708-09,
1725, 1738-39, 1747, and 1753, and selected acts were performed at court
in 1703 and 1713. Its success was thus considerable, though it went for a
longer period in the 1680s without a revival than almost all the other Quinault-Lully operas and was one of the first to drop out of the repertoire in
the mid eighteenth century.

Contemporary reaction was mixed, if the circle of Mme de Sévigné was typical. Her daughter, as well as Mme de Lafayette, disliked
Quinault's text, but her son Charles admired it, especially the first two
acts:[3]

---

[3] This is an excellent example of how these libretti were read as independent texts.
See Morel, "Philippe Quinault, librettiste d'*Atys*": "La mère et le fils appréciaient donc
l'œuvre du poète à la simple lecture, privée des agréments de la musique" (22). As
Morel points out (25), Pierre Bayle did not share the Sévigné's enthusiasm for reading
libretti. He wrote to his brother on March 28, 1677, about *Atys* (he refers to a much earlier letter on the same opera that had been lost): "cet opera est si peu de chose, quand il
est dénué de sa musique et de l'actuelle représentation des changements de theatre et de
l'execution des machines, que vous plaindriez toute votre vie les 20, ou 30 sols qu'il
vous couteroit de port. Il n'est rien de plus languissant que cette sorte de vers. Les eve-
nemens et les intrigues ne sont rien à les voir ainsi decharnés; enfin il n'y a presque

> Je vous soutiens que ces deux premiers actes de l'opéra sont jolis, et
> au-dessus de la portée ordinaire de Quinault; j'en ai fait tomber
> d'accord ma mère, mais elle veut vous en parler elle-même. Dites-
> nous ce que vous y trouverez de si mauvais, et nous vous répondrons,
> au moins sur ces premiers actes, car pour l'assemblée des Fleuves, je
> vous l'abandonne. (2: 233; Charles, Feb. 2, 1676)

His mother found much to admire, but still preferred *Alceste* (to which, in
1674, she had preferred *Cadmus et Hermione;* but this is perhaps because
of the influence of the cabal against *Alceste;* see chapter 3, *Alceste,* 94-
96):

> [...] il y a des choses admirables. Les décorations passent tout ce que
> vous avez vu, les habits sont magnifiques et galants. Il y a des endroits
> d'une extrême beauté; il y a un Sommeil et des Songes dont l'inven-
> tion surprend. La symphonie est toute de basses et de tons si assoupis-
> sants qu'on admire Baptiste sur nouveaux frais [...]. Et cependant on
> aime mieux *Alceste*. (2: 285-86; May 6, 1676)

The *Gazette d'Amsterdam* of January 21, 1676, reported that "le
ballet et l'opéra" d'*Atys* met with so little success that the king ordered
Lully "d'y travailler encore pour y augmenter le divertissement." La
Gorce (*Opéra* 56) suggests that it was simply a matter of some problems
with the first performances, since several sources report Louis XIV's admiration of *Atys,* which became known as "l'opéra du roi." His approba-
tion could explain both the initial success (a first run of almost a year)
and the lack of overwhelming success at the Académie Royale after 1678,
since his own interest in opera had begun to diminish by the early 1680s.

With the exception of the comments on the final scene of *Atys,* to
which I will return toward the end of this first section, we have few other
contemporary judgments on *Atys,* except for almost universal appreciation of the *sommeil* in act III and of the touching scene between Atys and

---

personne qui achette ces pieces, sinon ceux qui vont a la representation, afin de suivre de
l'œil les paroles qui se chantent sur le theatre" (f. 130ʳ). Given the number of editions of
Atys published in Paris and in Amsterdam in 1676, Bayle must have been in the minority; even he mentions a cheap edition in Toulouse (f. 199; Aug. 24, 1676).

Sangaride in I.vi.[4] The opera would be quite popular in the eighteenth century, when Voltaire referred to it as "la charmante tragédie d'Atys" ("Art dramatique" 7: 383), and several critics considered it one of Quinault's best libretti, along with *Armide* and *Roland* (Gros, *Quinault* 751-59). By the time Marmontel revised the libretto in 1780, he could complain that Quinault had not put enough violent passion into *Atys,* though his younger contemporary La Harpe found that Quinault had put too much "barbarie" into the last act (1: 665B; Gros, *Quinault* 753).

In short, it would seem that, as successful as *Atys* was in the seventeenth and eighteenth centuries, it met with more consistent approval from spectators, buyers of recordings, and critics in the late twentieth. If today we find it to be the most dramatic, the closest to Racinian tragedy, and therefore the best, and our opinion is somewhat different from that of spectators at the time when Quinault and Racine were both writing for the Parisian stage, there are several possible explanations for the difference:

1. our idea of the dramatic in general;
2. our idea of Racinian tragedy in particular;
3. the assumption that the opera that most resembles Racinian tragedy is the best;
4. our application of our ideas of drama and tragedy to the libretto of Atys.

To proceed somewhat along the lines of Arnauld and Nicole, the authors of the Port-Royal *Logique,* which was undergoing its third revision in the 1670s, the origins of difference or misunderstanding are more likely to lie in our principles and assumptions (*jugements*)—possible explanations one, two, and three—than in a reasoning process that involves a series of applications of these principles to a given work (21, 177-78). In other words, I do not deny that *Atys* is the most tragic of Quinault's libretti, nor that it is the one that can most successfully be compared to Racinian tragedy. However, as I suggested in the introduction, I am not convinced that our modern notion of drama is well suited to the esthetics of opera, and especially of baroque opera, nor that the Racinian model of tragedy was

---

[4] On the *sommeil,* see the Sévigné letter quoted above. On the scene between Atys and Sangaride, see Lecerf 2: 13, quoted below, p. 170; Clément and Laporte 98; Le Brun 26.

solidly established in the 1670s. The "querelle d'*Alceste*" is one example of the debate about tragedy, the arguments over the appropriateness of comic and burlesque elements in *Cadmus et Hermione* and *Alceste* are another; as Deshoulières said in his discussion of Villégier's staging of *Atys*, "N'oublions pas que l'harmonie des règles classiques fut en son temps un objet d'avant-garde, l'enjeu de violents débats" (41). To the extent that it is possible to know how the first spectators reacted to *Atys*, an analysis of the many qualities of the libretto from the point of view of what was most likely to please early audiences and from that of what pleased twentieth-century ones can be enlightening.

§ § §

After the success of *Thésée* and the failure of his rivals to furnish Lully with a suitable libretto (see the beginning of chap. 4), Quinault could consider that his place as Lully's librettist was secure. He had found a successful combination of heroism, love, and the supernatural, with a minimum of divine intervention and of comedy. The emphasis on the human, the noble, and the tragic (in the seventeenth century a tragedy did not necessarily have an unhappy ending) could be considered concessions to the regularity advocated by Boileau and Racine, but the complexity of structure and the multiple centers of interest are still far from Racinian simplicity.

Quinault's choice of a subject is somewhat unusual. The myth of Atys (Attis) was fairly well known, but had not been the subject of important works of literature or painting. It is only mentioned briefly in Ovid's *Metamorphoses*, Quinault's main source for all his other libretti based on classical myths (with the obvious exception of *Alceste*, taken from Euripides). He took the metamorphosis of Atys into a pine tree from the *Metamorphoses*, but based the rest of the opera on Ovid's account in the *Fastae*.[5] There, Atys inspired a chaste love in Cybele, who made him

---

[5] Quinault took the names Sangar and Sangaride from another version of the myth (especially Pausanias's *Graeciae Descriptio*, VII. 17.9-12 and VII. 20.3) in which an almond tree sprang from the emasculated member of the hermaphrodite Agdistis. The daughter of the river god Sangarios picked an almond, placed it against her breast, became pregnant, and gave birth to Attes (Attis). Details vary, but the madness and emasculation of Attis are common to all.

promise to remain a virgin. He betrayed her, however, with the nymph Sagaris. Cybele killed Sagaris by cutting a tree associated with her, and caused Atys to go mad. During his madness he castrated himself, and the priests of Cybele have since then followed his example.

In addition to making some changes in order to stay within the *bienséances* (there is no reference to castration, nor any explicit mention of the consummation of the love between Atys and Sangaride),[6] Quinault had some filling in to do (see Gros, *Quinault* 553-55). In fact, as Beaussant points out (*Lully* 571), it could be the freedom that Quinault had in setting a less well-known myth that allowed him to construct a libretto that is more like a spoken tragedy. Among the characters he created are of course the usual confidants, of whom, as we will see below, Quinault makes especially good use. His most masterful stroke, however, was in filling out the two-couple structure that he had used in *Thésée* by inventing the character of Célénus. In one person we have a king at whose court the action takes place, a friend and protector for Atys, a potential husband for Sangaride, a rival to Atys, and finally his persecutor. His role is not unlike that of Égée in *Thésée*, in that his plans to marry Sangaride are at the origin of the avowals of Atys and Sangaride (separately, then to each other) that put the plot into motion and in that he is powerless at the end to marry the woman he loves.

What Quinault did not add to the story is a hero, even though Cadmus, Alcide, and Thésée had been essential characters in his first three libretti. Atys is not only of humble birth and not at all inclined to heroic deeds, but he betrays his best friend and dishonors his position as Grand Sacrificateur. Other Quinault heroes (especially Roland and Renaud) will temporarily abandon their duty for love, but none will stoop as low as Atys does. Nor does any of them come to a tragic end because of love, though Phaéton's excessive ambition leads to his death. It is as if, in this special form of tragedy that is the *tragédie lyrique*, tragic endings and heroism are meant to be incompatible—in an artform in which Louis XIV sought reflections of his own glory, it would hardly do to have a true hero meet a tragic end.

---

[6] It does not take much imagination, however, to see beyond Cybèle's lines "J'y viens d'être témoin de leur amour extrême" and "Tous deux s'abandonnaient à des transports si doux, / Que je n'ai pu garder plus longtemps le silence" (V.i.870 and 879-80). This is as direct as any reference in Quinault to physical love.

Seen as a successor to *Thésée*, *Atys* can be said to mark the beginning of what Gros calls Quinault's second period, what one could call his
maturity, or at least his putting to use the lessons he learned in the first
three libretti he wrote for Lully. As Gros says,

> *Atys* se distingue de *Thésée* et des livrets antérieurs par deux caractères
> essentiels: il ne contient aucun élément comique; il ne comporte au-
> cune intrigue secondaire. L'œuvre est une: elle est une au point de vue
> du ton, et elle est une au point de vue de l'action. (Quinault 603)

However, one can also say, as Bassinet has, that *Atys* also represents the
end of a period, as far as Quinault would go in a certain direction:

> Quinault y fait preuve d'un véritable projet dramatique et atteint le
> sommet d'une des voies qui s'ouvraient à lui dans la réalisation d'une
> cohérence théâtrale. En effet, *Atys* clôt la première période de l'œuvre
> de Quinault pour Lully qui conduit l'opéra d'une simple traduction du
> modèle italien de l'abbé Buti vers une intégration maximale du modèle
> tragique. Pourtant cet aboutissement demeurera sans postérité jusqu'à
> la mort de Rameau qui met un terme au genre de la tragédie lyrique,
> sans doute parce qu'*Atys* rompt l'équilibre anthologique constitutif de
> la tragédie en musique pour donner à la tragédie une importance
> écrasante. (19-20)

Without looking quite so far ahead, one has only to look at Quinault's
next libretto, *Isis,* to see that Quinault did not see *Atys* as the obvious
model to follow in the rest of his libretti.

There is some truth in both views—*Atys* is different from the three
earlier libretti but also from the following ones. As Gros says, the comic
scenes disappear; the secondary characters are not only not comic, they
are involved in the main action and do not, as they had in the earlier operas, have scenes devoted to their own feelings. Idas and Doris are excellent examples of confidants who first bring out the true feelings of their
friends (I.ii; I.iv) and then devote themselves to their friends' happiness.
Their conversation with Atys in III.ii convinces him to put his love for
Sangaride before his debt to Célénus. If their decision reveals a less than
heroic moral strength ("Le plus juste parti cède enfin au plus fort,"

III.iii.437), it is realistic and, more important from a dramatic point of view, this decision leads directly to the crucial confrontation with Cybèle at the end of the act (III.vi). And, I should add, more important from an operatic point of view, it leads to the famous *sommeil* in the following scene and to Cybèle's poignant monologue in III.viii ("Espoir si cher et si doux"). In sum, we have in this third act an excellent illustration of why *Atys* is so successful from the standpoints of *tragédie* as well as of *lyrique*. After an opening monologue by Atys, the supposedly secondary characters bring about an important change in direction. But before Atys—after another scene alone—can put this decision into practice, a long and musically complex *divertissement* informs him of Cybèle's love. A change of plans is called for, but it is too late, and Sangaride rushes in (after having spoken off stage with Idas and Doris). Instead of winning the goddess's pity, according to the plan devised in III.ii, she incurs her divine wrath, which will dominate the last act. But not, however, before, Cybèle expresses her very human pain in a monologue that by no means sacrifices dramatic intensity to musical expediency.

§ § §

The fourth act offers another example of the key role of the secondary characters, as well as of the continuity and unity of action that one finds in this remarkable libretto. In the first scene, Doris and Idas again influence the decision of one of the principal characters: they keep Sangaride from rejecting Atys completely, enough to make possible her reconciliation with him in IV.iv but not enough to prevent her hesitations in IV.ii-iii. Much as in act III, their plans are delayed by a *divertissement*, in this case the preparations for the wedding between Sangaride and Célénus (IV.v). Coming immediately after Atys and Sangaride have reaffirmed their love for each other, this *divertissement* is an effective means of creating suspense but hardly as effective, musically or dramatically, as the dream sequence in act III, which added a new complication to the plot.

The fourth act is thus very much an integral part of a dramatic whole, even if the acts that precede and follow it last considerably longer. One finds a similar alternation of long and short acts in acts I-III,[7] which

---

[7] In the Christie recording, acts I-V last, respectively, 34, 23, 37, 25 and 31 minutes. In Quinault's text, the five acts have, respectively, 246, 153, 218, 231, and 231 lines.

suggests a conscious decision by Lully but presents a potential problem of
proportion. Before looking at some comments on this problem, one that is
due more to Lully's music than to Quinault's text, it is important to look
at another aspect of act IV, one that plays a key role in making *Atys* different from most of Quinault's other libretti.

Quinault has often been criticized for his fourth acts, especially in
Armide, where many spectators feel that the journey of Ubalde and the
Chevalier Danois detracts from the dramatic effect, in spite of the obvious
parallel between the temptations they undergo and those that Renaud has
undergone (see chap. 12, 342-44). Several other libretti have fourth acts
that involve new characters and a radical change of scene:

> *Alceste:* Alcide descends to Hades to bring back Alceste.
> *Isis:* Io undergoes a series of sufferings.
> *Proserpine:* Aréthuse and Alphée rejoin Proserpine in Hades
> *Phaéton:* Phaéton visits the palace of his father the Sun.

The fourth act of *Roland,* with its famous mad scene, is set in a pastoral
setting similar to that of the second act, but introduces a new set of
characters.

The fourth acts of the other Quinault libretti involve a false resolution, which makes for a final act that is full of action and sudden
changes of fate but that almost seems like an afterthought:

> *Cadmus et Hermione:* after Cadmus and Hermione are reunited,
>   she is carried off and then returned.
> *Thésée:* the troubles of Thésée and Églé seem over, before Médée
>   destroys the palace and Minerve builds a new one.
> *Persée:* Persée and Andromède are set to marry, but are inter-
>   rupted by Phinée and his band of rebels.
> *Amadis:* Amadis and Oriane are reunited, but still must pass
>   through the *arc des loyaux amants.*

The fourth act of *Atys* avoids both potential weaknesses—there is
no radical change of scene that interrupts the main action, and although
Atys and Sangaride are united, there is no sense of finality at the end of
the act. Quinault makes it clear that the flight of Atys and Sangaride

(IV.vi) will not lead to happiness—Cybèle has said that she intends to find out if Atys is indeed unfaithful to her, and the Zéphyrs that allow Atys to escape with Sangaride are under Cybèle's control (III.vii.600-01) and bring the unfortunate couple to a place where Cybèle can observe them (V.i.867-70).

Indeed, this intervention of the Zéphyrs has been carefully prepared. They participated in the *divertissement* of the second act (stage directions, beginning of II.iv) and were ready to help Atys at the end of act III. Atys says that he intends to use them (IV.iv.744-45), and they are present during the end of the *divertissement* of act IV (scene 6), before Atys claims Sangaride for himself and orders the Zéphyrs to carry them away (846-47). Furthermore, what is already a skillful incorporation of the *merveilleux* into the plot becomes a meaningful part of the emotional and moral impact of the fate of Atys and Sangaride, as zephirs give way to the violent winds of a metaphorical storm at two key moments. In the scene immediately preceding their flight, the chorus uses the image of a storm to suggest what happens to inconstant lovers:

> Jamais un cœur volage
> Ne trouve un heureux sort,
> Il n'a point l'avantage
> D'être longtemps au port,
> Il cherche encor l'orage
> Au moment qu'il en sort. (IV.v.814-19)

A similar image serves as a comment on the death of Atys:

> Atys, au printemps de son âge,
> Périt comme une fleur
> Qu'un soudain orage
> Renverse et ravage. (V.vii.1063-66)

It is perhaps going too far to apply the word "volage" to Atys and Sangaride, but, though they are faithful to each other, they have betrayed the people who love them. They have left the port in which they could have had a peaceful life, if not a happy one, to find storms and danger.

§ § §

The fourth act is an excellent example of how Quinault could take the bare elements of a myth and turn them into a tragedy that builds to a powerful conclusion. In *Atys,* the first three acts are characterized by avowals (Atys to Idas, Sangaride to Doris, Sangaride to Atys; Cybèle to Mélisse; Cybèle to Atys), and by the end of the third act the knot is not only tied but beginning to break—as soon as all the love relationships have been presented, Sangaride believes Atys has been unfaithful and is ready to start a new series of relationships by agreeing to marry Célénus. Once this problem is resolved in IV.iv, there is still the threat of Cybèle's vengeance, which begins immediately in the first scene of the last act. The spectator looks on in horror as first Sangaride and then Atys die a violent death. The metamorphosis of Atys into a pine tree hardly softens the tragedy, though the moving funeral scene (V.vii) brings about a kind of catharsis.

However, even if in a successful staging, such as that of Villégier, this final scene can be very much the climax, the emotional peak, it is not easy to maintain tension until the very end. The scene is quite long,[8] and one could say that nothing happens while the chorus laments the death of Atys and honors the new tree. There is considerable repetition of both poetry and music, and one could understand how impatient spectators would think it was just one more example of the obligatory final *divertissement,* inherited from the *ballet de cour* and the comedy-ballet.

Indeed, contemporary reactions differ and offer interesting insights into different views of tragedy—spoken and sung—and its effects. Writing in the first years of the eighteenth century, Lecerf tells us that few people stay to the end of operas such as *Thésée* and *Atys,* which end with a *divertissement* (2: 14). It is not clear whether this was already the case in the 1670s, though Lecerf suggests as much by quoting two lines from Molière's *Les Fâcheux* to illustrate the tendency of "les petits Maîtres" to leave before the end, except in the case of *Armide* (2: 17).[9] It

---

[8] The final scene lasts twelve minutes in the Christie recording, which is approximately 40 percent of the final act and almost 10 percent of the complete five acts. This goes against Le Brun's recommendation that funeral ceremonies and other *divertissements* which are "ni vifs, ni galans, ni enjoüez, doivent être encore plus courts que les autres" (16).

[9] Molière's first comedy-ballet, first performed at Vaux in 1661, opens with an account of an obnoxious spectator who left before the performance of a comedy was over,

is possible that many seventeenth-century spectators, who went to the Académie Royale for reasons more social than esthetic and who saw the same work many times, left after the death of Atys, just before the final scene.[10]

There must have been spectators, however, who stayed and who indeed felt that this scene represented an emotional peak. In the "Lettre de Mademoiselle** à une Dame de ses amies, sur le goust d'apresent," published in the *Mercure Galant* in November 1714 (pp. 170-208), the author complains about people who leave before the end, which suggests that at least some people did not. According to her, the only Quinault-Lully operas that still maintain their "premier éclat" are *Armide, Roland, Alceste*, and *Phaéton*. She adds quickly, though, that *Thésée, Atys*, and *Belléro-phon* are not inferior to the first four:

> *Thésée* & *Atys* sont les chefs-d'œuvres de Quinault pour la regularité du Poëme, & pour l'exactitude de la versification, l'un & l'autre sont remplis de sentiments & de pensées [...]; cependant, [...] on a trouvé *Thésée* languissant, & nous avons vû à la honte de nôtre siecle, les Dames sortir au cinquiéme Acte d'*Atys,* comme on auroit pû faire au cinquiéme Acte de *Roland*, malgré la difference qui se trouve entre ces deux derniers actes. (199-200)[11]

For her, long scenes are often the best, in Corneille and Racine as well as in Quinault, and she likes to be led gradually to moments "qui jettent le trouble dans l'ame des Spectateurs" (206). In short, her preferences are the opposite of those who leave before the end: "le beau les accable, il ne leur faut que du joly" (207).

"Car les gens du bel air, pour agir galamment, / Se gardent bien surtout d'ouïr le dénouement" (I.i). It is quite possible that this practice was still current in the 1670s at the opera. The 1705 *Satire sur quelques personnes étant un jour à l'Opéra* quoted by La Gorce (*Opéra* 136) mentions several spectators who make a noisy exit "un peu devant la fin."

[10] According to Parfaict, the last scene of *Atys* was cut in the 1738 production: "On retrancha la fete du 5e acte qu'on celebre pour l'espèce d'apotheose d'Atys. Malgré tout l'art de l'incomparable musicien ce divertissement a toujours paru superflu après une si triste catastrophe" (*Académie Royale* 348; see Rosow, "Lully" 243).

[11] The entire fifth act of *Roland* was cut during the 1728 revival; see Beffara 449.

Those spectators who left before the end would perhaps agree with Lecerf's other example of how *Atys* does not maintain an increasing interest from beginning to end. As in the case of the final scene, *Atys* is found inferior to *Armide* because the spectator's interest peaks in the first act:

> Une des plus grandes perfections d'un spectacle est que la beauté croisse d'Acte en Acte, & à mesure que l'intrigue avance. Regle bien établie dans ces discours d'une sincerité si noble & d'un bon sens si instructif, que le grand Corneille a faits sur ses propres Tragedies. [...] *Atys, Amadis,* &c. sont sans doute des Piéces excellentes [...]; mais le premier Acte d'Atys est sans difficulté le plus beau, & il est trop beau. La Scene d'Atys & de Sangaride
>> Sangaride, ce jour est un grand jour pour vous.
> [i]nspire à l'Auditeur des mouvemens qui s'affoiblissent necessaire-ment ensuite, l'attention se refroidit, parce qu'on retourneroit toûjours volontiers à cette Scene. (2: 13)

Lecerf's comments on this scene remind one of what he and Sévigné (1: 59; May 6, 1676, quoted above, p. 160) say about the *sommeil* in the third act: its length and beauty continue to hold the attention of the spectator while the action continues.

In both these accounts, the scenes that are cited as examples of interruptions in gradually increasing "beauty" are scenes that involve the emotional effect ("mouvements" or "trouble dans l'âme") on the specta-tor. It is this emotional effect that should build to a peak, more than, or at least as much as, tension and suspense concerning what is going to hap-pen next. As Lecerf suggests by saying that the beauty of an opera should increase "à mesure que l'intrigue avance," plot is, if not secondary, a ba-sic building block for the creation of emotional effects. As I pointed out in the introduction, there is more than one way to interpret the term "dra-matic" as it is applied to opera.

- II -

I offer these varying opinions of *Atys* not as criticisms of the libretto or of those who comment on it, but as examples of different concepts of the intended effects of tragedy. From any point of view, *Atys* is an effective libretto, an excellent place to study Quinault's skills as dramatist and poet. It is the most approachable of Quinault's libretti for the majority of modern readers, whose idea of seventeenth-century tragedy is, like that of Mademoisellle** in the 1714 *Mercure* and like that of most spectators, based on the plays of Corneille and Racine. In the inevitable comparisons between *tragédie lyrique* and "straight" tragedy, it is *Atys* that comes closest to meeting the criteria we have accepted for good drama and good tragedy. The comparison can help us understand the workings of *Atys*, as well as why seventeenth-century and twentieth-century reactions are different, but it is most useful if we remember that, from a seventeenth-century point of view, it is not necessarily a question of holding up a *tragédie lyrique* to a firmly established standard for approval or condemnation. The tradition of the *tragédie galante*, which is so prominent in the *tragédie lyrique*, is at the heart of an esthetic that coexisted with the more *savant* tradition that Corneille, Racine and Boileau represent.

With this in mind, let us consider why *Atys* is so successful from a dramatic point of view, why it can be so easily—I prefer to avoid the value judgment implied by "favorably"—compared to our modern notion of tragedy and of Racinian tragedy in particular. First of all, there is continuing interest in the two main characters from the first act, when we learn that Atys and Sangaride are in love but that she is engaged to the king (who is also Atys's best friend) to the last, when their love—after brief moments of hope (III.ii; IV.iv, IV.vi)—comes to a tragic and violent end. Seen in this way, the plot is an example of Corneille's recommended plot with beginning (act I), middle (acts II-IV), and end (act V):

> Il faut donc qu'une action pour être d'une juste grandeur ait un commencement, un milieu et une fin. Cinna conspire contre Auguste et rend compte de sa conspiration à Émilie, voilà le commencement; Maxime en fait avertir Auguste, voilà le milieu; Auguste lui pardonne, voilà la fin. ("Discours [...] du poème dramatique" 77)

At a very general level, the declaration of love between Atys and Sangaride could be compared to the scenes between Cinna and Émilie in the first act, the discovery of their love by Cybèle to the revelation of the conspiracy, and Cybèle's vengeance to Auguste's pardon. There are of course considerable differences between the two works, but they share this basic structure of the establishment of a situation involving some of the main characters, the complication of this situation, and its resolution (for better or for worse). The most important difference is perhaps the importance of love in the first act of *Atys,* a situation more like that Corneille presents in the sentence following the ones quoted above, in which he describes the basic three-part structure of comedy, which begins with "deux amants en bonne intelligence" who will be "brouillés ensemble" and finally reunited. If *Atys* begins like a comedy and devotes the first act to bringing the lovers together, it certainly does not continue and end like one.

The interest that this structure creates is of course heightened by concentration on the four main characters, due partly to the diminished role of the secondary characters and of comic scenes that I have already mentioned. In addition to this unity of action (one of the key "rules" of classical French theater), Quinault observes the unity of time, since the action could easily take place in a few hours. He does not, of course, observe strictly the unity of place, since the spectators expected a different decor for each act. Still, the five acts take place in sites that could be part of the same city, a license that Corneille favored ("Discours des trois unités" 150). The first three in particular are closely related, since Cybèle's temple and that of her Grand Sacrificateur would be close to her sacred mountain, and there is no reason why Sangar's palace and the gardens of the last act could not be nearby.

The most important reason, however, for the dramatic success of *Atys* for twentieth-century audiences is almost certainly the relative absence of the *merveilleux.* Between Cybèle's appearance on earth (I.viii) and her manipulation and transformation of Atys in the last act, she acts very much like a human, using her divine powers only to bring about Atys's dream and to use the Zéphyrs as a means of transport. She goes through periods of doubt, undergoes the torments of unrequited love and of jealousy, and gives vent to her jealous rage before realizing—too late—the consequences that even the mother of the gods cannot undo.

Cybèle, like Atys and Sangaride, is a character whom Racine could describe as "ni tout à fait coupable ni tout à fait innocente" (preface to *Phèdre*). Indeed, much of the dramatic tension in *Atys* comes from the hesitations of the characters before making a decision to act according to their desire rather than according to their duty or honor. Cybèle has obviously undergone considerable soul-searching before deciding to leave the heavens and to try to win the love of a mortal:

> Ce fut au jour fatal de ma dernière Fête
>
> Que de l'aimable Atys je devins la conquête.
>
> Je partis à regret pour retourner aux Cieux,
>
> Tout m'y parut changé, rien n'y plut à mes yeux.
>
> Je sens un plaisir extrême
>
> A revenir dans ces lieux;
>
> Où peut-on jamais être mieux,
>
> Qu'aux lieux où l'on voit ce qu'on aime? (II.iii.338-45)

She has resisted "trouble" and "tendresse" in vain and must have given considerable thought to the justification of her choice of a mortal, since she has a response ready for Mélisse's reproach:

> MÉLISSE
>
> Mais vous pouviez aimer, et descendre moins bas.
>
> CYBELE
>
> Non, trop d'égalité rend l'amour sans appas. (II.iii.357-58)

In the case of Sangaride and Atys, they have nobly decided to hide their love from each other, but Atys gives in first to the temptation to reveal his love, believing naively—or disingenuously—that his intended suicide justifies his avowal. He is literally *dying* to tell someone of his love: "Qui n'a plus qu'un moment à vivre, / N'a plus rien à dissimuler." (I.vi.152-56).[12]

Sangaride is now equally incapable of keeping her love secret, and their mutual avowal (I.vi), more or less in spite of themselves, not only sets the strategic plot in motion but presents them as characters with

---

[12] These two lines serve as the epigraph to Poe's "Ms. Found in a Bottle."

noble intentions and very human frailties. In fact, their subsequent actions will be considerably less than noble—Atys betrays his best friend and Cybèle, both of whom have bestowed considerable wealth and honor on him, while Sangaride goes against her father's wishes and breaks off her engagement with Célénus. Such ignoble actions on the part of major characters, which are quite rare in Quinault's libretti, suggest another unusual—and effective—feature of *Atys:* in spite of deceit, betrayal, and lies, Atys and Sangaride maintain our sympathy to the end. Since this sympathy is established in the first act, is it any wonder that many contemporary critics found this act to be the most effective, indeed too effective? Carefully structured, elegant in its simplicity and directness, this act attains a degree of beauty and of emotional power worthy of comparison to the best operas of any period. And, in its own way, it is a worthy rival of the best efforts of "le tendre Racine" who, in 1676, was writing his own play about the guilty love of a powerful woman for a young man who knows more about love than everyone thinks; as Truchet points out, "L'amour, en cette tragédie en musique, apparaît, en fait, aussi cruel qu'il apparaîtra, l'année suivante, dans *Phèdre*" (*Théâtre du dix-septième siècle* 1050).

§ § §

This first act, like the opera as a whole, builds to a peak just before the *divertissement* that concludes it. The seemingly simple first line will, by the time it has been repeated four times—including at the beginning of the next two scenes—become rich in significance: Atys is alone, but will soon be joined by his compatriots and by Cybèle, precisely the people who will oppose his happiness:[13]

> Allons, allons, accourez tous,
> Cybèle va descendre.
> Trop heureux Phrygiens, venez ici l'attendre.
> Mille peuples seront jaloux

---

[13] The first two of these lines will be repeated at the beginning of scenes ii (7-8) and iii (48-49), again a few lines later (55-56), and for the last time at the end of scene iii (90-91). As in frequently the case in an opera, except in recitatives, these lines are repeated by the composer at least once each time they occur in the libretto.

Des faveurs que sur nous
Sa bonté va répandre. (I.i.1-6)

Left alone, he and Sangaride would have eventually discovered their mutual love, but the Phrygians want her to marry their king, and Cybèle wants him to be faithful to her. The theme of jealousy is sounded, and we will soon perceive the irony of the last three lines of the scene (4-6), the illusion of happiness which cannot exist in the presence of jealousy. As in so much of Quinault, and of his source Ovid, the interventions of the gods in human affairs rarely bring happiness.

The second scene begins like the first, and Atys's lyrical outburst (9-13) continues the festive, pastoral mood. His conversation with his friend Idas is at first quite conventional, until Idas switches from maxim-like couplets to a direct injunction to Atys to be honest with him:

Tôt ou tard l'Amour est vainqueur,
En vain les plus fiers s'en défendent,
On ne peut refuser son cœur
A de beaux yeux qui le demandent.
Atys, ne feignez plus, je sais votre secret. (23-27)

Nature quickly goes from a source of beauty and life (9-13) to a refuge for unhappy lovers (29-32), and the light sounds of "vive" and "émail" give way to "solitaire" and "sombre," which lead quickly to "feindre," "rigoureux," and "plaindre" (41-43). Lully's music matches the mood exactly, furnishing at first almost nothing but light, carefree-sounding airs as Idas makes fun of Atys's "badineries" (9-26). After "Atys, ne feignez plus," however, there is more recitative, as the discussion becomes more serious, and the two brief airs (29-32, 39-44) sound much more tender and sincere.[14]

---

[14] Duron, "Commentaire musical et littéraire" 43; he isolates five brief airs in the twenty lines of this section. The two brief airs that follow are better described as what Duron calls "récits lyriques" in "L'Instinct de M. de Lully"; see the introduction, p. 26.

I am deeply indebted to Duron's analysis for insights into Lully's creative process and to his collaboration with Quinault, and I refer the reader to his article for much more detail than I can include here. If I tend to give a little more of the credit to Quinault than he does to Lully, it is because I am convinced, as he says himself at the beginning of his article, that "*Atys* en effet n'est pas un opéra, mais une tragédie-lyrique dont le maître

The third scene makes a somewhat different use of similar principles. It begins and ends with "Allons, allons, accourez tous, / Cybèle va
descendre," marking both a continuity with the first two scenes and the
end of a larger section (scenes i-iii). These two lines even enclose a sub-
section of formalized exchanges between Atys and Sangaride, obviously
afraid to speak their true feelings (48-56). Quinault then returns to a description of nature, with Sangaride talking of birds much as Atys had of
the sun in scene ii. Atys manages to use the songs of the birds as a transition from Cybèle to Sangaride's upcoming marriage, and thus to love, but
their exchange never gets beyond banalities and cliches, which Quinault
expresses in another series of maxim-like airs (70-81). Unlike Idas, however, neither Atys nor Sangaride is bold enough to say "Ne feignez plus,"
and when the conversation finally reaches Atys's personal situation (83-
87), he breaks off and returns to the public celebration that was announced in the first lines, repeated here for the last time.[15]

The transition from generalities to personal situation is brilliantly
done. The first lines that Quinault offered Lully, obviously intended to be
an air, continue the theme of nature (70-77) and contain mostly light-
sounding words appropriate for such lyrics (*pleurs, belles, aimables
fleurs, roses nouvelles,* etc.). The second air (78-81) abandons the theme
of nature to express the pleasures of love with words of a negative con-
notation (*péril, alarmer, mal*) that, while not overly harsh in sound, are
considerably more so than the liquid consonants at the end of each of the
eight preceding lines. The vowel /a/ becomes especially prominent,
whereas /è/ and /ou/ had dominated lines 70-77. There is definitely a
movement toward a more serious discussion.

This movement is even more obvious in the line-lengths that Quinault has chosen. The first air (70-77) consists of four octosyllables followed by four seven-syllable lines. This regularity seems to continue in
the second air, which begins with three octosyllables, but the last line has
only six syllables. There is a strong effect of interrupted rhythmic regularity, and it is only with the next line (82) that one recognizes its function

d'œuvre n'est pas le musicien (Lully), mais le poète (Quinault)—il ne s'agit pas non
plus d'un livret, mais d'une tragédie" (32).
[15] A director is faced with an interesting choice here. Does Atys change the subject
because he sees some people gathering, or simply because he is afraid to take the conversation any farther?

as a transition to the alexandrine with its two halves of six syllables. Atys continues with an air (83-87), but—in keeping with his troubled state— the relative regularity of the two preceding airs gives way to a much more varied group consisting of lines of eight, twelve, eight, six, and six syllables.

I insist on these details of prosody because they constitute an excellent example of Quinault's skill and of his collaboration with Lully. One cannot read Quinault—or any librettist—as an uninterrupted series of lines of verse. Even within individual speeches, the metrical structure suggests pauses and changes of direction to which the reader should be attentive. Lully certainly was, especially when he decided to follow Quinault and combine Sangaride's last line with Atys's response (82-87): "Peut-on être insensible aux plus charmants appas?" (82) not only rhymes with the following line "Non, vous ne me connaissez pas," but fits in better with the twelve- and six-syllable lines that follow.[16] To make the transition clear, Lully turned lines 82-87 into a chaconne by repeating the same descending bass line beneath them. This same structural device, used here to create unity within a part of a scene, is then used to create the transition to the next scene; after the now familiar interruption of the preparations for the arrival of Cybèle, a similar chaconne bass line is heard again at the beginning of the next scene, before Sangaride's heart-rending cry.

Scene iii ends with the last repetitions of "Allons, allons, accourez tous," marking the end of the first section of act I, which began with these same lines, and offering another example of the extraordinary collaboration between Quinault and Lully. By beginning the first three acts and by ending the third with the same lines, Quinault has at the same time given unity to this first section of his libretto and provided Lully with an opportunity to organize his musical discourse around a repeated melody, introduced in the *ritournelle* that begins the act. During this first section of act I, the spectator has sensed that, in spite of outward calm and public joy, both Sangaride and Atys are troubled by a secret passion. They have as much as said so to each other:

---

[16] I must disagree here with Duron, who suggests that it was perhaps "à l'insu de Quinault" that Lully linked these two lines ("Commentaire" 43).

Est-ce un grand mal de trop aimer
Ce que l'on trouve aimable?
[...]
Si j'aimais un jour, par malheur,
Je connais bien mon cœur,
Il serait trop sensible. (I.iii.80-81, 85-87)

It is now time for scenes in which they admit their love to their confidants or to each other, for the *aveux* that so often constitute high points in seventeenth-century French literature.[17]

§ § §

As scene iv begins, Sangaride is alone with her good friend Doris, talking mostly for herself, much as Atys was with his friend Idas in scenes i and ii. Her "Atys est trop heureux" would seem almost to come out of nowhere, but the attentive spectator remembers that he/she has already heard the words "trop heureux" three times: in the third line of scene one and especially in scene ii when Idas repeats the *regrets* that he has overheard from an Atys who thought he was alone, a passage that begins and ends with "Amants qui vous plaignez, vous êtes trop heureux" (39, 44). The full impact of the juxtaposition of the two phrases requires that the spectator remember that, whereas Sangaride thinks Atys is truly happy, like the Phrygians in line three, and whereas Doris thinks that Sangaride is truly happy (I.iv.95-97), Atys considers himself even less happy than complaining lovers, which is exactly his situation and that of Sangaride. Some elaboration is in order, and Sangaride repeats "Atys est trop heureux," which becomes the beginning and end of a passage that obviously demands special musical treatment (I.iv.98, 103).

Lully does not let us down. In a new but closely related key (D minor, after G minor), the repetition of the bass line similar to the one that underlay "Peut-on être insensible aux plus charmants appas? / Non,

---

[17] Three of the most famous scenes in the canon of French classicism, Phèdre's admitting her love for Hippolyte first to Œnone (I.iii) and then to him (II.v) in Racine's *Phèdre* (1677) and the oft-debated scene between Mme de Clèves and her husband in Lafayette's *La Princesse de Clèves* (1678), were being written at the time *Atys* was performed.

vous ne me connaissez pas" takes us back to the subject of potential love
that ended scene iii. Then, on top of the same bass, he gives Sangaride a
brief melody of magical effect, in spite of its apparent simplicity.

This is not the place to try to explain how Lully achieves such emotional
effect with means that, to ears that have heard the immense orchestral and
vocal forces unleashed by composers such as Wagner and Strauss, seem
almost childlike. It is the place, however, to point out that he most likely
would not have achieved them without Quinault, who gave him a line that
can stand on its own but that is also related to words and themes from
earlier scenes, that can lead naturally to a full avowal of Sangaride's love.
Even more important for the composer, Quinault has provided a line that
requires repetition and elaboration, since Doris does not understand what
Sangaride meant the first time she said it. It is thus the perfect text and
context for a monologue similar in structure to those of Médée that I described in the chapter on *Thésée* (II.ix.491-97, for example; chap. 4, p.
143):

> Atys est trop heureux.
>
> Souverain de son cœur, maître de tous ses vœux,
>
> Sans crainte, sans mélancolie,
>
> Il jouit en repos des beaux jours de sa vie;
>
> Atys ne connaît point les tourments amoureux,
>
> Atys est trop heureux. (I.iv.98-103)

Doris now begins to understand the meaning behind Sangaride's words,
and she will soon learn of her friend's secret love.

The first act of *Atys* is so full of similar examples of how Quinault
provided Lully with text suitable for a variety of musical treatments that I
must refer the reader to analyses such as that of Duron and limit myself to

a brief description of the structure of the rest of this remarkable act. After Sangaride admits to Doris that she loves Atys, another interruption by the preparations for the arrival of Cybèle not only provides a familiar structural element and a brief slackening of the emotional tension, but offers Doris an excuse to leave Sangaride and Atys alone for the scene in which they will finally admit their love for each other. This interruption is not accompanied by repetitions of "Accourez, accourez tous," as were earlier ones, for Sangaride and Atys are by now less concerned with the upcoming ceremony than with their own situation.

In the scene between Sangaride and Atys (I.vi), Quinault has provided much more recitative than text for potential airs. Rather than groups of lines with a similar metrical structure, he has used a variety of line lengths and a freer rhyme scheme (a rhyme is often continued from one speech to the next). Even the repeated "Vous me condamnerez vous-même, / Et vous me laisserez mourir" (159-60, 165-66) does not really suggest an air; the two lines do not rhyme, and both characters speak twice before the lines are repeated. Atys is explaining his actions, not expressing his feelings, and the conversation needs to continue until Sangaride can no longer hold back her tears, nor her secret. After three occurrences of the verb *perdre* in four lines (I.vi.178-81), there is nothing left to say but "vous êtes aimé." Lully sets these words to a high, beautiful melody (see fig. 2, p. 29), but resists the temptation to dwell on these tender feelings. Their love is impossible, "aveu favorable" is inevitably followed by "misérable" and "affreux," and the "devoir impitoyable" (I.vi.197) that keeps them apart also forces them to pretend to be happy.

The lines with which Atys ends the scene,

> Aimons un bien plus durable
> Que l'éclat de la Beauté.
> Rien n'est plus aimable
> Que la liberté.

have been criticized for introducing a light, bantering tone inappropriate to the tragic situation,[18] but these lines are completely in keeping with

---

[18] See Bassinet's edition of *Atys*, pp. 74-75, n. 22, where he quotes Villiers's criticism and, somewhat abridged and adapted, Le Brun's response: "Ce sont deux amans

Atys's public image as someone indifferent to love and with the form of the act. They also serve as a transition to a *divertissement* that is well integrated into the action, having been mentioned from the beginning. No secondary characters are needed, and Atys and Sangaride have a well-defined role to play in the celebration (I.vi.142-43). The *divertissement* also serves to introduce the important character Cybèle and to present an atmosphere of joy that makes the suffering of Atys and Sangaride all the more poignant.

Is it any wonder, then, that this first act is so effective, and that for spectators who appreciated emotional impact as much as, if not more than, the working out of the plot, it was the high point of the opera and thus, for some, a structural fault? Such an opinion depends on how one views the overall structure of *Atys* since, as in the case of *Thésée*, it does not have a single obvious structure. From one point of view, one can discern a structure that builds steadily toward a tragic conclusion, presenting the principal characters in the first two acts and then working through complications, hope, and disappointment, up to the death of Atys and the funeral scene that follows. Such a structure is very much like what one finds in several tragedies of Racine, in which most of the main characters are presented in the first act but with at least one more reserved for the first scene of the second act. The third act then begins the real working out of the drama, sometimes starting with the same characters who were present in the first scene of the first act.[19] Duron's analysis of the tonal structure of Lully's score reveals such a structure, since at the end of the second act the music

> retourne au sol mineur qui ouvrait et le prologue et l'acte I, comme si,
> là, au centre de l'œuvre, après le divertissement de la gloire d'Atys, un
> premier opéra s'achevait, celui des portraits, pour laisser la place à un
> second, celui du drame. ("Commentaire" 52)

---

malheureux, quoy qu'aimez, qui ont raison de feindre, & de changer de langage, de crainte que leur secret ne se découvre. Je ne dirai rien davantage là-dessus, si ce n'est qu'il y a un peu de témérité à vouloir attaquer des endroits dont les beautez sont presque inimitables" (26).

[19] *Andromaque* is a good example. In *Atys,* of course, Cybèle appears in the last scene of the first act rather than in the first of the second, but, coming after the *divertissement,* this final scene of act I is very much like a beginning of a new act.

Similarly, the curtain of the third act

> se lève sur Atys seul, comme à l'acte I, et comme la première fois, il
> est précédé d'une *ritournelle* en trio, à trois temps et en sol mineur.
> Tout concourt donc pour créer là, à nouveau, l'événement; une nou-
> velle pièce s'élance, qui s'appuie, prend son essor sur le souvenir de
> l'autre. ("Commentaire" 57)

The opera returns to G minor with the death of Atys, although the tonal
orientation is a bit less clear than in earlier acts, and the key of the last
scene, C minor and then C major, is rather unexpected, creating "une
certaine angoisse," "non pas une conclusion, une péroraison, mais une
ouverture, un grand point d'interrogation" ("Commentaire" 75). Or, to
return to the letter in the 1714 *Mercure*, it is the kind of scene capable of
creating "le trouble dans l'ame des Spectateurs" (206). Anyone who left
before the end would not be someone who appreciated tragedy, who felt
the effect of catharsis; it would be someone who preferred the "joli"
rather than the beautiful.

There is at least one other way to see the structure of *Atys*, however, a way that makes the emotional climax in the first act less of an
anomaly without deemphasizing the final scene. Couvreur (*Lully* 340-41),
for example, sees a circular structure similar to that of *Thésée*, especially
from the point of view of the decors, an opposition between the exterior
scenes in acts I and V (a mountain, gardens) and the interior scenes in the
three middle acts (temples and palaces). While this structure based on decor is perhaps not as organic to the overall concept of the opera as is one
built on disposition of characters and on tonal structure (and similar to the
structures used by Racine and Corneille), it does have the advantage of
juxtaposing the moving avowals of Sangaride and Atys with their deaths,
thus making their love a frame that encloses the efforts of Cybèle and
Célénus to separate them.

From such a point of view, the open-ended final scene could suggest a return to the beginning, both to the first act in which Atys and Sangaride revealed their feelings and set the tragedy in motion and to the
prologue which, alone among those of Quinault's first six libretti, contains an explicit reference to the theme of the tragedy that is to follow
(see chap. 1, p. 64). Melpomène, the muse of tragedy, announces the

subject of the spectacle that is to follow, demanding that Flore and the "agrément rustique" of her games yield to her "spectacles pompeux." However, Cybèle sends Iris to insist that Flore and Melpomène work together to praise Louis XIV, suggesting that, while this new opera will, unlike its predecessors, be firmly in the tradition of tragedy, it will neglect neither the pleasures of love nor those of the pastoral tradition that was so important in its development. *Atys* is indeed a work that incorporates many of the familiar, traditional features of tragedy and of pastoral into what Quinault has by now established as the basic form of the *tragédie lyrique,* but at the same time it merits Duron's description as an "experimental" opera ("Commentaire" 34). The emotional impact of the first act, the combination of tender love with violent tragedy, the lack of a true hero, the less than noble main characters, the relative absence of divine intervention, and the final scene that is less a denouement than a return to the beginning, all these features make *Atys* rather unusual and should lessen the surprise that many commentators have expressed at the next Quinault-Lully work, *Isis,* which puts aside most of the features that made *Atys* so successful as traditional tragic drama. The least one can say is that Quinault and Lully were obviously not trying, with each successive opera, to make their *tragédies lyriques* more and more like spoken tragedy.

SANGARIDE.

Quand le peril est agreable,
Le moyen de s'en allarmer?
Est-ce un grand mal de trop aimer
Ce que l'on trouve aimable?
Peut-on estre insensible aux plus charmans appas?

ATYS.

Non vous ne me connoissez pas.
Je me deffens d'aimer autant qu'il m'est possible;
Si j'aimois, un jour, par malheur,
Je connoy bien mon cœur
Il seroit trop sensible.
Mais il faut que chacun s'assemble prés de vous,
Cybele pourroit nous surprendre.

ATYS, & IDAS.

Allons, allons, accourez tous,
Cybele va descendre.

SCENE QUATRIESME.

SANGARIDE, DORIS.

SANGARIDE.

A Tys est trop heureux.

DORIS.

L'amitié fut toûjours égale entre vous deux,

6

Isis

Beyond Tragedy

- I -

ISIS IS ONE OF THE MOST TALKED ABOUT, and least often performed, of the Quinault-Lully operas.[1] Of the two main reasons for this combination of notoriety and neglect, one is anecdotal and concerns the literary and musical merits of the work only in terms of the choice of subject, whereas the other involves the very nature of the *tragédie lyrique* and its relation to other theatrical forms of the seventeenth century. It is the latter—its emphasis on spectacle, its structure characterized by juxtaposition rather than by linear plot development—that is of primary concern here, but the former, which involves Mme de Montespan's anger and Quinault's subsequent disgrace is so well known and so little understood that a brief review of the situation would be useful.

    Isis opened January 5, 1677—the same week as Racine's *Phèdre* (Jan. 1)—at Saint-Germain-en-Laye, where it had less success with the court than had their four previous operas. Some spectators found fault with certain characters, such as the Fury Érinnis, who was "trop tranquille" (Parfaict, *Académie Royale* 122), while some earlier critics found

---

[1] The only modern performance was a concert version at Birmingham, England, in November 1995; this was probably the first performance since 1733.

it too "savant" and not natural enough.[2] Louis XIV was not completely happy with the new work either, especially in comparison with the preceding Quinault-Lully opera, *Atys,* which he liked so much that it came to be known as "l'opéra du roi" (Lecerf 1: 102). He asked Lully to make some changes, which was perhaps one reason why the Paris premiere did not take place until August. By that time, however, *Isis* had become a *succès de scandale* and its esthetic merit was relegated to secondary status in contemporary discussions of the work.

In 1677, Françoise [-Athénaïs] de Rochechouart-Mortemart, marquise de Montespan had been the reigning—and I do not use the word lightly—royal mistress for ten years. Described by her contemporaries as proud and ruthless, Mme de Montespan did not have queen Marie-Thérèse's ability to suffer in dignified silence when the king became interested in another woman. As Primi Visconti said, specifically about the affair in question, "La Reine était habituée désormais à ces infidélités, mais Mme de Montespan enrageait davantage" (106). The subject of her rage in this case was Mme de Ludres (Marie-Élisabeth de Ludres, chanoinesse de Poussay, one of Madame's *filles d'honneur*) with whom the king was infatuated and who immediately became identified with the persecuted Io, while Mme de Montespan became "Junon tonnante et triomphante" (Sévigné 2: 479; June 30, 1677). These events, as described by Sévigné and others, took place in June and July 1677, well after the fairly short run at court in January and February and before the opening at the Palais-Royal in August. They represent an eloquent testimony to the popularity of Quinault's libretti, not only because his contemporaries immediately made the connection between scandals at court and the plots of his operas, but especially because they could quote numerous passages.

---

[2] Lecerf de la Viéville says that "*Isis,* le plus sçavant de tous, sans contredit, a été un de ceux qui a eu le moins de succés, quand on l'a representé d'abord, & est encore un des moins aimés" (1: 89-90). Lecerf cites as an example of "musique savante" the *trio des Parques* in IV.vii, that Lully "estimoit tant luy-même" (1: 66). Lecerf's Chevalier prefers the more widely admired passages: "[...] il y a dans Lulli deux cens morceaux d'expression qui touchent la multitude, que je ne craindrai point de préferer à l'admirable trio, *Le fil de la vie*. Un des plus parfaits morceaux de science, & des plus au gré des Sçavans, qu'ait laissé Lulli" (2: 325).

Such familiarity could not come from a few performances at court and reflects the wide distribution of printed copies.[3]

The king's involvement with Mme de Ludres had begun well before 1677, however, and one must look at the situation in 1676—when Quinault wrote the libretto—to attempt to answer the question of what Quinault intended to suggest—if anything—by portraying royal infidelity and bitter jealousy.[4] Mme de Ludres had been the object of the attentions of several members of Louis's court, including Mme de Montespan's brother the marquis de Vivonne, as early as 1673,[5] and Primi Visconti writes of the King's infatuation—and Mme de Montespan's anger—with her in 1674 (33, 35). This infatuation was perhaps the cause of Louis's temporary separation from Mme de Montespan in 1675,[6] but the royal mistress was back in full favor, "une triomphante beauté," by July 1676 (Sévigné 2: 352; July 29, 1676).

By this time (July 1676), Quinault would certainly have begun working on his next libretto, hoping to match the success of *Atys*. One thing is obvious, and that is that Quinault had no intention of offending Mme de Montespan, even though she had worked to have him replaced as librettist by Racine and Boileau (chap. 4, *Thésée*, 129-30). As much as Louis's court enjoyed finding allusions to current events in plays, and especially in operas, with the overt references to the political situation, it would have been out of the question for Quinault to risk his lucrative and prestigious situation as Lully's librettist by attacking Mme Montespan. Nor can one imagine he would have been naive enough not to realize that the story of Isis and Juno would immediately be compared to that of Mme de Ludres and Mme de Montespan. Nevertheless, the allusions are there, and Beaussant sums up the situation well: "Il n'y a pas, il ne peut pas y

[3] There were at least six editions or printings in 1677, five of which were probably for performances at court early in the year. See Quinault, ed. Norman, 1: lvi.

[4] Rehearsals began November 19 (La Gorce, *Opéra* 55), and Quinault read the prologue to the Académie Française on Dec. 23: "hier [...] Quinault a lu le prologue de l'opéra que nous verrons les premiers jours de l'année prochaine. On en a trouvé les vers fort beaux" (duc de Saint-Aignan à Bussy-Rabutin, Bussy 3: 194; Dec. 24, 1676).

[5] Bussy 3: 246-47 (Mme de Montmorency to Bussy, May 6, 1673, and Bussy's response); Sévigné 1: 637 (Dec. 11, 1673); Primi Visconti 57, 103-04.

[6] Sévigné 2: 98 (Sept. 11, 1675); Primi Visconti 66; Gros, *Quinault* 119. According to Duchêne, Louis's affair with Mme de Ludres began in 1676 (Sévigné 2: 1317, n. 4).

avoir d'allusion critique dans *Isis.* Cela n'empêche pas les allusions" (*Lully* 588).

Everyone at court would have known the subject of the new opera. Mme de Montespan could certainly have prevented an opera that would have caused her embarrassment, and Lully was much too skillful a courtier to risk offending his royal patrons. As Gros says,

> on ne s'attaque pas impunément aux favoris de Jupiter [...]. Voit-on Quinault, poète officiel, critiquant la maîtresse encore en titre de Louis XIV? Voit-on l'Académie Française, la Petite Académie, Lully lui-même, approuvant et laissant faire? [...] Mme de Montespan qui, sans aucun doute, connut la pièce avant qu'elle fût jouée, en aurait-elle permis la représentation? (121-22)

What no one could have predicted in mid-1676 is that the "triomphante beauté" of Mme de Montespan would again be challenged by the charms of Mme de Ludres. Primi Visconti tells us that, sometime before the spring military campaign in March 1677, "Mme de Montespan, qui avait d'abord persécuté Mme de Ludres, croyant le crédit de celle-ci définitivement perdu, l'avait rappelée auprès d'elle. Mais ce retour avait réveillé les désirs du Roi" (103). From what Sévigné and others tell us, if Mme de Montespan had persecuted Mme de Ludres before 1677, what the latter had to endure during the summer of 1677 must have been more like torture. The precise chronology is not clear, but Mme de Montespan apparently found out for sure in June that her rival had indeed regained the favors of the king.[7] Sévigné and her family often mentioned Mme de Montespan's anger and "la pauvre *Io*" or "la belle *Isis*" between June 11 and July 28: "Ah! ma fille, quel triomphe à Versailles! quel orgueil redoublé! quel solide établissement! [...] quelle reprise de possession!" (2: 462; June 11, 1677). Mme de Sévigné reported July 28 that "*Isis* est retournée chez Madame, tout comme elle était, belle comme un ange" (2: 506), but she soon retired to a convent.

---

[7] Sévigné 2: 1317, n. 4. Bussy mentions in February a rumor that "Madame de Montespan étoit fort baissée dans les bonnes grâces du roi" but doubts that she is "sur le point de tomber" (3: 213; Feb. 7, 1677).

One of the results of Mme de Montespan's anger was two years of disgrace for Quinault. There are no contemporary documents that give an official reason, but it was clearly because Mme de Montespan did not like being portrayed in the "heavy" role of an unnaturally cruel Juno. However, it was not Quinault who portrayed her as Juno, but the courtiers who were familiar with the opera and made the easy connection. Mme de Montespan's discovery of the renewed affair with Mme de Ludres, her anger and revenge are all *after* the opening run of *Isis* in January 1677:

> [...] Madame de Montespan se m[i]t à jouer le rôle de Junon à la perfection, alors que l'opéra était déjà représenté à la cour [...]. C'est donc la petite chronique de la cour qui, en quelque sorte, recopiait l'opéra: et non le contraire. (Beaussant, *Lully* 590)

But enough court gossip. Aside from its *succès de scandale, Isis* is a remarkable work, unique in Quinault and Lully's collaboration and key to an understanding of the *tragédie lyrique*. If opera theaters have always been a place where courtiers and socialites could observe each other, exchange stories and start rumors, the performance itself is considerably more interesting, a privileged expression of the esthetic, moral, and political values of a society. Like Beaussant, I find the Ludres-Montespan affair of little consequence for an understanding of *Isis:*

> Mais il ne m'intéresse pas vraiment de savoir si oui ou non cet opéra est une œuvre "à clefs". Bien sûr, il l'est, comme le sont les autres. [...] L'opéra n'avait pas à être une œuvre "à clefs": c'est d'une manière entière et globale, comme genre, comme forme, comme style, comme figures, attitudes, sensibilité, comme conception de la vie et de l'homme, de la société, de la gloire et de l'amour, que l'opéra de Lully n'avait qu'une seule clef, et que les spectateurs s'y reconnaissaient. (*Versailles, opéra* 114-15)

I would add only that, in the case of *Isis,* opera reveals a conception of art as much as it does of life.

§ § §

Isis is a unique work with an unusual performance history. Lully certainly intended to use it to reopen his theater after the Easter closing, as he had with *Thésée* and *Atys,* but instead he revived *Thésée.*[8] The reasons are probably esthetic as well as political: the work had not been very well received at court in January, the king had asked for changes, and it was probably considered expedient to wait until after the resolution of the fate of Mme de Ludres, who retired to a convent in July. Parisians finally had a chance to see *Isis* in August 1677, and it ran continuously until the Easter closing in March of 1678;[9] apparently Lully made some important changes, or else the work was not as bad as the court had thought. On the other hand, it had only one revival during the rest of the reign of Louis XIV (1704), which makes it the only Quinault-Lully opera not to be revived in the seventeenth century. In addition, with only two revivals in the eighteenth century (1717-18, 1732-33), it was the least often performed of any of their works and the first to go out of the repertory.

One could attribute the lack of success during the seventeenth century in part to a lack of enthusiasm on the part of Louis XIV, who was not pleased with the first performances and who can hardly have enjoyed the gossip about Mme de Montespan/Junon and Mme de Ludres/Io. Furthermore, he could not have been very pleased with the inevitable associations between himself and Quinault's Jupiter, who was tricked by Junon into giving up his new favorite, unable to protect her from the ensuing persecution, and finally forced to admit the errors of his ways.[10] Louis, thinking back on a much more favorable portrayal as an adulterous Jupiter in Molière's *Amphitryon* (1668), was perhaps more than willing

---

[8] April 27, 1677. It would not have been possible to have a series of performances at the Palais-Royal immediately after the performances at court, since the theater was closed during the Jubilee from February 20 to April 25. See La Fontaine, "A M. de Niert": "Avec mille autres biens le jubilé fera / Que nous serons un temps sans parler d'opéra" (*O.D.* 620).

[9] *Isis* shared the stage with *Alceste, Thésée, Atys,* and perhaps with *Cadmus et Hermione* in September 1677 and with all four in the first months of 1678, after the performances of these same operas at court.

[10] See Couvreur 377 and Rémond de Saint-Mard, who criticized the role of Jupiter: "Quelle figure fait-là Jupiter? Et lui qui avoit tant d'autorité, ne devoit-il pas en prendre un peu sur sa femme, & laisser moins souffrir cette malheureuse Isis, qu'il aimoit tant?" (31).

for Mme de Montespan to take the blame for Quinault's temporary disgrace.

Lully's numerous enemies certainly contributed to the mitigated success of *Isis*. Much as in 1674, when *Alceste* inaugurated the new theater at the Palais-Royal, his near monopoly on the musical theater angered many of his rivals, and his remarkable ascension from servant to royal favorite had made many people jealous. Although La Fontaine certainly exaggerated somewhat in writing in "Le Florentin" (1674) that

> [...] tout le genre humain,
> Petits et grands, dans leurs prières,
> Disent le soir et le matin:
> "Seigneur, par vos bontés pour nous si singulières,
> Délivrez-nous du Florentin" (*O.D.* 614)

there was probably a concerted effort by Lully's enemies to keep *Isis* from being a success at Saint-Germain-en-Laye in early 1677. It was perhaps the same group that circulated songs such as the following,

> Les vers d'*Isis* sont pitoyables,
> Lully mal en Cour crèvera
> Et Bigarani [sic] se pendra
> Avec un des ses câbles. (La Gorce, *Opéra* 61)

La Fontaine, whose libretto *Daphné* had been refused by Lully in 1674, contributed his poem to Niert "Sur l'opéra" to the effort, deploring the success of opera at the expense of the *air de cour* and of a separation between tragedy, ballet, and song. His comment that "De Baptiste épuisé les compositions / Ne sont, si vous voulez, que répétitions" (*O.D.* 619) proved to be wishful thinking.

However, neither royal displeasure nor jealous rivals can completely explain the relative lack of success of *Isis* at the Académie Royale after 1678. Audiences and critics alike continued to admire the music— *Isis* became known as "l'opéra des musiciens" (Lecerf 1: 102)—and to enjoy excerpts from the work, such as the "chœur des trembleurs" (IV.i) and the "plainte d'Io" (V.i), but complete performances were rare. In the eighteenth century, Rémond de Saint-Mard found Quinault's libretto "ridicule" (31), while La Harpe found that the last two acts "languissent par l'uniformité d'une situation trop prolongée [...]" (1: 665B) and that the manner of tormenting Io "semble n'avoir été imaginée que pour des effets de décoration" (1: 666A; see Gros, *Quinault* 753, n. 2). About 1742, Claude Parfaict, in his manuscript history of the Académie Royale, wrote that "on ne sent point dans la pièce cet intérêt qui doit être l'ame de tous les ouvrages de Théatre." Parfaict did not blame Quinault, however; rather, he sympathized with him: "Plaignons-le d'avoir été obligé de traiter un fond ingrat et sterile, dont il a été contraint de remplir les vuides de scènes épisodiques" (122-23).

Parfaict is assuming—perhaps incorrectly—that Quinault had little or no role in the choice of his subject and that he and Lully were trying to write another opera that, like *Atys,* could be compared favorably to Racinian tragedy. Indeed, by such standards, the plot of *Isis* is weak, its characters one-dimensional. Still, it has many qualities that can make it effective theater, and one can attribute its mitigated success less to any weaknesses the work might have than to its experimental nature, to Quinault and Lully's obvious decision to try a new approach to the *tragédie lyrique*. I will discuss this in more detail in section 2, after a brief look at some other ways *Isis* is similar to but also different from Quinault's other libretti.

§ § §

If the choice of the myth of Io did not present Quinault with a plot full of traditionally dramatic possibilities, it is a particularly rich myth and one that has numerous connections with his other libretti. Io is the ancestor—through her son Epaphus, who will play a large role in Quinault and Lully's *Phaéton*—of the Danaans, who repopulated Greece, and of Hercules, whose triumph is celebrated at the end of *Alceste*. Furthermore, Io is the character chosen by Aeschylus to dominate a third of his *Prometheus Bound,* to be the second example of someone whom Jupiter has made to suffer. Like this great Greek tragedy, *Isis* is a work that stages "la nécessité d'un certain renoncement pour mettre fin aux conflits qu'engendre sans cesse la violence égoïste des passions" (Mazon 153). Renunciation, self-control, cooperation, these are the themes that one finds not only in the libretti that feature the descendants of Io (*Alceste,*

Phaéton) but also in *Thésée, Atys, Proserpine,* and *Persée,* as well as, in a different context, *Roland* and *Armide.* From this point of view, the choice of *Isis* to follow *Atys* is hardly surprising.

The subject of *Isis* is also similar to that of *Atys* in that both deal with a divinity who descends to earth to trouble the love between two mortals. The major difference, of course, is that Cybèle is passionately in love with Atys, whereas Jupiter, in spite of his protestations of true love, seems interested in Io only because of her beauty: "Il n'est rien dans les Cieux, il n'est rien ici-bas, / De si charmant que vos appas" (II.ii.232-33). If it is true that "[Il sort] avec plaisir de [s]on suprême empire" (II.ii.210), he does not become involved, as Cybèle does, in a truly desperate struggle for the love of a mortal. He does not suffer, nor does he run any risk in being involved in a tragic denouement.[11]

He does cause Io to suffer, however, at the hands of his jealous wife, in much the same way that Thésée unwittingly causes Églé to suffer at the hands of a jealous Médée (*Thésée* III.vi-viii). Like Églé, Io is "guilty" because she is lovable. Médée reponds to Églé's "Je prétends ne rien faire / Qui vous doive irriter" with a succinct "Et n'est-ce rien que de trop plaire?" (III.iii.556-58). Similarly, Argus tells Io:

> Vous êtes aimable,
> Vos yeux devaient moins charmer;
> Vous êtes coupable
> De vous faire trop aimer.
> [...]
> C'est une offense cruelle
> De paraître belle
> A des yeux jaloux.
> L'amour de Jupiter a trop paru pour vous. (III.i.454-57, 461-64)

---

[11] Although she uses words similar to those of Jupiter, Cybèle emphasizes her reluctance to return to the heavens rather than the pleasure of a temporary visit to earth:
> Ce fut au jour fatal de ma dernière Fête
> Que de l'aimable Atys je devins la conquête.
> Je partis à regret pour retourner aux Cieux,
> Tout m'y parut changé, rien n'y plut à mes yeux.
> Je sens un plaisir extrême
> A revenir dans ces lieux. (II.iii.338-43)

One can see easily in these quotations one of the main differences between Io and Atys. Both suffer because they are loved by a god or goddess, but Atys is in a truly tragic situation, faced with choices that can
lead only to unhappiness. Io, though she deserves our pity as a more or
less innocent victim, remains passive and is ultimately pardoned. Again,
the comparison with Églé is enlightening: the main character in *Isis* is in a
situation similar to that of a secondary character in *Thésée*.

If *Isis* has much in common with earlier Quinault-Lully operas,
one can—with hindsight, at least—notice significant differences as early
as the first scene. Although *Cadmus et Hermione, Alceste,* and *Atys* begin
with the presentation of a hero who is unhappy in love, the lyrical out-
pourings of Hiérax in the first scenes of *Isis* are more extensive than
anything Quinault had written before.[12] In response to Pirante's evocation
of a peaceful pastoral setting:

> Regardez ces flots argentés,
> Qui, dans ces vallons écartés,
> Font briller l'émail des prairies.
> Interrompez vos soupirs;
> Tout doit être ici tranquille;
> Ce beau séjour est l'asile
> Du Repos et des Plaisirs. (I.ii.18-24)

Hiérax responds:

> Depuis qu'une Nymphe inconstante
> A trahi mon amour et m'a manqué de foi,
> Ces lieux, jadis si beaux, n'ont plus rien qui m'enchante;
> Ce que j'aime a changé, tout est changé pour moi.
> [...]

---

[12] This passage is often called "les plaintes" d'Hiérax" and singled out for special
praise. See Girdlestone, *Tragédie en musique* 35 and Gros, *Quinault* 713-14, where he
compares it to Lamartine; he looks more closely at the comparison in "A propos de
Lamartine et de Quinault." Gros also quotes Sévelinges's *Biographie universelle:*
"D'autres poètes ont possédé les grâces et l'élégance du style, mais nul d'entre eux n'a
été doué de cette mélodie enchanteresse, qui permettait de dire que les vers de Quinault
étaient déjà de la musique avant d'être livrés au musicien" (714).

L'inconstante n'a plus l'empressement extrême
De cet amour naissant qui répondait au mien,
Son changement paraît en dépit d'elle-même;
Je ne le connais que trop bien;
Sa bouche quelquefois dit encor qu'elle m'aime,
Mais son cœur ni ses yeux ne m'en disent plus rien.
[...]
Je ne les crus que trop, hélas!
Ces serments qui trompaient mon cœur tendre et crédule.
Ce fut dans ces vallons, où par mille détours
Inachus prend plaisir à prolonger son cours;
Ce fut sur son charmant rivage,
Que sa fille volage
Me promit de m'aimer toujours.
Le Zéphyr fut témoin, l'Onde fut attentive,
Quand la Nymphe jura de ne changer jamais;
Mais le Zéphyr léger, et l'Onde fugitive,
Ont enfin emporté les serments qu'elle a faits.
                    (I.ii.25-28,38-43,46-56)

The harmony of nature and of pastoral love has been interrupted by Jupiter's pleasure seeking. Nature changes almost instantly from faithful and attentive witness to the happiness of Io and Hiérax to a flighty, inconstant force that takes away that happiness. At the same time, Quinault's poetry—especially the use of the rhyming words *attentive* and *fugitive* to describe the personified *Onde*—evokes the change in Io.

In the third scene, in response to Io's protestations of continuing love, Hiérax returns to the nature imagery:

Vous juriez autrefois que cette Onde rebelle
Se ferait vers sa source une route nouvelle,
Plutôt qu'on ne verrait votre cœur dégagé.
Voyez couler ces flots dans cette vaste plaine,
C'est le même penchant qui toujours les entraîne,
Leur cours ne change point, et vous avez changé. (I.iii.72-77)

This use of water imagery takes on added significance in light of the importance of Neptune and of France's naval successes in the prologue and of the attempts of Syrinx (III.vi) and Io (IV.iv) to put an end to their troubles by plunging into water.[13] What was once a source of pleasure and refreshment becomes a source of danger, as the "mille détours" and "charmant rivage" become "fugitive" and "rebelle," as dangerous as the apple presented by the sinuous, undulating serpent, whose charms and "détours" brought about the end of Adam and Eve's stay in paradise.[14]

The commentators on this famous passage have not offered any detailed analysis of its formal beauty.[15] Quinault does not, as one would expect, give Hiérax the lilting lines with an uneven number of syllables that he uses so effectively elsewhere. Instead, it is Pirante who begins the second scene with a lyrical passage that ends with four seven-syllable lines (lines 21-24, quoted above). Hiérax cannot share these pastoral pleasures, and he responds with the first of several parallel structures that serve either to emphasize his feelings:

> Depuis qu'une Nymphe inconstante
> A trahi mon amour et m'a manqué de foi,

or to contrast his continuing love to the love that Io once shared:

> Ces lieux, jadis si beaux, n'ont plus rien qui m'enchante;
> Ce que j'aime a changé, tout est changé pour moi.

His sounds are rather harsh, especially in "A trahi" and the sibilant "jadis si," and his well-organized alexandrines suggest a spurned lover who has had time to formulate his reproaches. In fact, he will continue to use

---

[13] *Isis* contains eleven of the thirty-two occurrences of *onde* and *ondes* in Quinault's libretti.

[14] To complete this quite unflattering portrait of Jupiter-Satan-Louis, Mercure reveals to Io that Jupiter's interest in the "bonheur du Monde" is only "Pour abuser des Dieux jaloux" (I.v.150, 157). Is it any wonder that *Isis* was not Louis XIV's favorite opera?

[15] Girdlestone mentions "la répartition des longueurs" but goes on to say that "son secret se dérobe à l'analyse" (*Tragédie en musique* 35). Courville (88) singles out another passage of *Isis* for special praise: "Voyez ses yeux noyés de larmes, / Que l'ombre de la mort commence de couvrir (V.iii.864-65).

mostly alexandrines in these two scenes (approximately 60 percent of his lines in I.ii-iii), hardly the most lyrical arrow in Quinault's quiver. He begins to sound more lyrical in lines 35-36 ("Cette Nymphe légère / De jour en jour diffère"), but reverts quickly to the alexandrine, ending with three hemistichs with a regular 3-3 rhythm, suggesting Io's lack of enthusiasm (42-43).

Even in his last speech in scene ii (lines 46-56, quoted above), brief passages of soft sounds and varied rhythms are interrupted by words with unpleasant sounds ("Inachus" and "volage," for example) or meanings ("crédule") and, finally, by "mais," which introduces another parallel structure that emphasizes his pain through repetition and by the ironic use of lyrical words with soft sounds ("le Zéphyr léger, et l'Onde fugitive") to describe the forces that carried off Io's oaths and his happiness. Just when the spectator is settling in for poetic beauty and the evocation of tender love, the very forces that witnessed their happiness become agents of their separation. When Io appears at the beginning of scene three, the pastoral mood evoked by Pirante is gone; in speaking to her, Hiérax will not even intersperse short, lyrical lines and tender sounds with his complaints. In short, the poetry of scene ii, widely admired as some of Quinault's most beautiful, is far from being a collection of beautiful lines. Things are neither what they once were nor what they seem, and Lully's music makes this all too clear when he sets Io's "Non, je vous aime encor" (I.iii.82) to a most unconvincing melody. Quinault has captured this atmosphere perfectly by combining lyrical passages with harsher sounding ones, and it is fitting that what is perhaps the *tendre* Quinault's most successful portrayal of love is by no means all *tendresse*.

§ § §

Hiérax's nature as an eloquent complainer, rather than as a hero such as Cadmus, Alcide, and Thésée who will overcome tremendous obstacles to win the woman he loves, suggests that he will not be a primary actor in what is to come. Instead, his role is largely to sing some of the most beautiful and lyrical lines in any of Quinault's texts, and in so doing to set the tone for what is the least dramatic of his libretti. Indeed, after his duet with Io in act I scene iii, he does not reappear until the second scene of the third act, aware that his happiness is past ("[...] la félicité que vous m'avez ravie," III.ii.504) and interested only in punishing Io and in freeing himself from the chains of love. He is turned into a bird of prey in act III scene vii and is not mentioned again. With Hiérax gone, there is no mortal male character left, no one to compete for Io's affections and to create a potentially tragic situation.

It is also evident from the less than grave tone of the male gods, Jupiter and Mercury, that neither of them is likely to replace Hiérax as the tragic protagonist. Without going as far as Couvreur, who sees Jupiter as "presque une caricature" and *Isis* as parody and "farce mythologique" (*Lully* 374-75), one can safely say that Jupiter is interested in pleasure, not in love, and the delightful scene of banter between Mercury and Iris (II.iv) suggests that Mercury does not take love too seriously either.

The women certainly do, however. Iris is tempted by a loving and trusting relationship, though she is rightly skeptical of Mercure's intentions. If he is willing to be faithful, she will be an obedient partner:

> MERCURE
> Si je fais ma première affaire
> De vous voir et de vous plaire?
> IRIS
> Je ferai mon premier devoir
> De vous plaire et de vous voir. (II.iv.280-83)

He is only using the appeal of love to get information from her about her mistress Junon, and Iris soon sees through his ruse, concluding a delightful scene that would not be out of place in a comedy. Quinault and Lully are clearly not yet ready to cast all their operas in the tragic mold of *Atys*.

Unlike Iris, Junon and Io are already committed and thus take the situation more seriously; that is, they both have to deal with Jupiter's power and infidelity. Quinault did not need to develop Junon's character, since her role as jealous wife and protector of wronged women was known to anyone slightly familiar with classical mythology. She announces in her first speech that she is not "[...] une crédule épouse / Qu'on puisse tromper aisément" (II.v.323-24) and enters immediately into a war of wits with her husband. She shows extreme cruelty to Io, punishing her incessantly during the last three acts until Jupiter agrees to mend his ways. Her cruelty makes her an unsympathetic character, yet, from a traditional moral point of view, she is in the right. This ambiguity is typical of *Isis*, which lacks a main character who is both sympathetic and heroic.

Io seems sincerely divided between her love for Hiérax and her infatuation with Jupiter. While she clearly enjoys "l'avantage / De plaire au plus puissant des Dieux" (II.i.202-03), her protestations do not strike the reader, or the listener, as empty:

> Que sert-il qu'ici-bas votre amour me choisisse?
> L'honneur m'en vient trop tard, j'ai formé d'autres nœuds.
> Il fallait que ce bien, pour combler tous mes vœux,
> Ne me coûtât point d'injustice,
> Et ne fît point de malheureux. (II.ii.218-22)[16]

She continues to resist: Lully's shifting harmonies and chromatic lines make her "Contentez-vous, hélas" (243) and "Je n'ai que trop de peine" (253) sound as if she is truly struggling with herself, and her "Écoutez mon devoir" (249) is set to a firm cadence. However, by the end of the scene it is clear that, as she says, she has waited too long and it is too late to flee: the dissonant melodic intervals and rapid harmonic movement of "Je devais moins attendre; / Que ne fuyais-je, hélas! avant que de vous voir!" (II.ii.254-55) suggest considerable instability. She is still fleeing, according to the stage directions at the end of act II scene iii, but by the time Lully has repeated "vous m'arrêtez" three times, the sensuous melody and sweet, consonant cadence of the last repeat have transformed the phrase from a complaint to an expression of anticipated pleasure:

> Le devoir veut que je vous quitte
> Et je sens que vous m'arrêtez. (II.ii.258-59)

Jupiter and Io are singing together, in similar rhythms, for the first time and, as at the end of the famous duet between Don Givoanni and Zerlina,

---

[16] See also I.iv.138-41:
> Lorsqu'on me presse de me rendre
> Aux attraits d'un amour nouveau,
> Plus le charme est puissant, et plus il serait beau
> De pouvoir m'en défendre.

the outcome is no longer in doubt—we suspect that Jupiter and Io are doing more than talk of love while Mercure delays Iris (II.iv). We also suspect that there is no happy future in it for Io; like Iris, who contrasts her "devoir" to Mercure's "première affaire" (II.iv.282, 280; quoted above), it is Io who has to worry about duty and commitment, who will have to suffer. Women are not doing well in the battle between the sexes, and although Junon has her way in the end and Io becomes a goddess, these triumphs seem hollow; Jupiter will certainly continue to be unfaithful, and Io cannot have happiness on earth.

- II -

   This combination of passion and suffering (Junon, Hiérax, Io) with almost ironic detachment (Jupiter, Mercure, Iris) makes *Isis* more than a reflection of an insouciant, male-oriented concept of love. It also moves the Quinault-Lully collaboration in a new direction—a *tragédie lyrique* that is extremely *lyrique* but far from *tragique*. In addition, it does not develop one of the standard elements that one finds in all of Racine's tragedies from *Alexandre* to *Phèdre* and in Quinault and Lully's first four operas—after Hiérax is turned into a bird of prey in act III scene vii, there is no character who can be said to be truly in love. Nor do we ever have a united couple threatened by rivals in love, since the love—not very strong, apparently—between Hiérax and Io is a thing of the past before the opera begins. Audiences expected to find a loving couple at the beginning and to follow their trials and tribulations to the end, but they hardly found it in *Isis*. In fact, it is not hard to see why many critics have found the plot of *Isis* to be disappointing and weak, since

   1. Hiérax, who at first appears to be the male lead, does not appear in the second act and disappears near the end of the third;
   2. The fourth act does little to advance the plot, but is devoted to a series of scenes featuring divinities and strange peoples;
   3. The last act resolves very little, other than the quarrel between Jupiter and Junon. There is no real-life solution for Io, who becomes a goddess.

Why would Quinault and Lully write a *tragédie lyrique* that places little emphasis on the development of a standard plot and on realistic, individual psychological portraits, and this one year after *Atys*, the closest thing they wrote to a "regular" tragedy, which had precisely these more expected qualities?[17] Almost every critic who has dealt with *Isis* in some detail has struggled with the same question:

---

[17] Another difference between *Isis* and Quinault's earlier libretti is that the last two acts contain no events—no peripeteia, no heroic or divine intervention—that are likely to change Io's unfortunate situation. In this way *Isis* adheres to what Forestier calls, in his *notice* to Racine's *Britannicus,* "le principe esthétique le plus caractéristique de la dramaturgie de Corneille," one that Racine rejected: "chaque étape de l'action referme davantage l'impasse dans laquelle se trouve placé le héros, suscitant ainsi un pathétique

Atys venait au terme d'une évolution caractérisée par le progrès du dramatique et de l'humain. *Isis* marquera un violent coup de barre. Quinault et Lully abandonnent la voie qui menait leur genre à une forme plus strictement dramatique. Ont-ils compris la vanité de faire de l'opéra une doublure de la tragédie additionnée de chant et de danse? (Girdlestone, *Tragédie en musique* 77)

A persévérer dans la voie où il s'engageait avec *Atys,* Quinault devait être amené à s'éloigner de sa conception première de la tragédie lyrique. *Atys,* en tant que livret d'opéra, est une œuvre sobre. Le spectacle y tient une place beaucoup moins importante que dans les livrets précédents, et si les danses y sont encore relativement nombreuses, la part des machines est strictement limitée: l'action, très nettement, tend à s'intérioriser, l'intérêt à se concentrer sur l'intrigue, l'attention à s'attacher aux personnages et aux sentiments. Dans *Isis,* au contraire, l'action s'extériorise de nouveau; le spectacle reprend une place prépondérante, les danses sont plus nombreuses et la mise en scène est plus somptueuse que jamais [...]. (Gros, *Quinault* 607)

Après le resserrement progressif de la tragédie lyrique, l'effort constant et conjoint de Quinault et de Lully pour se rapprocher de la tragédie—et ils y parviennent, l'un et l'autre, dans *Atys,* compte tenu de la nature du spectacle qu'ils proposent—voici tout à coup une œuvre sans force proprement dramatique, sans volonté d'en avoir, sans unité d'action, avec un retour au ton léger et même au comique. Une régression? Ou une diversion? Les deux auteurs ont-il pensé que l'excès de rigueur d'*Atys* risquait de durcir leur théâtre? Ou de lasser leur public? (Beaussant, *Lully* 579)

The most obvious answer to these questions is that Quinault and Lully wanted to try a new approach to the *tragédie lyrique. Isis* has many qualities that can make it effective theater, and one can attribute its mitigated success less to any weaknesses the work might have than to its

---

intense, et appelant inéluctablement un événement ou une décision inattendue qui vienne trancher ce nœud inextricable et mortel" (1415). While I would by no means call *Isis* Cornelian, Forestier's description applies very well to its last two acts.

experimental nature, to Quinault and Lully's decision to give a larger role to spectacle[18] and to the music (especially Lully's instrumental music, or *symphonies*) and dance that were so popular with their audiences. This they did, but hardly at the expense of unity, structure, and drama.

Instead of a love interest or true unity of action, Quinault used thematic unity to structure his libretto. Io's suffering, which dominates the final acts of the opera, can best be understood in the context of the restrictions that are placed on her freedom and on that of most of the other characters. Io apparently made a free choice to enter into a relationship with Hiérax: "Mes vœux sont engagés, mon cœur a fait un choix" (I.v.165). Pirante says that her father approves of the match but emphasizes Io's preference, not her father's wishes:

> La fille d'Inachus hautement vous préfère
> A mille autres amants de votre sort jaloux;
> Vous avez l'aveu de son père. (I.ii.29-31)

Jupiter's attentions do not of course *force* her to change her choice, but it is as if Jupiter represents a force that cannot be resisted:

> C'est un amant qu'on n'ose mépriser;
> Et du plus grand des cœurs le glorieux empire
> Est difficile à refuser. (I.iv.135-37)

As we saw at the end of section 1, she sincerely tries to remain true to her choice of Hiérax, but she seems trapped in a hopeless situation, doomed to lose Hiérax, to be abandoned by Jupiter, and to be punished by Junon. Once the gods begin to intervene in human affairs, there is no more freedom for mortals.

Examples of characters who limit the freedom of other characters can be found throughout the libretto. Jupiter is of course the most powerful of the gods, but even he cannot simply impose his will; as Junon says,

---

[18] As Girdlestone points out (*Tragédie en musique* 80), there are eight different sets and eight appearances of divinities.

Sous sa toute-puissance il faut que tout fléchisse,

Mais puisqu'il ne prétend s'armer que d'artifice,

Tout Jupiter qu'il est, il est moins fort que moi. (II.v.328-30)

There are certain conventions that even Jupiter must obey. He does not simply abduct Io, as Pluton will do in *Proserpine,* nor does he openly flaunt his new passion. Similarly, Junon has the power to imprison and punish Io for as long as she likes, but her "courroux fatal" and "injuste fureur" finally must give way to "une juste pitié" (V.iii.869, 881, 868). Even though Jupiter's actions have left her little recourse except artifice and emotional blackmail, her jealousy and anger cause her to impose excessive punishment on a relatively innocent victim. Furthermore, there are "laws" of the theater that govern her behavior as well as that of Jupiter and the other characters. If there were too many scenes portraying Io's sufferings, they would bore the audience and would create such a portrait of injustice that it would go against the principles of *vraisemblance* and *bienséance.* Jupiter and Junon must do something to resolve their conflict, else the opera could not end.

There are numerous other examples of characters with limited freedom, such as Mercure and Iris ("Jupiter et Junon nous occupent sans cesse," II.iv.277), Argus, who puts his duty to Junon above brotherly love (III.ii.486-87), or the Fury Érinnis, who executes Junon's orders without question. Most important, however, for the thematic unity of the opera, is the example of Syrinx, who is pursued by Pan in the same way that Io is by Jupiter. Among its other functions, to which I will return toward the end of this chapter, this episode serves as another example of a man forcing his attentions on a woman while making explicit the theme of freedom that was more indirectly present in the first two acts. The word *liberté* occurs eighteen times in act III, and even more often when one counts all the repetitions in the score, serving as a sort of refrain for Syrinx and her nymphs.[19] It is introduced, however, by Argus (III.ii.514) following the "Heureux qui peut briser sa chaîne" that he sings with

---

[19] *Liberté* occurs eighteen times in *Isis,* which represents 37 percent of the fifty-three occurrences in Quinault's eleven libretti; the other two occurrences in *Isis* are in Hiérax's speech in I.i. A similar repetition of *liberté* by the chorus is found in the first act of *Thésée* (I.vi.138-46) which, as I pointed out above (pp. 193-94), also features—like *Isis*—an innocent female character who suffers at the hands of a jealous woman.

Hiérax, thus linking Hiérax's desire to be free of his love for Io to Syrinx's desire to be free from any amorous engagement. At the same time, the theme of liberty becomes linked to imprisonment and forced suffering, as Io is first locked up (end of III.i) and then forced to undergo a series of punishments (IV.i-V.i). Finally, the last scene brings us back to the theme of freedom of choice, as Jupiter and Junon decide to put their quarrel aside.[20]

Isis is thus much more than a collection of episodes designed to provide opportunities for spectacle and dance. Is it, however, effective drama? If one takes the definition of a dictionary such as the *Nouveau Petit Robert* (1994), "Qui est susceptible d'émouvoir, d'intéresser vivement le spectateur, au théâtre," there would be no problem; after all, we all know that "la principale règle est de plaire et de toucher" (Racine, *Bérénice,* preface), that is, "intéresser" and "émouvoir." However, one finds in all too many critical works the idea that nothing is worthy of interesting the spectator, of moving him/her, except the linear development of a well-constructed plot. To take the example of Kerman, whom I mentioned in the introduction—and whose *Opera as Drama* has *interested* a large number of people and *moved* many of them to fairly emotional reactions—he both denies that the dramatic has a necessary link to plot and talks about plot all the time.[21] He bases his concept of the dramatic on the reactions of the characters in a play or opera, rather than on those of the spectators: "What is essentially at issue is the response of the persons in the play to the elements of the action" (5). As a result, how these characters react and interreact, which is all too often the same thing as how the plot works out, is considered more important than the effects these characters have on the emotions of the spectators.

To take another example, closer to the time of Quinault and Lully, Charles Perrault, in his *Critique d'Alceste,* devoted most of his small book to "la conduite du sujet," in spite of having promised near the beginning to discuss versification and music. It is clear from this defensive

---

[20] Roger Shattuck offers an interesting discussion of music and sublimation in relation to the myth of Pan and Syrinx. See chapter 4 of *Forbidden Knowledge,* "The Pleasures of Abstinence," in particular p. 110.

[21] See above, p. 16, n. 16 and p. 17, n. 18. Patrick Giles reopened the debate in "Leap of Faith: Embracing *Tosca,*" with a welcome emphasis on "charged, extreme representation of events" and "real music drama" (48, 51).

strategy, as well as from most of the criticisms of Perrault's arguments in Racine's preface to *Iphigénie* (1674), that opera's detractors could not argue that the new *tragédie lyrique* did not please or move their audiences; their best strategy was to criticize it because its plot did not always meet the standards of Racinian tragedy, especially in terms of *vraisemblance*.

Quinault and Lully seem to have wanted to have it both ways. They had showed that they could write a near-Racinian tragedy with *Atys*, which could hardly be criticized for the working out of its tightlyknit plot. Then, with *Isis*, they seem to have decided to pay considerably less attention to plot and to a narrow definition of the dramatic. In agreeing to take the myth of Io as his subject, Quinault obviously realized that an opera based on this subject would have a form quite different from that of *Atys*, that it would represent an experiment with a different concept of the *tragédie lyrique*. This concept involves a structure that can accommodate a series of *divertissements*, that can bring the audience to recognize and feel the emotions, the suffering of Io—and to think about what caused them—as much through these *divertissements* as through the unfolding of the plot. At the same time, this concept represents what one could call an apotheosis of *divertissement*, an apology for the power of music, dance, and spectacle to move audiences even if they are not caught up in a tightly woven plot. Girdlestone seems to have understood this, though he did not seem to appreciate its advantages: "Nous sommes en présence d'une esthétique qui vise à produire l'émotion et qui ne se soucie ni d'action ni de structure. Il y aura juxtaposition d'états d'âme, non d'avance linéaire" (78).[22] He is exaggerating of course, especially about the structure of *Isis*, which has a strong thematic unity that makes the representation of the emotions of Io and the other characters more than just "juxtapositions d'états d'âme." When seen from the point of view of *divertissement* and dance, it also has a very carefully elaborated structure. One way of seeing this structure is as follows:

> **Act I**: Jupiter descends to Earth, after a quarrel between Io and Hiérax. He pursues Io.

---

[22] Beaussant says *Isis* "se présente comme une mosaïque" (*Lully* 583). His comment is in the context of how easy it is to excerpt scenes from the opera.

> **Act II**: Junon's nymphs await Io. She arrives, but cannot stay (Junon will have put her under lock and key by the beginning of the next act).
>
> **Act III**: Actors replace the gods and stage an opera within the opera, a work that demonstrates the power of opera.
>
> **Act IV**: The Fates are waiting for Io. She arrives, asks them for death, but must continue her torments.
>
> **Act V**: Jupiter descends to Earth again, after a quarrel with Junon. Io is no longer pursued or punished but immortalized as Isis.

In this ABCBA structure, Jupiter's pain-causing intervention (act I) and his moment of self-mastery (act V) frame the sufferings of Io, who is pursued by Jupiter before becoming a member of Junon's court (act II) and by Junon before becoming a goddess (act IV). Act III, which could seem a digression, functions as a variation on these themes of intervention, self-control, freedom, pursuit, and transformation.

The best example of Girdlestone's "juxtaposition d'états d'âme" as a means of evoking intense emotional response is the fourth act, where Io, as in Ovid and Aeschylus, goes from Scythian cold to the burning forges of the Chalybes[23] to the den of the Fates (Parques). What a series of opportunities for the composer, choreographer, and stage designer, what a series of reactions on the part of the spectator! Pity for Io, of course, and anger at Junon and Érinnis, but also fear, uneasiness in the face of the arbitrariness of Destiny and of the Fates, frustration at the refusal or inability of Jupiter to end Io's suffering, disorientation caused by the unfamiliarity of all these exotic settings, or simply cold and heat. Does one really have to regret, as Girdlestone did, that the emotional and the spectacular come to the fore here, at the expense of a notion of the dramatic that is little more than linear plot development? Does one really have to regret that, at least during part of this fourth act, the spectator is as interested in the unusual characters that surround Io as in the heroine herself?

Io's fate and the working out of the plot are hardly forgotten while Quinault and Lully dwell on the variety and intensity of her suffering. In

---

[23] The Chalybes, who lived in the Black Sea region, were known for their iron mines and forges.

the long run, however, Io is less important that what the spectator feels and learns. Is the goal of the theater not to please, to touch, to instruct? This fourth act does it all, asking questions about liberty, human suffering, fate, justice, and power, both domestic and political, while at the same time offering just what the public loved: spectacle, music, and especially dance. Why, I hear Quinault and Lully asking themselves, should this kind of opera not be as effective and as successful as *Atys*, which was truly a *tragédie en musique*? In other words, just how independent of traditional theatrical forms can, or should, opera be?

§ § §

I see evidence that this question is more than rhetorical in the great *divertissement* of the third act of *Isis*, where Mercury and a group of *sylvains* put Argus to sleep by staging, and especially by singing and dancing, the story of Pan and Syrinx. One could say that Quinault was just following Ovid, or that Lully was glad to have an occasion for another *sommeil* (slumber scene), after the huge success of the one in *Atys* the year before, but I prefer to think they had more artistic reasons for developing this scene—easily the longest in Quinault's libretti—to such an extent.[24]

Io, Syrinx, and pipe-like instruments are already associated in *Prometheus Bound*, although Syrinx does not appear as a character. Io enters, pursued by the gadfly and bemoaning her fate, and Aeschylus gives her these beautiful—in Mazon's edition at least—lines: "Et sur mes pas le roseau sonore à la gaine de cire fait entendre son assoupissante chanson" (lines 574-75). In the *Metamorphoses*, Mercury, disguised as a shepherd, meets Argus, makes some pan pipes (also called syrinx), and begins to play. Argus is charmed and invites the stranger to sit down:

> [...] Mercury joins him,
> Whiling the time away with conversation

---

[24] Scene vi contains 134 of the 918 lines of *Isis*, which is 15 percent of the total. The three preceding scenes can also be considered part of the *divertissement*, which brings the total to 167 lines (18 percent). The only other scene in Quinault's libretti with more than 100 lines is IV.vii of *Thésée*, which contains 112.

And soothing little melodies, and Argus
Has a hard fight with drowsiness [...]. (1: 681-83)

Argus does not go to sleep, however, and asks Mercury to tell him the history of the pan pipes, which had just been invented. Mercury begins the story of Pan and Syrinx, but Argus nods off well before the end. It is music that charms Argus and makes him sleepy, but it is the tale of Pan and Syrinx that closes the hundred eyes. Both music and words are necessary to accomplish this near-miraculous feat.

The only example in Quinault's libretti of a play within a play, his version of Pan and Syrinx is a true miniature opera, complete with a prologue where Mercury promises a "spectacle touchant."[25] In the context of the affair between Jupiter and Io, the goal of this scene, as in the *Malade imaginaire* or the *Barbier de Séville*, is to use music to put to sleep the obstacle-character who threatens the happiness of the young couple. But the levels of representation are much more complex here: the lovers are not present (Argus has locked Io up at the end of the first scene of the act), and Argus represents the absent Junon; even Pan and Syrinx are absent, since they are represented by a *sylvain* and a nymph who do not appear in the rest of the opera. Mercury, who works for Jupiter, plays the role of the director.

One could thus see the scene as an example of *mise en abyme:* at one level an actress plays a nymph who plays the nymph Syrinx who is in a similar situation to that of Io, who is trying to resist the amorous advances of a god. More generally, Jupiter delegates Mercury who hires *sylvains* and nymphs to represent a story that will allow Jupiter to outwit Junon and sneak off with the nymph whose situation is so similar to that of Syrinx. One can also see in this sequence of representation and delegation the king who delegates Quinault and Lully to hire actors to represent

---

[25] MERCURE déguisé en Berger, parlant à Argus
            De la Nymphe Syrinx Pan chérit la mémoire,
            Il en regrette encor la perte chaque jour:
            Pour célébrer une fête à sa gloire,
            Ce Dieu lui-même assemble ici sa cour;
            Il veut que du malheur de son fidèle amour
            Un spectacle touchant représente l'histoire. (524-29)
One could compare these lines to lines 114-17 of the prologue to *Persée*.

stories that will silence anyone daring to impose limits on royal preroga-
tives, be they amorous or political.

But let us leave the political aside for now, as we have left aside
the possible references to Mme de Montespan. Scenes iii-vi (lines 515-
681) constitute a *divertissement* chosen to accomplish the near-impossible
task of overcoming the vigilance of a hundred-eyed watchman. It was
fairly easy for a few flutes to close the two eyes of the mortal Atys, especially when they were playing by order of the powerful goddess Cybèle,
but considerably more difficult in the case of Argus. One can infer that, to
please Louis XIV, and to amuse his court, instrumental music is not
enough; it requires poetry, staging, music, and dance, that is, the *tragédie
lyrique*.

Let us look a little more closely at these remarkable effects of
music. According to Quinault's stage directions, "Argus commence à
s'assoupir" as he listens to the "concert de flûtes" played on the reeds that
once were Syrinx. If flutes have the place of honor at the end of this
miniature opera, one of the reasons is certainly that the flute takes us back
to the origins of music and of opera. It is not only one of the first musical
instruments, but the one that accompanied the actors of Greek tragedy—
as Mercury, in the *Metamorphoses*, accompanies himself on a kind of
flute—and that helped create the effects that the creators of opera at the
beginning of the seventeenth century in Italy wanted to imitate.[26] The
flute is also associated with the pastoral, a genre in great favor earlier in
the century, that played an important role in the development of opera,
and that is evoked in the opening scenes of *Isis*.

We thus have a reflection on the origins of opera, but especially
on its power. It is only at the end of a *representation*, where music,
words, and dance have played the major role—the first thing Argus and
Hiérax say when they see the nymphs approaching in III.iii is "Quelles
danses, quels chants, et quelle nouveauté!"—that the flutes *accompanying*
the representation succeed in putting Argus to sleep. Furthermore, this
reflection is found in the Quinault-Lully opera that "strays" the farthest

---

[26] More specifically, the aulos—often confused with the flute—led the chorus in
Greek tragedy. The *Oxford Companion to Musical Instruments* describes the aulos as "a
reed instrument and particularly the pair of slender pipes played together by one musician." It adds that "[i]t is for poetic euphony that in later literature 'aulos' has generally
been translated 'flute' rather than 'pipe.'"

from the conception of theater that stresses the unfolding of the plot and the psychological development of a love conflict.[27] It is as if they said to themselves: "In *Atys,* we gambled on drama and won; we created a *tragédie lyrique* that can hold its own with spoken tragedy. We reduced the spectacular to a minimum, had the goddess Cybèle interact with the other characters as if she were a mortal, put music and dance at the service of plot. Now, let us try something different, even the opposite: plot at the service of music and dance." Gros had more or less the same view of *Isis:*

> Tandis que dans *Atys* l'opéra, sans rien abandonner de ce qui lui était propre, se rapprochait de la tragédie et tendait vers une conception plus dramatique et plus sobre, vers une conception plus proprement tragique; tandis qu'avec *Atys* l'opéra s'intériorisait, il s'orientait, avec *Isis*, vers une conception infiniment plus libre et plus fantaisiste, où les éléments extérieurs, la mise en scene, les danses et les machines, tendaient de nouveau à envahir l'action et à se réserver, dans cette action, une part excessive. (*Quinault* 614)

Excessive? Perhaps. As I said earlier, the work was, if not a failure, not a great success. Still, the contemporary criticisms that have come down to us involve the music (too "savante") or the characters (Érinnis is not cruel enough), not the general conception of the work. The opera is not really flawed, just different. To quote Gros again,

> l'intrigue n'est plus qu'un prétexte dans l'action, *Isis* est l'un des meilleurs livrets de Quinault; *Isis* est une œuvre d'art; mais *Isis* ouvrait la porte à un excès. (*Quinault* 614)

The excesses that Gros mentions are those of the *opéra-ballets* of the early eighteenth century, many of which were hardly more than a string of dances with very tenuous links among them.

---

[27] Kintzler ("*Platée:* la comédie, vérité de la tragédie") points out that Le Valois d'Orville and Rameau's *Platée* (1745), another unusual opera, can be seen both as a reflection on the operatic tradition and as a remake of *Isis.*

Perhaps Quinault and Lully saw this danger; at any rate, they would not write another opera—and they wrote six more together—that gave so much importance to dance and to spectacle. The *tragédie lyrique* remains, after all, *tragédie,* inspired by Greek tragedy. On the other hand, music and dance are essential parts of the *tragédie lyrique,* and one can understand that the creators of a new type of theater would want to see how far one could tip the drama/spectacle scales toward spectacle. *Isis is* a unique work, hardly deserving of the neglect it has known. It is not only capable of giving great pleasure and of causing us to reflect on power, cruelty, jealousy, justice, and self-control; it can remind us of the relativism—if not the biases—of our assumptions about art and about reality. Could its critics be like Hiérax at the beginning of act I, overly eager to criticize a beautiful creature who has been unfaithful to their idea of how things should be and too ashamed to admit that they really like *Isis?* Perhaps if they listened to it more carefully, they too might say "Hélas! malgré moi je soupire!" (I.i.6).

7

Proserpine

Prudent Sexual Politics in a Patriarchal World

- I -

IN 1678, after six consecutive years of collaborating with Lully to create a new work for the court and for the Académie Royale de Musique, Quinault found himself in temporary disgrace (see chap. 6, 186-89). We have little information about what he did in 1678 and 1679,[1] but we can be sure that he gave considerable thought to the merits and defects of the libretti he had already written and to what he would do once he returned to favor. In particular, he must have followed very closely the collaboration of Lully and Thomas Corneille on *Psyché* (1678) and *Bellérophon* (1679).[2]

The former was an adaptation of the 1671 tragedy-ballet, for which Molière had called in Pierre Corneille to write the last three acts

---

[1] As Gros says (*Quinault* 123), it is unlikely that Quinault was in disgrace before June 12, 1677, when, as Directeur de l'Académie Française, he delivered the harangue to Louis XIV "sur son heureux retour & sa glorieuse Campagne" (*Recueil des harangues* 435-39). In September 1677, he read a sonnet and the "Poème de Sceaux," which is published in the 1811-17 edition of his *Œuvres choisies*. See the *Mercure galant,* October 1677, and Gros, *Quinault* 129.

[2] Lully considered a *Narcisse* by Frontinière, who had written lyrics for Lambert (*Mercure galant,* July 1677, 101) and *L'Amour guéri par le Temps* by Segrais; see Gros, *Quinault* 128. Corneille received help from Fontenelle (his nephew) and perhaps from Boileau, but there is considerable debate as to the extent of this help. Parfaict says it was common knowledge that Fontenelle was responsible for the role of Amisodar in *Bellérophon* (*Académie Royale* 134). See Reynier 57-60.

and Quinault to write the French verses that were to be sung to Lully's music in the *intermèdes*. The operatic *Psyché* opened in April 1678, after the Easter closing, with little success and was never given at court. Nevertheless, Lully (and possibly Louis XIV, at the instigation of Boileau and Racine, who did not want to see Quinault return to favor) convinced Thomas Corneille to write another libretto, *Bellérophon,* on the same subject as a tragedy by Quinault that had probably had its premiere, curiously enough, the same week as the earlier *Psyché* of 1671.[3]

According to Boscheron's biography of Quinault, (Thomas) Corneille had trouble with the second and third acts of his *Bellérophon* and, on the advice of Lully, consulted Quinault, who

> commença par lui retrancher la moitié de sa Piece, tellement que pour sept ou huit cent Vers qu'elle contient, Corneille fut contraint d'en faire deux-mille, malgré le desespoir où il étoit. Quinault ne laissa pas de le tirer d'embarras, en lui dressant le sujet de sa Piece. (41; see also Lecerf 2: 215)

The huge success of *Bellérophon* would thus be due at least in part to Quinault's collaboration, and the inability of Corneille—or any other dramatic poet of the time—to write a successful libretto without basing it on an earlier work must have been so obvious that the decision to return to Quinault was inevitable. Nevertheless, the decision was certainly made easier by the decline of Mme de Montespan's favor with the king and the rise of Mlle de Fontanges (Primi Visconti 115-21).

Quinault had certainly returned to grace by the spring of 1679, since a letter from Saint-Aignan to Bussy-Rabutin dated June 24 (4: 395) announces that an opera called *le Ravissement de Proserpine* will be ready for the following winter. There is no specific mention of Quinault, but it seems safe to assume that he was already at work on the *Proserpine* that is announced and specifically attributed to him in the *Mercure galant* of October 31 (pt. 1, 224-25, 351). The new opera was ready by Carnival of 1680, but Louis XIV ordered Quinault and Lully to wait until the arrival of the Dauphine (Marie-Anne de Bavière), who was to marry the

---

[3] Parfaict, *Académie Royale* 131; Quinault, *Bellérophon,* ed. Brooks, xiii; Boscheron 41.

king's son. She did not arrive until March, however (they married on March 7), and it was apparently decided that this would be too long to wait. The first performance was at Saint-Germain-en-Laye on February 3, where it continued at least until March 18, when the Dauphine finally saw it.[4]

It is not clear why *Proserpine* did not open at the Palais-Royal until November 15. The continuing success of *Bellérophon* was certainly one factor, as was the preparation of new sets and costumes for *Proserpine* by Berain.[5] Once it did open, the success was considerable. Sévigné said it was "au-dessus de tous les autres" (2: 833; Feb. 9, 1680), even though she had not seen it: "Je ne l'ai point vu (je ne suis point curieiuse de me divertir), mais on dit qu'il est parfaitement beau" (2: 857; March 1, 1680). Performances continued until the Easter closing in 1681 and began again the following November. This second run, which continued until the end of January 1682, was marked not only by new machines but "par les entrées que l'on a rendues plus belles en y meslant la plupart des filles qui ont dansé tout l'été dans *le Triomphe de l'Amour*."[6] *Proserpine* had only a modest number of revivals, which is probably a reflection of the numerous shortcomings mentioned by contemporary commentators.[7]

---

[4] The Dauphin (Louis, 1661-1711; often called the Grand Dauphin but usually referred to as Monseigneur) was a frequent spectator at the opera. The *Mercure* (March, pt. 2, 224) gives Monday, March 18, for this performance, but the *Gazette* (March 23) and Spanheim say March 19. Since there would normally have been a performance at the Académie Royale on Tuesday, March 18 (a Monday) is more likely.

[5] A contract dated Aug. 24, 1680, marked the end of Lully's association with the machinist and set designer Vigarani, possibly for artistic reasons but more probably because Lully no longer wanted to share the profits. On Dec. 26, 1680, Lully and Quinault signed a new contract for sharing profits (*Mercure galant,* Nov. 1680, 192; La Gorce, *Berain* and *Opéra* 68-70; Beaussant, *Lully* 602).

[6] *Mercure galant,* Nov. 1681, 319. The ballet *Le Triomphe de l'Amour* was Quinault and Lully's offering for 1681, the only year during their collaboration in which Lully did not compose a *tragédie lyrique*. When it opened in Paris, it featured *danseuses* for the first time in the history of the Académie Royale; see chapter 8 (*Persée*), 237-40.

[7] There were revivals at the Palais-Royal in 1699, 1715, 1727, 1741-42, and 1758-59, and performances at Marly in 1705 and 1709. The criticisms listed by Gros (*Quinault* 133), attributed to Parfaict's manuscript history, are from the *Mercure de France* about the 1727 revival: "on ne trouve pas l'intérêt principal pas assez vif. Les regrets d'une mère à qui on enleva une fille bien chère, n'ont pas produit dans l'esprit des spectateurs l'effet que l'auteur avoit attendu"; see Vialet and Norman 63-64.

Quinault followed Ovid's *Metamorphoses* closely,[8] but Beaussant is probably correct in saying that the choice of the Persephone myth could be considered a mistake: "C'est peut-être un bon sujet pour une scène de ballet de cour, mais ce n'est pas un bon sujet d'opéra" (*Lully* 597). If it is true that, as Gros says (*Quinault* 546), in Ovid's version "l'intérêt, éveillé dès le début et concentré autour de Proserpine, se maintenait dans le cours du récit, jusqu'à la fin," one can hardly say the same of Quinault's plot. The first act leaves the spectator confused as to what will be the principal action. Two couples have been presented, Jupiter-Cérès and Alphée-Aréthuse, but so far Proserpine is little more than a happy, flower-gathering nymph and dutiful daughter, impervious to the charms of love. The struggle between Jupiter and the Giants also seems a possible center of attention, since it is featured at the beginning and end of the act and fits in perfectly with the prologue's theme of peace and discord.

In the first two acts Proserpine has no real dialogue and interacts only with the chorus until she is abducted by Pluton at the end of act II. It is only in act IV that she takes on some personality as she argues with Pluton and Ascalaphe, and though she is present in the last act, in which her fate is decided, she does not speak. She has fewer scenes and fewer lines than Aréthuse, who forms half of the only united couple in the opera, and her reactions are much less emotionally charged than those of her mother Cérès, who for Beaussant is the true heroine of the opera. Cérès is already touching in the opera's second scene, when she complains to Mercury that Jupiter's feelings from her have gone from love to esteem (I.ii.43-44), but in the last three acts she is also a

> mère éplorée, qui n'apprendra qu'à l'extrême fin de l'acte V ce qui a
> pu arriver à sa tendre fille, bonne déesse bienfaisante qui sème ses
> dons par toute la terre, révoltée par l'injustice du sort, émue, angois-
> sée, elle est touchante dans tous les sentiments qui la bouleversent tout
> à tour. Quinault a trouvé de belles expressions pour le dire, et Lully
> s'y est laissé prendre. (*Lully* 598).

---

[8] Book V, lines 341-641. Ovid also presents the Persephone myth in the *Fasti,* book IV, lines 417-620.

This is precisely the kind of role that can create the most powerful effects in an opera, and not just because the spectator is fascinated and moved by the variety of situations in which Cérès finds herself; the spectator also begins to think about what he or she would do in a situation similar to that of Cérès, who is so desperate to recover a lost child that she goes from "déesse bienfaisante" to ravager of the earth:

> Du monde trop heureux je veux troubler la paix:
> Brûlons, ravageons-tout, détruisons mes bienfaits. (III.vii.643-44)

It is also the kind of role that can create catharsis, in the sense that the spectator can experience the kind of violent overreaction that is so tempting when one feels one has been treated unjustly.

There is no need to go farther into the details of the plot to show that the spectator's attention is often diverted from the fate of Proserpine, especially at the expense of the secondary plot involving Aréthuse and Alphée and of the efforts of Cérès to find her daughter. Girdlestone suggests that Quinault has returned to the "déroulement d'aventures" that he used in *Cadmus et Hermione* and *Alceste*, but immediately admits that "Seulement il n'y a qu'une aventure unique [the abduction of Proserpine by Pluton]" (*Tragédie en musique* 82). A better comparison might be to *Isis*, in which the mutual love between two characters (Hiérax, Io) is replaced by the conflictual relationship between a nymph and a god who forces his intentions on her (Io, Jupiter). In both operas all the major characters are divinities (unless one considers Hiérax in *Isis* to be a major character), a situation Quinault avoided in his other libretti. Such operas provide a wealth of opportunities for moving scenes and impressive spectacle,[9] but one can understand why Rémond de Saint-Mard found *Proserpine* boring (31).

However, as was the case with *Isis*, *Proserpine* is boring only if one is expecting one's attention to be held by the gradual progression of a unified plot and by careful development of the psychology of the principal characters, that is, if one is expecting a typical classical tragedy. In the first place, *Proserpine* is not as "irregular" as *Isis*. Even if Proserpine is

---

[9] "[...] cette variété sans disparate, qui est de l'essence de ce spectacle" (La Harpe 1: 666A); Gros, *Quinault* 545, 616; Beaussant, *Lully* 597.

not necessarily the most interesting character, the action of the last three acts still revolves around her disappearance and anticipated return—the secondary couple of Aréthuse and Alphée soon becomes involved in the search for her, while Cérès's complaints about being abandoned by Jupiter now include pleas for the return of their daughter. In the second place—and more important—it is fitting that an opera that has as one of its main themes the role of women in a male-dominated society (see section 2) feature a heroine who is dependent on others.

Furthermore, *Proserpine* contains a number of well-constructed, moving scenes. Lecerf (2: 325-26) mentions two scenes that were great favorites with the public, act II scene vii and act IV scene iv, which he considered superior to "la sçavante scene des *Ombres heureuses*" (IV.i) preferred by the experts. The first (II.vii) features Pluton's account of how this unlikely *galant* fell in love with Proserpine, a scene that inevitably evokes the famous scene in Racine's *Britannicus* where Néron describes the night he was smitten by Junie, as well as Aricie's accusatory look at the heavens:

> J'ai trouvé Proserpine en visitant ces lieux.
> Les pleurs coulaient de ses beaux yeux.
> Elle fuyait, interdite et tremblante;
> Pour implorer l'assistance des Dieux
> Elle tournait ses regards vers les Cieux. (*Proserpine* II.vii.393-97)

> Cette nuit je l'ai vue arriver en ces lieux,
> Triste, levant au Ciel ses yeux mouillés de larmes,
> Qui brillaient au travers des flambeaux et des armes,
> Belle, sans ornements, dans le simple appareil
> D'une Beauté qu'on vient d'arracher au sommeil.
> Que veux-tu? Je ne sais si cette négligence,
> Les ombres, les flambeaux, les cris et le silence,
> Et le farouche aspect de ses fiers ravisseurs
> Relevaient de ses yeux les timides douceurs.
>   (*Britannicus* III.ii.386-94)

> Par un triste regard elle accuse les Dieux. (*Phèdre* V.vi.1584)

The second scene also features Pluton, this time as a much more gentle lover pleading with his heartless beloved, opposing his *larmes* to her *soupirs* (IV.iv.821-22). Audiences apparently enjoyed the unusual spectacle of the lord of the underworld hopelessly in love, as well as the unusual musical spectacle of a tender lover sung by a bass. In addition, the scene between Pluton and Ascalaphe (II.vii) includes Lully's only duet for two bass voices (Lecerf 1: 115-16).

These are not the only scenes that various commentators have singled out for praise. Most recently, Beaussant (*Lully* 597-98) praises the same scene on the Champs Élysées admired by Lecerf's experts (IV.i), the destruction of Earth by the followers of Cérès (III.viii), as well as much of the last act, where "Cérès [...] nous réserve de touchantes larmes et de belles horreurs [...]" (598). Quinault's contribution is often praised explicitly. Beaussant calls the beginning of the second scene of the last act ("Déserts écartés [...]") "d'une perfection à la fois littéraire et musicale inégalée," while Voltaire compares the first scene of the first act to a Pindaric ode: "Y a-t-il beaucoup d'odes de Pindare plus fières, plus harmonieuses que ce couplet ['Les superbes géants [...]']" (*Dict. phil.* 7: 383; see also La Harpe 1: 666B). Marmontel admired the combination of elegance and energy of Pluton's appearance on Earth in act II scene vi (14: 437), an indication of the fondness that he, Voltaire, and other eighteenth-century readers felt for the more "heroic" passages in Quinault's libretti, which were less frequent than the more "tender" ones. When one adds to these scenes that of the complaint of Cérès at the end of the third act (III.vii) that Marmontel, La Harpe, and most other commentators single out both for its poetry and for it poignant musical dissonance, one realizes how much excellent writing there is in this libretto, even if its plot and characerization are not up to the standards of the best classical tragedies. As Beaussant (*Lully* 597) and Boscheron (manuscript version of his *Vie*, cited by Gros, *Quinault* 133) point out, *Proserpine* contains some of Quinault's best poetry. La Harpe goes as far as to say that it is in this opera that "l'auteur s'est le plus élevé dans sa versification [...]" (1: 666A).

§ § §

In short, *Proserpine* has much to recommend it but is open to criticism from several points of view. Quinault was obviously in no hurry to return to the tight dramatic structure of *Atys*, and he must have found much in the Persephone myth that he thought would make a successful opera. For one thing, this myth was already a popular subject on the musical stage by the time of Louis XIV. In the fifty years following the creation of what is considered the first opera, Peri's *Dafne* of 1597, there were four libretti called *Proserpina rapita*, two for operas and two for smaller-scale works.[10] There was of course no French opera in France in the first half of seventeenth century, but there were two plays called *Le Ravissement de Proserpine*, one by Alexandre Hardy around 1611, frequently revived, and another, based on Hardy's play, by Jean Claveret in 1639. Claveret's work, with scenes set in Heaven and Hades as well as on Earth, was especially spectacular and has been seen as a step on the way to opera.[11] The existence of these Italian and French works, in addition to the enormous popularity of Ovid's versions of classical myths,[12] makes it hardly surprising that the creators of French opera would eventually turn to the Persephone myth. Indeed, the Persephone myth had already been the subject of ballets danced by the king earlier in his reign (Gros, *Quinault* 578, 585 n.1), and Quinault had proposed it as a subject for a machine play in 1670, only to see Molière's *Psyché* preferred (Clément and Laporte 2: 443; Néraudeau, *Olympe* 121-22, 144).

Another measure of the popularity of the Persephone myth, and especially of Ovid's version, is a long tradition of burlesque versions (Anton). There was an anonymous *Enlèvement de Proserpine* written in 1430 and an anonymous *Ravissement de Proserpine* published in Lyon in

---

[10] Of the two for operas, one libretto was by Giulio Strozzi in 1630, with music by Monteverdi, and the other was by O. Castelli in 1645, with music by Pompeo Colonna. There was also a prologue plus four "intermedii in musica," probably by Ridolfo Campeggi with music by Girolamo Giacobbi, published in Bologna in 1613, and an "intermedio per musica" by Benedetto Ferrari dalla Tiorba, first performed at Venice in 1641 (Sartori; Loewenberg; Sonneck 899).

[11] See Lancaster, vols. 1 and 2, especially 2: 170-71 and 1: 158, and Rigal 419.

[12] Ovid's *Metamorphoses* were read in Latin by most educated men, and by the general reading public in the translations of Renouard (1651) and Du Ryer (1666). Benserade's adaptation of the *Metamorphoses* in rondeau form, published in 1676 by the Imprimerie Royale, guaranteed that all of Louis's courtiers would be familiar with them. For more information, see Néraudeau, *Olympe* 16-18, Apostolidès, *Roi-machine*, 79, and Gros, *Quinault* 544-52.

1556. Closer to Quinault's time is a burlesque comedy *Le Ravissement de Proserpine*, "performed" in Sorel's *Le Berger extravagant* (published in 1627 and revised as *L'Antiroman ou l'Histoire du berger Lysis* in 1633). In 1656, at the time Quinault was writing his first plays, D'Assoucy, who had already published *L'Ovide en belle humeur* in 1650, published a burlesque poem *Le Ravissement de Proserpine*.

In addition to being popular with the public, the Persephone myth was also well suited to the spectacular side of the *tragédie lyrique*. As Gros says, the myth "semblait être fait exprès pour les décors multiples et successifs de l'opéra" (*Quinault* 545). Berain could contrast the pastoral setting of Proserpine and the other nymphs (the palace and then the gardens of Cérès, acts I-II, and Mount Etna for act III[13]) to the Elysian Fields and the palace of Pluton, and he would have an abundance of possibilities for impressive stage machinery: Cérès's chariot pulled by winged dragons (I.vii; III.iii), the chariot in which Pluton abducts Proserpine (II.ix), the descents of Mercury (I.ii; V.v) and Jupiter (V.v) from the heavens, and the destruction of earth by the followers of Cérès (III.viii). There would also be the metamorphoses of Cyané into a brook and of Ascalaphe into an owl and, since Quinault worked in the revolt of the Titans, an earthquake at the end of the first act.

There are certainly other reasons behind the choice of this popular and ready-made subject. One could take into account—along with the obvious, but all too often forgotten desire to create a good opera—Quinault's need to advance his own career, to reflect current social and political concerns, to please the king, and to adapt to Lully's needs. For example, one could see in Proserpine's disappearance and subsequent return a reference to Quinault's temporary disgrace. In this light, Mercure's efforts to convince Cérès that Jupiter still loves her could be read as reassurance that Louis still appreciated Quinault's talents:

---

[13] Most of the action in act III takes place in the area around the mount itself, but the decor showed the volcano "vomissant des flammes" in the background, which provides the fire for the torches of the followers of Cérès who burn the crops on Earth. The volcano also creates an appropriate atmosphere of danger and destruction as well as a foreshadowing of the mysterious and frightening realm of Pluton that will be the site of most of the last two acts.

> Dans les soins les plus grands dont son âme est remplie,
> Il se souvient toujours que vous l'avez charmé;
> Il est malaisé qu'on oublie
> Ce qu'on a tendrement aimé. (I.ii.28-31.)

This of course adds little to our understanding or appreciation of the opera. I am not sure that all the possible references to current events do either, but they do help us understand the place of opera and other types of dramatic entertainment in seventeenth-century society. From this point of view, it is interesting to consider why Quinault (and Lully), after Mme de Montespan's reaction to *Isis,* would have presented another opera that featured the violent reaction of a former royal mistress. Perhaps they had no choice, and the Persephone myth was imposed on them, either precisely because of the possible relevance to current events or because of the popularity of the myth and its possibilities for spectacular effects. Whoever made the choice, the Quinault-Lully *Proserpine* contained plenty of material for court gossip and, as Sévigné wrote, "Il y a une scène de Mercure et de Cérès qui n'est pas bien difficile à entendre. Il faut qu'on l'ait approuvée puisqu'on la chante" (2: 833; Feb. 9, 1680). The reference is to the second scene of the first act, in which Mercure makes excuses for the lack of attention paid by Jupiter/Louis XIV to his former lover, Cérès/Mme de Montespan. If "on"—the King? the Académie Française? the Petite Académie?—approved this scene, it is most likely because, as Gros suggests (*Quinault* 132), the portrait of the lonely former mistress is not negative and because it was probably true that Cérès/Mme de Montespan retained Jupiter/Louis's esteem if not his love:

> Peut-être qu'il m'estime encore,
> Mais il m'avait promis qu'il m'aimerait toujours. (I.ii.43-44)

Most important, as I will discuss in more detail in section 2, Cérès remains willing to obey Jupiter:

> Allez, à ses désirs il faut que je réponde.
> Je quitte une paix profonde

> Qui m'offre ici mille appas.
> Que ne quitterait-on pas
> Pour plaire au Maître du Monde? (I.ii.68-72)

She only takes things into her own hands and begins what one could call a revolt when her daughter has been abducted and she cannot find out where she has been taken. She feels that her only recourse is to take back the gifts that, as the protectress of agriculture, she has bestowed on the Earth. She answers violence with violence, but does not explicitly disobey Jupiter.

The representation of a goddess inflicting punishment on innocent victims makes one think of *Isis* and Mme de Montespan's reaction to her association with the jealous Junon, but there would be no reason for Mme de Montespan to object, for the comparison is not exact—Cérès reacts not as a lover but as a mother. This is the first time Quinault has portrayed a positive mother figure, much more admirable than the murderous Médée in *Thésée*. The image is not entirely positive, however, and numerous contemporaries found her love excessive and compared her and Proserpine to Sévigné and her daughter Mme de Grignan:

> Bien des gens ont pensé à vous et à moi. Je ne vous l'ai point dit, parce qu'on me faisait *Cérès,* et vous *Proserpine;* tout aussitôt voilà M. de Grignan *Pluton,* et j'ai eu peur qu'il ne me fît répondre vingt mille fois par son chœur de musique:
> > Une mère
> > Vaut-elle un époux? [IV.v.846-47]
> C'est cela que j'ai voulu éviter, car pour le vers qui est devant celui-là:
> > Pluton aime mieux que Cérès,
> je n'en eusse point été embarrassée. (2: 857; March 1, 1680)

Yet another aspect of *Proserpine* that could start tongues at court wagging was the situation of Louis XIV's illegitimate children. Louis had legitimized his two children by Louise de La Vallière in 1667 and 1669, two from Mme de Montespan in 1673, and two others in 1681 (Bluche 392-94; see Couvreur, *Quinault* 378). For Saint-Simon, at least, whose hatred of the "bâtardeaux" is well known, the legitimization and marriage of these children was a burning issue. He referred to their ascent in the social hierarchy as an "apothéose," and it is quite probable that he and other courtiers saw the deification of mortals at the end of an opera or machine play as a most unwelcome glorification of the process.[14] This would have been especially true of *Psyché*, performed soon after the first two legitimizations and less than a year after the birth of Mme de Montespan's first son, and of *Proserpine*, performed the year the last two of these children were legitimized. The latter opera also features the marriage of Proserpine to her father's brother, a degree of interbreeding that even the Bourbons did not normally practice. Twelve years later, however, Louis would marry his illegitimate daughter by Mme de Montespan to his nephew, the duc d'Orléans, and this time it would be the mother of the groom, the princess Palatine, who would be compared to Cérès:

> Madame [...] marchoit à grands pas, son mouchoir à la main, pleurant sans contrainte, parlant assez haut, gesticulant, et représentant fort bien Cérès après l'enlèvement de sa fille Proserpine, la cherchant en fureur et la redemandant à Jupiter. (Saint-Simon 1: 37)

---

[14] 4: 835; 5: 345, 355. Couvreur (*Lully* 379) attributes the phrase "apothéose d'opéra" to Saint-Simon in the first of these quotations.

- II -

Kings, mistresses, mothers, children; the references to contemporary events seem easier to find in *Proserpine* than in any of the earlier Quinault-Lully operas. There are even more in the prologue, to which I will turn in a moment, but I have already discussed enough of them to suggest that *Proserpine* is an excellent work in which to emphasize the political and the social aspects of seventeenth-century opera. The references are impossible to miss, and *Proserpine* reaches its conclusion only after a political council meeting in Hades and a final decision—much like a modern press conference—by Jupiter. All of this tends to make *Proserpine* seem rather heavy and massive, an opera in which the fates of individuals are clearly in the hands of higher powers who are more power brokers than protectors. Gros noticed this aspect of *Proserpine* and suggested that Quinault was following the example of Thomas Corneille in his immensely successful *Bellérophon,* the libretto of which Gros found "plus somptuex, plus solennel, plus massif" than those of Quinault.

> *Proserpine* a une allure plus majestueuse que les opéras précédents et
> en quelque sorte plus royale. La conception académique de l'art Louis
> XIV s'y précise, non seulement dans le prologue, [...] mais dans le
> cours du livret. (*Quinault* 615)

Lully himself (or perhaps Quinault; it is not sure who wrote these dedicatory texts) said much the same thing in the 1680 edition of the score; his desire was to make his works "dignes, s'il est possible, de l'attention du Vainqueur de mille Nations différentes, du Pacificateur de l'Europe, de l'Arbitre souverain du Monde."

The celebration of a victorious king, arbiter, and bringer of long-awaited peace is hardly new in Quinault's prologues (see chap. 1, 49-54). The theme was particularly appropriate in late 1679, when Quinault was writing his libretto, for the Treaty of Nymwegen had been signed in August and September, ending the Dutch Wars (which had offered Louis the opportunity for the victories celebrated in earlier prologues). If this treaty did not literally make Louis the arbiter of Europe, it showed that he could withstand a powerful coalition; in addition, it added Franche-Comté to the kingdom and solidified its northern borders (Wolf 265).

The prologue to *Proserpine* is, as Parfaict suggests (*Académie Royale* 139) a play in itself, complete with exposition, *nœud*, peripeteia, and denouement. As the prologue begins, La Paix has been enchained by La Discorde, who is confident that the *héros* is too occupied with war to heed her captive's pleas (P.11-16). Soon however, to the sound of trumpets and cymbals, La Victoire descends to free La Paix and her followers and to cast La Discorde into a "gouffre plein d'horreur" (74). The ensuing celebration sings the praises of love and pleasure, and the lesson, of course, is that "Le vainqueur [...] s'est servi de la Victoire / Pour faire triompher la Paix" (P.82-85). The allegory could hardly be more clear.

This prologue is unusual in its length and in the elaboration of its allegory, but its subject is hardly surprising. What is surprising is that the theme of military victory leading to peace is continued in the opening scene of the opera:

> Les superbes Géants, armés contre les Dieux,
> Ne nous donnent plus d'épouvante;
> Ils sont ensevelis sous la masse pesante
> Des monts qu'ils entassaient pour attaquer les Cieux.
> [...]
> Jupiter est victorieux,
> Et tout cède à l'effort de sa main foudroyante.
> Goûtons dans ces aimables lieux
> Les douceurs d'une paix charmante. (I.i.3-6, 11-14)

The connection between Jupiter's triumph over the Giants and the Persephone myth is already present in Ovid,[15] but Quinault takes full advantage of it, returning to the Giants and their last effort at rebellion at the end of the first act. In this way Jupiter is established as the bringer of peace from the very beginning, preparing the return to the establishment of peace at the expense of discord in the opera's closing lines:

---

[15] Typhœus (II.vi.364) had led a revolt against Jupiter, who buried him under Mount Etna. Pluto, afraid an opening had been created that could let light into Hades, was surveying the situation when he was smitten by Cupid and fell in love with Persephone (II.vi; *Metamorphoses* bk. I, 347-83). Quinault probably confused the Giants and the Titans (V.i.930).

Que l'on enchaîne pour jamais
La Discorde et la Guerre.
Dans les Enfers, dans les Cieux, sur la Terre,
Tout doit jouir d'une éternelle paix. (V.vi.1020-23)

This is the most explicit return to the themes of the prologue in all the
Quinault libretti, one that is also expressed musically. The *ritournelle* for
oboe in the final chorus is quite similar to the one in the final chorus of
the prologue, and there are also similar *ritournelles* for trumpets in the
prologue and in the last act. The arrivals of Victory and Jupiter, which
bring about the final resolution in the prologue and the last scene, are
both preceded by trumpets and in C major ("gai et guerrier," according to
Charpentier's *Règles de composition;* see Cessac, *Charpentier* 456-57).

If there were ever any doubt that a politico-social reading of *Proserpine* is appropriate, this exceptionnaly tight link between prologue and
five acts, unique in Quinault's libretti, would remove it. Whatever else
the opera might be about, the theme of peace and harmony imposed by an
all-powerful ruler pervades it. It is no wonder that there is no strong love
interest, no heroic couple happily united at the end, in a work in which
individual desires are acknowledged but subordinated to the common
good. The secondary characters Alphée and Aréthuse are the only complete couple, while Proserpine and Cérès are reunited only for half of the
year, just as Pluton can spend only half the year with his queen.

This compromise comes about only after considerable warfare and
negotiation. Pluton carries Proserpine away by force, and her mother re-
sorts to the same scorched earth tactics Louis would soon use against the
Palatinate (1688-89). Pluton then holds a council and decides to send his
troups to war (V.i), where they are opposed by Jupiter (V.iv.990-91).
Only after all this violence can Mercure announce that "Tous les Dieux
sont d'accord" (V.v.1001). Jupiter's ruling is a model of diplomatic success—given the delay with which he intervened, each participant can believe his or her request was heard. In short, Jupiter is the true beneficiary
of Proserpine's abduction. Having withstood revolts by the Giants and by
Pluton, he can afford to temper his power with diplomacy and justice.
Harmony reigns, but only at the expense of limited personal freedom and
after order has been imposed from above.

Proserpine represents on stage what Louis/Jupiter's courtiers saw
every day in the Gardens of Versailles. For the area in front of the central
facade, dominating the long central axis, which at this time included the
king's bedroom, Le Brun had designed in 1674 the *parterre d'eau,* a ba-
sin which was to have Apollo at the center and, in the four corners,
larger-than-life statues of rapes from classical mythology. Each rape was
to represent one of the four elements, with the rape of Persephone by
Pluto representing fire. The full explanation of the allegorical meanings
of these statues is lost, but Nivelon's biography of Le Brun states that the
statues were intended to represent the universe and its harmony: "toute la
masse de la construction universelle, [...] l'enchaînement de ce qui compose l'univers" (Marie 160-61). Le Brun probably took much of his plan
from Jean Baudouin's French translation of Cesare Ripa's *Iconologia,*
which, like earlier court ballets, has the same groupings as Le Brun's plan
and follows the presentation of the four elements with: "C'est à peu près
ce qu'on peut dire succinctement des quatre Éléments, les principales
puissances desquels, selon Empedocle, sont l'amitié & la discorde, dont
l'une unit ensemble les choses, & l'autre les sépare" (Ripa 2: 5). Rape is
thus idealized as a representation of separate entities that achieve unity by
force—the same elements that are characterized by violence and injustice
also contain the potential for ordering the universe and holding it together. The individual—and particularly the woman—hardly seems to
matter.

Issues such as harmony and diplomatic power were hardly abstract considerations, and the events of 1679, when Quinault was writing
Proserpine, feature a striking illustration. The treaty of Nymwegen (see p.
225) included a forced marriage, that of Marie-Louise d'Orléans, daughter of the late Henriette d'Angleterre and Monsieur, Louis XIV's brother,
to the young but gloomy and degenerate king of Spain, Charles II, son of
Philippe IV. When Louis XIV agreed to the plans on June 30, Monsieur
rejoiced at having his daughter become the Queen of Spain, but Marie-
Louise, who was seventeen and had never imagined leaving the French
court she loved (she hoped to marry the Dauphin), shed torrents of tears.
She did not move her uncle the King, however, who entrusted her with
the mission to be as good a Queen of Spain as Marie-Thérèse of Spain
had been of France. Before Marie-Louise's departure on September 20,

1679, the king firmly stated his goodbye: "Madame, je souhaite de vous dire adieu pour jamais; ce serait le plus grand malheur qui vous pût arriver que de revoir la France" (Sévigné 2: 688; Sept. 27, 1679; Van de Cruysse 246; Primi Visconti 134; Bassenne 28). Quinault could not have been unaware of this situation as he wrote the libretto, and it is quite possible that this marriage played a role in the choice of the subject of the new opera. No one at the court would have dared take Marie-Louise's side. Even Sévigné, a mother herself who cried her heart out whenever her daughter departed for Provence and who, like the princess Palatine upset by another royally imposed marriage, was compared to Cérès (see p. 223-24), is quite pitiless when she describes the sorrow of the Queen of Spain:

> La reine d'Espagne crie toujours miséricorde, et se jette aux pieds de tout le monde; je ne sais comme l'orgueil d'Espagne s'accommode de ces désespoirs. Elle arrêta l'autre jour le Roi par delà l'heure de la messe; il lui dit: "Madame, ce serait une belle chose que la *Reine Catholique* empêchât le *Roi Très Chrétien* d'aller à la messe." On dit qu'ils seront tous fort aises d'être défaits de cette catholique. (2: 680; Sept. 18, 1679)

A lasting peace with France's neighbors requires this marriage, and Marie-Louise's happiness is of secondary importance.

Needless to say, strict political sense demanded a positive treatment of this parallel, as well as of other aspects of the opera that contained references to current events. Quinault and Lully's opera had to show Proserpine happy, or at least reconciled, with her imposed marriage and her new life as a queen. Similarly, Cérès's grief and anger, which was so pathetically represented in the body of the opera, had to be dissolved in reconciliation and gratitude. The rape, the violence by which the marriage had been born, could not cast its shadow over the final scene, for Jupiter's glory required the happy submission of mother and daughter alike. A woman's fate was not to be an issue in the balance.

§ § §

The opera is carefully designed to present and then reconcile all these conflicting forces. The loving relationship uniting Cérès and Proserpine receives a prominent treatment throughout the opera, yet, in spite of a sensitive development of maternal and filial love orchestrated at several levels (poetic, musical, visual) to move the audience to sympathy, the opera sanctions the breakup of the mother-daughter couple. The performance ends on the happy mood of Proserpine's marriage as everyone rejoices at the reconciliation of Cérès, Pluton, and Jupiter. The music of the two final scenes is harmonious, cheerful, and celebratory, suggesting neither distress nor an ironic countertone covering Proserpine's sorrow with the joy of the dances. The feelings of pity and fear that Cérès and Proserpine's plight had aroused among the spectators vanish as the final *divertissement* helps the spectator believe in the solution imposed by Jupiter. We are almost in the world of comedy, where a couple is united in spite of the objections of a ridiculous parent.

Throughout the first four and one half acts, the opera highlights the distress that Proserpine's abduction causes both mother and daughter. Proserpine's refusal of love is stressed in act I by Aréthuse's description to Alphée of Proserpine's pride ("Si Proserpine est belle / Son cœur est fier et rigoureux," I.v.166-67) and later to Pluton:

Cette fière Beauté s'obstine

A fuir les amants et l'Amour.

Dans l'innocent repos de cette solitude,

Elle évite les Dieux

De la Terre et des Cieux; (II.vi.377-81).[16]

When Pluton's infernal divinities emerge from the underworld to abduct Proserpine at the close of act II, Cyané complains of the eruption of their

---

[16] In a duet with her nymphs, Proserpine herself sings of the happiness of not having a sensitive heart: "Le vrai bonheur / Est de garder son cœur" (II.viii.458-59). It is true, however, that she does not go as far as her nymphs in expressing a proud defense against love ("Pour nous défendre / D'un amour tendre / Avec fierté / Nous avons pris les armes" (II.viii.485-88). One could interpret her remaining apart from them to gather flowers as a figuration of a subconscious longing for something other than the "belles fleurs" and "charmant ombrage" she described as the only worthy object of love (II.viii.432-33).

"barbare violence" into the idyllic setting of Cérès's retreat. Proserpine, previously shown gathering flowers for the return of her mother and singing of the simple happiness of her life free from love, calls in vain for help. Cyané is threatened with losing her voice should she denounce Pluton (II.ix). The musical treatment contrasts Proserpine's plaintive song, Pluton's firm desire, and Proserpine's cries for help, though the chorus tries to sound reassuring.

To accentuate the sudden disruption of happiness caused by the rape, act III contrasts the grief of Proserpine's companions to the anticipation of Cérès, who returns from her mission to Phrygia unaware of any problem. Looking forward to seeing her daughter, she describes her love as a "tendresse maternelle" whose "empressement" is greatly increased by her love for Jupiter because, as she admits to herself, "C'est Jupiter que j'aime en elle" (III.iv.565-66, 569). She does not seem, however, to treat Proserpine as a compensation for Jupiter's neglect, but rather as a dear proof of Jupiter's past love for her.

The spectator is made to feel for the mother's and the daughter's distress alike. Proserpine's disappearance deeply affects Cérès. She progresses from inquisitive disbelief to affliction (III.v), then to a pitiless devastation of the trees and crops she normally bestows on humanity, and finally to a willingness to ally herself with the rebellious forces of Hades (V.iii). Her maternal sorrow is exasperated by the silence with which she is met whenever she inquires about her daughter, especially when she witnesses Cyané's metamorphosis into a brook (III.vi). This powerful figuration of silence subsumes the other forms of silence her calls receive, starting with Proserpine's literal silence (III.iv.577) and the nymphs' lack of information (III.v.589-90). One of the most poignant moments in the opera is when musical discord breaks through as Cérès expresses her mounting rage in the monologue "Ah! quelle injustice cruelle" (III.vii.619-40). No less touching is "Déserts écartés, sombres lieux" (V.ii), which follows a somber prelude and which Cérès sings in a setting of bare desolation ("Le Théâtre change et représente une solitude"). Her jagged melody, marked by the highly dissonant tritone on "cachez," and the frequently shifting harmonies emphasize her distress. Acknowledging her ultimate defeat, she begs deserts and darkness to hide the tears that her immortal condition condemns her to shed forever.

Proserpine expresses in a more reserved, although no less touching, manner her distress at being separated from her mother and companions. However, her burden of solitude differs from that of her mother
in that she is lonesome in the midst of the attentive companions Pluton
has given her. Her sorrow contrasts sharply with the happy Shades' celebration of Hades's "bienheureuse vie" (IV.i.666), as well as with their
advice to accept Pluton's love (IV.ii-iii). Nostalgia and discouragement
dominate Proserpine's monologue bemoaning her captivity:

> Ma chère liberté, que vous aviez d'attraits!
> En vous perdant, hélas! que mon âme est atteinte
> De douleur, de trouble et de crainte!
> [...]
> Faut-il vous perdre pour jamais? (IV.ii.685-98).

In the following scene, her grief increases as she discovers that
Ascalaphe has betrayed her trust: he showed her the dangerous fruit that
could quench her thirst but failed to disclose the power of the seeds. Her
outrage finds expression at the end of scene iii, where she condemns Ascalaphe to live in darkness and fright and changes him into an owl
(IV.iii).

To Pluton who pleads for a chance to teach her love, the young
captive calls forth her right to "le bonheur qui m'était destiné," which is
to live "sans amant" (IV.iv.814, IV.ii.708), and she denounces his cruelty.
Pluton is moved enough to decide to win Proserpine's love and starts by
suspending all pain in Hades (IV.v.828-30), but he will go to war with his
brother Jupiter and risk the destruction of the universe rather than allow
Proserpine to return to her mother (V.i).

§ § §

As it is lived by Cérès and Proserpine, the mother-daughter relationship appears to be a strong bond that has been fed by happy times and
a serene independence from other love relationships (this is true equally
of mother and of daughter). Deprived of each other's company, they both
lose the source of their happiness: life has become death, an emotional

reality for Proserpine and Cérès that the myth expresses with the destruction of life-giving crops and the juxtaposition of Earth and Hades. However, in spite of its intensity, the mother-daughter relationship seems at quite a disadvantage when the situation calls for voicing it on its own merit. Cérès does not confront Jupiter in Quinault's libretto, as she does in both Ovidian accounts. Rather, she implores him once *in absentia*, almost apologetically ("Sans troubler votre paix," V.iv.995) after she has learned of his failed attempt to set Proserpine free:

> Grand Dieu! c'est votre fille aussi bien que la mienne;
> C'est votre fille, hélas!
> Ne l'abandonnez pas. (V.iv.998-1000).

One possible interpretation of this departure from the Ovidian accounts is to view Cérès's silence as pride: she will not stoop to move Jupiter by her tears. Another is to attribute it to a pragmatic analysis of the rape: she will not address Jupiter if she suspects him of complicity with Pluton (after all, her journey to Phrygia, which was made at Jupiter's request, helped make the abduction possible) or if she knows that a mother's rights carry no weight among the gods when opposed to those of a brother in love. While both explanations could be supported, the happy tone given to the denouement points to a larger frame of interpretation. In renouncing aggressive behavior, Cérès leads the way to the acceptance of Proserpine's new fate. While the Persephone myth features a strong mother-daughter relationship challenged by the violence of rape sanctioned by the rule of the father, the libretto emphasizes the possibility of an acceptable compromise, underlaying the treatment of Proserpine's rape with a subtle interpretative subtext that tends to relegate violence to the background.

What could lead the spectators toward a more positive interpretation of Proserpine's forced marriage is the development of Aréthuse's love story and of Cérès's relationship with Jupiter. These two departures from Ovid serve to prepare and legitimize the marriage of Proserpine to Pluton by providing alternatives to the life that seems to be in store for Proserpine. Far from being digressive fillers that have a detrimental effect on the unity of action, as some critics have argued, these developments make the denouement psychologically and socially acceptable.[17] The scenes that contain them do not follow the preceding scenes out of Corneillian *nécessité*, yet they are essential to an understanding of the whole, as is the case in several other libretti, especially *Isis*. Their ties to the action are not causal but interpretational, for they are linked to the story of Proserpine and Pluton through the views they offer on the dominant roles played by men in love and marriage.

Aréthuse moves from the private world of women that one finds in the opening scenes to the public, male-dominated world that is the norm in the closing scenes. Long attached to "fierté" and "rigueur" towards love (she had obtained Diana's protection to escape her suitor Alphée, I.iii), she finally gives in to love (I.iv) and to Alphée (II.v), who could be said to have forced his love on her ("Alphée à mon repos a déclaré la guerre," I.iii.81). Later on, when she visits Proserpine in Hades, she encourages her to accept Pluton's love (IV.iii). Her reversal is complete in the last act, where she tries to present to Cérès a positive image of Pluton's love for Proserpine (V.iv), just as Cérès had tried to do for her when she was pursued by Alphée (I.iii).

Cérès proposes a more complex model in her own relationship with Jupiter. Unlike Aréthuse or her own daughter, she takes no stand against love. She is the one who had told Aréthuse:

> Aimez sans vous contraindre;
> Aimez à votre tour.
> C'est déjà ressentir l'amour,
> Que de commencer à le craindre (I.iii.106-09).

Through her life, she also gives the example of her faithfulness to the unfaithful king of the heavens, stating that she finds happiness in cherishing her daughter, evidence of Jupiter's love, and suggesting that such behavior can win back a lover's attention.

It is, however, her response to Jupiter's ruling on her daughter's abduction that is most telling. She has been angry enough to devastate the earth and to welcome the support of the forces of Hades (above, p. 231),

---

[17] La Harpe, however, says the episode of the love between Alphée and Aréthuse "est agréable, et bien adapté au sujet" (1: 666A).

and when she finally learns what has happened to Proserpine, she refuses
to listen to the arguments of Aréthuse and Alphée (V.iv.974-89). However, as soon as she learns that Jupiter has taken up arms against Pluton,
her anger seems to subside as she begs Jupiter (*in absentia*) not to abandon their daughter (V.iv.990-1000); she neglects the possibility that Jupiter is much more interested in his own power than in the fate of his
daughter. Then, in the next line Mercury announces the compromise that
will allow Proserpine to be with her mother and with Pluton, and all signs
of Cérès's anger vanish:

> Qu'un bien qu'on avait perdu
> Est doux, quand il est rendu
> Par les soins de ce qu'on aime! (V.v.1009-11).

Cérès finds the compromise surprisingly satisfactory, although as a
mother she must renounce both her wish to spend all her days with her
daughter and the promise made by destiny that Proserpine would remain
unwed. She acts more as Jupiter's lover than as Proserpine's mother.

The submission of Aréthuse and Cérès to the will of a lover parallels the submission that is required of Proserpine. From a structural
point of view, the three female characters developed in the opera are
similarly moved from resistance to acceptance of men's love practices,
where love is a rhetorical figure for men's desires. What is at stake, of
course, goes beyond the fulfillment of male sexuality. It is rather a model
of social order where women are to accept the call of love, "L'Amour qui
vous appelle," as Cérès puts it to Aréthuse (I.iii). According to this view
of Aréthuse's and Cérès's behavior in *Proserpine,* for a woman to accept
the call of love is to accept her lover's point of view and to agree to retain
her love for him even after his ardor has cooled, because maternity can be
viewed as an acceptable substitute for the departed father/lover.

Significantly, when Proserpine appears in the final scenes of the
opera, she is not given voice either in favor of or against her marriage.
Nor does Pluton comment on the ruling, contenting himself with attend-
ing the ceremony at the side of his bride. Given this silence, the function
of submission to love (Aréthuse) and to compromise (Cérès, Pluton) is
not only to reassure the spectator by removing the certainty of lasting
distress for Proserpine and for the universe, but also to propose a

consensus on the conditions under which relationships between men and women, like those between rulers, can operate harmoniously. Thus, by intertwining Aréthuse's story with that of Proserpine and Pluton and by making Cérès an exemplary advocate of love and compromise, Quinault and Lully soften the myth of Persephone. Rationalizing its violence, they transform it into the prelude to an auspicious marriage that seals peace among all parties while bringing each his or her measure of contentment.

§ § §

It is interesting, but ultimately futile, to speculate on the reasons behind these changes in the Persephone myth, changes that could explain why *Proserpine* is one of the few Quinault-Lully operas that has had no recent performances or recordings, in spite of some remarkable poetry and music. It is quite possible that Quinault did not condone violence or flagrant inequality between the sexes, but in 1680 a literary text was not generally considered a vehicle for the expression of personal opinions, and a text destined for performance at court and subject to approval at several more or less official administrative levels was certainly not the place for making a strong statement about one's political or social views. Quinault may have been under considerable pressure to present a positive picture of the use of power by men and a negative one of the "femme forte" (DeJean, "Amazons" and *Tender Geographies* 70), whatever his own views might have been, and all we can say for sure is that the libretto of *Proserpine* offers a carefully worked out treatment of a delicate political and social situation. In addition, it provided not only situations for spectacle and dance but also numerous scenes which, combined with Lully's music, contain striking effects and evoke strong emotions. *Proserpine* is similar to *Isis* in that, lacking a true hero and a heroic couple, it uses thematic unity to give structure to a rather disparate series of scenes that feature a rather important secondary couple (Alphée and Aréthuse). While *Isis* emphasized individual freedom, or the lack of it, *Proserpine* is constructed on a more global scale. Harmony and universal peace are presented as supreme values, yet this harmony requires an acknowledgement of the male power structure, of women's submission to men's desire in the name of universal peace.

8

Persée

Rivals All Around

> Quand on a lu l'*Andromède* de Quinault, on ne
> peut plus lire celle de Corneille.
> (Voltaire, *Commentaires* 55: 561)

- I -

THE SUCCESS OF *PROSERPINE* in 1680 marked Quinault's definite return to favor as Lully's librettist. He would write five more libretti—the same number he had written before his disgrace in 1677—but not until after a brief interlude. In fact, 1681 is the only year during Lully's career as a composer of operas (1673-88) in which he did not compose a *tragédie lyrique*. Instead, he and Quinault wrote the ballet *Le Triomphe de l'Amour,* a work that, as Beaussant puts it, is not an opera but is much more than a ballet.[1] The libretto devotes almost as much space to stage directions and to lists of participants in the twenty entrées as it does to the 346 lines of text, described by the *Mercure* of December 1680 as "les dialogues qui séparent les Entrées en plusieurs endroits" (317). It is close

---

[1] *Lully* 622. The *Mercure galant* of October 1680 (part 1, 280) says "ce n'est point un Opéra. Il n'y aura point de Comédie" (i.e., there will be no staged action, as in a straight play or an opera); the December 1680 issue repeats that it is not an opera, but only a "Mascarade" (317). On the other hand, Gros, following Prunières (*Lully 52*), calls it a "véritable opéra" (*Quinault* 134). Beaussant calls this ballet a turning point in the history of opera, in light of the innovations that I will discuss below.

enough to an opera, however, to merit a brief discussion here, especially since it contains several innovations that will become important features of later operas.

The obvious reason for the choice of a ballet was the arrival at court of the new Dauphine, a lover of all the arts and of dance in particular (see chap. 7, pp. 214-15). The last major *ballet de cour* had been the *Ballet de Flore* in 1669, a few months before Perrin's *privilège* for the creation of the Académie Royale de Musique. Although 1681 was still fifteen years before the vogue of the *opéra-ballet* would begin to replace that of the *tragédie lyrique*,[2] *Le Triomphe de l'Amour* can already be seen as a model and predecessor, if not the first example. After Venus sings a kind of prologue on the familiar theme of the peace that Louis XIV has brought to his kingdom ("la Paix est le temps destiné pour faire éclater la gloire de son fils," p. 867, opening stage directions),[3] she extols the charms and power of her son. In the following *entrées* Mars, Amphitrite, Borée, Bacchus, and especially Diane give in to Love, before Mercure sums it up:

> D'une affreuse fureur Mars n'est plus animé,
> Et les Amours l'ont désarmé;
> Amphitrite à son tour brûle au milieu de l'onde;
> Au milieu des glaçons Borée est enflammé;
> Diane et Bacchus ont aimé;
> L'Amour doit vaincre tout le monde. (890, entrée XIV)

---

[2] The best example of the *opéra-ballet* is La Motte and Campra's *L'Europe galante,* which had a tremendous success in 1697. However, in 1695 the *Ballet des saisons* by abbé Pic and Pascal Collasse "avait révélé au public la structure de ce nouveau spectacle, caractérisée par une succession de petites intrigues indépendantes les unes des autres, et développées à l'intérieur de chaque acte ou entrée. Seule une idée vague reliait ces différentes parties entre elles, assurant à l'ensemble une certaine unité. Dans le *Ballet des saisons,* chaque période de l'année était illustrée par un comportement amoureux qu'adoptaient ses propres personnages" (La Gorce, *Opéra* 102).

[3] Quotations from *Le Triomphe de l'Amour* follow the text of Canova-Green's edition of Benserade's libretti (he wrote the *vers pour les personnages*), which is based on the 1681 edition. I have modernized the spelling, in conformity with the quotations from Quinault's operas.

Love finally appears in the next to last *entrée*, preceded by Zéphyr and
Flore and followed by La Jeunesse,[4] before Jupiter appears in the last *entrée* to acknowledge the triumph of Love and to preside over the final
ballet that unites all the "divinités assemblées dans le Ciel" (895).

The theme of the triumph of love is certainly not new in Quinault's libretti. Passages such as "Si quelquefois l'Amour cause des
peines, / Que c'est un danger qu'il est doux de courir!" (869, entrée I) can
be found in almost every Quinault-Lully opera, and the vain resistance of
Mars (874, entrée IV), Amphitrite ("Ah! qu'un fidèle amant / Est redout-
able," entrée V), and Diane ("Un cœur maître de lui-même / Est toujours
heureux. / C'est la liberté que j'aime," 877, entrée IX) recalls that of
Pluton, Aréthuse, and Proserpine. *Le Triomphe de l'Amour,* however,
could be said to represent the high-water mark of love in the Quinault-
Lully libretti, for the following operas will place considerably less emphasis on the pleasures of love—of Quinault's last five heroes (Persée,
Phaéton, Amadis, Roland, Renaud), only Persée and Amadis find love
and happiness, and songs such as:

> Pour un amant
> Tendre et fidèle,
> Pour un amant,
> Tout est charmant. (*Persée,* IV.vii.776-79)

will become less and less frequent.

The emphasis on love in *Le Triomphe de l'Amour* is less characteristic of the later libretti than is the importance of youth. If the addition
of the role of La Jeunesse for Mademoiselle de Nantes was an afterthought, it was a good one, changing a rather banal sequence of victories
of Love into a celebration of the same youth from which were drawn
many of the royal dancers who contributed so much to the success of performances at court. Similarly, this emphasis on youth makes the appearance of Louis/Jupiter in the last entrée more than just another scene of
royal flattery. The king was well past forty, his son had married, and it

---

[4] This role, written for the nine-year-old Mademoiselle de Nantes (the daughter of
the king and Mme de Montespan), seems to have been added during rehearsals, probably
at the request of the king (Beaussant, *Lully* 618).

was time to showcase the new generation while at the same time emphasizing that power rests firmly in the hand of the older generation: "Ainsi, peu à peu, c'est toute la progéniture royale—légitime et autre, ensemble, de la manière la plus évidente et la plus harmonieuse—qui célébrait le Triomphe de l'Amour" (Beaussant, *Lully* 618). There was no doubt about who was in charge, as Jupiter oversaw the final celebration, and this reaffirmation of the hierarchy prepares the spectator to see in the following libretti more and more examples of lessons to young nobles, such as Phinée and Phaéton, who become overly ambitious, or Roland and Renaud, who put love before duty.

The new ballet was a huge success. Eagerly anticipated by Sévigné as early as September 29, 1680 (3: 29), mentioned several times by the *Mercure* in late 1680,[5] postponed because of the illness of the Dauphin in December 1680, it opened at Saint-Germain-en-Laye in January 1681 and at the Palais-Royal the following May.[6] It continued there until a revival of *Proserpine* in November and returned in January 1682 until the Easter closing in March. Its single set was spectacular and "d'une invention toute singulière" (*Mercure*, Dec. 1680, 318), the machines impressive, and the costumes magnificent. A special attraction at court was the participation of numerous nobles, especially Louis's children. Singing roles were taken by professionals from the Académie Royale, but much of the dancing was by a host of princes and princesses, including the Dauphin, the Dauphine, and the princesse de Conti. These roles were taken by professional dancers at the Paris performances, the first time *danseuses* had appeared on stage. This important innovation was less for reasons of *vraisemblance* than to give the Paris audiences some idea of the spectacle as it had been presented at court; there is no evidence that the public had been complaining about the practice of having male dancers take the roles of nymphs and goddesses.

---

[5] October, pt. 1, 280-82; November, pt. 1, 191-95; December, 317-28.

[6] The accounts of the Menus Plaisirs show at least one rehearsal per day from December 16 to January 20, involving singers, dancers, twenty-five "grands violons," twenty-two "petits violons," and twenty-one flutes and oboes, not to mention impressive quantities of food and wine. The discovery of the document (Archives Nationales, Menus-Plaisirs O¹2984) is discussed by Tessier; see also Beaussant, *Lully* 629-33.

Several sources, including Parfaict's *Académie Royale* (155), give April 15 as the date of the Paris premiere of *Le Triomphe de l'Amour*, but the *Mercure* of May 1681, pp. 200-01, states categorically that performances began May 10.

Another innovation in *Le Triomphe de l'Amour* is the use of what Beaussant calls "récitatif accompagné et mesuré" (622), a kind of recitative that is very close to an air, following a more regular meter and accompanied by an instrumental ensemble.[7] In his continuing efforts to develop the musical means at his disposal, while remaining close to the intonations and rhythms of Quinault's verses, Lully seems to have used this intermediate form between ballet and opera to experiment with new musical forms and structures. His later operas are more and more complex musically, offering independent musical forms that add a considerable amount of structure and unity to the work, whereas the earlier operas had been closer to what one could literally call a *setting* of a literary text, adding music to an existing form. The addition of regular meter to a passage of verse adds a musical structure that does not always coincide with that of the literary text, and the use of the orchestra during a recitative allows for the addition of independent musical ideas that "comment" on the situation, whereas the small group of continuo instruments that usually accompanies recitative does just that—accompanies the poetic text.[8]

§ § §

---

[7] Lully's recitative up to this point had generally been accompanied by the continuo only and rarely gave a strong impression of regular meter. He had also used what Beaussant calls arioso, or what Duron calls *récit lyrique* (see the introduction, p. 26), closer to a melody with regular rhythm but accompanied by the continuo. The best examples of this "récitatif accompagné et mesuré" can be found in the remarkable entrée X, which features Diane, Le Mystère, La Nuit, and Le Silence. See the opening lines of Le Mystère, "On ne peut trop cacher les secrets amoureux," or La Nuit's "L'Amour veille quand tout repose," followed by Diane's "Malgré tous mes efforts un trait fatal me blesse," which includes several changes of meter.

[8] This basically literary study is not the place to enter into the details of Lully's music. For examples from later operas, see Beaussant, *Lully* 611-12, 666, 672-75, 697; Anthony, "Lully" 34-35; and La Gorce's text in the booklet that accompanies the Minkowski recording of *Phaéton*.

When the Académie Royale reopened after Easter in 1682,[9] *Le Triomphe de l'Amour* was replaced by Quinault and Lully's new opera, *Persée;* Louis XIV himself had chosen the subject. Performances continued until the revival of *Alceste* in August or September, including a free performance on August 11 to celebrate the birth of the duc de Bourgogne, the Dauphin's son for whom Fénelon would write *Télémaque*. It was revived once during Quinault's lifetime, in April 1687, and ran, in alternation with *Amadis,* until November of that year. It was revived fairly regularly during the first half of the 18th century, more often than *Proserpine* and *Isis* but less than most of the other Quinault-Lully operas.[10]

The first performances of *Persée* at court did not take place until July 1682. The premiere was probably planned for earlier in the year, during Carnival like most of the other operas at this time, but instead there was a series of performances of *Atys,* which the new Dauphine had never seen, in January and February.[11] Perhaps Lully did not finish *Persée* in time, or perhaps she preferred to see *Atys,* of which her new father-in-law was so fond; at any rate, the first performance at Versailles, where the court had moved in May, was somewhat miraculous, since a change in the weather forced Lully to transform the riding school (*Manège*) into a theater in less than eight hours. The opera was performed without machines, since Versailles did not yet have a suitable theater, but was nevertheless a great success. According to the *Mercure,* "Le Roy dit à M^r de

---

[9] The Dauphin and Dauphine attended the first performance, which was probably Friday, April 17, although some copies of the 1682 libretto have the date of April 18. This latter date is confirmed by the *Mercure,* but specifically rejected by Beffara; it would have been quite unusual for a performance to take place on a Saturday. According to Parfaict's manuscript history of the Académie Royale, the first performance was the 18th, and "Lully ne put resister à l'impatience du public qui souhaitoit avec d'autant plus d'ardeur de voir cet Opera que n'ayant point encore paru à la Cour comme la plupart des précédents, c'étoit un spectacle neuf" (1: 162).

[10] There were revivals in 1695, 1703, 1710, 1722, 1737, and 1746. It also had at least two performances in March 1727, according to the *Journal de l'Opéra.*

[11] The libretti of 1722, 1737, and 1746 say June, and Beffara insists that June, not July, is the correct date. However, it is the *Mercure* of July 1682 (354-58) that contains the description of the event, and it explains that the rush was in order to have the performance before the Dauphine went into labor (her son would be born August 6). Madame's letter of July 21 specifies that day as the day of the performance (Brooks and Yarrow 98). On the performances of *Atys,* see the *Gazette* of Jan. 1682, p. 278, and Sourches 1: 68 (Dufourcq, *Musique à la cour* 10).

Lully, qu'il n'avoit point vû de Piece dont la musique fust plus egalement belle par tout que celle de cet Opéra" (July 1682, 358).

Persée would continue to be associated closely with the Dauphins and Dauphines of the Ancien Régime. It was revived, with a new prologue by La Bruère (music by Bury), at Versailles in March 1747 to celebrate the marriage of Louis XV's son to the daughter of the Elector of Saxony, Marie-Josephe de Saxe.[12] Then, on May 17, 1770, *Persée* was the work chosen to inaugurate the new theater at Versailles, this time for the marriage of the new Dauphin (Marie-Josephe's son, the future Louis XVI) to Marie-Antoinette (Couvreur, *Lully* 364-65, 396).

It is not hard to explain this association of *Persée* with three Dauphins. If, after the celebration of youth and love in *Le Triomphe de l'Amour*, Louis chose the story of Perseus for the first opera performed after his son's marriage, it was certainly because of the widely accepted allegorical interpretation of the deliverance of Andromeda as a representation of the heroic tasks that a new Dauphin would undertake, in particular the "Grand Dessein," the liberation of the Holy Land from Turkish control.[13] To cite but one example, Charles Perrault included in his 1661 *Ode au roy sur la naissance de Monseigneur*, written for Louis XIV's son the Grand Dauphin, a reference to the first Crusade:

> Quand ce jeune foudre de Guerre
> Sur les traces de Godefroy,
> Ira dans l'infidelle terre
> Porter le carnage & l'effroy [...].[14]

---

[12] Here is a sample of Bruère's prologue:
> Dieux immortels, pour faire son [Louis XIV's] bonheur
> Rendez heureux un fils qu'il aime.
> Que ce jeune Héros, des mains du tendre Amour,
> Reçoive une Nymphe charmante;
> Que l'Hymen la lui présente
> Pour enchanter son cœur et pour orner sa Cour.

[13] France had been allied with the Turks against the Hapsbourgs, but in 1682 Louis was leading the European alliance against a new Turkish threat. See Karro, "L'Empire ottoman" 251-54 and 256-58.

[14] *Recueil de divers ouvrages* 175. Godefroy is Godefroi de Bouillon, leader of the first crusade, who will be mentioned in *Armide* (I.i.18, II.i.176).

More generally, the legend of Perseus was interpreted as an image of the hero-king, much like Hercules, blessed by the gods with virtue as well as with super-human powers.[15] Even without going into detail about seventeenth-century theories of government, one can see easily how *Persée* could serve as a "mirror" in which Louis XIV could see—and show—himself as he liked to be seen. The dedication to the 1682 Ballard edition of the score, ostensibly by Lully but quite possibly written by Quinault, could hardly be more explicit:

> Le sujet m'en a paru si beau, que je n'ay pas eû de peine à m'y at-tacher fortement; si je ne pouvois manquer d'y trouver de puissants charmes, Vous-mesme, SIRE, Vous avez bien voulu en faire le choix, & si tost que j'y ai jetté les yeux, j'y ai découvert l'image de Vostre MAJESTÉ. En effet, SIRE, la Fable ingenieuse propose Persée comme une idée d'un Heros accomply: Les faveurs dont les Dieux le com-blent, sont des misteres qu'il est facile de developper: Sa naissance di-vine & miraculeuse, marque le soin extraordinaire que le Ciel a pris de le faire naistre avec des avantages qui l'eslevent au dessus des autres Hommes. L'Espee qui luy est donnée par le Dieu qui forge la foudre, represente la force redoutable de son Courage: Les Talonnieres ailées dont il se sert pour voler où la victoire l'appelle, monstre sa diligence dans l'execution de ses desseins: Le Bouclier de Pallas dont il se cou-vre, est le symbole de la Prudence qu'il unit avec la Valeur; & le Casque de Pluton qui le rend invisible, est la figure de l'impenetra-bilité de son secret. Il repond dignement aux graces qu'il reçoit du Ciel. Il n'entreprend rien que de juste: Il ne combat que pour le bien de tout le Monde: Il détruit la puissance effroyable des trois Gorgones: Il ne se repose pas, apres avoir assûré le repos de la Terre: Il surmonte sur la Mer un Monstre terrible; & il contraint enfin la jalousie que sa gloire a excitée, à ceder à son invincible Vertu. [...] je m'apercoy qu'en decrivant les Dons favorables que Persée a receus des Dieux, & les Entreprises estonnantes qu'il a achevées si glorieusement, je trace un portrait des Qualitez heroïques, et des Actions prodigieuses de VOTRE MAJESTÉ.

---

[15] See Delmas's introduction to Corneille's *Andromède,* lxxxiii-lxxxiv, and Wagner. See Blanchard (28) on Persée and the monster as the Kingdom of France and the Fronde.

The "héros accompli" is of course Louis XIV, known as "Dieudonné" because of his near-miraculous birth at a time when the kingdom had almost given up hope for an heir to the throne. He is born to his task, according to the theory of the divine right of kings, and if the first of his special powers are the courage and diligence necessary to carry out his grandiose projects, his prudence and other virtues come right behind, for all of his efforts are in the name of justice and the general good.

This emphasis on virtue is particularly strong in *Persée*. The idea is certainly not absent from the other Quinault-Lully operas, but it rarely receives the attention that it does here. For example, the prologue to *Persée* is the only one in which la Vertu appears as a character. The word "vertu" (in its abstract sense or referring to a personification) appears fourteen times in this prologue, but only twice in the others (once in *Isis*, once in *Phaéton*). Whereas the other prologues had coupled glory with love, the prologue to *Persée* mentions only la Vertu as the "plus chères amours" of the king (P.92), as if Virtue had replaced Love as the latest royal mistress. Could one not expect to find (except for the number of syllables) "l'Amour" in the place of "la Vertu" if the following lines had appeared in an earlier prologue?

> La gloire où la Vertu conduit
> Est la parfaite gloire. (P.11-12)

In fact, la Vertu dominates this prologue from the beginning: "Sans la Vertu, sans son secours, / On n'a point de bien véritable." (P.5-6). Even la Fortune—accompanied by l'Abondance et la Magnificence—yields to her: "Un auguste Héros ordonne à la Fortune / D'être en paix avec la Vertu" (P.82-83). La Vertu and la Fortune unite to sing the praises of Louis XIV, in terms very similar to those of the Dedication:

> Les Dieux ne l'ont donné que pour le bien du Monde.
> Que ses travaux sont grands! Que ses destins sont beaux!
> [...]
> Les Dieux, qui méditaient leur plus parfait ouvrage,
> Autrefois dans Persée en tracèrent l'image (P.108-09, 115-16)

It seems clear that Quinault had recognized a changing attitude at court, where there was indeed a new royal mistress, as Mme de Maintenon replaced Mme de Montespan and the court became—in appearance, at least—more concerned with virtue and religion. "Vertu de façade, si l'on veut, sous laquelle se cachaient bien des ambitions et des intrigues, dévotion un peu spéciale qui consistait surtout 'à observer les péchés d'autrui', mais vertu et dévotion tout de même."[16]

The five acts that follow the prologue will of course give considerable importance to love, with the eventually-to-be-happy couple of Persée and Andromède framed between the violently jealous Phinée and the plaintive, pitiable Mérope; even Méduse remembers the time when she enjoyed the pleasures of love:

> J'ai perdu la beauté qui me rendit si vaine;
> Je n'ai plus ces cheveux si beaux
> Dont autrefois le Dieu des eaux
> Sentit lier son cœur d'une si douce chaîne. (III.i.441-44)

Yet, even if the opera ends with a line that could have ended *Cadmus et Hermione* or *Thésée* ("Héros victorieux, Andromède est à vous," V. viii.916), there is considerable emphasis on virtue and duty, a foreshadowing of the themes of *Roland* and *Armide*. Persée is concerned for the welfare of the Ethiopians in general almost as much as he is for his beloved Andromède, and she is a model, obedient daughter, even willing to die for crimes she did not commit.[17] Similarly, Mérope can not bring herself to participate in the violent revolt against Persée, even though, at the

---

[16] Gros, *Quinault* 142. He quotes the memoirs of Primi Visconti, who wrote of these changes at court in the same part of his memoirs in which he describes the new Dauphine. The complete quotation from Primi Visconti is "Tout le monde, en effet, fait ici profession de dévotion, particulièrement les femmes, mais toute la dévotion consiste à observer les péchés d'autrui" (153).

[17] Persée's act is not quite "purement généreux," as Couvreur suggests (*Lully* 356), since, as in the *Metamorphoses*, he has asked for the hand of Andromède as his reward if he is successful in killing Méduse ("Ma fille est le prix qu'il demande," II.ii.248). Still, Quinault chose not to show this slightly ungenerous scene, and Persée can say honestly to Andromède "J'ignorais votre amour, et j'allais vous défendre" (II.vi.366) and—perhaps somewhat less honestly—to Mercure that glory and public service are more important to him than love: "Un peuple infortuné m'engage à le défendre, / C'est à la Gloire que je cours." (II.vii.380-81).

beginning of the last act, the happiness of her rival Andromède makes her implore death to end her "destin déplorable" (V.i.792, 798, 803). Only Phinée lets his baser passions get the better of him and cause the death of many people on both sides in his desire for a "douce vengeance" (V.ii.812, 826, 833).

When one reads with this emphasis on virtue in mind and remembers the applications of the Perseus myth to Dauphins and to kings, one realizes how skillfully Quinault has combined a tender love story and heroic exploits with moral and political lessons. I cannot agree with Girdlestone, for whom the principal theme of *Persée* is "la suppression par des moyens merveilleux des fléaux envoyés par Junon pour désoler l'Éthiopie," a theme to which the "rivalités amoureuses" take second place: "C'est moins une tragédie d'amour qu'un récit de hauts faits qui fournissent des spectacles palpitants" (*Tragédie en musique* 84-85). If it is true that the young lovers in *Persée* move us less than Sangaride and Atys, one could say the same of any Quinault-Lully opera, and there is much more in *Persée* than a two-way opposition between love and heroic exploits.

Persée triumphs over Méduse and the monster not just to impress spectators and win the hand of Andromède, but to prove himself worthy and at the same time confront the limitations of his mortal powers. Like any prince in a political system that accepts the divine right of kings, Persée has received from the gods special powers which he must use wisely for the good of his people while remembering that, as strong and courageous as he is, he still needs divine help. Toward the end of act II, Persée rushes off to kill Méduse, full of youthful fervor and noble intentions (and love). Mercure stops him, to assure him of divine help but also to remind him that he needs it:

> [Jupiter] reconnaît son sang à l'effort généreux
> Que vous allez tenter, d'une ardeur héroïque,
> Pour secourir des malheureux,
> Mais ce n'est point en téméraire
> Qu'il faut dans le péril précipiter vos pas.
> L'assistance des Dieux vous sera nécessaire. (II.vii.387-92)

Persée then receives from the gods the sword, winged sandals, shield, and helmet necessary to carry out his mission. These three scenes constitute the *divertissement* of the second act, which not only forms a logical part of the action but also corresponds to a pause that the rash Persée needs to make to prepare himself for his dangerous task.

Having proved himself in his triumph over Méduse, Persée is ready to save Andromède from the monster and stop the revolt that threatens his life as well as the kingdom of Céphée. Quinault does not give much importance to whatever ambitions Persée might have to succeed Céphée as king, though Phinée does encourage his fellow rebels by referring to Persée as "Cet étranger audacieux / Qui prétend régner en ces lieux" (V.vii.890-91). This theme of royal ambition will be much more explicit in Quinault's next libretto, *Phaéton,* but it is certainly latent here, as Quinault presents for the first time two young male rivals.[18]

§ § §

Before looking in more detail at this new element in the plot of the *tragédie lyrique* (section 2), it will be helpful to look briefly at Quinault's sources and at how he structured the libretto of *Persée.* His main source, as usual, is Ovid's *Metamorphoses,* where the story of Perseus occupies the end of book IV and the beginning of book V, immediately after the account of the end of the lives of Cadmus and Hermione and shortly before the story of Ceres and Proserpina. Quinault followed Ovid rather closely, though he of course put the Medusa episode in its chronological place, rather than have Persée describe it during the wedding feast, and gives only two scenes to the battle between the troops of Phinée and those of Persée (V.v and vii), whereas it occupies a third of book V of the *Metamorphoses.*

A perhaps more interesting comparison, at least from a seventeenth-century point of view, is that between Quinault's libretto and Corneille's *Andromède,* first performed in 1650 and revived by the rival

---

[18] For a much fuller treatment of how "la quête de légitimité des futurs souverains est transposée dans le monde des tragédies en musique," see Couvreur, *Lully,* part 6, chapters 2 and 3, especially pp. 354-56. See also Goodkin's study of the representation of primogeniture in tragedy; Persée and Phinée are not brothers, but the former could be said to represent the "meritocracy" that challenges the "heritocracy."

Comédiens Français in 1682, with new incidental music by Charpentier.[19] The two versions are fairly similar, though Corneille does not stage Persée's conquest of Méduse and Quinault leaves out the oracle of Amnon. Both depart from Ovid in having Persée at the court of Céphée and in love with Andromède from the beginning (though in Corneille Andromède loves Phinée during the first three acts, and Persée's identity is not known until the third act), rather than having him come upon her by chance as he was flying over the country, and in not showing Andromède exposed naked on the rocks. Corneille, however, took more pains than Quinault to adapt Ovid to contemporary taste, to make the tale less cruel, the characters more *galants*,[20] in part because his play is twice as long as Quinault's. Corneille's characters have more to say, for example, in their scenes with their lovers, and the more they say the more they sound like members of the court of the young Louis XIV. Quinault's lovers, on the other hand, speak in more general terms and seem more like Ovid's characters. Quinault perhaps came to regret some of these similarities when, as we shall see, many of his readers and spectators found Phinée too cruel, far from the perfect lover.

The overall structure of *Persée* is one of Quinault's best, in spite of the unusually large number of characters.[21] In addition to Andromède and Persée and their rivals Mérope and Phinée (similar groupings of four characters are found in *Thésée* and *Atys*, where these four are the only

---

[19] See Delmas's introduction to his edition of Corneille's *Andromède*, 190-214, Cessac, *Charpentier* 95-103, and the London Baroque recording of Charpentier's music.

[20] Gros is of a similar opinion (*Quinault* 579-80), but Couvreur finds that Quinault "avait pourtant fort adouci l'*Andromède* de Corneille dont il s'inspirait" (*Lully* 107). Rather than go into a detailed comparison of the two works, I refer the reader to Gros, *Quinault* 579-84, and to Delmas's excellent edition of *Andromède*, especially pp. lxxxi and xcix-ci. La Harpe considered Méduse's monologue (III.i), along with the opening scene of *Proserpine*, "[...] ce qu'il y a dans Quinault de plus fortement écrit" (1: 666B).

With all due respect to Corneille, I tend to agree with Girdlestone that the poetry of *Andromède* has neither the power of Corneille's great tragedies nor the lyrical grace of Quinault's libretti: "A son [Corneille's] mieux la tirade peut être une source de richesses inaccessibles à la tragédie en musique, mais au-dessous du plus haut niveau la réplique courte et le monologue ramassé de la scène lyrique l'emportent sur elle comme un précis bien rédigé l'emporte sur un article long et touffu" (*Tragédie en musique* 88).

[21] Schneider comments on how the tonal structure of the score contributes to the harmonious composition of *Persée*: "L'harmonie parfaite de *Persée* n'est pas seulement apparente par sa conception dramatique, mais aussi par la disposition sévère tonale qui inclut le prologue" ("Persée" 549). For details on this tonal structure, see Legrand.

truly important characters), Céphée, Cassiope, Méduse, and several gods play important roles. All except Persée are presented in an exposition (I.i-ii) that is especially well handled,[22] giving the spectator all the necessary information before Mérope's monologue in scene iii and the confrontation between Phinée and Andromède in scene iv. Persée's first appearance, on the other hand, is delayed until act II, scene iv, where the mutual love between him and Andromède forms a stark contrast to the corresponding scene in act I (each comes toward the end of the act, immediately before the *divertissement*) that opposed Andromède to Phinée. Persée is mentioned frequently by the other characters, but Quinault takes the time to develop each of the other five characters well before bringing the hero on stage, thus keeping a better balance among the principal characters. The status of both Phinée and Mérope as major actors in the drama makes *Persée* stand out among Quinault's libretti as the only one in which four mortal characters are involved in a love relationship and play truly important roles.

The *divertissements* do not interrupt the development of the plot, in part because the myth of Perseus makes it "natural" to show the gods who appear at the end of act II to prepare Persée for his struggle with Méduse, the monsters who spring from the blood of Méduse (III.iv), or the combat between Persée and the monster that threatens Andromède (IV.vi).[23] Even the games and the apotheosis that form the *divertissements* of the opening and closing acts—if somewhat more conventional in the world of the *tragédie lyrique*—are well prepared and integrated into the action. For example, the games that we see in the fifth scene of the first act are mentioned four times in the four preceding scenes (see lines 21, 76, 94, and 174) and then interrupted by the news that Méduse has claimed more victims, so that the act returns to the dangers that were

---

[22] Lecerf singles out the opening of *Persée* for special praise: "Qu'y a-t-il qui fasse plus de plaisir, & qui ouvre mieux un Opera que ce commencement de Persée?" (1: 101). His remarks are directed in particular at Lully's recitative, but the general context of the discussion is that of the superiority of French opera over the Italian, a superiority due largely to "la conduite, l'intrigue, l'art du Théatre" and to Quinault's "belles paroles," which are "les premiers fondemens de la Belle Musique" (1: 99). See also Girdlestone, *Tragédie en musique* 86.

[23] Technically, the *divertissement* of act IV would be scene vii, the celebration of Persée's victory. Beaussant calls this "la scène la plus brillante, la plus mouvementée de tout le théâtre de Lully et, pour longtemps, de l'opéra" (*Lully* 607).

announced in the first scene and that will continue to be discussed in the beginning of the second act.

The action builds gradually toward the last act. Gros criticizes act III as being "en dehors de l'intrigue" (*Quinault* 622) and concentrating for too long on Persée and Méduse at the expense of the other characters, but Quinault has been careful to make this act more than just an excuse for spectacular effects. As we will see later in this chapter, he creates some sympathy for Méduse as a victim—like Cassiope and Andromède—of a vengeful goddess, so that the introduction of another character does not distract from the general thematic development. Furthermore, in the context of a royal marriage and the expectation of a successor to the throne, Quinault wanted to show that Persée needed both to prove his worth and to recognize his limits before his more spectacular combat to save Andromède.

One might expect the opera to end with the well-deserved celebration of the happiness of Persée and Andromède at the end of act IV. The fact that it does not, that mortals pose threats to the happiness of the young lovers and that these threats are as dangerous as those posed by the gods, is an indication of how *Persée* is similar to earlier operas such as *Cadmus et Hermione* and *Thésée,* in which the young hero is finally reunited with his beloved, but also to later ones such as *Phaéton* and *Armide*, in which duty or ambition means more to some characters than love.

- II -

　　It is especially the presence of the young hero who accomplishes, with divine help, superhuman exploits in order to triumph over obstacles created by other gods and win the hand of his beloved that links *Persée* to earlier Quinault-Lully operas such as *Cadmus et Hermione, Alceste,* and *Thésée.* If the basic relationship among the characters is that of *Thésée* and *Atys,* it is the resemblance to *Cadmus et Hermione* that is especially striking: a hero arrives from afar, falls in love with the princess, receives gifts from the gods in order to triumph over monsters and his rival, and finally wins the hand of the princess after a temporary setback in the last act. Love and glory win out over jealous gods in a classic boy-kills-dragon-and-saves-girl plot, and it does not take much imagination to see in Cadmus and Persée a Louis XIV triumphant on every front, in love as well as in war. Nor does it take much imagination to see why such operas were such huge successes with aristocratic—or would-be aristocratic—audiences who still dreamed of heroic exploits in spite of the increasing absolutism of Louis's rule.

　　Yet a lot had changed between 1673 and 1682, and *Cadmus et Hermione* seems considerably more naive, less anchored in reality than *Persée. Atys* had already moved the emphasis from heroes to tender lovers, and then *Isis* paid little attention to either, at least not after the first two acts. Quinault must have given considerable thought to the political realities at court during his two years of disgrace, for when he returned in 1680 with *Proserpine* the atmosphere was often dark, and not just because parts of it take place in Hades. There were no heroes, no noble lovers, and women posed a threat to the existing order. One can see in Pluton (if not already in Jupiter in *Isis,* unable to satisfy his own desires or to guarantee the happiness of those he favors) a new type of character who has the same desires and goals as a Cadmus or a Thésée without their noble, generous nature. He is as concerned with his own power as he is with his love,[24] as angry at Jupiter for having received the best share when the

---

[24] Pluton is the only principal character in Quinault's libretti who loves only because he has been chosen as a target for one of Cupid's arrows. There is nothing in particular in Proserpine that has caused him to fall in love with her, and he does not know the proper way to love.

universe was divided as he is at him for taking Proserpine away for six months each year. In short, he is the protagonist and the principal male character, but hardly a hero or a perfect lover.

This dark side continues to be present in *Persée*, in spite of the re-appearance of heroism and requited love. We find the first happy mortal lovers since *Thésée*, but to achieve happiness they must overcome not only obstacles created by the gods but also a violent mortal whose legitimate claims to the princess and to the throne were supplanted by those of Persée.[25] The suffering and death caused by Méduse and the monster are terrible, but the real carnage occurs during Phinée's attack on the royal palace.[26] In the earlier operas, heroes such as Cadmus and Thésée seem safely distant, the dangers placed in their way by gods or magicians seem somewhat unreal, more general moral lessons than specific dangers to avoid. In *Persée*, however, and even more so in *Phaéton*, the rivalry between young males would be well known to every courtier, the struggle for power closer to home than a more idealized quest for glory or love.

As in *Le Triomphe de l'Amour*, the emphasis is on mortals and on youth, after the older divine protagonists of *Isis* and *Proserpine*. In *Persée*, and in *Phaéton* as well, the king is older and weak, in need of the support of a young hero. The situation is similar to the one in *Thésée*, except that now there are *two* young heroes. In *Thésée*, as in *Cadmus et Hermione* and *Atys*, the king (or tyrant, in the former) was also the hero's rival in love, but in *Persée* the presence of two heroes allows Persée to punish his rival Phinée without threatening royal power; instead, it is Phinée who leads a political revolt in hopes of winning back Andromède. The tyrant in *Cadmus et Hermione* was of course defeated (with the help of Pallas), but the situation is more delicate in *Thésée* and *Atys*, where Égée and Célénus are not only rightful monarchs but also father or friend. Problems of succession are avoided in the former when Égée yields to his son, and Atys, who is not a candidate for the throne, would probably have been pardoned by Célénus had Cybèle not wreaked her terrible vengeance

---

[25] Lycomède in *Alceste* is also a violent mortal who poses a threat to the lovers' happiness, but he is clearly a villain from the beginning. Furthermore, he plays no role in the action after act II, scene iv.

[26] The description of this carnage is especially graphic in book V of the *Metamorphoses*, which Ovid clearly meant to recall Homer and Virgil. Otis calls it a "hollow pretense of epic" (163); see pp. 159-65 and 350-51.

before he had a chance to get over his initial anger and deception. The presence of a hero and of a king did not present serious problems, and Louis and his propagandists could choose the best elements of both when polishing the royal image. The presence of two heroes, however, of two princes, was a more dangerous situation, one that could lead to violent revolt. Perhaps Louis was thinking ahead to the potential difficulties of multiple heirs when he chose the subject of *Persée,* shortly after his son's wedding?

Be that as it may, what we have in this libretto is a new situation, a different kind of character for Quinault and Lully to depict. Almost all critics note not only the large number of interesting characters but that their psychological motivation is more developed than in many other libretti, evoking in the spectators considerable interest in these characters, be they cruel or sympathetic.[27] The emotions of the characters lead directly to their actions, such as Persée's combat with the dragon or Phinée's revolt, and their hesitations help create suspense or move the action in a different direction. Andromède, for example, finally admits that she loves Persée (II.vi), giving him additional incentive to fight Méduse and the dragon. Phinée hesitates during the first four acts before finally taking arms,[28] and Mérope's decision to warn Persée of Phinée's attack moves the last act from celebration (V.iii, a scene the spectator could at first think was the final *divertissement*) to conflict and ultimate resolution (the apotheosis in V.viii, the true final *divertissement*).

If Persée and Andromède are not very different from earlier couples, except perhaps for a greater sense of generosity and of duty, their rivals represent something new for Quinault. Indeed, Phinée, vengeful

---

[27] See, for example, Gros, *Quinault* 622, 652; Girdlestone, *Tragédie en musique* 86; Beaussant, *Lully* 604-05.

[28] He threatens first Persée (I.iv.144-47), then (in a somewhat veiled manner) Céphée (II.ii.230-32), and refuses to believe that Persée will be able to kill Méduse ("Le succès n'est pas sûr, souffrez que je l'attende; / Souffrez que cependant mon amour se défende," II.ii.250-51). He awaits the outcome of Persée's combat with the monster (IV.iii.649-50), and finally, after having watched the people celebrate Persée's victory, decides to take action:

> Il faut nous éloigner du peuple qui s'avance;
> Ce superbe appareil, ces riches ornements,
> Tout ici de ma rage accroît la violence.
> Allons hâter l'éclat de nos ressentiments. (V.ii.829-32)

enough to wage war against his brother and so cruel as to prefer to see Andromède devoured by the monster rather than in the arms of his rival (IV.iii.646-48), shocked many spectators to the point that the *Mercure galant* posed the question to its readers "Si le sentiment de Phinée dans l'Opéra de Persée est d'un veritable Amant, lors qu'il dit qu'il aime mieux voir Andromède devorée par un Monstre, qu'entre les bras d'un Rival." The response was that Phinée was brutal and cruel, though he would have been considered less guilty if Andromède had been unfaithful to him.[29]

Mérope, on the other hand, is one of Quinault's most sympathetic characters (see Newman 76). His own invention, she fills the role in the two-couple structure, which we have already seen in *Thésée* and *Atys*, of the woman with a hopeless love for the hero. In the two earlier works, however, this was the role of a powerful and vindictive sorceress (Médée) or goddess (Cybèle), while here it is the mortal Phinée who has the aggressive role. Mérope is more like the tender Égée (also of Quinault's invention) and Sangaride (filled out by Quinault from brief references in various versions of the myth), except that her love is unrequited. She evokes our pity in large part because, unlike her counterparts Médée and Cybèle, she is human and thus lacking the superhuman powers that allowed them to remain in control after they had lost their beloved. She is like Cybèle in that she regrets her past happiness, before she knew love (I.ii.58-62; *Atys* II.iii.351-52), but she has none of her vengeful nature. She of course hopes that Phinée will be allowed to marry Andromède, so Persée will pay some attention to her (II.i.219-22), and she is tempted briefly by Phinée's plans for vengeance (V.ii.833-35), but her remarkably steadfast love (I.iii) continues even after she knows that the love between Persée and Andromède is mutual (I.ii.54-57; II.v). She cannot bring herself to share Phinée's cruel desire for Andromède's death (IV.iii.642), and in V.iv she rushes in to warn Persée of the approach of Phinée and his army. By having her killed during the ensuing battle (V.vi.881-82), Quinault not only spares this remarkable character the pain of witnessing

---

[29] October 1682, Extraordinaire, pp. 168-70. Quinault was not alone in painting this cruel portrait of Phinée, since Lully used the extremely dissonant leap of a tritone to set the last two syllables of Quinault's rather harsh "Est-ce à moi que l'Amour l'arrache?" (IV.iii.643); see Newman 105-06. The best known example of a cruel character in Quinault's libretti is Phaéton, whom Lully found "dur à l'excès"; see chapter 9, p. 268.

Persée and Andromède's ultimate happiness but creates a touching moment that suspends the fury of the battle and leaves the spectator in doubt
a bit longer about its outcome.

Mérope is not the only sympathetic female character. Andromède,
of course, wins our pity because she has to hide her love for Persée and
because she is condemned to an unjust death. She is especially touching
in her farewell scene with Persée (II.vi), trying to convince him that she
loves Phinée, in hopes of keeping him from risking his life to kill
Méduse. Quinault also presents Cassiope in a mostly positive light, even
though her pride is at the source of Junon's anger (I.i.14-19). He shows
her aware of her guilt and repentant, even willing to die in her daughter's
place (IV.v.674-76), but does not go into the details of her crime, as Corneille does.

Even Méduse is, if not sympathetic, human and interesting. Mercure agrees with her that "[...] un fatal courroux / A trop éclaté contre
vous" (III.ii.492-93), and the spectator can believe that her current fury
conceals a justifiable grief:

> Ah! quand on se trouve effroyable,
> Que c'est un cruel souvenir
> De songer que l'on fut aimable! (III.ii.501-03)

Méduse is also the victim of a vengeful goddess, punished by Pallas for
having defiled one of her temples during a night of love with Neptune.
Her situation is thus similar to that of Cassiope, who also offended a goddess—one has lost her beauty and become a monster, the other almost
loses her beautiful daughter to a monster. The vengeance of these goddesses affects not only Méduse and Cassiope, who offended them, but
also the innocent Andromède and Mérope, rivals for the love of Persée. If
one is saved, thanks to Persée and Pallas, the other would only have a
chance for happiness if Junon and Pallas had not intervened.

There is thus considerable female rivalry to go along with that
between Persée and Phinée. The presence of several willful female characters—mortal and divine—could be seen as a hint of Angélique and Armide still to come, but *Persée* is more like *Proserpine* and earlier operas
in that the women who take the most active role (Cassiope, Méduse,
Junon) are punished or forced to renounce some of their goals. In many

ways, *Persée* is—like *Proserpine*—quite sexist, offering a perfect model for young males put posing a considerable number of questions for women. Throughout the opera, there are women who cause problems for men and must be taken care of in some way. Cassiope is blamed as the cause of the Ethiopians' problems, and Junon is portrayed as overly vengeful. Méduse is first a victim of the sexual double standard of Olympus, then dies "in the service" of Junon. The latter is eventually forced to put aside her quarrel, and Mérope is a victim of the struggle between Persée and Phinée. Finally, Andromède, the cause of a dangerous revolt, is reduced to an object to be possessed, as the libretto ends with "Héros victorieux, Andromède est à vous."[30]

In spite of the rejoicing at the end, there remains a sense that Persée's victory has been won at considerable cost—in addition to Méduse's victims, the king's brother and the queen's sister are dead, as are a large number of Ethiopians on both sides of a bloody civil war. The emphasis is as much on the unfortunate results of rivalry as on the—probably temporary—resolution, an emphasis that will be even stronger in *Phaéton,* where there is no mention of love or happiness to allay the tragic consequences of Phaéton's literally unbridled ambition. Neither the glittering facades of the court's new residence at Versailles, nor the too often insincere piety and devotion, could conceal the bitter jealousies and rivalries among courtiers and princes, just as neither Lully's joyous final *divertissement* nor Quinault's graceful verses could quite erase the memory of Phinée's spiteful character and the sometimes harsh sounds that they placed in his mouth.[31] Did Quinault sense that the installation of the court in the "golden bird cage" of Versailles could only intensify the already bitter rivalries, that the glory years of the Sun King were already behind

---

[30] This is not the place for a more complete discussion of the particularly interesting case of Andromède. Oppressed, repressed, objectified, she never has the chance to become a true partner to Persée. See, for example, Delmas's edition, where he writes of the "angoisse existentielle de la femme devant la possession amoureuse, éprouvée comme une mort de l'être" (ciii).

[31] The sounds of Phinée's lines often offer a striking contrast with those of Mérope. In IV.ii, for example, his lines 584-88 contain several harsh consonants such as /k/, /p/, and /f/, and the bright vowels /a/ and /i/ are prominent. Just before this passage (lines 575-83), Mérope's rather rare harsh sounds are tempered by the softer sounds that follow ("m'arrache des soupirs," for example). There are no harsh sounds at the rhyme, and the dominant vowel sounds are those of /ène/ and /ent/.

them? *Persée* marks in many ways the end of an era for the young *tragédie lyrique*, the last appearance of happy lovers in a Quinault-Lully opera taken from classical mythology.[32]

---

[32] I will return to this suggestion of new directions for the *tragédie lyrique* at the end of the following chapter and in chapter 10 (*Amadis*), especially in section 2.

9

Phaéton

Ambition Leads to a Fall

Talis per auras non suum agnoscens onus
Solique falso creditum indignans diem
Phaethonta currus deuio excussit polo.

[Just so, not recognizing their wonted burden,
and indignant that the day had been entrusted to
a pretended Sun, the horses flung Phaeton far
from his heavenly tract.]

(Seneca, *Hippolytus* 1090-92)

- I -

QUINAULT AND LULLY'S LAST OPERA ON A MYTHOLOGICAL SUBJECT was
so successful it became known as "l'opéra du peuple."[1] It opened at Versailles on January 6, 1683, the first to have its premiere at the new palace,
which had recently become the home of the court (May 1682). There was
still no appropriate theater at Versailles, and, as in the case of *Persée*, performances took place in the *salle de manège*, without machinery but with
sumptuous costumes. According to the *Mercure* of January 1683,

---

[1] Lecerf 1: 102; he does not explain the origin of the label, but one can assume from
other accounts that it must have been because of the considerable popularity of *Phaéton*
and its machines. Lecerf also says that *Armide* was known as "l'opéra des femmes," *Atys*
as "l'opéra du roi," and *Isis* as "l'opéra des musiciens."

> Comme il n'y a point encor d'assez grande salle à Versailles pour y
> faire des Machines, il n'y en a point dans cet Opéra; de sorte que la
> grandeur du Spéctacle dépend des Habits. Mr Berrin Dessignateur or-
> dinaire du Cabinet du Roy, n'en a pas seulement fait les Desseins,
> mais il a aussi pris soin de les faire exécuter. (323)

Lully was especially proud of the costumes for *Phaéton*, since this aspect
of the productions of his operas was now under his control (see chap. 7,
Proserpine, p. 215, n. 5). In the Dedication to the 1683 edition of the
score, he thanked Louis XIV for having allowed him to "estendre mes
soins jusqu'aux Habits, qui sont une des principales parties de ces sortes
de Spectacles."

After a series of performances at court throughout the Carnival,
Phaéton opened at the Académie Royale on April 27, 1683, when the
theater reopened after Easter. Performances continued uninterrupted until
the premiere of *Amadis* in January 1684, except for a month (July 30-
August 30) when all theaters were closed during a period of mourning for
queen Marie-Thérèse.[2] It would not be revived in Paris or at court during
the lifetimes of Quinault and Lully, though it would be performed—with
Lully's permission, of course—in Marseille in 1686, Avignon in 1687,
Lyon in 1688, and Rouen in 1689; in the latter two cases, *Phaéton* was
performed for the opening of an Académie Royale de Musique in those
cities.[3] It would have a typical number of revivals, including 1692, 1702,
1710, 1721-22, 1730-31, and 1742. All of these revivals were successful,
and the one in 1721 was the first performance at the Académie Royale
attended by Louis XV (Nov. 16). A less typical "revival" took place in
1952, when Paul Hindemith added to his opera *Cardillac* a new third act
that included extracts from Lully's score.

In many ways, *Phaéton* seems like an obvious choice for a libretto
for an opera in 1683; indeed, Racine and Boileau had chosen the same

---

[2] The *Mercure* of August 1683 reports that the July 30 performance was interrupted
by the news of the Queen's death: "On jouoit déjà l'ouverture; on ne continua pas et M
de Lully ayant fait rendre l'argent qu'il avoit reçu renvoya l'assemblée fort triste" (37-
38). The *Journal de l'Opéra* states that performances recommenced in late August after
thirty days of mourning.

[3] See Schmidt, "Geographical Spread" 85-94. *Phaéton* was also performed to inaugurate the new opera house in Lyon in 1993.

myth when they tried to write a libretto for Lully.[4] The myth offered the chance to present the Sun and his palace, a spectacular ride through and fall from the skies, and the dangers of excessive ambition. Homage to the new palace, impressive special effects, royal allegory, a social/moral lesson, the subject is indeed rich. Yet it lacks two key ingredients of the *tragédie lyrique,* a love interest and a true hero. Quinault did his best, but, as we shall see in section 2, Phaéton is a problematic hero and hardly the perfect lover.

Quinault, as usual, followed Ovid rather closely (Gros, *Quinault* 552, n. 6), but only in his last three acts. Ovid's version of the myth begins, at the end of the first book of the *Metamorphoses,* with the presentation of Phaeton as the companion of Epaphus, the sun of Jupiter and Io/Isis, whose story Ovid has just told (this was Quinault's major source for his *Isis*). Three lines later Epaphus doubts Phaeton's account of his divine birth, and the latter begs his mother Clymene for proof. From this point Quinault's version is similar to Ovid's, except that Quinault had to abridge considerably the 400 lines of book II that Ovid devotes to Phaeton's visit to his father's palace, his fatal ride, and the lamentations of his family.

Quinault does not present Épaphus and Phaéton's quarrel over their glorious births until act III, after he has invented a love story and linked Phaéton and Épaphus to it. He introduces two young women, Libie and Théone. The former is presented as the daughter of king Mérops[5] and the nymph Climène (whom Quinault found in Ovid), though the best-known princess of this name is the daughter of Epaphus. Théone is the daughter of Proteus, whom Quinault introduces to the story perhaps to furnish the *divertissement* of the first act.[6] In inventing or borrowing so

---

[4] This was probably in 1674, when Quinault's place as Lully's titular librettist was less secure, or perhaps in 1677, after Quinault's disgrace following *Isis;* see chapter 4 (*Thésée*), 129-30.

[5] Gros suggests that Quinault may have taken Mérops from the 1639 *Chûte de Phaéton* by l'Hermite de Vauzelle, the brother of Tristan l'Hermite (*Quinault* 578, n. 1).

[6] See Gros, *Quinault* 552, n. 6. There is no obvious link between the myths of Phaeton and Proteus, although it is possible that Quinault was familiar with the scene in Virgil's *Georgics* (IV.386-453), in a similar setting, in which Proteus goes through a series of metamorphoses in a vain effort to avoid Aristæus (the son-in-law of Cadmus and Hermione). This episode is linked to the legend of Orpheus, so important to early opera, because it was Aristæus who was chasing Euridice when she was killed by the sea

many characters and episodes to add to what was already in Ovid's version of the myth, Quinault created something of a hybrid, different in many ways from his earlier libretti. The various episodes are remarkably well tied together, but the result is somewhat unsettling.

Perhaps the myth of Phaeton, full of ready-made spectacle and allegory but lacking in heroes and lovers, was not the ideal choice it seemed to be at first glance. For one thing, Phaéton's spectacular ride and fall were so impressive that they often overshadowed the rest of the opera. Berain's famous "machine effrayante" (Lecerf 2: 16) was a highlight of the Swedish architect Nicodemus Tessin's visit to the Palais-Royal in 1687:

> Ce qu'il [Berain] me raconta de l'Opéra de *Phaéton* était très intéressant. Comment apparaissaient les nuages clairs et comment se levait ensuite le soleil qu'il a représenté en encastrant une lampe au milieu d'un demi miroir d'acier. [...] Après la disparition du soleil, Phaéton est tombé. Sur le côté, Jupiter paraissait, au moyen de la foudre, faire voler la voiture en éclats. Phaéton, en remuant le pied, détachait une petite corde, ce qui faisait basculer rapidement les quatre chevaux et lui-même "culbutait" à l'aide d'une machine, dont une des petites roues était d'un diamètre supérieur à l'autre.[7]

It would be hard to concentrate on the emotional reactions of the other characters when such a spectacular fall ends the opera. The author of the 1743 *Lettre [...] sur les opéra de Phaéton et Hippolite et Aricie* exaggerates somewhat, but much of what he says is true: Quinault

> a donc prodigué les beautés du Spectacle; mais en travaillant trop pour les yeux, il a cessé de parler au cœur: l'ame ne peut suffire à deux sentimens fort vifs; elle quitte l'un pour embrasser l'autre: on s'occupe

---

monster, leaving Orpheus to sing alone on the shore. The gods punished Aristæus by sending an epidemic to destroy his bees, and he consulted Proteus in order to determine the cause of this epidemic and a solution.

   [7] Weigert 33; quoted in Beaussant, *Lully* 612, from p. 250 of the original publication in the *Bulletin de la Société de l'Histoire de l'Art Français* (1933, pp. 220-79). *Phaéton* was not being performed in Paris when Tessin was there from July 21 to Oct. 17, 1687, but he visited the Palais-Royal theater thoroughly with Berain; he did see *Persée*.

de la pompe du Soleil ou de l'évenement de la chùte de Phaëton, &
l'on néglige les interêts de l'Amante qu'on ne revoit plus. (7)

§ § §

Another aspect of *Phaéton* that makes this myth a somewhat
unusual choice for a *tragédie lyrique* is the complexity of the representation of royal power. For one thing, Mérops is the last and probably the
weakest of a series of weak—or otherwise less than ideal—monarchs in
Quinault's mythological libretti, beginning with the tyrant Draco in *Cadmus et Hermione.*[8] The kings of the next three Quinault-Lully operas,
Admète, Égée, and Célénus, are unable to take things into their own
hands and must rely on younger heroes (Alcide, Thésée) or on divinities
(Cybèle). *Isis* contains no kings at all, another mark of its unique nature.
The king in *Proserpine,* Pluton, is not weak, but he abuses his power in
abducting Proserpine. In *Persée* and *Phaéton,* Céphée and Mérops are
similar to Admète and Égée, dependent on younger heroes. Mérops appears only in the *divertissements,* in largely ceremonial roles, speaking
only to gods or to assembled crowds, never to another individual character. Clearly, we are not to associate Louis XIV with these weak kings, but
rather to understand that he is unlike any other monarch, "au-dessus des
louanges ordinaires."[9]

The association of Louis the Sun King with Apollo is complicated
by two factors. One, if *Phaéton* presented a perfect opportunity to evoke
the splendid new residence of the court, and if Louis was certainly flat-
tered by lines such as:

Sans le Dieu qui nous éclaire,

Tout languit, rien ne peut plaire.

Chantons, ne cessons jamais

De publier ses bienfaits, (IV.i.588-91)

[8] See the introduction, pp. 32-35, and chapter 3 (*Alceste*), 105. The last three operas,
with subjects drawn from chivalric legends, present special cases, since the rulers there
derive much of their power from magic. In addition, they contain only one king—Hidraot, Armide's uncle—unless one counts Médor in *Roland,* whom Angélique makes a
king but who is never seen to rule.

[9] *Cadmus et Hermione,* prologue, opening stage directions. The panegyric literature
of the period is full of such mentions of Louis's uniqueness.

he was perhaps less eager to be portrayed as a father unable to restrain the excessive ambition of his illegitimate children. Second, the librettist's task is made complex by the presence of both Apollo and Jupiter. As I suggested at the end of the preceding chapter, by 1683 Louis was no longer presented mainly as the Sun King, and allegorical representations of the king were more overtly political, with less emphasis on Louis's resemblance to mythological heroes and more on his own accomplishments. If he were to be compared to a Greek god, it would more likely be to Jupiter, master of the universe (this tendency is already present in *Isis*) than to Apollo.

Indeed, the last representation of Louis in the Quinault-Lully mythological operas is as Jupiter, clearly more powerful than the Sun. The king of the gods saves the earth from destruction, punishes Phaéton, and issues the rather obvious warning to overly ambitious courtiers, "Sers d'exemple aux Audacieux" (V.viii.875). His intervention is well integrated into the action and, for once, the intervening divinity maintains his or her decorum and does not act out of jealousy or vengeance (Gros, *Quinault* 622). It is an effective royal portrayal, but at the expense of the hero of the opera and also of the type of conclusion that had been so effective in earlier operas.

§ § §

Without going farther into the extremely complex question of mythological representations of Louis XIV, or into speculation about why Quinault and Lully chose this moment to emphasize the dangers of ambition,[10] I would rather concentrate on the libretto itself, and especially on its problematic hero. As in *Persée*, we have two rivals for the hand of the princess, and thus for the throne. Three of the four rivals in the two operas are the result of an adulterous relationship between a mortal woman and a powerful god, and there are doubts about the divine paternity of the two eponymous heroes.[11] The rivalry was already bitter in *Persée*,

---

[10] There was hardly a more ambitious person at Louis's court than Lully himself!

[11] *Persée* II.ii.234-42; *Phaéton* III.iii.500-09. Questions of royal succession, including the status of the illegitimate children of the king, were always important, and especially in this time following the birth of the duc de Bourgogne (see chap. 8, *Persée*, 243-45).

especially when Phinée, in spite of his love for Andromède, led a violent revolt against Persée and king Céphée. Quinault takes this predominance of politics over love a step farther in *Phaéton,* where from the beginning Phaéton has put away his love for Théone in hopes of marrying Libie and thus succeeding to the throne. What has happened to the *tragédie lyrique* when the hero puts love in second place?

- II -

The question of the role of love is especially appropriate in light
of the considerable changes the *tragédie lyrique* would soon undergo.
Phaéton was Quinault's last libretto with a mythological subject, and in
five years both he and Lully would be dead. Soon thereafter, the *tragédie
lyrique* would begin to lose favor to the opera-ballet and other less serious
forms of musical theater that became so popular during the early eighteenth century. The next truly great operatic composer after Lully would
be Rameau, whose first opera, *Hippolyte et Aricie* (1733), would have as
its hero another famous charioteer of the French theater. To discover the
characters of Racine's great tragedy in an opera that features the two
young lovers as much as Phèdre—and that has a happy ending—is
enough to make it clear that the public no longer had anything near the
same expectations in 1733 that it did in 1677. This in itself is no surprise,
but it is indicative that the tendency that one finds in the last four Quinault-Lully operas to place ambition (*Phaéton*) or duty (*Roland, Armide*)
ahead of love was hardly the beginning of a lasting trend.

What a difference between these two heroes, Hippolytus and
Phaeton, in spite of the similar circumstances of their deaths that led Seneca to compare them, in the lines that serve as the epigraph to this chapter. Both are killed when they lose control of a horse-drawn chariot, but
Hippolytus is an innocent victim, destroyed by a god avenging a credu-
lous father (Thésée, the hero of Quinault and Lully's third opera),
whereas Phaeton brings his fate on himself and dies because he has
placed the universe in danger. The former deserves all our pity, and
Racine evokes it eloquently in Théramène's great *récit* (V.vi), which is
often described as an aria; the latter is hardly mourned at all.

Or, at least, he is hardly mourned in Quinault's version. After his
death, there remain only two more lines:

CLIMENE ET THÉONE
O sort fatal!
MÉROPS, LIBIE, ET LE CHŒUR
          O chute affreuse!
O témérité malheureuse!

Ovid, on the other hand, not only describes the grief of Phaeton's father, mother, sisters, and cousin; he offers a noble epitaph for Phaeton, giving him true heroic status:

> Here Phaeton lies
> Who drove his father's chariot: if he did not
> Hold it, at least he died in splendid daring. (2: 327-28).

The less than heroic status of Quinault's Phaéton is what creates much of the special character of this libretto, of which one could say that the hero is not a hero. Based on the first seven Quinault-Lully operas, it would have been hard to imagine, in late 1682, a *tragédie lyrique* without a model, faithful lover. If *Isis* and *Proserpine* did not have a hero-lover who could be considered the main character, at least Hiérax and Pluton were constant in their love,[12] and *Persée* seemed to mark a return to the type of hero found in Quinault's first four libretti. Phaéton, however, breaks all the rules of the genre, and one could suggest that he is punished as much because of his unworthiness as an operatic hero as because of his exaggerated ambition.

Obviously, one cannot deny that the tragic end of Phaéton can be read as a lesson for courtiers who strive for too much power, as a reminder of Fouquet's tragic end. Still, it is not his role as an ideological anti-model that makes him, for Girdlestone at least, "le héros le plus intéressant de leur [Quinault and Lully's] théâtre" (91);[13] it is because he is so different from their earlier heroes; operatic heroes, at least in 1683, were supposed to be in love. Quinault's Phaéton is as interesting as a

---

[12] Hiérax makes half-hearted efforts to forget his love for Io (*Isis*, I.i.1; III.ii.513), but he remains an "amant jaloux" (III.vii.686) until his last scene. It is interesting that Hiérax says much the same about Io that Théone says about Phaéton. Compare, for example, "Sa bouche quelquefois dit encor qu'elle m'aime, / Mais son cœur ni ses yeux ne m'en disent plus rien" (*Isis,* I.ii.42-43) to *Phaéton,* I.iii.78-79: "Ingrat, le moyen de vous croire? / Vos regards inquiets démentent vos discours."

[13] Pascal Paul-Harang, in his essay accompanying the Minkowski recording, also warns against reading *Phaéton* as "une simple allégorie politique" or a "panégyrique servile à la gloire de Louis XIV" (22). He too finds Phaéton one of Quinault's most interesting characters, responsible for his fate and characterized by *aliénation,* striving more—in this libretto, at least—for recognition by others and for proof of his worthiness than for power. See also Néraudau, *Olympe* 178.

rebel against what had become norms for seventeenth-century French opera as he is as a rebel against accepted standards of political and social
behavior.

Quinault and Lully were apparently aware from the beginning that
their title character was different from their previous heroes. Lecerf's famous account of how Lully corrected Quinault's texts mercilessly, even
after they had been examined by various colleagues and academies (see
the introduction, pp. 27-28), cites the example of the role of Phaéton, with
emphasis on his status as a less than zealous lover:

> [Lully] examinoit mot à mot cette Poësie déja revûë et corrigée, dont il
> corrigeoit encore, ou retranchoit la moitié, lors qu'il le jugeoit à pro-
> pos. Et point d'apel de la critique. Il faloit que son Poëte s'en retournât
> rimer de nouveau. Dans Phaëton, par exemple, il le renvoya vingt fois
> changer des Scenes entieres, approuvées par l'Académie Françoise.
> Quinaut faisoit Phaëton dur à l'excés, & qui disoit de vrayes injures à
> Theone. Autant de rayé par Lulli. Il voulut que Quinaut fît Phaëton
> ambitieux, & non brutal; & c'est à Lulli, Mesdames, que vôtre sexe
> doit le peu de galanterie que conserve Phaëton, qui, sans lui, auroit
> donné de fort mauvais exemples. (2: 214-15)

Is Phaéton brutal, like Phinée in *Persée* (see chap. 8, 255), or just ambitious? Just what is the "peu de galanterie" that he retains? What kind of
emotional response does he evoke in the spectator? And, ultimately, what
kind of opera can be constructed around such a title character?

§ § §

Before looking directly at Phaéton, it is essential to note the background of peace and tranquillity against which he will appear. The prologue, in which Louis XIV reestablishes the golden age of humanity's
"siècle fortuné," of the "Univers naissant" (P.21, 22), begins with the
goddess Astrée's "Cherchons la Paix dans cet asile."[14] She will not have

---

[14] Astrée, the daughter of Zeus and Themis (Justice), encouraged justice and virtue
on Earth during the Golden Age. When evil began to prevail, she left Earth and became
the constellation Virgo. La Fontaine uses her in two odes on peace, "Le noir démon des

to search long, since Louis will bring her back to a new era of peace: "Il calme l'Univers" (P.44). An imagery of peace dominates the eighty-five lines (506 words) of the prologue, where one finds *paix* five times, *repos* four times, *tranquillité* twice, and *paisible, reposer,* and *calmer* once.

The theme of a return to a happier time and the imagery of peace and rest also characterize the beginning and the end of the first act. The opera begins with a monologue by Libie, who fears that love is not compatible with political necessity and that her father's choice of a husband for her will not be the choice of her heart:

> Heureuse une âme indifférente!
> Le tranquille bonheur, dont j'étais si contente,
> Ne me sera-t-il point rendu?
> Dans ces beaux lieux tout est paisible;
> Hélas! que ne m'est-il possible
> D'y trouver le repos que mon cœur a perdu? (I.i.1-6)[15]

At the end of the act, the *divertissement* in which Protée predicts Phaéton's tragic end begins with an evocation of "la douceur du repos" (I.v.162), as Protée suggests avoiding the fate of "Ceux qui sont dans l'horreur d'un dangereux orage!", that is, "les malheureux amants" (I.v.150-51).

Between these two evocations of peace—one in which love is threatened by politics, the other in which general peace is threatened by love—we meet Phaéton who, perhaps on purpose, does not even see Théone as he looks for his mother. His first line, "Je vous aime, Théone, et ce soupçon m'offense" (I.iii.55), is an excellent indication of his character, of how his single-mindedness convinces him that he is telling the truth when it is clear to others that he is not. Or rather, truth is somewhere in between, in this age that is no longer golden, where transparent language and unambiguous truth are as rare as the peace and innocence bemoaned by Astrée in the prologue. In this new golden age, guaranteed by

---

combats" (1659) and "Loin de nous, Fureurs homicides" (1679); *O.D.* 501-02, 628-31. His libretto *Astrée* features not this goddess but the shepherdess of d'Urfé's novel.

[15] In the first act, one finds *repos* and *tranquillité* three times each, *paix* and *indifférence* twice each, and *paisible, calme,* and *calmer* once each.

Louis XIV, "truth" emerges more often from royal degree than it does from dialogue.

Judging from what he says later to his followers (III.ii.447-49), his statement that he loves Théone is true to a certain extent. He does not love anyone else (I.iii.66-68), and his heart loves Théone "autant qu'il peut aimer" (I.iii.88). Phaéton loves Théone in his way, since he finds her "belle" and "charmante," but less so than the throne: "Si Théone me paraît belle, / La couronne est encor plus charmante à mes yeux" (I.iv.129-30). His "non, je vous aimerai toujours" (I.iii.77) does not sound nearly so unconvincing as the "je vous aime encore" that Io offers to Hiérax (*Isis*, I.iii.82), for he is not under the charm of another lover, but only of ambition. What is striking, musically, about this passage, is Théone's reply in the following line, with the "forbidden" interval of the tritone between the two notes of her "Ingrat." Though this dissonant outburst is prepared somewhat by the same interval of a tritone between the base and the /rai/ of Phaéton's "Je vous aimerai toujours," its harshness suggests that Théone is unwilling to listen to Phaéton's explanations. It is true that he has broken her promise to him, but she sees only her point of view, underlining again the difficulty of communication and of establishing truth.

By the third act, however, this "love" has become pity:

Je plains ses malheurs,

Je m'attendris par ses larmes;

Ah! que de beaux yeux en pleurs

Ont de puissants charmes!

Je n'avais jamais vu l'éclat du sort des Rois

Quand je m'engageai sous ses lois;

Rien n'était à mes yeux si beau qu'un amour tendre.

La Grandeur m'appelle aujourd'hui,

L'Amour me parle en vain, je ne puis plus l'entendre,

La fière Ambition parle plus haut que lui. (III.ii.443-52)

Up to this point, Phaéton remains somewhat sympathetic, ambitious but not totally brutal, still able to speak as a *galant homme* ("[...] que de beaux yeux en pleurs / Ont de puissants charmes!"). The ten lines of this air are divided into two sections, with the first four lines sounding much like a tender hero while the following six sound more vigorous, like a hero ready for action.

He retains some feelings for Théone, and is certainly not ready to see her devoured by a monster, as Phinée was once he had lost her to Persée (IV.iii.646-48). Still, the rapid transition within this air (III.ii.446 to 447) reminds us that he is already what one could call a monarch-in-training, dismissive of those whom he does not want to see, all too willing to talk to a person who favors his ambitions but unwilling to listen to warnings from the same person (Climène in I.iv and II.i). When he comes into contact with those who oppose his plans, he quickly changes from bold and assertive to brash and whiny.

Indeed, the "action" that follows the second section of his air is a sacrifice to Isis that Phaéton intends to carry out, not out of piety and respect, but because of custom and duty (III.ii.453-56). What could have been a positive step toward consolidating his power quickly becomes a confrontation with his rival Épaphus, who is the son of Isis. Phaéton is arrogant ("Quel sort est plus beau que le mien?," III.iii.466) and contemptuous, gloating over his victory: "Plus mon rival est jaloux, / Et plus mon bonheur est doux" (III.iii.476-77). His duet with Épaphus sounds like two adolescents vying for bragging rights, and Phaéton will soon "run to Mommy" to demand proof of his divine birth (III.vi).

In the meantime, he not only insults the goddess by being disdainful of her son, but also by refusing to accept, in spite of his mother's warning, the omen of the doors of the temple that close by themselves:

MÉROPS
Dieux! Le Temple se ferme!
PHAÉTON
                         Allons, il faut l'ouvrir.
Les Dieux veulent souvent qu'on ose les contraindre
A recevoir les vœux que l'on doit leur offrir.
CLIMENE
Ha! mon fils, arrêtez.
PHAÉTON
                    Suivez-moi sans rien craindre. (III.iv.545-48)

This is the second time he has refused childishly to listen to his mother's advice, the first being after Protée's prediction of his tragic end ("Non, non, je ne puis vous quitter / Que vous ne m'assuriez du bonheur où j'aspire," II.i.262-63). Now he has offended the woman he loves, his rival, and the tutelary goddess of his country, and has certainly lost what little sympathy he had earlier evoked in most spectators. By the end of act III, when he leaves for the palace of the Sun, it is hard to deny that he is deserving of the fatal fall that awaits him. This is particularly important because the spectators, almost all of whom would be familiar with the myth, would know how the opera must end, and it would violate one of the principal rules of tragedy to have an innocent hero meet an undeserved death.[16]

However, again as in classical tragedy, the fate of the hero should evoke some admiration and pity in the spectator, even if that fate is largely deserved. While it is impossible to know Quinault's exact intentions, the author of the *Lettre [...] sur les opéra de Phaéton et Hippolite et Aricie* states the problem well:

> Si Quinault a eu pour objet de rendre l'ambition odieuse, & d'en faire desirer la punition, son objet n'est pas entierement rempli. L'indignation que l'on conçoit contre Phaëton, est assez légere; son inconstance ne paroit guéres criminelle, & l'ambition, ce me semble, y jouë un plus beau rôle que l'amour. (6)

In particular, Quinault seems to have been careful to present Phaéton in a relatively positive light in the last scene in which he has a speaking role (in the last act, he appears only in his chariot, above the stage). He is welcomed to the palace of the Sun by one of the Hours of the Day, who encourages him to persevere in the paths of glory:

---

[16] See chapter 13 of Aristotle's *Poetics.* Racine, in the preface to *Phèdre,* mentions an ancient commentator who criticized Euripides for having portrayed Hippolytus without any imperfections, with the result that "la mort de ce jeune Prince causait beaucoup plus d'indignation que de pitié" (818). See also Forestier's discussion of Racine's idea of the "héros imparfait," with its welcome emphasis on the evocation of emotion, in the introduction to his edition of Racine, xxxv-xxxviii.

Bravez l'Envie

[...]

La Gloire est belle,

Ne tardez pas,

Suivez ses pas.

Vous la cherchez, sa voix vous appelle,

Vous êtes fait pour aimer ses appas;

L'amour constant que l'on a pour elle

Porte un grand nom au-delà du trépas. (IV.i.618, 626-32)

This exhortation—as is often the case with Quinault—is expressed in terms as appropriate to love as to glory ("belle," "aimer ses appas," "amour constant"), which serves not, as in other operas, as a reminder that the hero can satisfy the demands of both, but as an indication that Phaéton has left love behind. When he reveals his feelings with a sigh before he says anything (IV.ii.639), it is not a sigh of love, but of wounded pride. One would be tempted to speak of childish pride, of a less than noble desire for revenge against his "jaloux ennemis" (IV.ii.648), if, at the court of Louis XIV, the ancestry of a prince such as Phaéton was not of such crucial importance for questions of succession and of general prestige. In keeping with his ambitions, which the court of the Sun finds appropriate until he makes his fatal request to drive his father's chariot, Phaéton expresses his courage in heroic terms:

Si je suis votre fils, puis-je trop entreprendre?

[...]

La Mort ne m'étonne pas,

Quand elle me paraît belle;

Je suis content du trépas

S'il rend ma gloire immortelle. (IV.ii.673, 679-82)[17]

The unusual nature of the hero of *Phaéton* is certainly related to its unusual conclusion. The love scene is a sad one between two "minor"

---

[17] His courage here resembles that of other heroes in Quinault's libretti, from Cadmus ("Malgré le péril qui m'attend," II.iv.316) to Persée ("Quel péril peut m'alarmer," III.iii.536).

characters (V.iii), the title character does not return from his dangerous adventure, and, in particular, there is no *divertissement* at the end:

> fait unique à l'opéra avant *Armide,* la pièce se termine brusquement après le foudroiement du héros, sans que ce foudroiement soit suivi d'aucune danse ni d'aucun divertissement. (Gros, *Quinault* 623)

One can imagine several reasons for this arrangement of the last act. First, Quinault, Lully, and Berain must have wanted to save the spectacular machinery of Phaéton's ride and fall for the end, rather than have its effect diminished by the dancing and elaborate staging of a *divertissement.* Second, it makes for effective drama to interrupt a *divertissement* that is a scene of rejoicing (V.iv) with the announcement of Phaéton's impending fall (V.v). More specific to *Phaéton,* however—saving the spectacular for the end and interrupting a scene of false hope are general dramatic techniques that could be used in almost any opera—is the difficulty of presenting an appropriate response to the death of a young heir to the throne, a person loved by several important characters (especially Théone and Climène) and admired by the people as a "soleil nouveau" (V.i.716 and eleven other times). A tribute to Phaéton's "splendid daring," as in Ovid (see page 267 of this chapter), would hardly be appropriate for a "hero" who has been shown to abandon his fiancée and insult his nation's gods. Furthermore, his death was necessary for the common good (V.viii.874), and it would not do to display displeasure with Jupiter's decision to destroy him.

The issue of the common good, of the need to set an example for "Audacieux" (V.viii.875), brings us back to the rather obvious political implications of this final scene. It also tends to make us forget, however, the unusual dramatic situation. Not only is the hero dead, and deservedly so; the fate of the other characters is left hanging, which goes against one of the principal rules of classical dramaturgy: the denouement is supposed to explain what happens to all the main characters.[18] But will Épaphus

---

[18] Bray (324, n. 1) cites several sources, including Racine's preface to *Britannicus:* "j'ai toujours compris que la Tragédie étant l'imitation d'une action complète, où plusieurs personnes concourent, cette action n'est point finie que l'on ne sache en quelle situation elle laisse ces mêmes personnes" (374).

marry Libie and ascend to the throne? What will happen to Théone? Will Climène be punished for having, in a way, been responsible for Phaéton's death and the danger he caused to the earth?

§ § §

The question of whether or not Épaphus and Libie will end up together underlines the new direction Quinault has taken in the treatment of love in the *tragédie lyrique*. Before *Phaéton*, only *Atys* among the Quinault-Lully operas had ended without some kind of happy couple, though it is perhaps stretching the point somewhat to see Jupiter and Junon in *Isis*, or Pluton and Proserpine in *Proserpine*, as truly happy couples. The latter are only together six months of the year, and Proserpine has not expressed her approval, but the conclusion nonetheless appears to favor the couple as a fundamental social structure, a structure that will be emphasized in the following opera, *Persée*, as well as in the intervening ballet *Le Triomphe de l'Amour*. One could see in the reunited couple Jupiter-Junon in *Isis* a strong endorsement of the need for couples in society, but at the same time a deemphasis of the need for a happy couple among the principal characters of the opera, of the couple as an operatic necessity.

In *Phaéton*, the young couple Épaphus-Libie is not present at the end of the opera. Épaphus does not reappear after their famous duet "Une chaîne si belle" at the end of V.iii,[19] and although Libie returns in the last two scenes, her only role is to join her father Mérops and the chorus in singing the concluding "O chute affreuse! / O témérité malheureuse!" Quinault's plan for this last act thus draws on the emotional and dramatic potential of a meeting between seemingly doomed lovers (even though the audience knows that Phaéton will die, it is not certain that Épaphus and Libie will be united) without including them in the denouement. The emotional high point is in the middle of the act, where it would seem to take second place to the spectacular conclusion, which, although it would evoke pity for Phaéton and admiration for the machines, would be less moving for most spectators than the *tendresse* of the love duet. Quinault's decision not to include the young lovers at the end, or even to explain

---

[19] Lecerf called it "ce fameux Duo du 5. Acte, que tout le monde a admiré et admire" (1: 69).

what will happen to them, not only goes against the rules of classical dramaturgy, but removes love from the climactic moment of the opera.

Absent from the denouement, love also receives a fairly critical treatment during the last act, as well as throughout most of the opera. If love can be seen in V.v as a positive force that causes Théone to take pity on the man who betrayed her ("Hélas! je ne vois plus sa trahison cruelle, / Son funeste péril est tout ce que je vois," 840-41), it hardly brings happiness to her or to Épaphus and Libie. Furthermore, the images involving the dangers of fire and heat (*embraser, feu, ardeur,* V.v) serve double duty as warnings against the dangers of love, often expressed through the same imagery. Even the song of the shepherdess in V.iv places love in an unfavorable light, singing the praises of love only when "Ce n'est que pour rire " (V.iv.807 and 827), and concluding

> Jeunes cœurs qui cherchez à vous rendre,
> N'aimez pas tant;
> Un amour trop tendre
> N'est jamais content. (V.iv.810-13 and 830-33)

This tendency toward hedonism seems to contradict what could otherwise be seen as a reflection of a court—under the growing influence of Mme de Maintenon—moving toward (often insincere) devotion and away from love and its pleasures. This "contradiction" is not new, however, since a "morale lubrique" coexists with a sense of duty, honor, courage, and fidelity in almost all the Quinault-Lully operas (see chap. 3, *Alceste,* 106-09). One must remember that what can be considered immoral is almost always found in the *divertissements,* and that the presence of a cheerful tribute to pleasure is not only an established literary topos but a sentiment that is no more incongruous in an opera featuring noble heroes than is the presence of opera itself at the court of a king devoted to duty but fond of pleasure.

In sum, it is, as usual, far from easy to find a single point of view from which one can read a Quinault libretto. One could even read *Phaéton* as a work in favor of love, since Phaéton would have avoided his tragic fall if he had remained in love with Théone. For example, as Girdlestone (*Tragédie en musique* 93) and Couvreur point out, we are far from "la vieille gloire cornélienne," from a conception of the theatrical

hero who not only puts duty and honor above love but who is openly ambitious: "Ce qui aurait été considéré en 1650 comme le fait d'un cœur
aristocratique est ressenti en 1683 comme celui d'un ambitieux égoïste"
(Couvreur, *Lully* 357).[20] On the other hand, if *Phaéton* is not Cornelian, it
hardly resembles Racinian tragedy, where the hero—except in *La Thébaïde*—is never able to resist the power of love. Indeed, in *Phèdre* Racine
went out of his way to present Hippolyte as deeply in love, when most of
his sources had portrayed the son of the all-too-loving Thésée as totally
opposed to love.

Phaéton does not resemble the typical Quinault libretto any more
than it resembles a typical play by Corneille or Racine. It has elements of
the two-couple structure discussed in chapter 4 (*Thésée*), but different relations, complicated by an attraction to power that is stronger than the desire for the beloved. Whether Quinault felt pressure from the king and
soon-to-be morganatic wife[21] or a need for artistic renewal—or both—
Phaéton represents an effort to experiment with the structure of the
tragédie lyrique, to try new means of pleasing, instructing, and moving
his audience. From this point of view, the move away from classical
mythology in his next libretto (*Amadis*) is not so surprising. *Phaéton*
announces the end of the perfect hero-lover, a new emphasis on duty together with a de-emphasis of the ennobling powers of love, a need for
divine—or magical—intervention to protect the world from the errors of
the mighty, and at least a suggestion that women can succeed where
overly ambitious or jealous males fail. It is also an indication that
Quinault is placing more importance on the development of character. If
Phaéton is not, as Girdlestone suggested (*Tragédie en musique* 91),
Quinault's most interesting hero, he stands out not only as a character
with unique motivation but also as one of the most skillfully drawn, a
worthy companion to some of Quinault's greatest creations that are still to
come, such as Angélique, Roland, and Armide.

§ § §

---

[20] The best example in Corneille of a character who puts ambition above love would
be the title character in *Othon* (1665), a play of failed love and ambition that lacks a true
hero; see Baker 118.

[21] Louis XIV married Mme de Maintenon in October 1683, during the first run of
Phaéton.

We thus come to a turning point in the *tragédie lyrique,* a moment at which it is useful to look back at the first seven libretti and forward to the last three. I suggested near the end of section 1 of chapter 2 (76-77) that the operas from *Cadmus et Hermione* to *Phaéton* could be seen as, if not a true cycle, a series of texts that have a global perspective, in which divinities intervene not only for their own pleasure but also for the good of the universe. Cybèle is concerned for the happiness of her worshipers, as are Cérès and Jupiter (in *Phaéton*), and there are numerous examples of gods and goddesses who help worthy heroes accomplish deeds that bring them happiness in love but at the same time rid their country of tyrants (*Cadmus et Hermione*), sorceresses (*Thésée*), and monsters (*Persée*). *Phaéton* comes at a moment in Quinault's career as librettist and in the reign of Louis XIV when this optimistic, heroic ideal, along with its close association with love, is at the same time called into question and admired as a nostalgic ideal. I will discuss this moment of questioning and nostalgia in more detail in section 2 of the following chapter (especially pp. 296-99), but it is important to turn first to a more obvious way in which *Phaéton* represents a turning point in the Quinault-Lully collaboration.

After this opera with a most unoperatic—and in many ways unheroic—hero, the mythology that had served the French monarchy and French opera so well gives way to a source of ideals, worthy deeds, and moving scenes that is more modern and more French. It is not really, as least as far as the *tragédie lyrique* is concerned, a radical change, for the basic elements of the form that Quinault and Lully created will remain the same, especially in their next opera, *Amadis.*[22] If the five acts of *Phaéton* can be seen as an example of the move toward the substitution of "l'allégorie ouvertement politique" (Himelfarb, "Versailles" 252; see chap. 10, *Amadis*, 302) for the incarnation of contemporary ideals in mythological characters, this politicization will be less obvious in the last three libretti. They do contain overt moralizing, especially in *Roland* and *Armide* when Roland and Renaud forgo love and return to their patriotic

---

[22] The prologues of Quinault's last three libretti are not very different from those of the first eight, for allegorical characters continue to extol the noble qualities of Louis XIV. See, for example, La Gloire and La Sagesse in *Armide*. These prologues do differ in one important way, however, from earlier ones, in that they are linked much more closely to the five acts that follow; see chapter 10 (*Amadis*), 292.

duty, but nothing quite like the direct intervention of Jupiter/Louis XIV in the affairs of the kingdom. *Phaéton* also prefigures these last two operas in the sense that its hero puts the kingdom at risk and that love and glory are no longer compatible, but first there is *Amadis*, which hardly de-emphasizes love or continues with the theme of rivalry between heroes.

10

Amadis

New Directions and Familiar Themes

> J'admirerai tout air triste qui imitera *Bois épais,*
> tout air emporté qui tiendra de celui d'*Amadis,*
> que toute la France, depuis la Princesse jusqu'à
> la servante de cabaret, a tant chanté, *Amour que*
> *veux-tu de moi.*   (Lecerf 2: 312)

- I -

IT IS PROBABLY NOT UNFAIR TO SAY THAT, at least from a literary point of view, *Amadis* (1684) is less interesting in itself than for the changes it reflects. These changes, which will be the subject of section 2 of this chapter, go far beyond the change in subject matter—*Amadis* is the first Quinault libretto to have a subject based on chivalric romance instead of on classical mythology—and are part of a shift in taste that characterizes the end of what has been called the "classical moment" (Turnell).

The subject of *Amadis* was chosen by Louis XIV who, some time before the death of Queen Marie-Thérèse on July 30, 1683 (Quinault wrote her epitaph), ordered Quinault to prepare a libretto based on the famous novel (Boscheron 52). Lully would probably have followed the familiar pattern and premiered the new opera at court early in the year, but this was impossible in 1684, since Louis XIV was still officially in the year-long period of mourning following the death of the queen (*Mercure,* March 1685, 222). There is some doubt as to exactly when the first performance at the Académie Royale de Musique took place, but it was probably Sunday, January 16.[1] It was still playing June 23 and July 7, when the Dauphin saw it (Dangeau 1: 29-30, 34), and there is no evidence that it did not continue until the first Paris performance of *Roland* on March 8, 1685.[2] The first performance at court took place at Versailles on March 5, 1685, following a series of performances of *Roland.*

Amadis was a considerable success, in spite of criticisms of the libretto, to which I will return shortly. It was one of the most frequently revived Quinault-Lully operas during Louis XIV's reign and the Regency,[3] and was heard in Marseille in 1689, Rouen in 1693, Brussels in 1695 (with a new prologue), and Lunéville in 1709 (Schmidt, "Geographical Spread" 186, 193, 204, 196). The libretto was still popular in the late eighteenth century, after Lully's music had begun to go out of style, and it was reset by La Borde in 1771 (choruses, dances, and *divertissements* only) and by J.C. Bach in 1779 (reduced to three acts by Devismes).

Much of the success was due to the popularity of the subject. Herberay des Essarts's 1540 translation of Montalvo's *Amadís de Gaula* was a true best-seller, "livre favori des dames, bréviaire des courtisans, manuel d'éducation pour les jeunes gentilshommes," read by Saint Ignatius and Saint Teresa in spite of its condemnation by the Church (Giraud, introduction 3).[4] Des Essarts's translation was known as the "Bible of Henri IV" and retained its popularity in spite of Cervantes's brilliant

---

[1] This is the date found in all the libretti that give a precise date (Ballard 1701, 1731, 1740, 1759; Delormel 1759, 1771) and by the *Journal de l'Opéra.* Most modern authorities prefer Jan. 18 (Parfaict, *Dictionnaire;* La Vallière; Crapelet; Clément and Laporte; La Laurencie; Prunières, *Lully;* Ducrot; Mélèse; La Gorce, *Opéra;* Anthony, "Lully"), but Parfaict's manuscript *Académie Royale* (179) gives Jan. 14. Gros (*Quinault* 147) prefers Jan. 15, the date given by Boscheron, p. 53; this date is unlikely, since the Académie normally did not perform on Saturday. This preference for Jan. 15 is based on the *Mercure* of Jan. 1684, pp. 326-28 (and not p. 229), which says only "depuis quinze jours"; this approximate date would match either Jan. 15 or 16.

[2] The *Journal de l'Opéra* for 1685 says "On reprit *Amadis* à Paris au mois de février au lieu de *Roland* retardé jusqu'au 8 mars" but does not mention what *Amadis* would have replaced. This is a problematic entry, with almost certainly an error concerning the date and/or place.

[3] There were revivals in 1687, 1701, 1707, 1718, 1731, 1740, and 1759.

[4] Written around 1492 and first published in 1508. His sources, which can not be identified with certainty, include lost Portuguese, Spanish, and perhaps even French versions. See Giraud, introduction 5.

parody in *Don Quixote*. Beaussant put it well when he said that Amadis was the Rhett Butler of the popular imagination of Quinault's time (*Lully* 657), and of course the perfect knight was the perfect vehicle for praising Louis XIV. As La Fontaine said in the dedication he wrote for the score published by Ballard in 1684,

> Du premier Amadis je vous offre l'image;
> Il fut doux, gracieux, vaillant, de haut corsage.
> J'y trouverais votre air, à tout considérer,
> Si quelque chose à Vous se pouvait comparer.
> [...]
> En Vous tout est enchantement.
> [...]
> Vos beaux faits ont partout tellement éclaté
> Que Vous nous réduisez à chercher dans la Fable
> L'exemple de la vérité.[5] (*O.D.* 621)

If it was easy for Quinault to flatter Louis XIV by comparing him to Amadis, there is evidence, both anecdotal and internal, that he had some difficulty in crafting a coherent libretto out of a sprawling novel. Boscheron's *Vie* mentions a rumor that "Quinault étoit fort embarrassé comment il exécuteroit le dessein du Roi" (52) and that he wrote a clever madrigal explaining that the "Opéra [...] fâcheux" was not "l'Opéra que je fais pour le Roi," but rather finding husbands and dowries for five daughters.[6]

§ § §

---

[5] La Fontaine and Lully had reconciled their differences, which went back at least to 1674-75; see chapter 4 (*Thésée*), 128-29. La Fontaine would also write the dedication for the score of *Roland* in 1685. His poem confirms that Louis had suggested the subject of *Amadis*.

[6] This "Madrigal," which is reproduced in Boscheron 52 and Gros, *Quinault* 145, was first published in Bouhours's *Recueil de vers chosis* in 1683; see Lachèvre 3: 119, 495. Bayle included it in letter XXI of his *Nouvelles lettres de l'auteur de la critique générale de l'histoire du Calvinisme*, *O.D.* 2: 306-07. It is described there, in a letter dated Oct. 3, 1684, as a madrigal by Quinault that was circulating the previous year, which is when he would have been writing *Amadis*.

It was obviously difficult to reduce the first five long books of the Amadis story into the five brief acts of a *tragédie lyrique*.[7] Quinault borrowed freely from each of these books, added some scenes of his own, rearranged the chronology, and did his best to work in all the familiar scenes that his audience would expect. As Gros aptly puts it, "son livret, pourrait-on dire, est écrit et conçu 'en marge' de l'*Amadis de Gaule*" (*Quinault* 567). To take but a few examples, there is nothing in the libretto of Amadis's birth, of why Urgande protects him, of how he met Oriane, of why he fought Ardan Canille, and little of his rivalry with Arcalaüs. Oriane's engagement to the Emperor of Rome comes in book IV, after the end of her jealousy of Briolanie; the two situations are simultaneous in Quinault's act I. Florestan is able to pass successfully under the Arc des Loyaux Amants in book II, but not in Quinault's last act. There is nothing in the novel about Arcabonne's love for Amadis. And there is of course a happy ending that, in the novel, comes only in book IV, after many trials and tribulations.[8]

In spite of these difficulties, Quinault completed a libretto that, although somewhat hard to follow if one is not familiar with the Amadis tradition,[9] suggests that, in fact, "Quinault avoit été fort peu embarrassé" (Boscheron 53). Or rather, as in the case of *Isis,* that he had not been too concerned with writing a libretto that would have the unity of action, steadily building intrigue, and profound psychological insights that are associated with classical tragedy. Once the King had chosen the subject of Amadis, Quinault must have realized that, even if he could reduce the novel into one concentrated action, it would make for good theater to include the two best-known couples (Amadis and Oriane, Florestan and Corisande) and the two main magicians (Arcalaüs and Urgande, one evil and one good). More important, he must have realized that such a series of emotion-packed scenes involving love, chivalry, jealousy, revenge, and

---

[7] There were eventually twenty-four books, but books I-IV "racontent l'essentiel de son histoire jusqu'au mariage avec Oriane" (Giraud, introduction 21).

[8] For more examples, see Gros, *Quinault* 565-67 and Newman 77-79. For details about the Amadis legend, see Bourciez, O'Connor, and Baret.

[9] Gros (*Quinault* 625) exaggerates considerably the difficulty of following the plot in the first act. The last act offers examples of a need for familiarity with the novel, since the origins of the Arc des Loyaux Amants and of the Chambre Défendue are not explained.

magic would allow Lully to exploit his musical imagination to the fullest. Lully responded with some of his most successful music, what Beaussant describes as "une musicalité inégalée" (*Lully* 666).

Prunières probably goes too far, but his enthusiasm bears quoting as an example of the impatience many musicologists have felt when dealing with what they consider the "constraints" of the literary tradition.[10] Rather then look forward, as Beaussant does, to "le chef-d'œuvre [...] au bout de leur plume" (*Lully* 666), to works such as *Roland* and *Armide* that combine tragedy with great music, Prunières prefers to appreciate *Amadis* purely as a musical work:

> [Lully] a oublié les scrupules littéraires qui le retenaient et s'ést aban-
> donné à la joie de créer de souples mélodies aux lignes expressives
> sans s'embarrasser de la césure et de la rime.[11]

With all due respect to Prunières, who has done so much for Lully studies, it is not true that Lully pays no attention to the rhythmic structure of Quinault's lines. He does, however, give an increased role to the orchestra, and he allows the music to flow more freely than in earlier operas. The vocal lines take on more of an independent melodic structure than did his earlier recitative; he often uses a *récit lyrique* where he would earlier have used recitative, and it is often difficult to distinguish the former from a full-fledged air.[12]

---

[10] Bassinet organizes his introduction to *Atys* around this notion of *contraintes,* though he of course devotes more attention to the demands placed by the composer on the librettist. In a similar vein, many literary critics, especially in the romantic period, have seen the rules and unities of classical tragedy as unfortunate constraints on Corneille or Racine. One can of course argue that Racine flourished under the pressure to concentrate the action of his plays in a brief period of time or to use only the most noble words, and that Quinault and Lully worked better as a team than as individuals.

[11] *Lully* 101. See also Prunière's introduction to his edition of *Amadis;* he was especially eager to publish the score before his health interrupted the edition.

[12] See Beaussant, *Lully* 664-65; he calls "arioso" what I am calling *récit lyrique*. He cites lines 10-13 of the first act where, in the midst of the exposition, one would expect recitative but finds a simple air: each pair of two lines is repeated, and the vocal line has a larger melodic range and more regular rhythms than what one normally finds in recitative. In no case, however, does Lully fail to observe the pause at the *césure* or at the end of a line. In the two passages I discuss in the next paragraph, there are a few examples of Lully's being somewhat more free with Quinault's rhythms. In "Bois épais," the long note on the first syllable of *être* in "Tu ne saurais être assez sombre" (II.iv.248) does not

Two passages were particularly successful, "Bois épais" (II.iv) and "Amour, que veux-tu de moi?" (II.i). The latter had the reputation of being sung by "toutes les Cuisinieres de France" (Lecerf 2: 328), and the former is one of the rare Lully airs to have remained in the standard recital repertory. Its emotional power was so great that one of Lecerf's interlocutors bursts in to interrupt the Chevalier, who had hypothesized that any person "avec un naturel heureux" and with "une connoissance raisonnable de la langue" would have enough taste to cry out "Ah! l'aimable chanson" after having heard Lambert's song "Les beaux yeux de Climène": "& aprés avoir entendu *Bois épais,* interrompit Madame du B. que diroit-elle? [...] Je croi qu'elle ne diroit rien, Madame, & qu'elle pleureroit" (2: 285). This is the supreme compliment for an art form that depends so heavily on a thorough understanding of language but ultimately leaves the spectator speechless.[13]

The success of *Amadis* is attested not only by the popularity of some of its airs[14] and of its long run. The chaconne from the last act was excerpted for performances at court, such as one in November preceding

---

fall on the first beat of the measure. In "Amour, que veux-tu de moi," there is a string of nine notes with the same value in "Je suis accoutumée à ressentir la haine" (II.i.176), which takes the singer across the *césure* without much of a pause. Even here, however, Lully suggests a slight pause between syllables six and seven (a pause that is accentuated by the permitted hiatus "accoutumée à") by setting them both to the same pitch in the middle of a line that otherwise climbs steadily for more than an octave.

[13] "Bois épais" was also one of Lully's favorite airs: "Lulli, qui distinguoit souvent *Amadis* de ses autres Opera, distinguoit *Bois épais, &c.* entre les meilleurs morceaux d'Amadis; & citoit cét air comme un des ceux de ses grands airs, qu'il estimoit davantage" (Lecerf 2: 150). Grimarest cites "Bois épais" as an example of Lully's skill in setting words to music: "Quand, par exemple, il a voulu exprimer la situation d'un Amant qui se plaint, il a donné à ses tons une longueur proportionnée à cette situation. Mais il n'a point disproportionné l'étendue de ses intervales, comme font les Compositeurs ordinaires, qui se mêlent de mettre des paroles en musique" (125).

[14] At least one passage seems to have won a rather unwelcome notoriety. In Lecerf's *Comparaison,* "Consolez-vous dans vos tourments, / La mort n'est pas un mal si cruel qu'il le semble" (III.ii.412-13) is mocked by the Chevalier's Italophile nemesis the Comte as being unnatural, "faux," and "puéril" (2: 33), and the Chevalier agrees that Lully was not always "également juste & exact." I have never heard this scene performed, but it is true that, out of context at least, the simple harmonies and long series of quarter notes on the same pitch could sound contrived. Lully's idea, apparently, was to underline the falseness of the pity that Arcabonne is expressing.

a performance of Racine's *Mithridate*.[15] The sleeves worn by the actors became a hot fashion item,[16] and Quinault's additions to the basic Amadis story were well enough known that Madame de Grignan—who, like her mother, could put quotations from Quinault's libretti to good use—could count on her allusion to act III scene 4 being understood. When she realized that one of the *commissaires* in a suit against her was M. de Moulceau, whom she admired very much, she wrote, "Toute la colère allumée contre le premier a disparu à ce nom, et les armes me sont tombées de la main comme celles d'Arcabonne quand elle reconnaît Amadis" (Sévigné 3: 130; June 13, 1684). Furthermore, the frequent parodies of *Amadis* in the 1680s and 1690s are a sure sign of its success.[17]

§ § §

There are certainly aspects of the libretto that one can criticize from a literary point of view, but these do not seem to have diminished the pleasure of the first audiences—why complain about a lavish setting of a beloved story, full of moving scenes containing beautiful dance and music?[18] Still, Beaussant is probably right when he says of the first act that the abundance of opportunities for musical development in the libretto is perhaps a sign of its "mauvaise construction *dramatique*" (*Lully*

---

[15] Dangeau 1: 62 and 67, Oct. 22 and Nov. 5, 1684; *Mercure,* November 1684, 228-29. Dangeau mentions dancing between the acts and the *Mercure* says that the chaconne "servit de Prologue à la Tragédie de *Mithridate*." See also Brooks and Yarrow 104. Such performances, where dance and opera alternated with spoken tragedy, are an excellent indication that the separation of the arts was less than airtight.

[16] A note in Beffara's copy of Parfaict's *Académie Royale* (183, n. A) attributes the design of these sleeves to Berain. The Littré Dictionary quotes Ménage to explain why this type of sleeve became known as "Amadis."

[17] Moureau lists parodies of *Amadis* in 1684, 1693, and 1694. Parfaict (*Académie Royale* 269, note A) suggests that the performance of *La Naissance d'Amadis* in February 1694 is an indication that *Amadis* was revived in 1694, but no contemporary documents mention a revival at that time. Moureau points out that these and other parodies of operas often appeared several years after the opera first appeared (236), and that certain scenes were well enough known by the theater-going public for a parody to be successful, even if the opera was not being performed at the time.

[18] See Gros, *Quinault* 627 and Pitou 1: 150: "In short, it became evident once again that the average purchaser of a ticket to the Palais-Royal before 1700 was much more interested in moving music, breathtaking spectacles, and picturesque episodes than in appraising works on the basis of codified principles of esthetics."

664, his emphasis; see also Gros, *Quinault* 625). Two couples are presented in what Pitou calls a "double exposition" (148), and then the opening scenes of act II introduce two more characters, one of whom is in love with an unknown knight. This knight will turn out to be Amadis, but in this case previous knowledge of the story would not help, since the love of Arcabonne for Amadis is the main new element that Quinault introduced. The spectator is perhaps slightly confused at this point, but Quinault begins to pull things together thanks to a device common in chivalric romance but that would push the requirements of spoken tragedy for *vraisemblance* too far—after Arcabonne leaves, Amadis wanders into the same place where Arcalaüs is waiting and where Corisande is bemoaning the enchantment that has fallen on Florestan. Only Oriane is missing, and Arcalaüs will soon make Amadis think she is there as well. No one is surprised at all these coincidences, nor should the spectator be. Rather than fault Quinault's dramatic construction, one could praise him for following the spirit of the genre and for cleverly creating a large cast of characters and bringing them all together within two acts.

Most of the other "weaknesses" of the libretto can be better understood as inherent characteristics of an opera about Amadis: episodic action, secondary characters who are as involving as the principal ones (Lecerf thought the role of Oriane was "admirable [...] quoiqu'un peu trop pleureur," 2: 5), a final act that is more of a celebration than a denouement. Parfaict's criticisms are typical:

> L'Épisode de Florestan et de Corisande tient si peu à la pièce, qu'on souhaiteroit qu'il ne fût point du tout. [...]
>
> Toute la pièce est bien versifiée, mais elle n'est pas conduite avec cet art ordinaire à cet ingénieux Auteur, quoique l'unité d'action ne soit pas essentielle au Théatre de l'Opera, cependant elle est icy si mal observée qu'on ne sçait le plus souvent ou elle se passe. Au reste la Tragedie paroit finie au 4ᵉ acte qui ainsi que le 5ᵉ ont toujours paru languissants en comparaison des trois premiers. (*Académie Royale* 180, 181)

It is certainly not Quinault's "ordinary" way of constructing a libretto. But *Amadis* is not an ordinary libretto. The traditional view is that he was finding his way with a new type of subject matter, a way that he would find quickly with *Roland* and *Armide*. However, *Amadis* is in many ways more like the preceding libretti than the two following ones, in spite of the change from mythology to chivalry. Quinault's mythological characters always sounded a bit like chivalric heroes anyway, much more *tendre* and *galant* than the often brutal gods of the Greek sources.[19] Love and duty are still reconcilable in *Amadis,* a very different situation from what we will find in the next two operas. The material is thus familiar, but the length and complexity of the Amadis novel imposed a different kind of structure.

Some of the other criticisms of the libretto are more understandable. Parfaict (*Académie Royale* 181) and others wondered why Amadis did not explain to Oriane right away that he did not love Briolanie, rather than waiting until the last act, which is the first time Quinault has them together. (Oriane still thinks he is dead at the end of act IV and the beginning of act V.) Parodists such as Morambert did not miss the chance to poke fun at this situation:

> Est-il un amant plus tendre
> Et plus malmené que moi?
> Je ne vois qu'au dernier acte
> Celle qui fait mes malheurs.
> Il faut ce ce soit un pacte
> De ces malins enchanteurs.
> [...]
> Adieu donc, car s'il demeure,
> Je trahirai mon secret;
> Mon cœur doit être discret
> Pour le moins encore une heure.
> Si les amants s'expliquoient
> Les Opéras finiroient. (See Gros, *Quinault* 762)

Artificial it may be, but such situations are hardly unheard of in romance.

---

[19] See Beaussant, *Lully* 659. Gros is a bit harsher: "Fidélité, tendresse, vaillance, tout cela n'était pas sans charme; mais c'était la moule où Quinault coulait indifféremment ses héros, qu'ils fussent romains, grecs ou français" (*Quinault* 568).

This means of keeping the main plot going leaves plenty of room for the secondary characters, and Quinault has been criticized for making them more interesting than the main ones. Indeed, Arcalaüs and Arcabonne dominate the three middle acts, from their appearance in the first two scenes of act II to their defeat in the last scene of act IV. The spectator feels some pity for Florestan, Corisande, and the other captives (though he/she can hardly believe that Amadis is really dead), but the drama of Arcabonne's hesitations between love and hatred is considerably more captivating. Like Armide, she falls in love with her sworn enemy and, in a moving scene (III.iv), is unable to strike him when the long-awaited opportunity finally arrives.[20] To consider this shift of interest from primary to secondary characters a defect is to accuse Quinault of an unthinkable blunder, since he chose to introduce Arcabonne's love for Amadis into a story that already had more than enough material for a dozen operas. There is too much evidence of Quinault's craftsmanship to think he introduced this new love element without good reason, and I consider it more appropriate to search for this reason than to leap to the conclusion that he is incompetent. True, Racine would not have done it this way; but then, Racine would not have agreed to write a tragedy about Amadis, nor would Louis XIV have suggested it. Quinault needed not only a means of saving Amadis and the prisoners, but a character with a true interior conflict that linked her to the main as well as to the secondary action. It is Arcabonne's hate that first places Amadis in danger, then her love that spares his life; parallel to this vacillation between love and hate, Oriane reacts to the danger in which she sees Amadis by revealing that she truly loves him, even though she says she hates him (IV.iii). It is this series of close parallels that keeps Arcabonne from being a truly secondary character and that links the third and fourth acts so well to the first two:

---

[20] Arcabonne has fallen in love with an unknown knight, who of course turns out to be Amadis, whom she has sworn to kill in order to avenge her brother, Ardan Canille. This scene is strikingly similar to the famous scene in *Armide* (II.v), where love keeps the heroine from stabbing the sleeping Renaud. There are several other points of comparison between *Amadis* and *Armide,* including the temptation of Amadis with the image of Oriane (II.vii) and the similar, but unsuccessful, temptations of Ubalde and the Danish Knight in the fourth act of *Armide.*

[Arcalaüs] n'est intéressé que par la haine dans l'action épisodique mais Arcabonne s'y trouve attachée tout à la fois par la reconnaissance l'amour et la haine, et c'est ce qui fait que le troisieme et le quatrieme actes sont les plus intéressants. (Parfaict, *Académie Royale* 181)

Arcabonne and Arcalaüs are vanquished by Urgande at the end of the fourth act, as the Demons of the Air overcome the Demons of the Underworld, and all that remains is for Amadis and Oriane to be reunited. This type of structure could be said to result in a lessening of interest in the fifth act but, on the other hand, it refocuses the spectators' attention on the main characters. This is a compromise that Quinault was obviously content to accept—he reunites Amadis and Oriane, then concludes with their triumphant passage under the Arc des Loyaux Amants and into the forbidden Chamber.[21] He could hardly have denied this famous scene to his audiences, and the overall effect is not unlike that of the final ballet at the end of *Le Bourgeois gentilhomme* and *Le Malade imaginaire*, where the young couple is united after a series of obstacles and the play ends with music and dance.

In short, there is much in *Amadis* that is familiar, especially at the level of plot, structure, and characterization. We still have heroes faithful to both their love and their *gloire,* supernatural forces that thwart and aid them, heroines who bemoan their fate but are ultimately saved, and a willingness to try means of pleasing and moving the audience that would not be accepted in spoken tragedy. The new subject matter, however, and the considerable effort that Quinault made to adapt the *tragédie lyrique* to it, are an indication of a general change in taste and attitude, especially at court. Before looking more closely at this change, however, a brief look at the prologue will help understand what is new and what is old.

§ § §

---

[21] See the last acts of *Cadmus et Hermione, Persée,* and *Roland,* or of Pellegrin and Rameau's *Hippolyte et Aricie,* for other examples of a final act that could be considered anticlimactic. Lecerf found that "les deux derniers Actes d'Amadis sont languissans en comparaison des trois premiers" and noted that, as at performances of *Atys* and *Persée,* audiences left before the end of the final chaconne (2: 13, 14; see chap. 5, *Atys,* 168-69).

For Lecerf (2: 231) and Parfaict, the prologue of *Amadis* was the best of all the Quinault-Lully prologues. "Le prologue de cet Opera fut universellement approuvé. [...] Il est relatif à la pièce et travaillé avec un art infini tant de la part du poète que du musicien" (Parfaict, *Académie Royale* 180). It contains the praise of Louis XIV[22] and of love that one finds in the earlier prologues but, like the opera that follows, no mythological characters. The prologues to *Atys* and to *Persée* had mentioned the title heroes briefly, but there was no specific reference to the five acts other than the standard use of the myth of Perseus to praise kings and dauphins. In *Amadis,* however, it is as if the mention of a hero who was thought (mistakenly) to be French allows a much tighter connection. Urgande, Alquif, and their followers are awakened from a spell by the appearance on earth of a hero even more glorious than Amadis (P.39), inaugurating a new age similar to the Golden Age that returns in the prologue to *Phaéton.*[23]

Urgande and her followers will return at the end of act IV to rescue Amadis from the sorcery of Arcalaüs and Arcabonne. She saves what La Fontaine called "le premier Amadis," is in turn revived by Louis/new Amadis, and revives the original Amadis to glorify Louis. The connection could hardly be tighter, and this is the only Quinault-Lully opera in which a character from the prologue (Urgande) appears in the following five acts.

The two following operas will continue to have prologues with specific references to the hero of the opera and to how he is related to Louis XIV, but they will omit the praise of love. From this point of view, *Amadis* is very much a transitional work, having made the shift to chivalric subjects but not to the praise of duty at the expense of love. Duty is important in *Amadis,* and the *gloire* that it brings is an essential requirement for a hero to be loved (I.ii.91-94), but it also takes the hero away

---

[22] There is also praise of the palace of Versailles, where Louis had recently installed the court (May 1682): "Nous ne saurions choisir de demeure plus belle" (P.52).

[23] The similarity between the two prologues is emphasized by the use of the expression "reprenez tous vos charmes" (P.23), which had first appeared in the prologue to *Phaéton:* "Reprenez pour jamais vos charmes les plus doux" (P.63, 65). It also occurs in the prologue to *Roland:* "Doux Plaisirs, reprenez vos charmes" (P.14). The opera-lover can hardly resist thinking about Siegfried awakening Brunnhilde from her long sleep (Wagner's *Siegfried*) or, in the last act of the opera, about the trials that Tamino and Tamina must undergo in Mozart's *The Magic Flute.*

from his beloved (I.ii.83-86). The last act suggests that this separation is temporary and unfortunate, since Florisande rejoices that "Je puis vivre pour vous, / Que mon bonheur est doux!" (V.v.827-28). One could not be farther from the emphasis on duty and the condemnation of love that one finds in *Roland* and *Armide*.

- II -

If *Amadis* hearkens back to earlier operas in many ways, the shift from mythological to chivalric subjects nonetheless reflects a profound shift in the taste and attitudes of the court, a shift that will soon be evident in all the arts. The extremely tight link between the prologue and five acts of the tragedy not only emphasizes a tradition that is modern and French; it solidifies the relationship between the hero of the prologue and the hero of the tragedy. No matter how historically false might be the notion that the Bourbon monarchy is descended from Amadis, the idea of a new Amadis stepping out of the pages of history to reign gloriously over seventeenth-century France is more plausible than the idea of Louis as a reincarnation of Apollo or Perseus. Furthermore, Amadis comes from a Christian tradition, and it had always seemed incongruous, if not completely inappropriate, for Le Roi Très Chrétien to be depicted as a pagan god.

The first scene of *Amadis* contains an explicit criticism of classical mythology and, implicitly at least, of opera based on this mythology:

> J'ai choisi la Gloire pour guide,
> J'ai prétendu marcher sur les traces d'Alcide;
> Heureux si j'avais évité
> Le charme trop fatal dont il fut enchanté![24]
> Son cœur n'eut que trop de tendresse,
> Je suis tombé dans son malheur;
> J'ai mal imité sa valeur,
> J'imite trop bien sa faiblesse. (I.i.22-29)

This will be the last mention of a mythological hero in the Quinault libretti, a kind of goodbye both to mythological representations of Louis

---

[24] Alcide (Hercules) was involved in numerous amorous adventures. His affair with Iole aroused the jealousy of his wife Dejanira, who gave him the poisoned garment that led to his death. In this passage, "charme" could refer to the charms of love and to the blood of the Centaur Nessus with which Dejanira poisoned the vest. (Nessus had tried to abduct Dejanira; Hercules killed him, but the dying Nessus convinced Dejanira that his blood could be used as a charm to keep her husband faithful.)

XIV and to operas such as *Alceste*, in which Alcide, like Amadis, is suffering from love. In the 1674 opera, Lychas asked Alcide

> L'Amour est-il plus fort qu'un Héros indomptable?
> L'Univers n'a point eu de monstre redoutable
> Que vous n'ayez pu surmonter. (*Alceste* I.i.26-28)

In *Amadis*, Florestan asks Amadis

> Le grand cœur d'Amadis doit être inébranlable;
> Quel malheur peut troubler un Héros indomptable?
> Vainqueur des fiers tyrans et des monstres affreux... (I.i.6-8)

The similarities are striking—the "Héros indomptable" can defeat monsters but not Love, and jealousy is the cause of the suffering of both heroes, although in *Alceste* it is Alcide who is jealous and not, as in *Amadis*, his beloved.[25]

There is nothing like this comparison in the eight earlier operas, since a mythological hero was unlikely to compare himself unfavorably to another hero. Now it is the hero of the tragedy who is compared to Alcide, not the king in the prologue. It could hardly be otherwise, of course, since the comparison is no longer favorable, but the inclusion of an unfavorable comparison to the hero of one of the earlier operas is a striking indication that something fundamental has changed. At the same time that he begins to exploit a new source of imagery for the praise of the king, Quinault calls attention to the fact that heroes are not perfect and that the dream of combining love and glory is difficult to realize.

The inclusion of this unfavorable comparison in the opening lines of this new opera should not cause us to leap to conclusions. The comparison will turn out to be inaccurate, since the rest of the opera reveals that one cannot really criticize Amadis's valor and that he is far from having the weaknesses that led to the death of Alcide. He can be defeated

---

[25] Another similarity is the occurrence of the phrase "parfait modèle" in *Alceste* (III.v.596) and *Amadis* (P.55) but in no other Quinault libretto. A similar reversal is present, as one of the characters in the tragedy, Alceste, is the model in *Alceste*, whereas in the Prologue to *Amadis* it is the king.

only by sorcery (II.vi.299-300), and in the last act he and Oriane will be proven to be "parfaits amants." There is no real evidence in *Amadis* that either Amadis or the *tragédie lyrique* is moving away from love and *tendresse*. That will come soon enough, in the next two Quinault-Lully operas, in which the heroes Roland and Renaud will almost be undone by the weakness of Alcide; in *Amadis*, the shift remains one of subject matter and of royal representation.

The shift in subject matter and, as we shall see, a more general esthetic shift, is in reality less a move toward something new than a return to an earlier fascination with heroism and adventure, a refusal to accept the "demolition" of the hero that one finds in the works of Racine and other writers of the 1660s and 1670s.[26] Such a fascination is only natural in the nobility, who in the 1640s and 1650s still dreamed of glorious conquests on the field of battle as well as in the hearts of their princesses, but now found themselves relegated to deploying their sartorial *canons* in the gardens of Versailles, far (figuratively, at least) from the corridors of power. By 1684 Louis's power is solidly established, the institutions of centralized control by middle-class civil servants firmly in place, and visions of Amadis and Renaud dancing in the heads of courtiers no longer posed the threat they would have during the Fronde.

A lingering taste for heroic literature—and for the *galanterie* of heroic lovers—was equally present, as is clear in what Gros calls a "tournoi poétique" (*Quinault* 147) begun by a *ballade*—an appropriately medieval form—that Deshoulières wrote shortly after the first performances of *Amadis*. She complained of the brutal lovers of her day, both in Racine's tragedies and in real life, concluding each stanza with "On n'aime plus comme on aimoit jadis" which, in the *envoi*, rhymes with "Ramène-nous le siècle d'Amadis." Saint-Aignan, who had been organizing courtly entertainments since *Les Plaisirs de l'Ile Enchantée* in 1664, responded that, at least as far as he was concerned, "j'aime encor comme on aimoit jadis." The exchange continued and expanded to include works

---

[26] Bénichou 155-80, 214-56. McIntyre notes that *Amadis* "reeks of nostalgia" (13). For a discussion of a different type of nostalgia, see Donington's archetypal reading of *Amadis* (*Opera and Its Symbols* 43-50) in terms of projected fantasy, the eternal feminine, and a guide deep within the psyche.

by La Fontaine, Pavillon, and Montchesnay.[27] La Fontaine latter could not pass up the opportunity to poke fun at Deshoulières and to sing, in slightly archaic verse, the praises of a tradition that was so dear to him:

> On voit au monde assez d'amants discrets:
> La race encor n'est pas toute détruite;
> Quoi qu'en ait dit femme un peu trop dépite,
> Rien n'est changé du siècle d'Amadis.
> [...]
> Quand la dame est d'attraits assez pourvue,
> On aime encor comme on aimait jadis.[28]

It is clear that there were two coexisting traditions, both in style of courtship and in style of novel-writing, and that women were playing a more and more important role in both of these areas.[29] The older novels by writers such as La Calprenède and Scudéry had not been forgotten, in spite of more concise novels by Lafayette and Villedieu depicting more recent events and the dangers of love in a society where lovers were not always *parfaits* and *galants*.[30] What Bourciez says of the sixteenth-century reader was true of many readers in the late seventeenth century:

---

[27] The poems by Deshoulières and Saint-Aignan, along with a reply by the former to the latter, were published in the *Mercure* of January 1684, pp. 172-84, and then in Deshoulières's *Œuvres* of 1693, pp. 56-63. La Fontaine's contribution was not published until 1750, in the *Œuvres d'Étienne Pavillon*, vol. 2, pp. 150-51. This edition also includes the poems by Deshoulières and Saint-Aignan and one by Pavillon. Deshoulières's ballad is reproduced in the Grands Écrivains de la France edition of La Fontaine's works, vol. 9, pp. 36-38. Excerpts from these poems can also be found in Gros, *Quinault* 147-48 and Beaussant, *Lully* 658-59.

[28] *O.D.* 622-23. La Fontaine was perhaps still holding a grudge against Deshoulières from when they had been on opposite sides during the cabal surrounding Racine's *Phèdre* in 1677. In any case, he by no means always defended the *art d'aimer* of his contemporaries; see "Les Rémois" 49-51 ("Le seul plaisir est ce que l'on souhaite; / Amour est mort; le pauvre compagnon / Fut enterré sur les bords du Lignon," *Fables, contes et nouvelles* 490) and "Clymène" 3-4 ("Le siècle, disait-il, a gâté cette affaire: / Lui nous parler d'amour! Il ne la sait pas faire," *O.D.* 20).

[29] See DeJean, "Amazons and Literary Women" and *Tender Geographies*, Beasley, and the discussion of the role on Angélique in section 2 of the next chapter.

[30] DeJean documents this lasting success—and the reasons why it is not well known—in chapter 5 of *Tender Geographies;* see especially p. 168 and n. 8, p. 264. See also Sévigné's letter of July 12, 1671 (1: 294): "tout cela m'entraîne comme une petite

Ces complications infinies, ce perpétuel entrecroisement d'actions distinctes, trop prolongées au détriment de l'unité totale, sans autre raison d'aboutir que le bon plaisir du conteur, ne lassaient pas la complaisance des lecteurs du XVI° siècle; on aimait à se laisser bercer, à suivre tant bien que mal des héros fictifs, à travers un monde enchanté. (63)

There were also conflicting outlooks at court, as the pleasure-loving Louis XIV aged and came more and more under the influence of Madame de Maintenon, whom he had married in 1683. The glory years seem to have passed—the economy was in trouble, military expenditures were growing, Colbert had died, Louis had been seriously ill, and conflicts between Catholics and Protestants were intensifying.[31] Along with the military, economic, and social glory, the brilliant outpouring of the masterpieces that make up the canon of French classicism was almost over. Pascal's *Pensées* were published posthumously in 1670. Molière wrote his last comedy in 1673, Corneille his last tragedy in 1674, and Racine his last profane tragedy in 1677. Lafayette's *La Princesse de Clèves* appeared in 1678, as did the last edition of La Rochefoucauld's *Maximes*, and La Fontaine had published eleven of the twelve books of his *Fables* by 1679.

In light of all these changes, of these conflicting moral and esthetic points of view, the success of *Amadis* and of the following two operas based on chivalric romance can be seen as representative of a return to popularity of a type of literature that had lost the favor of some of the reading public during the past twenty or thirty years (since the 1650s). It is certainly more than coincidence that two of the few dramatists who had known success in the 1650s and 1660s, with their *tragédies galantes,* and

fille"). Adam (131, 132) comments on the pleasure that readers continued to find in La Calprenède's *Cassandre* (1642-45) and on the enormous success of Scudéry's novels (140, n. 1). Scudéry's *Clélie* (1654-60) was probably the best-selling book of the century (Chavardès 53; Cuénin, introduction xiii), and she continued to use parts of her novels in the conversations that she published from 1680 to 1692 (Wolfe 16-17). Good examples of this new type of novel are Villedieu's *Les Désordres de l'amour* (1675) and Lafayette's *La Princesse de Clèves* (1678).

[31] Colbert died in 1683. Louis had operations for a passage between his mouth and nose in January 1685 and for an anal fistula in 1686. The revocation of the Edict of Nantes was in 1685.

were still finding success in the 1680s were Quinault and Thomas Corneille, and that both of them had written libretti during the interval. They had always been in touch with the preferences of their public—Quinault's *Astrate* (1664 or 1665) and Corneille's *Timocrate* (1656) were more successful than any other tragedies of the second half of the century—and Quinault was becoming particularly adept at pleasing the king. Perhaps he even led Louis to choose the subject of *Amadis,* as he did in 1685 when he presented the king with a choice of Armide and two other subjects he would almost certainly not choose.[32]

These changes are perhaps best understood as a confirmation of what Philip Butler called "la réaction baroque" (245), a change that is evident in Racine's *Mithridate* (1673) and *Iphigénie* (1674) and that reflects "une nouvelle évolution du goût, qui se manifeste en particulier dans le succès de l'opéra," the "genre le plus en faveur" (250).[33] Racine's recognition that the success of the Quinault-Lully operas in the 1670s reflected the taste of his public is a clear indication that the glorious flowering of what we call French classicism was more the exception than the rule, that the taste for the "thèmes chevaleresques de l'art baroque" (Butler 250) was still strong. The first Quinault-Lully operas featured these themes but took their subjects from the mythology that was so important to classicism; the shift to chivalric subjects suggests that, as far as their public was concerned, they had been on the right track all along.

This evidence of a renewed interest in the baroque is of particular interest to musicologists who, unlike literary scholars, use the term *baroque* to refer to the period from 1600 to at least 1750. Beaussant refers explicitly to Butler's interpretation in the beginning of his chapter on *Amadis,* insisting on the "retour au baroque" and the brief duration of the "classical moment" (*Lully* 657). It is true that we are not far, in works such as *Mithridate, Iphigénie,* and *Amadis,* from the baroque. Still, even these most baroque of Racine's tragedies contain at least as much of what, in literature at least, we traditionally call classicism than they do of the baroque. While it is extremely important not to overemphasize the

---

[32] See chapter 14 (*Armide*), p. 327, n. 3.

[33] I have argued elsewhere that not only Racine's *Iphigénie* (the primary example given by Butler) but also *Mithridate* could be called "operatic," given their *galant* lovers and the compatibility they show between love and glory, "that it can be read as an effort to adapt to the prevailing taste at the time" ("Trailing Clouds of Glory" 31).

success, and especially the durability, of the classical esthetic championed by Racine, Boileau, and other Ancients, Butler was probably exaggerating when he said that the success of the *tragédie lyrique* "représente un échec très net pour les tendances qui avaient dominé la littérture durant les dix années précédentes" (250). Kintzler has demonstrated convincingly that there is a common, classical esthetic that stretches from Corneille to Rousseau, and characteristics such as *vraisemblance, nécessité,* and *propriété* remain constant, in spite of increased presence of such baroque characteristics as freedom, movement, and metamorphosis.[34] If one must have a common term to define the esthetic of the second half of the seventeenth century, *galant* would be more appropriate than either baroque or classical, which are constantly opposed to one another yet overlap chronologically. Defined by Furetière as "qui a de la bonne grâce, de l'esprit, du jugement, de la civilité et de la gaieté, le tout sans affectation," the *galant,* when applied to literature, is more flexible. Rather than follow strict principles, inherited from the past, the literary *galant* features mixtures that can assimilate contradictions. It incorporates a variety of styles and of genres, often considered "minor" or "small," but its presence is often felt in the "larger," more established genres favored by the partisans of the Ancients, such as tragedy. (Racine's *Alexandre,* 1665, is an excellent example.) Most important, the *galant* shares the goals of all the practitioners and theoreticians of what we call classicism: to please, to be beautiful, and to move. If it does not always appear to be deadly serious, it is not—in spite of some negative connotations of the words *galant* and *galanterie,* especially later in the century—immoral.[35]

§ § §

---

[34] See, for example, Kintzler, *Poétique* 25 and 134, and Louvat, "Les Spectacles musicaux." Butler does say "les procédés extérieurs, la structure formelle de sa [Racine's] tragédie sans doute ne changent pas" (245). Néraudau refers to the *tragédie lyrique* as a "démarche classique, à l'intérieur d'un genre baroque" (162).

[35] See the works by Viala included in the bibliography, especially *L'Esthétique galante* and "Galanterie et classicisme." The latter includes a similar appeal for a rethinking of the labels we apply to seventeenth-century literature (134). See also Denis; Bury, who situates the *tragédie lyrique* in the context of *l'esthétique galante* (*Classicisme* 87-88, 96-99); and Nédélec, who argues that it is the *esthétique galante*—and not classicism—that is the reference against which Molière's ridiculous characters are measured (136).

The choice of the subject of *Amadis* reflects one more important shift that was taking place in the mid-1680s, one that is intimately related to the *tragédie lyrique*, a royally sponsored art form that returns the favor by praising the monarch and portraying values dear to him. One can see, beginning about the time of Quinault and Lully's first operas, a move away from direct allegorical representation of Louis XIV toward more indirect types of representation that give more importance to him as a person rather than as royal essence and that give a larger role to contemporary history than to mythology. According to Édouard Pommier (208), the *fête* in 1674, during which *Alceste* was performed in the Cour de Marbre, marks the arrival of history at Versailles and foreshadows the moment when history of Louis's reign will replace mythology. Similarly, Néraudau shows how mythology and history were intertwined in Louis's triumphal entry into Paris in 1674 to celebrate the conquest of Franche-Comté.[36] Apostolidès also sees 1674-75 as the time when "l'idéologie mythistorique se défait" (*Roi-machine* 114). It is a gradual process, however, since, as Néraudau and Apostolidès point out, it is opera that supplants tragedy as the privileged means of representation of the monarch (Néraudau 118, 162-65; Apostolidès, *Prince sacrifié* 181), and opera will not abandon mythology until 1684.

Another indication that this move away from mythology is complete in 1684 can be found in the modifications of the central section of the palace at Versailles, and in particular the construction of the Galerie des Glaces, which did away with the symbolic arrangement of the king's apartment as seven rooms conceived and decorated as seven planets around the sun. Louis XIV moved into a room at a corner of the Cour de Marbre, out of the symbolic place of the sun at the center of the universe. At the same time, the Galerie des Glaces was adorned with scenes from recent history, with Louis as himself and not as a mythological god, and the king's apartments were decorated in true Louis XIV style, without

---

[36] *Olympe* 7-13. Néraudau finds evidence as early as the late 1660s of a "remise en cause [de] la métaphore mythologique" (109). He also discusses La Fontaine's hesitations about the use of mythology for political ends (70-72). At the time that Quinault wrote *Amadis,* La Fontaine had by no means abandoned references to mythology in his poetry. For example, his poem for the Comte de Fiesque (*O.D.* 620-21) and the "Discours à Mme de la Sablière" (added to Book IX of the *Fables*), both written in 1684, contain references to Mars, Neptune, Flore, and the Styx, as well as to Plato and Homer.

mythological paintings. As Beaussant suggests, echoing Néraudau (*Olympe* 228-31), "Tout se passe comme si la personne du roi n'avait plus besoin de la représentation mythologique pour s'exprimer" (*Lully* 682). The king can project his own image, without the help of Olympus. Or, as La Fontaine put it in 1679, "l'Olympe est partout où Louis tient sa Cour" ("Ode pour la paix," *O.D.* 629).

Images from classical mythology obviously do not disappear completely from Versailles or from the *tragédie lyrique* and other types of art.[37] Its systematic use does decrease considerably, however, and Himelfarb has suggested that Quinault and Lully helped show the way, that in the 1680s at Versailles the solar allegory will gradually be replaced by:

> tantôt l'allégorie ouvertement politique [...] et tantôt la juxtaposition
> hédoniste de sujets de la fable sans programme systématique, dans le
> choix et le rapprochement desquels on soupçonne une influence crois-
> sante de l'opéra lullyste et postlullyste, forme dominante sans doute de
> la culture française à la charnière des deux siècles. ("Versailles" 252)

Nor does Louis XIV cease encouraging comparisons between himself and great heroes, such as Amadis or Renaud. I have already quoted the passage from the dedication La Fontaine wrote for the 1684 score, in which he compares Louis to Amadis, and he will repeat the same kind of comparison in the dedication of the score of *Roland* the following year, where he will place Pâris, Helen of Troy, Mars, Apollo, and the Muses in the company of Charlemagne and Roland. What Quinault has done with *Amadis,* and what he will do with *Roland* and *Armide,* is to give concrete form to a general tendency, show how these subjects can make good theater and at the same time provide an image of Louis XIV that was more appropriate to the 1680s.

As important as the representation of the French monarchy was in the *tragédie lyrique,* Quinault and Lully's main objective remained the representation of emotion, the creation of pleasing, instructive, and moving spectacle. The choice of subjects from classical mythology was natural in

---

[37] See Néraudau, *Olympe* 232 for a description of the mythological décor of some of Louis's private rooms, which also date from 1684.

1673, when Racinian tragedy dominated the stage and when it was impossible to avoid having a tragedy compared to the great works of classical antiquity. Opera began as an effort to recreate the effects of Greek
tragedy and music, and Quinault and Lully certainly understood their task
to be in the same tradition. Eleven years later, the *tragédie lyrique* was
firmly established, and they had shown that they could be successful in a
variety of formats.[38] It almost seems natural now, with hindsight, that this
particularly French art form, the darling of the Moderns, should try taking
its subjects from a tradition closer to home in place and in time.

---

[38] See Couvreur, *Lully* 351: "En 1673, pour prouver que la tragédie en musique était
un grand genre et qu'elle était une reconstitution des spectacles antiques, Quinault et
Lully avaient jugé indispensable de recourir à l'Antiquité. Lorsqu'ils écrivirent *Amadis*
en 1684, la France avait pris conscience de son originalité et de la qualité de ses ar-
tistes."

11

Roland

Women, Madness, and Music

- I -

I POINTED OUT IN THE PREVIOUS CHAPTER (pp. 291-300) that although *Amadis* (1684) is the first Quinault-Lully opera with a subject taken from chivalric romance rather than classical mythology, it remains in many ways similar to their earlier works. Love, glory, and heroism remain paramount and reconcilable, and it is in the following year's opera, *Roland*, that we find another new direction, one that Quinault would continue to explore in *Armide* (1686). Indeed, since the latter is Quinault's last libretto and, for most critics, his best, it is tempting to see *Roland* as a crucial step that brings the early *tragédie lyrique* close to a kind of perfection. While such a teleological view is of course deceptive, *Roland* is one of Quinault and Lully's most important works, both in itself and as a transitional work between *Amadis* and *Armide*.

To put it briefly, *Roland* represents a new direction because the hero does not marry the princess; in fact, the princess—or Queen, in this case—is not even interested, and Roland's love for the beautiful Angélique, far from inspiring him to perform glorious deeds, as it had done for the eponymous heroes of *Persée* and *Amadis*, is seen as something that keeps him from carrying out his duty and thus from his *gloire*. There are several reasons for this new direction, and several important effects on the content and form of the libretto, but first it is important to look more closely at how Quinault adapted the well-known legend of Roland and at the public's initial reactions.

§ § §

It is possible that Louis XIV chose the subject of *Roland,* as he did for *Amadis* and *Armide.*[1] Whoever chose it, the choice is hardly surprising—no work of romance was more popular than Ariosto's *Orlando furioso,* no episode better known than Roland's madness when he discovers that Angélique prefers the lowly Médor. A great hero, a beautiful queen who is hopelessly in love, a pastoral setting, a mad scene, and the opportune intervention of a powerful fairy—what more could a librettist want? Given the increasing danger of foreign war and the tendency of Louis XIV—and thus of his court—to lead a more restrained life and to devote less time and money to elaborate entertainment, a librettist could also want a subject that featured a hero who put duty to his country above personal pleasure. Quinault will keep most of the features that made his earlier libretti so successful but he will also, in a manner of speaking, change his tune. No longer do his characters sing the praises of love; the prologue begins with a celebration of peace and the hope that "[...] nous verrons naître / De tendres Amours!" (24-25) but concludes on a different note:

> C'est l'Amour qui nous menace;
> Que de cœurs sont en danger!
> Quelques maux que l'Amour fasse,
> On ne peut s'en dégager. (P.52-55)

It must have come as a surprise to many spectators and readers, after the almost constant praise of love in his first nine libretti, that Quinault would announce his next subject in these words:

> Du célèbre Roland renouvelons l'histoire.
> La France lui donna le jour.

---

[1] Gros, *Quinault* 150-51. Parfaict says Roland was composed "pour le roy et par son ordre" (*Académie Royale* 185).

Montrons les erreurs où l'Amour
Peut engager un cœur qui néglige la Gloire. (P.37-40)

This new orientation is clear in Quinault's adaptation of Ariosto's long poem. For the first four acts, he followed his source fairly closely (especially cantos XIX, XXIII, XXIV, XXX, XXXIX): Angélique who heals Médor and then falls in love with him, her rejection of Roland, the magic ring that allows her to become invisible, the fountains of Love and Hate, the grotto in which Roland reads the happiness of the newly wedded couple written on the walls, the shepherds, and Roland's madness. The last act, however, is of Quinault's own creation. He certainly could not, in a brief libretto, include all of Roland's mad wanderings (cantos XXIX-XXX), nor Astolphe's long journey to the moon to recover Roland's reason (canto XXXIV), but his conclusion adds a strong dose of patriotism and restraint that he did not find in Ariosto:

Sauvez votre pays d'une guerre cruelle.

Ne suivez plus l'Amour; c'est un guide infidèle.

Non, n'oubliez jamais

Les maux que l'Amour vous a faits. (V.iv.1035-38)

§ § §

The new opera was a success, in spite of the King's declining interest. The premiere of *Roland* was January 8, 1685 at Versailles, in a theater set up in the *salle de manège,* without machines. Performances continued through March 3, but were given only once a week, whereas ten years earlier Louis would see a new opera three times a week. According to the journal of the Marquis de Sourches, "ce n'étoit pas que celui-là fût moins beau que les autres, mais le roi déclara que ces sortes de spectacles l'ennuyoient, quand il les voyoit représenter si souvent" (1: 168).[2]

---

[2] The "si souvent" is extremely important here. Louis was not tired of opera in general, and the *Mercure* reports that on March 5 he attended the first performance of *Amadis* at court. He wanted to see the work that he had been unable to see the previous year, when he was in mourning for the death of Marie-Thérèse (see chap. 10, *Amadis,* 281). Dufourcq (10) gives this quote under the misleading date of Jan. 5, 1685.

The Paris premiere followed almost immediately, since the public was eager to see the new work, especially with the decors and machines by Berain that gave "un nouvel éclat à cet Opera."[3] *Roland* was still being performed in November, when the haute-contre Duménil, who was playing the role of Médor, left the company temporarily. Performances were resumed when Duménil returned in January 1686 and continued until the premiere of *Armide* on February 15.[4] Even this immensely successful opera did not cool the enthusiasm for *Roland,* which was revived in late 1686.[5]

The fourth act was greatly admired, especially the tight integration of the *divertissement* with the main action.[6] Roland, full of "noirs soupçons" (IV.ii.770) after reading the inscriptions that Angélique and Médor have left on the walls of the grotto, goes to look for Angélique in the village where he hears the shepherds singing and dancing. The third scene at first appears to be no more than an excuse for singing and dancing, but then Coridon and Bélise begin to sing of Angélique and Médor, who have recently celebrated their marriage with these same shepherds. When Roland sees that Angélique has thanked them with a gift of the bracelet he had had presented to her in the *divertissement* of the first act, he can stand it no longer and lapses into madness. The famous mad scene follows, with some of Lully's most remarkable music.[7]

---

[3] *Mercure,* March 1685, 228. The account in the *Mercure* specifies March 8 as the first performance, though some authorities prefer March 9, when the Dauphin saw a performance.

[4] Parfaict, *Académie Royale* 190-91. The *Mercure* of January 1686, p. 284, mentions Duménil's return.

[5] There were also special performances in 1690 and 1691, as well as reprises at the Académie Royale in 1705, 1716, 1718, 1727-28, 1729, 1743, and 1755-56. Quinault's libretto was revised by Marmontel in 1778 for new music by Piccini.

[6] Parfaict, *Académie Royale* 185: "son quatrieme acte, ou il se surpasse dans l'interest qu'il a sçu y répandre et l'art du Divertissement qui fait corps de la pièce." Lecerf (2: 326) sides with the "peuple" who greatly admired "le desespoir de Roland," although the "savants" found it inferior to the "profondes beautez du rôle de Logistile."

[7] In general, the score of *Roland* contains some of Lully's best music, more than enough to offset the criticisms of the libretto that are discussed below, some of which are quite justifiable. Although Gros says (*Quinault* 154, n. 1) that Lecerf never mentions an air from *Roland* as having been a success with the public, the latter chose Angélique's "Je ne verrai plus ce que j'aime" (I.v) as his example of "un beau chant de Lulli" (*Réponse à la défense du parallèle,* appended to volume 3 of the *Comparaison,* p. 52); see also 2: 326. Beaussant calls Roland's monologue in IV.ii "la page la plus forte et la

The new opera was not without its critics, however. Boscheron's
Vie mentions several:

> Malgré un grand nombre de beaux morceaux, dont est composé cet
> Opéra, & quoiqu'il ait passé pour être assez régulier, quelques Cri-
> tiques n'ont pas laissé de dire qu'Angélique est trop souvent sur la
> Scene avec Médor; que Roland n'y paroît pas assez, & que la fureur de
> ce Héros devroit être employée à quelque chose de plus grand qu'à
> déraciner des arbres, à renverser des vases & à tirer son épée contre
> des figures inanimées, à qui il a tort de s'en prendre du malheureux
> amour qui lui fait tourner la cervelle.[8]

It is true that Roland is present in only two of the seventeen scenes of the
first three acts, but this is due in large part to the rather unusual structure
of the libretto, which I will discuss in more detail below. Roland is present in eight of the ten scenes of the last two acts, and, as Gros says (*Quinault* 630), it is clear at least as early as the second act that, as the title
suggests, Roland is the principal center of attention. As to the criticism
that his *fureur* should be "employed" in some nobler cause, one can easily
argue that, first, he is taking out his fury on whatever he can find and,
second, he seems even more desperate and pathetic precisely because he
is attacking objects he would not attack in his normal state.

The most frequent criticism was that the last act was superfluous,
that the action was over at the end of act IV.[9] This view ignores not only
the question of whether Roland will recover his sanity, which would seem
to be an essential part of the action, but also the emotional effect of

plus dense" in all of Lully's operas (675); see pp. 670-73 for his examples of the effective and moving music of the first act. Prunières (*Lully* 61) says Lully thought *Roland*
was his best work.

[8] P. 53. Parfaict (*Académie Royale* 186), which is perhaps following this biography,
says that *Roland* was well received at court except for the fact that Angélique and Médor
were on stage too often and Roland not enough. Clément and Laporte's *Dictionnaire
dramatique* repeats these criticisms and adds an amusing sonnet making fun of the opera, including a comment on the powers of music that I mention near the end of this
chapter (p. 321): "[Roland] va dans des Hameaux faire le Capitan; / Puis un doux
menuet lui remet la cervelle" (3: 70-71).

[9] See Parfaict, *Académie Royale* 185. It was not uncommon for spectators to leave
before the end of a play or opera. See page 291 and chapter 5 (*Atys*), 168-69.

celebration after depression and madness, the suggestions about the power of the arts, and the moral message of the opera, a message that was clearly important to the success of the work at court. Perhaps Parisian audiences were less inclined to give up the pleasures of love than was the king, were more interested in a love story than in a rather blatant appeal to duty and patriotism. A closer look at the structure of the libretto will be helpful in understanding the place of this last act in the overall framework of the opera and, more generally, the relevance of several of the criticisms I have mentioned. It will also be helpful in understanding the role of Angélique, which will be the main topic of section 2.

§ § §

From the point of view of the plot and the characters, the five acts of the libretto of *Roland* are divided into three distinct sections of unequal length:

> **Acts I-III**: The love between Angélique and Médor,
>   which is threatened by Roland.
> **Act IV**: Roland, the shepherds. Roland's madness.
> **Act V**: Logistille helps Roland recover his reason.

Or, and perhaps more neatly, one could see the first three acts as concentrated on Angélique and the last two on Roland. He is rarely present in the first three, and she and Médor are completely absent from the last two. The fourth act introduces Coridon, Bélise, Tersandre, and the other shepherds, who at first appear to be incidental participants in the *divertissement* but who quickly begin to play an important role in the action. Logistille appears only in the last act, the only act with supernatural and allegorical characters—troupes of fairies and heroes, la Gloire, la Renommée, and la Terreur.

This last act can be seen as forming the second part of a framework established by the prologue, which also features an important fairy and a chorus of supernatural beings—Démogorgon has the first word, Logistille the last. Louis XIV's victories have brought peace, a time for love and pleasure for Démogorgon and his followers but, at the same time, an occasion to recall the story of Roland and the misfortunes he endured because love caused him to neglect his *gloire* (P.39-40). The same chorus of fairies that was looking forward to "tendres Amours" (P.25) now sings of "l'Amour qui nous menace" (P.52, 58). It is no more a renunciation of love than are the similar verses in several other operas that evoke love's dangers along with its pleasures,[10] but it is a statement about priorities. Roland can serve only one mistress, and glory has its own charms:

> Roland, courez aux armes.
> Que la Gloire a de charmes! (V.iii.1031-32)[11]

The first four acts contain neither supernatural characters nor their moralizing. The action is unusually concentrated, as Quinault, for the first time, builds his plot around only three principal characters (Angélique, Médor, Roland). In his previous libretti, there were at least four characters with important roles: either two couples (*Thésée, Isis, Phaéton, Amadis*) or a couple whose happiness was threatened by at least two other characters (*Cadmus et Hermione, Alceste, Atys, Persée*).[12] Here, the action develops according to the decisions and reactions of the three characters, who are motivated by emotional and psychological reasons on a purely human level. There will be no unexpected arrivals, no surprising news; one of the three characters either enters or leaves, and the audience immediately understands what the reaction of the two other characters will be.

For example, in act I Angélique speaks, first alone and then with Témire, her confidante, of her love for Médor, a love that her "fierté"

---

[10] See, for example, *Alceste* I.vii.203-07; *Thésée* IV.vii.979 and V.vi.1101-02; *Phaéton* I.ii.38; *Armide* V.ii.653-54.

[11] I cannot agree with Couvreur ("le paladin vainc sa passion pour Angélique comme Louis vainc celle qu'il a pour la guerre," *Lully* 395). It is true that the prologue extols the virtues of peace, but the call to arms of act V would be an unusual way to convince Louis that he should give up his passion for war.

[12] *Armide* will be even more concentrated, with only two characters—Armide and Renaud—that one could consider principal. *Proserpine* is difficult to categorize, since there is no male-female couple who shares a reciprocal love. In *Cadmus et Hermione*, *Alceste*, and *Thésée*, characters that one could call secondary have quite important roles. See Gros, *Quinault* 604, n. 2, where he correctly points out that the need to create roles for the principal singers in the troupe often left Quinault little choice as to the number of characters in his libretto.

should overcome (i-ii). Médor appears and Angélique conceals herself to listen to him (iii). Then she speaks to him, only to tell him to leave (iv), and in the following scene is no more sure of herself than in the first scene. She is interrupted by the arrival of Ziliante with the bracelet Roland has sent her as a gift (vi).

The organization of each of the first three acts is remarkably similar. In the first scene of the second act, Angélique is speaking to her confidante about Médor, as in the first act. In the next scene Roland, the other man in her life, appears, and she again hides. After another conversation with Témire, the fourth scene of the act is again devoted to a conversation between Angélique and Médor. This time she does not send him away but, instead, admits her love for him; the structural function of the scene, however, is the same as in the first act—the two lovers talk of their future. The act concludes with another *divertissement* that interrupts their conversation.

The third act is not very different. It opens once again with Témire, who this time is talking to Médor. Then Roland talks to Angélique (ii, as in II.ii, although in II.ii she disappears without answering) while Médor listens to them. The act ends once more with a conversation between Angélique and Médor and a *divertissement,* but this time it is not an interruption of their love but a celebration of it. Their story is over, except for the wedding and its consummation in the grotto, which we will hear about in act IV.

This thrice-repeated structure, which very neatly brings Angélique and Médor from despair to happiness, would seem to leave little room for Roland. He only appears in two scenes, but he is the subject of conversation of seven of the remaining eleven scenes (excluding the *divertissements*) of acts I-III. His presence is implicit from the beginning, since Angélique is always aware that he is the obvious husband for her, and Médor is well aware of his rival. The only scene in which he speaks to Angélique (III.ii, at the center of the libretto) is of great importance, for it is Angélique's pretense of love for Roland that not only allows her to be rid of him but prepares him for his jealous rage and madness in the following act. Her pretended love for Roland at the same time protects Médor and drives him to despair (he is listening), setting up the tender scene that follows. The die is cast, and Angélique and Médor leave the stage to Roland. It is an unusual but effective means of setting up the act that every spectator was waiting for: "Roland furieux."[13] Furthermore, it is only fitting that this act be separate from the first three, in order to isolate Roland's madness in a solitude that is all the more unbearable because it was recently inhabited by Angélique and his happy rival. After a celebration of love that recalls the end of *Amadis,* which Beaussant calls "l'apothéose des parfaits amants," comes "la proclamation de la solitude du héros" (687).

The fourth act stands by itself, long enough to constitute a separate section between the first three acts and the last (which is "reinforced" by its connection with the prologue).[14] Roland is indeed isolated, able to be part of neither the world of Angélique and Médor nor of that of the shepherds. Quinault's libretto, with its separate sections through which Roland seems to wander, with its numerous parallel scenes,[15] presents a complex view of love and human relationships. It is one of his longest libretti, approximately 20 percent longer than *Amadis* and 35 percent longer than *Armide,* one that juxtaposes many points of view while suggesting a framework that can contain them all.

---

[13] The simple title of *Roland* was probably chosen not only in keeping with the titles of Quinault's other libretti but also to avoid confusion with Ariosto's masterpiece. By deemphasizing Roland's madness, Quinault leaves room for the moral message of the last act.

[14] The fourth act, as one would expect from an act that is juxtaposed to the first three taken as a whole, is particularly long (288 lines). Only act II of *Proserpine* (292 lines) is longer.

[15] In addition to the examples of parallel passages from the first three acts and from the opening and closing sections (prologue, act V), one could include the grotto that is occupied first by Angélique and Médor, then by Roland (IV.ii), the two fountains (II.i.229-36), and the two weddings (Angélique and Médor, Bélise and Coridon).

- II -

One key to understanding *Roland,* and one of its most interesting and unusual features, is the character of Angélique. She clearly dominates the first three acts and, although absent, can be said to be at the origin of most of the action in the fourth. In fact, she is the only woman in Quinault's libretti who can dominate a situation without being either a goddess or a magician. (She does have the magic ring that makes her invisible, but she uses it to avoid unpleasant situations rather than to change the course of events.) She is a powerful queen, loved and obeyed by her subjects. She has complete power over Médor, whom she has nursed back to health and plans to marry. She manipulates Roland, aware of his strengths and weaknesses. She organizes the three spectacles that make up the *divertissements* of acts I-III and is very much present in the thoughts of Roland and of the shepherds who celebrate her *grandeurs* and her *appas* in the *divertissement* of act IV.

When Roland goes mad, it is ostensibly because he has been rejected by Angélique, who prefers the lowly Sarasin Médor to the greatest of the Paladins. However, Roland is also mad—angry, frustrated, insane—because he cannot control the situation.[16] After all, he is the greatest of warriors, the greatest of heroes. Yet it takes him three acts to find Angélique (she disappears when he arrives in II.ii); and when he does finally talk to her (III.ii), she fools him completely. His wrath is to be feared, but she knows how to avoid it—she sends him to the Fountain of Love in order to get him out of the way so she and Médor can escape.[17] He is too enamored to listen to Astolphe's good advice (IV.i), and he is reduced to learning the truth about Angélique and Médor from some shepherds. Their comments on his impressive appearance ("Aisément on devine / Qu'il sort d'une illustre origine," IV.v.891-92) underline the incongruity of the situation: an armed and richly dressed knight listens to some pastoral songs that would normally have nothing to do with his own

---

[16] It must have been the reaction of some spectators that Roland was especially frustrated because he had been outsmarted by a woman. As modern opera-lovers are well aware, it is almost always the woman who is the victim of powers beyond her control and who has the mad scene (see Clément).

[17] This is more clear in the stage directions following act III scene v than it is in the text.

situation. But here two genres with incompatible values are brought together, the epic meets the pastoral, and the result—for Roland, but not for
the spectator—is madness.

Roland is certainly not used to finding out about key events in his
life from shepherds he happens to meet. Nor is he used to being rejected.
Clearly, in his mind, Angélique *should* love him, and no one else.[18] She is
the beautiful queen that so many men find attractive, he is a man of "rare
valeur" and of "amour extrême" (I.ii.23), a "guerrier invincible" who
abandons all, including his king and his army, for her (II.i.257; II.ii.280-
87). It had probably never occurred to him that Angélique would not love
him in return; he has covered himself with glory for her sake, sent her
fabulous presents born by conquered kings, and now he has come to
claim what he considers his reward ("[...] je touche à l'heureux moment /
Où je dois recevoir le prix de tant de peines," IV.i.706-07). Instead, she
avoids him, then sends him off to wait in vain, until he learns what everyone else in the countryside already knows.[19] He must feel hopelessly out
of control, that is, mad.

From a *galant* point of view, Roland loves badly, much like the
modern lovers of whom Deshoulières complained in her Ballade "On
n'aime plus comme on aimoit jadis," that is, in "le siècle d'Amadis" (see
chap. 10, 296). He expects to "win" Angélique thanks to his heroic deeds,
and indeed, earlier heroes of Quinault-Lully operas, such as Persée, did
just that. The princess seemed to love the hero "naturally," whereas here
Angélique does things in quite a different way. She falls in love with a
man who is far beneath her in rank and who owes his life to her; he is
obviously someone she can control, who must play the game of love according to her rules.

This is certainly a viable type of relation between the sexes—one
thinks, for example, of the rules of love imposed by the *Précieuses* on
their suitors—even if it was, as Deshoulières complains, somewhat out of
fashion in 1685. It is not out of fashion for Roland however, perhaps

---

[18] See Couvreur, *Lully* 366: "Se considérant, à juste titre, comme le plus glorieux de
tous les chevalier chrétiens, [Roland] ne conçoit pas que la reine de Cathay puisse
s'éprendre de quelqu'un d'autre que de lui."
[19] Parfaict (*Académie Royale* 184) criticizes Quinault's "faute de jugement" here.
Since Angélique, at the end of act III, has announced to the people her choice of Médor
as king, "Roland qui la cherche de tous cotés, peut-il ignorer un pareil événement?"

because of his temperament, certainly because of his role in society. He is not used to being subservient, neither to a woman nor even, in some situations at least, to his king, whom he has left "sans appui" (II.ii.280; see IV.i.686-90) to pursue Angélique. The resulting conflict between his personal and social (professional) life is at the heart of what one could construe as the moral message of *Roland*—he is not wrong to love, but he is wrong to love as he does, since he is neglecting his duty for love. In fact, he has gone astray in two ways: his kind of love has not gained him a place in Angélique's heart and his love has taken him away from his place in the king's army. He is truly isolated, out of his element.

Roland is wrong to love as he does, but neither Quinault's libretto nor Lully's music can be said to condemn love. There is no criticism of the love between Angélique and Médor (except from Roland), nor of that between Bélise and Coridon. As in the prologue (see above, pp. 306, 311), some characters can sing of "tendres amours" while others complain of love's dangers. These dangers are particularly strong for a character in a position such as that of Roland, who can afford neither to devote all his energies to pleasing his beloved nor to live simply in pastoral bliss. For him, the public must take precedence over the private, and he is excluded from many of the traditional domestic joys and from the pleasures of passionate love.

The idea of separation is present from the beginning of the libretto to the end.[20] Characters hide or avoid each other, lie and hide their true feelings. They distance themselves from their duty and their reason (Roland, a true "aliéné," both mad and alienated), from their *fierté* (Angélique), from their country (Médor). To take but a few examples:

Angélique hides from Roland, then lies to him (II.ii, III.ii).
Angélique orders Médor to leave (I.iv).
Angélique sends Roland away from the port from which she plans
    to embark (III.v).

---

[20] The French words *écart* and *écarté* (II.ii.530, V.iii.1020) suggest not only separation and distancing but also straying from the beaten path. This latter meaning is that applied to one of the most famous of all the opera heroines who are forced to give in to the male-dominated world, Violetta in Verdi's *La Traviata* (see Clément and below, p. 322).

Médor hides to eavesdrop on the conversation between Angélique
    and Roland (III.ii).

Roland abandons (temporarily) his king, his duty, his reason (I-
    IV).

Roland hopes to spend time with Angélique "en des lieux écartés"
    (II.ii.530).

Roland wants to hide his shame (V.iii.1017-22).

Isolation, that of the title character in particular, is characterized by an
important constellation of words that one finds more frequently in *Roland*
than in any of Quinault's other libretti. *Distance* appears only here
(I.iii.66), along with 50 percent of the occurrences of *lointain*, 31 percent
of *loin*, 29 percent of *éloigner* and 17 percent of *séparer* (one would expect about 10 percent, given the length of *Roland*).

    Such distances exist only in opposition to an obvious presence,
and the vocabulary reflects numerous oppositions, especially those between love and duty, happiness and despair, reason and madness. The
overall—for almost everyone except Roland—positive view of love described above is dominant: *amour* appears eighty-five times in the prologue and five acts (not counting occurrences in lines that are repeated),
gloire only twenty-one, *devoir* (as a noun) only once. Only a small percentage of the occurrences of *amour* are in a pejorative context, and
heureux is three times more frequent than *malheureux*, *bonheur* five times
more than *malheur*. Adjectives such as *beau*, *doux*, and *charmant* are
more frequent than *cruel* and *vain*. Still, whereas there are few words
with negative connotations that appear more than ten times,[21] there is an
important group of words such as *tourment*, *peine*, *funeste*, *fatal*, and
désespoir that occur between seven and nine times. The pleasures of love
dominate, but hardly reign uncontested.

    These oppositions can be seen as part of a more general one be-
tween agitation and repose.[22] The first instance of this opposition comes

---

[21] There are no nouns with negative connotations that occur more than ten times; the
adjective *cruel* occurs fourteen times, *malheureux* twelve.

[22] The word *repos* represents an important, polyvalent concept in seventeenth-
century French literature, crucial, for example, to Pascal's view of the human condition
and to the conclusion to Lafayette's *La Princesse de Clèves*, to which I will return in the
final paragraph of this chapter; see Stanton.

early in the prologue, where Louis XIV has established peace after the "fureurs affreuses" (P.7) of war and punished his enemies "en les condamnant au repos" (P.12). This *repos* is immediately seen as an occasion to enjoy the pleasures of love (P.17-32), but also to sing of "[...] les erreurs où l'Amour / Peut engager un cœur qui néglige la Gloire" (P.39-40) before closing with the *repos* that "Le Vainqueur" has brought to the world. Roland thinks he has found *repos* in the fourth act, since Angélique has promised to satisfy his desire; his illusion is quickly shattered, however, beginning with the writing on the wall in the grotto: "quelque envieux a voulu, par ces mots, / Noircir l'objet que j'aime et troubler mon repos" (IV.ii.765-66). For Astolphe, however, this *repos* is "honteux" (IV.i.699), and it will require all the skill and magic of Logistille in the last act to restore Roland's "parfait repos" (V.i.964).[23] Louis guarantees *repos* and peace, which is a time for love for some people but not for heroes like Roland; for them, love leads to a lack of heroic activity and thus to shame, and the *repos* that must be restored to such heroes is not what charms the chorus in the prologue or the shepherds in act IV—love is not a "parfait repos."

§ § §

A situation characterized by an opposition between agitation and rest, between love and heroism, with a cast of characters that include peasants as well as knights and queens, is ideal for a *tragédie lyrique* that often isolates the praise of love in the *divertissement* of each act while reserving the more heroic action for the other scenes. Before *Roland*, or rather before the fourth act of *Roland*, the particular love being praised was usually that of the characters in the same act. *Roland* follows that model for the first three acts, only to combine in one remarkable act the evocation of the happy moments enjoyed by Médor and Angélique, the anticipated bliss of Coridon and Bélise (who has never heard of the sufferings of love; IV.v.908-09), and the unrequited love of Roland, which

---

[23] This *repos* is "sa première paix," a peace "bannie" by love (V.ii.985), something to recover, not to discover. When Roland regains his reason, he is immediately conscious of the "désordre où l'Amour avait réduit [s]on âme" (V.iii.1013), as if his madness were a sort of parallel life that he can observe.

quickly goes from false hope to jealousy to madness. In the midst of these moments of past and future happiness, Roland suffers. As a hero from the epic tradition, he is ultimately out of place in a pastoral setting, as he is in a love triangle where the other two participants are relatively free from the call of duty and honor (Angélique is a powerful queen, apparently with few responsibilities, and Médor is basically an orphan). Yet, in this act where the *divertissement* is as tightly integrated with the action as one could wish, the epic and pastoral traditions coexist remarkably well in the rather rarefied world of the *tragédie lyrique*.

Quinault has done much more than just build an act that works well on an esthetic level and creates a background for the mandatory mad scene. In placing this fourth act between the love story of the first three acts (what could have been a complete opera in itself, if Roland had been a generic villain, such as Draco in *Cadmus et Hermione,* instead of a well-known hero) and the return to duty of the last act, he has given us a glimpse of the workings of three of the most important strata of seventeenth-century French society: the salons, rural villages, and the court. The subject of the first three acts could be from a Scudéry novel or a *précieux* debate (should a woman follow her passion and marry beneath her station?). The fourth is hardly a true portrait of rural life, but its village *fête* and happy peasants eager to please wandering nobles reflect the way many aristocrats must have liked to imagine life in the country. The last act, with its "Troupe d'Ombres d'anciens Héros" and its allegorical characters (La Gloire, La Terreur, La Renommée) and its emphasis on duty to king and country, is evocative of Versailles, with its paintings featuring heroic and allegorical subjects. The salons and the country are forgotten as Roland prepares for battle, thus bringing the opera back to the moment just before it began, the wars that brought peace and *repos*. The notion that war serves to bring peace, like the image of these three different worlds coexisting in such harmony, is certainly as idealized as that of the happy peasant, but it is appropriate for a work that had to please audiences at court as well as in Paris.

§ § §

In short, the opera, in the best classical tradition, pleases as well as instructs. No one would deny that the pleasure usually outweighs the instruction,[24] and most spectators look at *Roland* the way Angélique looked at Médor, or the way Rodrigue looked at Chimène.[25] They listen to the lessons about duty, glory, and morality, consider following *Fierté* rather than *Amour* (I.i.2), but eventually give in to the pleasures of love, and of music and poetry. From this point of view, the hero of *Roland* is not Roland, but Médor. Ariosto understood the power of the sympathy and pity that youth and beauty can evoke; Zerbino is about to kill Medoro, but he glances at the young mans's face: "Ma come gli occhi a quel bel volto mise, / Gli ne venne pietade, e non l'uccise." Médor begs for pity:

> Cosí dicea Medor con modi belli,
> E con parole atte a voltare un monte;
> E sí commosso già Zerbino avea,
> Che d'amor tutto e di pietade ardea.[26] (Canto XIX, st. 10, 12)

Angélique will have a similar reaction: she should follow her *fierté* and love Roland, but she only has eyes for Médor.

Boileau and other Ancients said the same thing of their contemporaries: they should prefer spoken tragedy, but they only have eyes—and ears—for opera. La Fontaine, who described this passion as "Hiver, été, printemps, bref, opéra toujours" ("A M. de Niert," *O.D.* 619), thought tragedy and opera should be distinct genres. Lully found his libretto

---

[24] May suggests that we should not take too seriously the claims of other genres to be primarily instructive (179-91) and that during the end of the reign of Louis XIV there was a "véritable doctrine [...] plaçant le plaisir au centre même de la création littéraire" (190-91).

[25] "En vain contre le Cid un ministre se ligue: / Tout Paris pour Chimène a les yeux de Rodrigue" (Boileau, *Satire* IX, 231-32).

[26]
> But as his eyes that beauteous face survey,
> Takes pity on the boy, and does not slay.
> [...]
> Medoro thus his suit with grace, preferred
> And words—to move a mountain; and so won
> Upon Zerbino's mood, to kindness turned,
> With love and pity he all over burned.

This scene, in which an emotional reaction keeps someone from killing his or her enemy, recalls *Amadis* III.iv and *Armide* II.v; see chapter 10 (*Amadis*), 290.

(*Daphné;* see chap. 4, *Thésée,* 128-29) too much in the pastoral vein, however, and one can find in the denouement of *Roland* a strong argument for this special mixture of tragedy and pastoral that is the *tragédie lyrique*.[27] When Logistille cures Roland, restores him to "parfait repos," it is "Par le secours d'une douce harmonie," by having the fairies dance, and by evoking "les Ombres des anciens Héros" (V.ii., line 982 and stage directions). That is, Roland becomes a spectator at a miniature opera, containing music ("harmonie"), dance, and heroic action, just as Angélique beheld the tender, touching charms of Médor. The shepherds of the pastoral tried to cure Roland but were not successful. One can almost hear Lully savoring his victory over Perrin and his pastorals that inaugurated his Académie Royale de Musique. Only the *tragédie lyrique* can restore Roland's reason, only the *tragédie lyrique* is a worthy spectacle for the glory years of the reign of Louis XIV.

If the hero is worthy of being cured by the spectacle created by Quinault and Lully, we should not forget that Angélique found Médor worthy of being cured. One is heroic and covered with glory, the other is touching and lovable; one follows (eventually) the moral paths of duty, the other the pleasures of love. For the typical spectator (if not for Roland) both can coexist, and the *divertissement* of act III considers Médor a hero in his own right:

> Heureux Médor! quelle gloire
> D'avoir remporté
> Une entière victoire
> Sur tant de fierté! (III.vi.626-29)

Angélique has not been able to control her emotions, but she has nevertheless been in overall control of the situation. Like the spectator of the *tragédie lyrique,* and in accordance with Aristotelian catharsis, she has fulfilled her emotional needs without losing control.

§ § §

---

[27] I suggested a similar argument for act III of *Isis;* see section 2 of chapter 6.

When I say that Angélique has been in overall control of the situation, I am not forgetting that she is absent from the final two acts. Her presence is very much felt in act IV (she is mentioned nine times), where things have gone exactly as she planned, but act V is devoted to causing Roland to forget her and to return to his *devoir,* to being the kind of person he should be. On a more global level, this return is a return to a world where things are as the powers that be think they should be and, in particular, where men are in control. A situation with a woman in control has led to madness and the structure of *Roland,* in which the last act is so different from the first four, seems designed to restore a situation in which masculine values are dominant. The first four acts constituted for Roland and, we can infer, for most male spectators, an embarrassing spectacle ("J'ai fait de ma faiblesse un spectacle odieux," V.iii.1015). In this last act, it is time for him to regain control of his life and to render valuable service to his country ("Sauvez votre pays d'une guerre cruelle," V.iv.1035).

This return to the patriarchal status quo does not negate the example of Angélique, nor of seventeenth-century women who, like Mme de Clèves in Lafayette's novel, were beginning to establish some control of their lives in a society in which women had few rights.[28] It does underscore the difficulty of such an effort, however, as does Quinault's next (and last) libretto, *Armide,* which features an even stronger woman. Armide leads the country in which the action takes place (Angélique is queen of Cathay, i.e., China), defeats the invading army, refuses to marry, and causes the great hero Renaud to fall in love with her and to neglect his duty. Seen from the seat of power, this is going much too far, and it should come as no surprise that Armide suffers a spectacular downfall at the end of the opera. It is hard not to see in this last libretto an example of what Clément calls "la défaite des femmes," but the portrait of Angélique

---

[28] For Stanton, *repos* "marks the triumph of lucidity over blindness, of order over disorder" (103). A comparison of the situations of Mme de Clèves and Roland is indicative of the complexity of this concept: both recover *repos,* which is opposed, along with *devoir,* to love, but Mme de Clèves's decision can be read as a rejection of the values of the patriarchal society that are praised in the final scenes of *Roland.* On Lafayette, see also DeJean, "Lafayette's Ellipses." Beasley and DeJean (*Tender Geographies*) describe the efforts of women novelists and memorialists to write new versions of history and new kinds of fiction. See Biet, "De la Veuve Joyeuse," on how some widows were able to control their own lives.

in *Roland* suggests that Quinault could at least envisage a situation that could be considered an improvement upon the present, just as he could suggest a need for peace in the midst of Louis's wars.[29]

---

[29] See chapter 1, 52-54, for a discussion of Quinault's "criticism" of Louis's wars in the prologues of some of his libretti. See section 2 of chapter 7 (*Proserpine*) for another treatment of sexual politics in a patriarchal world.

12

Armide

Charms and the Man

Si vous avez entendu Armide bien executé,
vous pouvez vous flâter d'avoir entendu le plus
beau morceau de Musique qui se soit fait depuis
quinze ou seize siecles.

[Act V of *Armide*] montre à merveilles combien
le Poëte contribuë à la sublime beauté ou à la
langueur d'un Opera, par la bonne ou mauvaise
consititution qu'il luy donne. (Lecerf 2: 10, 15)

Tout concacre cet Ouvrage à l'immortalité; tout
nous autorise à le proposer aux Poëtes du
Théâtre Lyrique comme un de ces points émi-
nens vers lesquels on doit toujours tendre,
même en désespérant d'y atteindre.
(*Mercure Galant*, Dec. 1761, p. 163)

- I -

EVEN IF ONE TAKES LECERF'S PRAISE of *Armide* with several grains of
salt—and perhaps one should not, since he makes these statements to
confirm his high opinion of this opera in response to his critics who had
suggested that he had praised it too highly in part 1 of his *Comparaison*—
his first statement is a good indication of the success of Quinault and

Lully's last opera. This success was both immediate and lasting. *Armide* ran from the premiere in Paris on February 15, 1686 until September, with further performances from December 1686 to March 1687; in fact, it is possible that performances continued throughout the period from February 1686 to March 1687, though in alternation with *Acis et Galatée* and *Roland* from September to December.[1] There were revivals in 1688, 1692, 1697, 1703, 1713-14, 1724-25, 1746 (with additional performances in early 1747 and 1748), and 1761-62 (with additional performances in 1764-65 and 1766).[2] Finally, perhaps the most impressive testimony to the widespread admiration for Quinault's last libretto came in 1777, when Gluck set it with only a small number of minor changes. Musical tastes had changed considerably (Rosow, "How Eighteenth-Century Parisians"), in large part due to Gluck's "reforms," but the new conception of opera could not acquire its *titres de noblesse* without coming to grips with the standard by which all libretti had to be judged.

Lully had reason to be disappointed, however, since he would never see *Armide* performed before Louis XIV. As he wrote in the Dedication to the 1686 edition of the score of *Armide,*

> De toutes les tragédies que j'ai mises en musique, voici celle dont le public a témoigné être le plus satisfait [...]. Cependant, c'est de tous les ouvrages que j'ai faits, celui que j'estime le moins heureux puisqu'il n'a point eu encore l'avantage de paraître devant Votre Majesté.

Lully appears to have planned for a performance at Versailles in early 1686, after performances of *Le Temple de la Paix* and *Le Ballet de la jeunesse;* after all, Louis had chosen the subject of Armide and Renaud,

---

[1] Parfaict (*Académie Royale* 208) says that performances of *Armide* continued until the death of Lully (March 1687) "avec un succès continuel"; a note by Beffara in his copy points out that there were some performances of *Acis et Galatée* (Lully's last complete opera, with text by Campistron) during this period. By May 30, 1686, the Dauphin (Monseigneur) had been to Paris at least nine times to see *Armide* (Dangeau 1: 296, 304, 311, 314, 315, 319, 325, 332, 342 and Sourches 1: 370). The Siamese ambassadors saw *Armide* on Dec. 20. They had also seen *Roland* at Versailles on Jan. 16, 1685 and *Acis et Galatée* on Sept. 24, 1686.

[2] Brooks and Yarrow ("Observations" 133-34) argue convincingly that Madame saw *Armide* on Jan. 13, 1705, even though the standard sources do not mention a revival in that year.

from Tasso's *Gerusalemme liberata,* himself.[3] However, *Le Temple de la Paix* was so popular during the court's residence at Fontainebleau in October and November 1685 that it received additional performances at Versailles in December 1685 and January 1686, which delayed the opening of the *Ballet de la jeunesse* until January 28.[4] Performances of the latter continued until February 25, by which time it was in alternation with *Endymion,* a *tragédie en musique* by Henry Desmarest.

This much is clear, but what happened between mid-January and mid-February 1686 is less so. The *Mercure* of January (284) says work is continuing on *Armide,* but Lully's Dedication says that, in spite of his illness, he finished the score "dans le temps que Votre Majesté le souhaitait." This would have been some time in January, probably before the 28th, but there was apparently an understanding that the *Ballet de la jeunesse* would be performed before the new opera. At that point (around the end of January), one of two things must have happened: either it was decided that waiting until after the performances of *Le Ballet de la jeunesse* would have meant a premiere of *Armide* at court too close to the end of Carnival (Mardi Gras was February 26), or Louis XIV's illness, from February 5 until some time in March, made a royal premiere during Carnival impossible. Lully's dedication suggests the second reason: "Votre Majesté ne s'est pas trouvée en état de les [ces nouveaux concerts] entendre," whereas the *Mercure* mentions only the first:

> Mr Quinault [...] estoit alors occupé par ordre du Roy à achever l'Opera d'*Armide* qui avoit esté commandé d'abord pour Versailles. Comme il n'a pû y estre representé, à cause de l'autre Divertissement

---

[3] See Dangeau's entry for May 16, 1685: "Quinault apporta au Roi chez Madame de Montespan trois livres d'Opéra pour cet hiver. L'un était *Malaric fils d'Hercule,* le second *Céphale et Procris,* le troisième *Armide et Renaud.* Le Roi les trouva tous trois à son gré et choisit celui d'*Armide.*" As Couvreur points out (*Lully,* 407-08), Quinault could be fairly sure that Louis would choose a subject involving Christian history. See Gros, *Quinault* 574-76, for details on Quinault's adaptation of Tasso, cantos IV, V, X (act I), XIV (acts II and IV), XV (act IV), and XVI (act V).

[4] *Le Temple de la paix* is a ballet by Quinault and Lully that premiered at Fontainebleau on Oct. 20, 1685, and at the Palais-Royal the following November. Another series of performances began at Versailles on Dec. 3 and continued until Jan. 21, 1686. According to the *Mercure* of Feb. 1686 (part 1, 312), original plans called for a brief run and for performances of the *Ballet de la jeunesse* (by Dancourt and Lalande) at Fontainebleau in December.

qu'on a commencé plus tard que l'on ne croyoit, il a paru à Paris dans
les derniers jours du Carnaval sur le Théatre Royal de Musique, avec
le succès qui suit tous ces grands Spectacles. (February, part 1, 295)

Since the *Mercure* of January—well before the king's illness—mentions
the expectation of Paris performances of the still unfinished *Armide* but
no performances at court, it seems likely that Lully's excuse of royal illness (nicely parallel to his own) was mostly wishful thinking.

We will probably never know the exact reasons for the cancella-
tion of the court premiere of *Armide,* which was apparently done at the
king's request (La Gorce, *Opéra* 75). The illnesses and scheduling problems were quite likely less important than the general mood at court, for,
even when concert versions of *Armide* were given at Versailles in the
spring of 1686, Louis apparently did not attend; he definitely did not
explicitly sponsor them.[5] The change from mythological to chivalric
subjects with *Amadis* in 1684 had suggested a change in the means of
projecting the royal image (see chap. 10, 301-02), and Mme de Maintenon seems to have convinced Louis not to spend excessive amounts of
time and money on such lavish theatrical entertainments. In fact, 1686
marks the end of large-scale operatic productions at Versailles (Gros,
Quinault 163).

This new direction at Versailles is also reflected in one of the
principal themes of *Armide,* a theme that it shares with *Roland,* produced
the year before: the dangers of love, especially when it comes into conflict with glory and duty. No longer can one say "Qui peut être contre
l'Amour / Quand il s'accorde avec la Gloire" (*Cadmus et Hermione*
I.vi.202-03). Love and glory are incompatible, and heroes are expected to
behave more like knights on a crusade than like adventurers pursuing love
and glory. The prologue to *Armide,* unlike most of the earlier ones,
downplays Louis's military accomplishments and emphasizes his "domestic policy," in particular the revocation of the Edict of Nantes on October 18, 1685, which marked the defeat of the Protestant "monster":

---

[5] La Gorce, *Opéra* 76. The first performance at Versailles, in a concert version, was
postponed from March 23 to March 30 because of the illness of the king, but there is no
indication that he attended the performance, which was organized by the Dauphine; see
Dangeau 1: 313 and 316. There were similar concerts April 29, May 13, and May 25.

> La Victoire a suivi ce Héros en tous lieux;
>
> Mais, pour montrer son amour pour la Gloire,
>
> Il se sert encor mieux
>
> De la Paix que de la Victoire.
>
> Au milieu du repos qu'il assure aux humains,
>
> Il fait tomber sous ses puissantes mains
>
> Un monstre qu'on a cru si longtemps invincible. (P.23-29)

The prologue leaves no room to doubt as to the "moral" of the story that is to follow:

> Nous y verrons Renaud, malgré la volupté,
>
> Suivre un conseil fidèle et sage;
>
> Nous le verrons sortir du Palais enchanté,
>
> Où, par l'amour d'Armide, il était arrêté,
>
> Et voler où la Gloire appelle son courage. (P.52-56)

and it ends with praise of a new combination, in which Wisdom replaces Love: "C'est à lui [Louis XIV] qu'il est réservé / D'unir la Sagesse et la Gloire" (P.66-67).[6]

It is almost too obvious that one can find additional clues about the circumstances surrounding the creation of *Armide* in the fact that it is Quinault's last libretto (see Beaussant, *Lully* 681). Writing for a king who was losing interest in opera, he suggested a subject that Louis could not refuse, that of a man who, after an infatuation with pleasure and diversion, returns to his duty—Renaud returns to Godefroi's camp and his military and religious duty, Quinault returns to his family and to religion, and Louis returns from extravagance and infidelity to his political and marital duty.[7]

---

[6] Karro ("Le Prologue d'*Armide*") proposes an interpretation of *Armide* as a celebration of Louis XIV's aspirations to establish a universal monarchy and, in particular, to conquer the Turks and the Protestants (Armide) and destroy their empire (Armide's palace).

[7] "Visiblement, l'œuvre avait été composée sous l'influence de Louis XIV ou, si l'on préfère, dans l'intention évidente de se conformer aux sentiments nouveaux et à l'attitude du roi" (Gros, *Quinault* 160). See also Couvreur, *Lully* 402: "Sa Majesté offre à ses peuples un divertissement auquel Elle vient de renoncer métaphoriquement."

This point of view quite probably reflects Quinault's thoughts at the time, even though it is dangerous to read *Armide* as an allegory of Quinault's career. By April 5, 1686, Quinault had asked for and received Louis's permission not to write any more libretti: "On sut que Quinault avait fait demander au Roi de le dispenser des Opéras, dans sa dernière maladie; il a eu des scrupules sur cela et Sa Majesté a trouvé bon qu'il n'en fît plus."[8] It is one thing, however, to draw conclusions about Quinault's career, and quite another to draw them about the esthetics of the *tragédie lyrique*. Unfortunately, it is all too easy to associate the two, and while it is true that, in many ways, with *Armide* the collaboration between Quinault and Lully reaches its zenith as it comes to an end, the fact that this is their last and their most respected opera does not mean that everything in *Armide* represents French baroque opera as it "should be."[9] In particular, the fact that much of *Armide* can be compared favorably to the best of classical French tragedy should not be taken as proof that the only valid criterion for judging opera is how close it comes to Racinian tragedy.

§ § §

Armide does share many elements with Racinian tragedy, such as clear structure, concentrated action, a minimum of exterior events that change the course of the action, and a heroine of considerable psychological interest. The elements of the *tragédie lyrique* that are usually considered incompatible with classical tragedy, such as the presence of the supernatural and the *divertissements,* with their dancing and elaborate

---

[8] Dangeau 1: 319. Quinault mentions having been seriously ill in two letters dated 1686 (La Gorce, "Proche collaborateur" 369). Boscheron's *Vie* suggests another reason for Quinault's retirement: "[...] je doute qu'il eût pu faire une Piece lyrique au-dessus de celle d'*Armide*. C'est peut-être cette raison qui l'engagea à ne plus travailler [...]" (56). The *Mercure* of Dec. 1761 (162) makes the same point. Similar arguments have been made about Racine's retirement from the theater after *Phèdre*. Clément and La Porte's *Anecdotes dramatiques* suggest that Quinault's retirement was due to his religious scruples or to the fact that Lully supposedly made him redo act V of *Armide* five times (1: 110).

[9] For example, see Gros, *Quinault* 632: *Armide* "est à la fois le terme vers lequel tendait sa conception de la tragédie lyrique et le couronnement de sa carrière de librettiste: autant dire qu'*Armide* est également le terme naturel de cette étude sur la structure de l'opéra: elle nous permettra d'en dégager la conclusion qui s'impose."

machinery, are especially well integrated into the overall context. And, last but certainly not least, Quinault's poetry paints a beautiful and moving picture of a fascinating heroine, a picture that is effective when read but even more so when heard in Lully's setting.

Quinault concentrated his tragedy on Armide and her emotions. The first act begins after her triumph over Godefroi's army of crusaders, emphasizing not the events but her reactions and feelings. In a scene that begins with the celebration of "un jour de triomphe," Armide's first line shows that her feelings do not reflect the exterior circumstances: "Je ne triomphe pas du plus vaillant de tous" (I.i.21). Much like Racine's Athalie, troubled by the young Joas, she can talk only of Renaud and of the dreams that have upset her.[10] Her two fairly long introspective speeches (I.i.21-29 and 38-56), which seem more like monologues than replies to her confidants Sidonie and Phénice, create an effective contrast with the latter's short, optimistic statements and questions.[11] Equally effective is Armide's brooding silence during the eighteen lines between Phénice's question in line two ("Qui peut vous inspirer une sombre tristesse?") and Armide's reply in line twenty-one.

Her obsession with Renaud continues in the second scene when, in reply to Hidraot's plea that she marry, she follows two fairly conventional excuses ("La chaîne de l'Hymen m'étonne," I.ii.78; "Mais je fais mon plus grand bonheur / D'être maîtresse de mon cœur," I.ii.93-94) with the real reason: she is waiting for the right man, one with *gloire* and *valeur*, such as "le vainqueur de Renaud" (I.ii.107-08). Furthermore, as Quinault suggests and as Lully brought out in one of the most famous

---

[10] This "songe affreux" is the first of several passages in *Armide* in which a situation is presented that will have a parallel later. Her dream represents a situation similar to that of her famous monologue in II.v, except that in the dream it is Renaud who wields the dagger. In both cases, she is "contrainte à le trouver aimable" (I.i.55). The most obvious example later in the opera is in act IV, where Ubalde and the Chevalier Danois resist charms—both magic and erotic—similar to those that have temporarily bewitched Renaud.

Thomas's "Opera, Dispossession, and the Sublime: the Case of *Armide*" takes up several of the points I make here: the decreasing importance of the supernatural after the first two acts (171-77), the concentration on "the inner scene of passion" (176), and Armide's dream (179-80).

[11] Beaussant (*Lully* 697) cites the second of these speeches as an example of how Quinault gave Lully a perfect opportunity to change the tone of the first act and suggest the tragedy that is to come. See also Gros, *Quinault* 683.

moments of his score ("si quelqu'un le peut être," I.ii.107), she is not sure
such a man exists. If he does not, she has a good excuse for not marrying,
but there is much more at stake. If one takes her first line ("Je ne triomphe pas du plus vaillant de tous," I.i.21) at face value, *she* wants to be "le
vainqueur de Renaud." If she can realize this desire, she can remain independent, though dangerously narcissistic—she alone will be worthy of
herself. If she cannot, she will be more than just independent: no one will
be worthy of her, she will never have a successful relationship with another person, and she will remain alone with her magic. It is of course
precisely this scenario that Quinault will develop in the last four acts—
she will try to conquer Renaud and to form a couple with him, but her
magic charms are the only ones that are effective; her personal, human
charms have no effect on Renaud, and he can leave her fairly easily when
another magic charm opens his eyes: "C'est un vain triomphe, un faux
bien" (III.ii.368).

    If I go into such detail about the implications of these six sylla-
bles, it is partly because this example of how Quinault could suggest so
much with so few words is singled out for special praise by most commentators. Lecerf and Rameau both admire this parenthesis, pointing out
that while one could take these lines as Armide's praise of Renaud's
valor, Lully's music underlines her doubts:

> Ce demi soûpir, ce ton bas & lent, me fait voir qu'elle doute qu'on
> puisse vaincre Renaud, qu'elle craint qu'on ne le puisse pas, ou peut-
> être qu'elle le souhaite. Tout fins, tout spirituels que sont ces traits
> pour Quinaut, ils le sont plus encore pour Lully: Les tons de celui-ci
> sont plus sensibles que les paroles de celui-là; et c'est là retoucher la
> peinture de la Poësie, c'est là en renforcer les couleurs. (Lecerf 2: 197)

> La musique semble lui faire prononcer cette réflexion avec une espèce
> d'humiliation, de mortification, comme si dans le moment la crainte de
> ne pouvoir triompher de ce héros lui venait à l'esprit [...]. Tel est sans
> doute le sens qui a guidé Lully: car si l'on voulait qu'Armide n'eût
> prétendu qu'exalter simplement la gloire de son héros, sans se rappeler
> en même temps la crainte de n'en pouvoir triompher, Lully n'aurait
> pas manqué de nous le faire sentir par un autre fonds d'harmonie.
> (Rameau 169)

The "demi soûpir"[12] that Lecerf mentions sets off the parenthesis
from the preceding "Le vainqueur de Renaud," and the "ton bas & lent"
refers to the three quarter notes C, C, and B flat on "si quelqu'un."
Rameau explains that, in contrast to the rising C major scale to which
Lully set "Le vainqueur de Renaud," the B flat brings us from the side of
the dominant (G above C) to that of the subdominant (F below C), a side
characterized by "regrets" and "pleurs":

> On donne tous les jours dans ce sens [...], lorsqu'on cite le bémol en
> signe de mollesse, de faiblesse, etc., lors enfin qu'on rabaisse la voix
> dans les mêmes cas. (168-69).

Six syllables, five short words, a temporary change of harmony (quite
subtle for modern listeners, but obviously striking to ears that had never
heard seductresses such as those in *Tannhäuser, Salome,* and *Lulu*), an
extremely complex character comes to life, and the tragedy begins.

The scene that follows (I.iii) offers an excellent example of a *divertissement* that is well integrated into the action. A formal celebration
of Armide's triumph is an obvious part of the "jour de triomphe" mentioned in line one, but Quinault has used it as more than just an excuse for
the dancing and choral singing that were expected in every act. Armide
has time to think about her failure to charm Renaud, about her dream, and
especially about what will happen if indeed no one is capable of being "le
vainqueur de Renaud." The spectator has time to think about these things
as well, since the dance music and the visual splendor of the *divertissement* do not necessary occupy the full attention of his/her more rational
side.[13] The content of such a celebration is standard, and many of the

---

[12] By "demi-soûpir," Lecerf does not necessarily mean literally an eighth-note rest.
There is no rest in the first two editions of the score (1686, 1713), though there is in the
example included in Rameau's *Observations* (which uses different time signatures and
note values). Rameau's example also includes hypothetical settings of "Si quelqu'un le
peut être" using harmonies of the dominant.

[13] Abbate makes a similar point, but in the opposite direction. She describes operatic
narration as a moment during which "the listener's attention is no longer captured by
either the material or the performance" (61), when the music does not command complete attention. This an excellent illustration of one of the key differences between baroque and modern opera; it would be unthinkable in seventeenth-century France for
music to occupy all of a spectator's attention for more than a few moments.

lines are repeated several times. Like Armide, he/she can watch the spectacle while continuing to think about what has just been said.

This *divertissement* also creates a change of atmosphere that makes the arrival of Aronte in scene four all the more effective. The "thrill of victory" gives way to the "agony of defeat," as Armide's fears become reality. Renaud is not only undefeatable, he is capable of undoing the work of Armide's charms. The parallel with the last act is clear (if one has already read or seen the last act, which would have been the case of many spectators):

ACT I	ACT V
Talk of victory, of charms (i)	Talk of love, of pleasure (i)
Armide talks to her magician uncle (ii)	Armide leaves to consult demons (end i)
Divertissement (iii)	*Divertissement* (ii)
Arrival of Aronte (iv)	Arrival of Ubalde, Chevalier Danois (iii)
Armide calls for vengeance (iv)	Armide hopes for vengeance (v)

This first act is truly masterful, very much in the mold of classical tragedy if one substitutes the staging of a victory celebration in I.iii for a *récit* such as the one in Racine's *Bérénice* ("De cette nuit, Phénice, as-tu vu la splendeur?," I.v.301-16). The exposition is concise, the complex psychology of the main character is presented with remarkable economy of means, and a *coup de théâtre* at the end of the act moves the action forward and leaves the outcome in doubt.[14]

The remaining acts will be somewhat different, though equally effective in their way, as we see Armide's magical powers at work instead of hearing about them as we do in act I. If we expect the other four acts to be exactly like the first, however, we will fall into the same trap as do numerous critics who see *Armide* as a model for the *tragédie lyrique*—because it is the closest of the Quinault-Lully operas to Racinian tragedy—while at the same time criticizing the fourth act, because it is so un-Racinian. I will return to the fourth act at the end of this section; for now, let us assume that Quinault knew what he was doing and that he could have cast the fourth act in a Racinian mold if he had wanted to.

---

[14] This is of course only true from a theoretical perspective. In practice, almost everyone in the audience in 1686 would know the outcome of the story of Armide and Renaud, either from familiarity with Tasso's poem or from having seen *Armide* or another work based on the same story.

The structure of acts II and III can easily be understood within the context of Racinian tragedy, but they introduce a new element, that of magic. As in so many classical tragedies, the first scene of act II introduces the one important character who does not figure in the first act. In this case it is Renaud, who, like Armide in act I, prefers liberty to love and *gloire* to *repos* (see Couvreur, *Lully* 390-91). Scene two returns to Armide and Hidraot, who are laying a trap for Renaud. Their invocation of the "Esprits de haine et de rage" (II.ii.219)—literally, as magicians, not figuratively, as troubled souls—is followed by the lyrical interlude of Renaud's arrival in a spot so charming that he cannot resist sleep, as Quinault juxtaposes *repos* in a literal sense (III.iii.247) to the *repos*-inaction rejected by Renaud two scenes earlier (II.i.191).[15] The act closes with Armide's famous monologue, expressing the hesitation and interior conflict that one so often finds in tragedy. However, rather than change her mind during a moment of introspection, alone on the stage, she makes her decision not to kill Renaud while holding a dagger over his sleeping body: "Plus je le vois, plus ma vengeance est vaine, / Mon bras tremblant se refuse à ma haine" (II.v.284-85). The act thus begins with the presentation of one main character, presents the passions and hesitations of the other, and ends with a *coup de théâtre*. A familiar structure, but quite different from spoken tragedy in its literal presentation of invocations of the supernatural (ii) and of the image of the beloved (v). Again, the *divertissement* (II.iv) is well integrated into the action and moved from its habitual place at the end of the act, to make way for the powerful closing scene.

One finds much the same type of mixture in act III. Like many tragedies, it begins with a situation similar to that of the beginning of the play, as Armide expresses her disappointment and her confidants wonder how she can be unhappy. With the last two scenes of the act, however, we are fully in the realm of the supernatural, as Armide asks for and then rejects the aid of La Haine in eradicating love from her heart.

---

[15] "Repos" has already been mentioned in conjunction with the peace brought by Louis XIV ("[le] repos qu'il assure aux humains," P.27) and with the image of Renaud that troubles Armide ("son [de Renaud] importune image / Malgré moi trouble mon repos," I.i.47). See chapter 11 (*Roland*), 317-18.

After a fourth act that does not involve any of the main characters, the last act, which Lecerf called "tout seul un Opera" (2: 15), shows us Armide and Renaud together for the first time. By this time, it is clear, even to those few who do not know Armide's story, that what should be a moment of great happiness is laden with irony and impending doom. We know that Ubalde and the Chevelier Danois are approaching with the diamond shield that can counteract Armide's magic, and she has told us herself that Renaud's love is not real, that it is the effect of her magic charms but not of her physical ones:

> Il m'aime? quel amour! ma honte s'en augmente.
> Dois-je être aimée ainsi? puis-je en être contente?
> C'est un vain triomphe, un faux bien.
> Hélas! que son amour est différent du mien! (III.ii.366-69)

Thus, as we listen to the great *passacaile* that underlies the *divertissement* of this last act (scene ii), we realize that one of Lully's greatest creations serves not to conclude a love story but to prepare the tragic end of Quinault's most fascinating heroine. With its beautiful melodies and harmonies above a literally obstinate (*basso ostinato*) bass line, it suggests the conflict between the sensuous variety of the pleasures of love and the straight line of duty that will come to a head in the next scene, when Renaud literally "sees the light":

> Que vois-je? quel éclat me vient frapper les yeux?
> [...]
> Ciel! quelle honte de paraître
> Dans l'indigne état où je suis! (V.iii.670, 673-74)

The opera concludes with two scenes that, by most contemporary accounts, could easily rival the emotional power of spoken tragedy. I will return to these scenes in section 2, but first it is important to look more closely at how Quinault combines lyrical passages and the supernatural with the traditional structures of spoken tragedy.

§ § §

The supernatural is certainly present in *Armide,* as magic underlies all the *divertissements*—indirectly in act I, where the people of Da-
mascus celebrate the victory won through Armide's charms, and directly
in the other acts (her spells in II, la Haine in III, the Demons and the
golden scepter in IV, the Plaisirs and the destruction of the palace in V).
Armide, however, is much more than a magician who uses her powers to
achieve her goals; in fact, at the beginning, rather than use magic to ensure her power over the man she loves (as did Médée in *Thésée*), she uses
her beauty to ensure her power over men whom she does not love. In both
cases, it is a matter of *charmes,* magical and physical, but Médée used her
physical charms in love, not in war. When Sidonie says "Vous allumez
une fatale flamme / Que vous ne ressentez jamais" (I.i.5-6), she is using
the *galant* vocabulary of love to describe a military victory. The *flamme*
lit by Armide can be literally fatal to her enemies who have been captured
and who will, quite possibly, be put to death. In fact, one of Armide's
most remarkable abilities is that of putting her physical charms to such
good effect that she does not need to use her magical ones nor resort to
military force:

> Ses charmes les plus forts sont ceux de ses beaux yeux.
> Elle n'a pas besoin d'emprunter l'art terrible
> Qui sait, quand il lui plaît, faire armer les Enfers.
> [...]
> Nous n'avons point fait armer nos Soldats,
> Sans leur secours Armide est triomphante. (I.iii.112-14, 137-38)

Love without love, victory without battle, a seemingly magical conquest
without magic, *charmes* without *charmes.*

Armide's magical charms only come into play once her physical
ones have failed. When she learns that Renaud has freed the captives,
who had followed her "beaux yeux," she and Hidraot cast a spell so the
"empire infernal" will lead their victim to them (II.ii.215-16). This time
fatal is clearly used in the sense of a deadly trap (II.ii.231) into which
Renaud will fall.[16] At this stage she is a magician because her physical

---

[16] As is appropriate for a *tragédie lyrique,* where lyricism and magic go hand in
hand, the trap takes the form of a "séjour [...] charmant" (II.iii.239) and of demons

charms have failed to make Renaud fall in love (he stated his "heureuse indifférence" in the first scene of the act), but she is not in love. Quinault has already made skillful use of the ambiguity of the *galant* vocabulary (*charmes, fatal, flamme, piège,* etc.). In much the same way as Racine, he takes these figurative terms literally (Biet, "La Passion des larmes" 168; Viala, "Racine galant"), since Armide's physical charms lead men not into chains of love but of captivity. Then, at the end of the act, he takes this ambiguity a step farther—if physical charms cannot bring Renaud into real captivity, then magical ones can. But when Armide is at the point of killing her captive, Renaud's physical charms make her "captive," make her fall in love. Her charms can not make him a military captive, but his can make her an amorous captive. As the demons change to "aimables Zéphyrs" and whisk them to the end of the universe (II.v.297, 301), she has her captive, but not the kind of captive she intended. She has lost her *paix,* her *repos* (I.i.7, 47; see p. 335 above) and has become a captive herself. As Beaussant puts it, "Armide ne sera plus magicienne *et* amoureuse: elle sera magicienne *en tant* qu'amoureuse et *parce* que amoureuse" (*Lully* 687; his emphasis). She cannot separate the two, and it will become painfully clear to her that magic has not brought her true love. When Armide reappears in the third act, questioned by her confidants about another hollow victory, "ce qui avait pu nous apparaître comme un jeu de langage, brusquement dépasse le jeu, et devient déchirant. Le jeu de mots devient tragédie."[17]

It is this shifting network of signs that integrates the supernatural into a tragedy. What is particularly interesting about *Armide* is that, in an opera ostensibly about the conflict between love and duty, or glory, the main interest lies elsewhere. As Rosow says, this conflict "is not the heart of the tragic conflict [...]. The conflict is all Armide's." [18] While it is true

---

which, "sous la figure des Nymphes, des Bergers, et des Bergères, enchantent Renaud, et l'enchaînent durant son sommeil avec des guirlandes de fleurs" (II.iv.260d).

[17] Beaussant, *Lully* 696. Beaussant also discusses how Quinault interiorizes the action, especially as compared with the fifth act of his *Comédie sans comédie* (1655), where the Armide-Renaud story is presented as a machine play in which Cupid appears to keep Armide from killing Renaud (686, 691, 694). See also Gros, *Quinault* 517-19.

[18] "Lully's Armide" 198. The theme of the opera is stated explicitly in the prologue:

Nous y verrons Renaud, malgré la volupté,
Suivre un conseil fidèle et sage;
Nous le verrons sortir du Palais enchanté,

that Renaud is divided between love and duty, he never goes through any soul-searching.[19] He falls in love because of one magic charm and returns to duty because of another.

Once Armide took advantage of her beauty and of her indifference to love as a weapon in war; now love has become a kind of war.[20] Both Armide and Renaud are in love with their enemy. She tries to hate him (III.ii.338), but only falls more deeply in love; he will realize that he is bound by duty to hate what he has come to love.[21] *Roland* had presented a great hero torn between love and duty, who descends into madness without achieving truly tragic proportions, and a strong woman with remarkable powers who always gets her way. *Armide* presents a similar situation, including a hero who temporarily forgets about his duty, and satisfies all the exigencies of the *tragédie lyrique,* but at the same time explores the contradictions and frustrations of a person who, like Racine's great heroes and heroines, is drawn inevitably toward something she cannot have.

Renaud, as almost all critics agree, is a weak and relatively uninteresting character.[22] We know more about his reputation than we do about him—he has a speaking role in only two scenes of the first two acts (II.i, II.iii) and is absent from acts III and IV. When he reappears at the beginning of the last act, he is under the influence of the charms (in both senses of the word) of Armide, quite the opposite of what we had seen

---

Où, par l'amour d'Armide, il était arrêté,

Et voler où la Gloire appelle son courage. (P.52-56)

This displacement of the spectator's interest from the ostensible theme, as announced in the prologue, to the emotional conflict within one of the characters is strong evidence that the allegorical, face-value subjects of these libretti should not be taken too seriously.

[19] ARMIDE

La sévère Raison et le Devoir barbare

Sur les Héros n'ont que trop de pouvoir.

RENAUD

J'en suis plus amoureux plus la Raison m'éclaire.

Vous aimer, belle Armide, est mon premier devoir. (V.i.619-22)

[20] See Beaussant, *Lully* 691, where he speaks of "deux métaphores croisées: celle de l'envoûtement et celle du combat."

[21] In a way, Armide's hatred is the equivalent of her duty, since it is her duty as an enemy of the Christian army to destroy Renaud. In this light, her hesitation between hate and love, expressed so powerfully in act III, is the equivalent of a hesitation between duty and love.

[22] See, for example, Couvreur, *Lully* 388-89.

and heard about him before. His speech here is characterized by *galant* clichés, yet his love appears real enough to prepare his sincere, if passing, regrets when he abandons Armide. It may seem odd to speak of "sincere" regrets that do not keep him from abandoning the woman he loves, but, as Armide has said (III.ii.366-72), his love for her is only the effect of her magic spells. His true love is glory,[23] and one could say that his love is real and false at the same time, since he has strong feelings based on artificial premises. These feelings will fade, but he hardly deserves the epithet of "perfide" (V.v.748, 762).

Armide of course knows this, but cannot admit it to herself in the final scene. She has been troubled since the first scene by the image of the invincible Renaud, and not only because he is the last obstacle to military victory. It is not just that "Les Enfers ont prédit cent fois / Que contre ce guerrier [ses] armes seront vaines" (I.i.38-39); she is convinced that she is doomed to love her enemy:

> Un songe affreux m'inspire une fureur nouvelle
> Contre ce funeste ennemi.
> [...]
> Et par un charme inconcevable,
> Je me sentais contrainte à le trouver aimable
> Dans ce fatal moment qu'il me perçait le cœur. (I.i.48-49, 54-56)

In this context, the suspicion, or fear, expressed in the famous parenthesis ("Si quelqu'un le peut être," discussed above p. 332) immediately suggests the fear of love. Renaud too has his charms, which have prevented Armide from killing him and which will, later in the third act, turn her hate to love, though without removing her hatred nor her desire for vengeance. Her monologue ends "Que, s'il se peut, je le haïsse" (II.v. 295), and early in the following act she will say "Il faut qu'un nouveau charme assure ma vengeance" (III.ii.322). Most of the third act will be devoted to her efforts to revive her hatred, efforts that end in failure

---

[23]   Vous brûliez pour la Gloire avant que de m'aimer,
          Vous la cherchiez partout d'une ardeur sans égale:
          La Gloire est une rivale
          Qui doit toujours m'alarmer. (V.i.608-11)

(III.iv.412-16), and when she reappears in the first scene of act V, she is hopelessly in love. It is no wonder than, that when Renaud leaves she is beside herself, dominated by love instead of by the hatred that filled her heart earlier.

One could say, aware of all the unfortunate ramifications of a distinction that was all too infrequently challenged in the seventeenth century, that she began the opera like a man and ended up like a woman, rejected by the male establishment and unable to control her passions. On a more symbolic level, Armide is less the victim of a misogynist society and more a failure in a desperate search for wholeness.[24] Not wholeness in the sense that "a woman needs a man," but in the sense that someone who relies on exterior, artificial means such as beauty and magic to attain happiness will always be lacking something. She wants something she cannot have, someone who rejects her charms. Yet, if Renaud succumbs to her charms, he will no longer be the hero who resists her charms, and he will thus no longer be what she wants (Beaussant, *Lully* 704). Like Chimène who cannot love Rodrigue if he does not avenge the insult to his father even if it means the death of her own father, or like Bérénice who could not, in the end, love a Titus who abandoned the duty she had taught him to respect, Armide could not continue to love a Renaud who would abandon his duty and glory for her love. In the end she is like Cybèle, the heroine of Quinault's other truly tragic libretto, who, in spite of her divine powers, cannot find happiness. The endings of the two operas are quite different, however, since Cybèle regrets her vengeance and mourns his death, whereas *Armide* concludes with "L'espoir de la vengeance" (V.v.766). I will return to this concluding scene in section 2, after a look at the infamous act IV.

§ § §

---

[24] I prefer this interpretation to that of an Armide who can only find happiness in love "when it is offered in response to the suit of a hero" (Howard 198). Armide is much more than a woman who is unhappy in love; she represents the Other, be it political, social, religious, or sexual.

As in the *Gerusalemme liberata*, Godefroi has decided to pardon Renaud for having killed Gernand[25] and sends two knights (the Chevalier Danois and Ubalde) to bring Renaud back. They first visit a wise old man (XIV.xxxiii-XV.ii) who tells them where Armide is hiding with Renaud and gives them a golden scepter and a diamond shield; the first is to protect them against Armide's enchantments on the way, the second to counteract the effect of Armide's charms, which have made Renaud fall in love and forget his duty. Quinault began with the two knights, equipped with the scepter and the shield, as they arrive in the desert that was the setting of act III. He then took the two lascivious maidens mentioned briefly by Tasso, whom the two knights resist (XV.lviii-lxvi) and created two parallel episodes in which first the Chevalier Danois, then Ubalde are tricked into believing they have met their beloved Lucinde and Mélisse. Each knight uses the golden scepter to dissipate the illusion that is threatening his friend, and they criticize each other's lack of resolve in nearly identical terms. They then continue on their way and, in act V scene iii, take advantage of Armide's temporary absence to show the shield to Renaud, who immediately rejects the "Vains ornements d'une indigne mollesse" (V.iii.682) and agrees to return with them.

Act IV is a traditional and integral part of the story, necessary to explain how Renaud escapes from Armide's pleasure palace, yet, as Cahusac put it, it is "l'endroit même qui depuis près de soixante-dix ans passe pour le plus défectueux de ses [Quinault's] Ouvrages" (3: 86).[26] Lecerf said that the act "manque de matière," that Quinault was "nû et sterile à l'excés" (2: 15; see also Parfaict, *Académie Royale* 193). In fact, the act is far from empty, and these critics really seem to be saying that the act was lacking in what they expected. Armide does not appear,[27] and her struggle with love and hate seems forgotten.

---

[25] Gernand was a knight in Godefroi's army, seduced (like many others) by Armide. When Renaud was preferred over him to replace the captain Dudón, Gernand defamed him, and an angry Renaud killed him, in defiance of Godefroi's orders. He leaves the Christian camp rather than become a prisoner and is thus an outcast when he encounters Armide. See canto V, stanzas i-lix.

[26] For other criticisms of this act, see Gros, *Quinault* 635-36; Couvreur, *Lully* 390; Rosow, "How Eighteenth-Century Parisians" 214-15 and "Lully's *Armide*" 239-40. Philippe Herrewegghe omitted act IV from his first recording of *Armide* (1984).

[27] There are practical reasons for Armide's absence. She has had four demanding scenes in act III, preceded by her great monologue, and she will have a demanding part

This struggle is of course not forgotten, as Cahusac explains quite well (3: 89-91). Armide, whose magic powers make her aware of the expedition to rescue Renaud, must do everything in her considerable power to stop it. She first conjures up "des bêtes farouches et des monstres épouvantables" (IV.i.434d), and when these cannot stand up to the golden scepter, she brings out what she must consider the ultimate weapon, the pleasures of love which have enthralled her as well as Renaud. There is more than enough stage action to hold the spectator's interest, if Quinault's intention is well executed (Cahusac 3: 87; Beaussant, *Lully* 718; *Mercure*, Dec. 1761, 169). While we watch Ubalde and the Chevalier Danois, the spectator should be thinking not just about the conflict between duty and passion, about the obvious parallels between Ubalde and the Chevalier Danois on the one hand and Renaud on the other, but about Armide's attempt to retain control over her lover.[28] A struggle that pits magic against magic is certainly not lacking in dramatic possibilities.

In short, one can justify each element of this much-aligned act, even perhaps the "replay" in scene iv of the Chevalier Danois's temptation in scene ii.[29] Each knight must undergo temptation and show himself as weak as the other, and as Renaud. On the other hand, the repetition does extend the act without adding anything new, and such a parallel, which allows one character to say "I told you so" to the other, is perhaps

---

in act V scene i, just before her two long and taxing scenes at the end of the opera. It is hard to imagine how a singer would have anything left for the fourth act. See the extract from the Dec. 1761 *Mercure,* quoted more extensively in English in Rosow, "How Eighteenth-Century Parisians" 233: "M. Quinault a laissé un vuide, dans le quatriéme Acte, trés-nécessaire pour le repos de l'Actrice qui représente *Armide;* nécessaire même pour ne pas offrir sans interruption les objets de l'intérêt principal" (168).

[28] See Couvreur, *Lully* 391: "A partir du moment où le spectateur a compris le fonctionnement de l'allégorie, les "longueurs" disparaissent, le sens et la structure s'éclairent." There were certainly no *longueurs* in the production at the Théâtre des Champs-Élysées in 1992-93, nor was the sense and structure of the act unclear. In addition to the allegorical representation of the conflict between love and duty, this act also lends itself to interpretations that emphasize Louis XIV's struggles against the Protestants and the Turks (see above, p. 329, n. 6).

[29] This scene was cut from the 1703 libretto and was probably no longer performed as early as 1697; see Rosow, "How Eighteenth-Century Parisians" and "Lully's Armide" 238-51. Rosow points out that the two episodes "differ completely in formal structure (division into airs, duets, and recitatives" ("How Eighteenth-Century Parisians" 215-16).

too reminiscent of comedy in the context of Armide's struggle.[30] In particular, the textual repetition of "Est-ce là cette fermeté / Dont vous vous êtes tant vanté?" (IV.ii.509-10, IV.iv.563-64) could be considered comical, especially in light of the thinly veiled off-color joke. On the other hand, as Gros points out (*Quinault* 634), a little *détente* is not out of place here, after Armide's monologue and the evocation of Hate and before the powerful final act.

---

[30] Parfaict refers to the "double rencontre" as a "jeu propre seulement à la comédie" (*Académie Royale* 193).

- II -

It is fitting that, in this the last section of the last chapter of a book devoted to Quinault's libretti, I should conclude with a consideration of one of his most universally admired passages: Armide's final scene with Renaud and the monologue that concludes the opera (V.iv-v). Most commentators would agree that, along with her monologue (II.5), these are the best examples of dramatic poetry in the libretti; Boscheron went so far as to say "Je ne sais ce que l'esprit humain pourroit imaginer de supérieur au cinquieme Acte d'Armide" (56).[31] Since the second-act monologue has been so frequently analyzed, I will limit myself here to the two concluding scenes.[32]

Lecerf is one of the commentators who single out these two scenes:

> Connoissés-vous quelque chose dans tout [sic] nos Opera qui soit plus
> en possession de saisir & d'attendrir tout le monde que ces deux en-
> droits d'*Armide*?
>> *Enfin il est en ma puissance, &c.*
> Et
>> *Renaud, Ciel, ô mortelle peine, &c.*
> Pour peu que cela soit bien chanté, on se trouble, on se laisse aller au
> plaisir d'une douce émotion, & il y a de beaux yeux, Madame, qui y
> ont pleuré. (1: 80-81)

Lecerf discusses these two passages as examples of the power of simple music, "un recitatif fort uni [...] une belle voix seule, avec un chant bien expressif, & un accompagnement net & proportionné" (as opposed to "un grand concert, [...] un grand assemblage d'instrumens"). If the music is

---

[31] The quality of the act is perhaps due to the fact that Lully, worried about the public's reaction to act IV, made Quinault rewrite the last act three times; see Parfaict, *Académie Royale* 193. See chapter 6 (*Isis*), 194-97, for a discussion of one of Quinault's most admired lyrical passages, the "plaintes d'Hiérax." Given the different natures of lyric and dramatic poetry, it is difficult to compare the two.

[32] The most important early analyses are those by Rousseau in the *Lettre sur la musique française* (1753) and by Rameau in his *Observations sur notre instinct pour la musique et sur son principe* (1754). More recent analyses include those by Malgoire and by Kintzler (*Poétique* 402-03, 458-60).

simple, it is because a large part of the emotional effect of seventeenth-century opera lies in the words and their declamation. There was no debate in the seventeenth or early eighteenth century, as there would be later in the history of opera, as to which was more important, words or music.

> On auroit honte de contester que la premiere beauté, la vraye beauté, la beauté unique d'un air ne soit d'être fait pour les paroles; surquoi une personne de bon esprit, disoit tres-juste, qu'une marque excelente de la bonté d'un air, est que nulles paroles n'y conviennent si bien que celles sur lesquels il aura été fait: [...] plus on épluche le sens des paroles, plus on est exact & difficile sur la fidélité à exprimer les pensées, & plus on demeure satisfait de la Musique de Lulli. (Lecerf 2: 141)

The best way to appreciate these dramatic passages, then, is to study the words, to "épluche[r] le sens des paroles."

If Lully's music could be simple, it is because there is already a certain musicality in Quinault's poetry, a musicality that would have been quite evident in the florid style of delivery of actors of the period. It is the same type of musicality that one finds in Racine's poetry, and the anecdote of Lully's basing his recitative on the declamation of La Champmeslé (see my introduction, p. 28, n. 42) reflects such an obvious approach on the part of a composer that, as the saying goes, one would have to invent it if it did not already exist. Anyone who had heard actors (except those who preferred Molière's more "natural" style) or orators would be used to the rhythms, pauses, rising and falling pitch, and *éclats de voix* that heightened the effect of a text. To analyze dramatic poetry then—and not just poetry written for the musical stage—one must pay attention to the sounds and rhythms as well as to more frequently discussed elements such as content, vocabulary, and structure.

In act V scene iv, Armide returns from her consultation with the infernal spirits, announced at the beginning of the act, to find that Renaud is leaving. At first she can do little but exclaim "Renaud! Vous partez" (V.iv.693), but then she calls on her demons to stop him. When she realizes she is powerless to stop him, all she can do is repeat her exclamations (V.iv.696, 698). Quinault has thus found a way to make the repetitions so often required by the composer seem natural, and Lully used the same music for the repeat that he did for the first two lines. However, Quinault has separated them the second time with "Mes cris ne sont pas écoutés!" (V.iv.697), which adds variety while ensuring closure.

Renaud stops to listen, and Armide's exclamations become desperate pleading. The theme of love as combat returns, as she offers to become his enemy or his captive, anything to be near him. Far from the powerful, independent woman of the first act, she can conceive of no existence of which he is not a part. Renaud's protestations of regret could be interpreted as hollow (see above, p. 340), but the simple, tender music to which he sings them make his regrets sound sincere.

Armide is not convinced, but she does not burst out with reproaches. Her next five lines (V.iv.716-20) are in a lyrical vein (*charme, soupirs, pleurs, larme, nœuds, doux*), as she seems to have decided to try Renaud's tender side first, before calling him inhuman, *barbare*, and *ingrat* (722-25) and then threatening him. They are not threats of overt violence, however, but of "Mon Ombre obstinée à te suivre" (727). Fittingly for a situation in which Renaud has had a radical change of heart, everything becomes reversed: the living Armide imagines herself dead (724-25), her ghost will take on the inflexibility of Renaud (729-30), and fury will become the equal of love (731-32). At this point Quinault simply added an elliptical three dots, signaling a pause and a change in direction. She begins to faint, thinking she is dying, and Renaud pities her to the point that Ubalde and the Chevalier Danois must drag him away, in spite of himself.[33]

When Armide regains consciousness at the beginning of scene v, Renaud has fled, a flight that is reflected in the sound /i/ in the rhyming syllable of the first eight lines of the scene. Armide regrets that she is still alive, mostly because her heart is still full of Renaud: "Tout perfide qu'il est, mon lâche cœur le suit" (748, 754). When she says that "L'horreur de l'éternelle Nuit / Cède à l'horreur de mon supplice" (751-52), it is more than a figurative comparison—she knows only too well what the horrors of eternal night are, having literally gone to the underworld at the end of the first scene. As in the examples mentioned earlier of *galant* vocabulary

---

[33] Lully effects this transition (V.iv.731-32) mainly by slowing down the rhythm: two whole notes follow the series of eighth and sixteenth notes to which the preceding five lines had been sung, and the quarter note becomes the principal note value for the next four lines.

being taken literally (p. 337), what is an image for ordinary people is vivid, terrible reality for Armide.

The realization that she still loves Renaud, that she can control real demons but not the figurative demons that are her passions, brings on regrets about her earlier decisions, especially the one in act II not to kill him (755-57).[34] At this point, it is hard to know whether she really sees Renaud nearing the shore that limits her domain, or if she imagines it, for, after a vain effort to drag herself to where he is, she imagines that she has recaptured him, that she is back in the situation of control in which she found herself at the beginning of act II scene v (762-63). She soon realizes her error (764-65), regains some control, and decides that vengeance is her only hope. She drives away everything associated with pleasure (which suggests that she will probably find no satisfaction in vengeance), destroys her palace, and departs in a flying chariot, hoping to leave love behind her.

The situation is thus very much the same as at the beginning, where a powerful Armide is bent on punishing Renaud, except that she now knows all the pleasures and pains of love. She also knows that both love and the magic charms at the disposal of the Christian camp are more powerful than her own charms, and one suspects that, in a later moment of reflection, she will resign herself to her fate. For now, however, the opera ends with the spectacular destruction of her palace and her departure. It is more than just a flashy finale:

> Cela finit par le Fracas du Palais enchanté, que les démons viennent détruire en un instant. Dans l'émotion que cause une machine, amenée & placée avec un art si unique, la toile tombe, & l'Auditeur plein de sa passion, qu'on a augmentée jusqu'au dernier moment, ne peut pas ne la point remporter toute entière. Il s'en retourne chez lui pénétré malgré qu'il en ait, rêveur, chagrin du mécontentement d'Armide. (Lecerf 2: 15-16)

This is not exactly the moral conclusion one would expect from an allegory of the triumph of duty over passion. While one can certainly read

---

[34] Line 755, "Quand le barbare était en ma puissance," is a clear evocation of the beginning of her monologue in II.v, "Enfin, il est en ma puissance."

Armide as the triumph of duty, or of Catholicism, or of France, or of other noble causes, Lecerf understood perfectly that, on a more human level, the emotional impact of *Armide* comes from our pity for a person who suffers from problems that we have experienced or can imagine ourselves experiencing.[35] This pity builds to a climax during the last two scenes, as Armide goes from shock to pleading to playing on Renaud's compassion to threatening him, working herself into such a furor that she faints. Renaud leaves, and she is left to live with her pain and regrets, still in love but crying for vengeance, hallucinating, trying to escape from everything that reminds her of Renaud.

Quinault used all the resources of his art in this portrait of a desperate woman, creating a text that provided Lully with a splendid vehicle for his music but that can easily stand on its own, partly because of its own music. He used almost exclusively lines of twelve and eight syllables, sacrificing some rhythmic variety for the sake of a more unified tragic tone. Variety is hardly lacking, however, as he frequently uses interjections to divide the longer lines into shorter sections (for example, 692-93, 733, 763-64). Some of the alexandrines contain hemistichs that express parallel ideas with parallel rhythms (703, 719),[36] whereas others place the two halves of the line in opposition (701, 748). The alexandrines all have regular caesuras, but the pause in the octosyllables can come after the second, third, fourth, or fifth syllable.

The lines of different lengths are used to good effect. Two six-syllable lines (734-35) suggest, by their brevity, that Armide is about to faint, and two decasyllables (755-56) serve as a transition between the air

---

[35] Lecerf seems to go against the standard interpretation of Aristotelian catharsis, in which the spectator is purged of passions and would not take them home. In particular, his description of the spectator as "rêveur, chagrin" does not seem to agree with Racine's statement about how tragedy removes what is "excessif" and "vitieux" from emotions such as pity and fear and brings them back to "un estat modéré et conforme à la raison" (*Principes* 12).

[36] These parallels are highlighted by Lully, who in both cases gives almost identical rhythms to the two hemistichs in the line: four eighth notes followed by a quarter note in each hemistich of V.iv.703, a quarter note surrounded by shorter notes on syllables three and nine, as well as on syllables six and twelve, in V.iv.719. The *Ménagiana* (2: 4) finds Quinault's "J'irai dans les combats [...] destinés pour vous" (703-04) preferable to Tasso's "Sarò [...] scudiero o scudo" (canto XVI, st. 50.)

at the beginning of the last scene (V.v.747-54, set off by the repetition of the first two lines) and the concluding passage.

Just as Lully organizes his pitches into patterns, so Quinault organizes his sounds. To take but three examples, if the first line of scene iv appears disjointed because of the interjections, the presence of three /è/ and two closed /o/ gives the line considerable unity; even the other vowel sounds, two *e muet* and one open /o/, are similar to the /è/ and closed /o/.[37] The lines with parallel syntax usually contain similar sounds in each section, such as the /k/ of *combats* and *coups* in line 703 or the /ou/ and /p/ in *soupirer* and *couler mes pleurs* in line 718. When Armide mentions her own name, it is usually followed by a repetitions of its vowels:

> Se peut-il que Renaud tienne Armide asservie? (III.i.310)
> Emmenez Armide captive (V.iv.702)[38]

Quinault also chose his sounds in function of the speed of delivery that would be appropriate for the content. For example, when Armide tries to drag herself to the spot where Renaud is about to leave her domain, the sounds become longer, like a person dreaming that he or she is unable to move: "Je fais pour m'y traîner d'inutiles efforts" (V.v.761).[39] The "extra" syllable represented by the *e muet*, the doubled consonant, the vowels lengthened by the following liquid consonants all suggest a decrease in speed, a suggestion that Lully did not miss—the last hemistich occupies two and a half measures, approximately the same number of measures as the twenty syllables of "Quand le barbare était en ma puissance, / Que n'ai-je cru la Haine et la Vengeance?" five lines earlier.

It is obvious that Quinault's lines imply rising and falling pitch, in a slightly more heightened way than does ordinary spoken French, but the art of choosing appropriate vowel sounds for desired pitches is too complex to allow detailed analysis here. Still, one can see that the

---

[37] For another example of a frequently repeated sound, see the eight rhymes in /i/ in lines 747-54, mentioned above, p. 347.

[38] In the only other case where she pronounces her name, "Que dis-je? où suis-je? hélas! Infortunée Armide!" (V.v.764), the /i/ and /a/ precede the name.

[39] The sounds of this line (the first four syllables, the word *inutile*) are quite similar to those in Mallarmé's famous sonnet, "Le vierge, le vivace et le bel aujourd'hui," where the swan is unable to move: "Que vêt parmi l'exil inutile le Cygne."

exclamation "ciel!" in the first line of scene iv would be sung at a high pitch, and Quinault provides a vowel that is easily sung at such a pitch. Similarly, the vowels suggest that "comme Ennemi" in line 701 would be sung higher than "comme Amant" with its nasal consonants and vowels, a drop in pitch that reflects Armide's dejection.

The care that Quinault took not only with the structure and psychology of his libretti, but also with rhythms and sounds, as well as the attention that theater artists gave to these sonorous aspects of dramatic poetry, is reflected in an anecdote about Adrienne Lecouvreur. When asked to declaim Armide's monologue from act II, "de ce ton et cette intelligence avec lesquels elle rendoit si bien la nature, [...] l'on fut agréablement surpris de voir jusqu'à quelle précision Lully, par sa musique, se trouva d'intelligence avec elle" (Clément and Laporte 1: 113). It is not just that Lully's music was in agreement with her interpretation, however; the experiment would hardly have worked if Quinault's text had not given her words and phrases, sounds and rhythms that suited the emotions evoked by the text and the music appropriate to them. It is a fitting tribute to Quinault's role in the creation of these magnificent closing scenes that Parfaict, in quoting Lecerf's praise of the last scene, modified his wording slightly, changing the next-to-last word from "Musique" to "Poésie": "On peut appeler cette scène pour le Pathétique, pour les grâces, pour la diversité des mouvements, le triomphe en abrégé de la Poesie françoise" (Parfaict, *Académie Royale* 194; Lecerf 2: 15).

SCENE CINQUIESME
& derniere.
ARMIDE seule.

LE perfide Renaud me fuit;
Tout perfide qu'il est, mon lâche cœur le suit.
Il me laisse mourante, il veut que je perisse.
A regret je revoy la clarté qui me luit ;
    L'horreur de l'éternelle Nuit
    Cede à l'horreur de mon supplice.
    Le perfide Renaud me fuit ;
Tout perfide qu'il est, mon lâche cœur le suit.

Quand le Barbare estoit en ma puissance,
Que n'ay-je crû la Haine & la Vengeance !
    Que n'ay-je suivy leurs transports !
Il m'eschape, il s'esloigne, il va quitter ces Bords;
    Il brave l'Enfer & ma rage ;
    Il est désja prés du Rivage,
Je fais pour m'y trainer d'inutiles efforts.

Traistre, atten .. je le tiens .. je tiens son cœur
    perfide ....
    Ah! je l'immole à ma fureur ....
Que dis-je! où suis-je! helas! Infortunée Armide!
    Où t'emporte une aveugle erreur?

L'espoir de la vengeance est le seul qui me reste.
Fuyez, Plaisirs, fuyez, perdez tous vos attraits.
      Demons, détruisez ce Palais.
Partons, & s'il se peut, que mon amour funeste
Demeure enseveli dans ces lieux pour jamais.

Les Demons détruisent le Palais enchanté,
    & Armide part sur un Char volant.

Fin du cinquiéme & dernier Acte.

Conclusion:

Representation, Imitation, and Recognition

ARMIDE STANDS, LIKE RACINE'S *PHÈDRE,* an acknowledged masterpiece at the end of a distinguished career (see Gros, *Quinault* 637). Twelve years earlier, Racine had attacked Charles Perrault's defense of Quinault's *Alceste* in his preface to *Iphigénie,* and the quarrel between Ancients and Moderns had entered into a new phase; it would enter its best-known phase less than a year after *Armide,* when Perrault would read his "Siècle de Louis le Grand" at a meeting of the Académie Française. Soon after the quarrel over *Alceste,* the two rivals had both written moving tragedies about the suffering of a jealous woman and the young couple she destroyed, about hopeful efforts to establish a new order after a catastrophe (*Atys* premiered in 1676, *Phèdre* in 1677). In some ways one can see Quinault as the more successful of the two: when he retired from writing for the stage later in 1686, Racine had not written a play in the nine years since *Phèdre,* and he would include sung choruses and instrumental music in the two plays he would write later, *Esther* and *Athalie* (1689 and 1691). Quinault would never see them, since he died on November 26, 1688, just over a month before the first performance of *Esther.*

We will of course never know for sure why Racine and Quinault stopped writing for the stage when they did, nor how much the works and the success of the one influenced the writing of the other. If I insist on this rivalry and on these dates, it is to emphasize that Quinault and Racine

wrote for the same audiences and that they both had great and lasting success with these audiences. Racinian tragedy and the *tragédie lyrique* may
seem quite different on the surface, but they both passed with flying col-
ors the supreme test of literary success in classical France, as defined by
Racine in the preface to *Bérénice:* "La principale Règle est de plaire et de
toucher" (542).[1] There is no need to declare a winner, to prefer one writer
or the other. But there is a need to understand the works of both, for a
deeper appreciation of their works and of the period as a whole.

There is a certain irony in the fact that the *tragédie lyrique* is the
perfect illustration of Racine's point. First of all, the numerous examples
given by seventeenth- and eighteenth-century writers of how audiences
were moved, often to tears, reinforces what is clear in the sentences before and after Racine's famous phrase: to please and to touch (move) are
almost the same thing. Note the emphasis on *toucher* in the following
quotations, taken from the same paragraph as "La principale règle est de
plaire et de toucher":

> [...] ils avouaient qu'elle [*Bérénice*] n'ennuyait point, qu'*elle les
> touchait même en plusieurs endroits,* et qu'ils la verraient encore avec
> plaisir. [...]

> Je les conjure d[e] [...] ne pas croire qu'*une Pièce que les touche,* et
> qui leur donne du plaisir, puisse être absolument contre les Règles. [...]

> Qu'ils se réservent *le plaisir de pleurer et d'être attendris* [...]. (my
> emphasis)

In the first example, "même" emphasizes "touchait," and "ils la verraient
encore avec plaisir" seems almost an afterthought. In the second example,
the parenthetical "et qui leur donne du plaisir" seems less important than
"qui les touche." Finally, in the third example, the pleasure of theater is
defined as "de pleurer et d'être attendris." The "tendre Racine" was most

---

[1] See also May 179-81 and one of the passages he quotes from Du Bos: "Mais le
mérite le plus important des poëmes & des tableaux est de nous plaire. Cest le dernier
but que les Peintres & les Poëtes se proposent, quand ils prennent tant de peine à se conformer aux règles de leur art. On connoît donc suffisamment s'ils ont bien réussi, quand
on connoît si l'ouvrage touche ou s'il ne touche pas" (2: 347).

certainly capable of bringing tears to the eyes of his audiences, if perhaps
not as often as Quinault and Lully did. Furthermore, of the tragedies
Racine wrote during the Quinault-Lully collaboration, it was *Iphigénie*—
which owes so much to the *galant,* the baroque, and the operatic—that
was most moving.[2] Again, my point is not to declare a winner, but to re-
emphasize the fact that this "classical moment," with all its rules, order,
restraint, and decorum, was—like its music—primarily about emotion,
and that there was more than one way to create this emotion.

   Second, if Racine wanted the perfect example of how to please
and move an audience without following all the rules, he had only to cite
Quinault's libretti. *Vraisemblance* is modified to accommodate the *merveilleux,* battles and combats are not relegated to *récits,* and the unities
are set aside to make way for set changes in almost every act, for the
passing of long periods of time between the acts, for secondary characters, and (for a while, at least) a mixture of comedy and tragedy. As
Kintzler has shown so well, everything seems different, but the basic
structure and the basic goals are the same.[3]

                              § § §

   How can the basics stay the same while so much seems to have
changed? One means of answering this question, and of gaining a more
complete appreciation of the esthetics of late seventeenth-century France,
is to look closely at one of the key elements of classical esthetics, imitation (mimesis). I discussed in the introduction (39-40) the awareness of
the artificiality of our systems of representation that is implicit in the
stylized nature of operatic representation.[4] The Aristotelian concept of the
imitation of nature, which is fundamental to all seventeenth- and eighteenth-century discussions of the arts, does not concern a reproduction of
external reality, but rather—for the theater at least— a presentation of

---

   [2] See chaper 10 (*Amadis*), 298-300. Biet's "La Passion des larmes" is an excellent
treatment of tears and classical tragedy.
   [3] See the introduction, especially pp. 15, n. 15, 21, 36-38.
   [4] The imitative and representational powers of music are the subject of immense and
complex debate, and I can only touch on them here as they relate to similar powers in
dramatic literature. For an excellent study of many of the aspects of this debate, see
Winn, especially pp. 194, 232, and Lindenberger, *Extravagant Art,* chapter 3.

events that reveal fundamental human truths.[5] In terms of the emotional power of theater, and of opera in particular, mimesis is best understood as the representation of reactions to emotional situations and as a means of arousing appropriate emotions in the audience. This kind of imitation is very much a re-presentation, or transformation (Gadamer 121), in which all the components of the *tragédie lyrique*—text, instrumental and vocal music, action represented on stage, dance, costumes, and decor—contribute to the stylized recreation of an emotional state in which the representation itself is ultimately less important than its effect on the spectator.

To understand how these components work together, it is helpful to see them as existing along two axes, one from the verbal to the musical (from narration of facts to strictly musical form and including ideological content, figurative or "poetic" language, recitative, and aria) and the other from the aural to the visual (from declamation to sets and including acting, singing, and dancing). Both axes have their origins in sounds that have been organized into a communicative system in which, ideally, a sign is an unambiguous representation of some aspect of external reality, fact or idea. This is rarely the case, of course, and from this common point of departure the *tragédie lyrique* uses two means of intensification of expression, of going beyond what can be expressed by a fairly straightforward system of verbal signifiers and signifieds—adding a visual element and adding figurative discourse; the latter includes music, as most seventeenth- and eighteenth-century practitioners and theoreticians understood it (see Kintzler, *Poétique* 512-20, 489).

In adding visual elements to aural ones, the *tragédie lyrique* is not that different from other staged genres in which the audience sees characters and settings, except in its emphasis on lavish sets, machines, and costumes and on stylized movements (gestures, dance). In addition to being beautiful and pleasing in themselves, lavishness and stylization, even more than acting and dance, call attention to the inadequacy of everyday means of expression.

The use of figurative linguistic and musical discourse can be understood in a similar way. Rather than add one sense (vision) to another (hearing), one adds an intermediary between the verbal and the non-

---

[5] There is an excellent summary of these notions in Kintzler's *La France classique et l'opéra*, 17-23.

verbal, between signifier and signified—*cœur* is no more directly linked to the attitude of a brave hero than is the steady, "martial" beat of a march. Metaphors and other tropes, rhythms and clusters of sounds, musical equivalents of linguistic tropes (*depths* of despair, *shaking* from cold), poetic and musical form, all are at least one step removed from nonfigurative discourse in which there is assumed to be a direct correspondence between signifier and signified. Classical tragedy uses all the figurative resources of poetry, and opera adds those of music.[6] Means of expression, of creating an emotional response, are diversified and intensified, and the everyday world is left farther behind. The verbal remains paramount, however, both because the libretto is the basis for all the other components and because poetry and music are conceived according to a linguistic model.

Seen in this way, opera in general and the *tragédie lyrique* in particular are indeed rather far removed from mimesis in the sense of imitation of external reality. Lindenberger posits an operatic principle, opposed to a verbal, or dramatic, principle and which stresses "an indifference or hostility to mimesis of the external world" (*Extravagant Art* 65). Drawing on several passages in Lindenberger's first three chapters, one can compare the following characteristics of the two principles:

VERBAL	OPERATIC
representational, mimetic	oriented toward esthetic pleasure
mimetic	gestural
referential	ceremonial
discursive (narrative)	affective (emotional)
corresponds to world	performative
restrained	histrionic
literary	extravagant
informative	strives for effect
prosaic	expressive
dramatic	musical

---

[6] It is obviously more than a simple matter of addition. Unless the length of a tragedy and of an opera are radically different (as in the case of a typical spoken tragedy compared to the fifteen hours of Wagner's *Ring*), more time for music and dance means less time for, less concentration on (for example) poetry. It is around such choices that much of the debate over the relative merits of opera and other genres rages.

This operatic principle, which strives for "the maximum possible effect on the audience" (76), corresponds quite well to the view of the *tragédie lyrique* I have presented, yet Lindenberger opposes it to the representational, the mimetic, and the dramatic.[7] While it is true that many operas are neither dramatic, representational, nor mimetic in a narrow, traditional sense of these terms, I prefer to give these terms a broader meaning that allows us to understand their special kinds of mimesis and of drama. Otherwise, there will always be the widespread tendency to follow Kerman's example and label many operas undramatic, and thus unsuccessful (introduction 16) without making a special effort to take these operas for what they are, to try to understand their special type of effectiveness.

For this special type of effectiveness, this operatic type of representation to have the desired effect on the spectator, one must add another important characteristic to the "operatic principle": emotions must be presented in such a way that the spectator can easily *recognize* them and find an emotional verisimilitude in the characters' reactions. Following Gadamer in his essay "Art and Imitation," I would like to present a way of understanding mimesis that privileges the importance of recognition and in particular of recognition of order.

§ § §

"Recognition" is a crucial aspect of epistemology and esthetics and, as Terence Cave has pointed out, is an extremely elastic term.[8] It includes most types of knowledge, especially those that involve the consideration of a definition, an example or analogy, or previous experience. For example, the tension and resolution discussed at the end of section 3

---

[7] My view is not really opposed to Lindenberger's but is rather a recombination of several ideas present in his excellent book. The recombination is implicit in his "dual" view of drama discussed toward the end of section 3 of the introduction, a view that includes emotional impact as well as sequence of events.

[8] *Recognitions* 5; "Corneille, Œdipus, Racine" 82-83. Cave's emphasis, like that of Kerman (see section 3 of the introduction), is more on recognition by characters than by spectators. Michel Poizat, in a rather different style, concludes his consideration of the special "persistante et énigmatique émotion" of opera (9) with the idea of recognition on the part of the spectator: "Et de cette Chose originelle, ces moments de jouissance, rares et fugaces, évoqués tout au long de ces pages ne sont-ils pas, pourrait-on dire pour finir, que le signal de l'instant où en est vécu l'impossible retrouvaille?" (285).

of the introduction cannot function if the spectator does not recognize the connection (or analogy) between the original situation and its resolution—one must recognize a disguised character for who he/she really is, recognize the return of a poetic or musical theme and remember its earlier associations. In literature and opera, recognition includes recognition scenes of many kinds (Œdipus realizes he has married his mother, Electra recognizes her brother Orestes), the realization of an important truth or of the true state of affairs (the end of *Phèdre* or of Proust's *Recherche*, a Joycian epiphany, or the end of almost any comedy), the awareness of intertextuality, the pleasure of recognizing a melody or quotation, and the desire to see or hear certain works many times. I use it here especially in the sense of establishing a connection between something one sees on stage and something one has experienced personally, and this is an important part of key aspects of theater such as verisimilitude and catharsis.[9]

Gadamer begins with the three "dominant aesthetic concepts" (93) of imitation, expression, and sign, which are basically the same as three of the main concepts I am dealing with here: imitation, emotional effect, and representation. He sees the traditional concept of the imitation of nature as inadequate for the modern age and being challenged by expression,[10] a development that "can be traced particularly well in the realm of musical aesthetics" (94). Traditional signs have an instantly recognizable meaning as "I now cognize something *as* something I have already seen." As part of the process of recognition "we see things in terms of what is permanent and essential in them, [...] for what imitation reveals is precisely the real essence of the thing" as well as a deeper knowledge of ourselves and familiarity with the world (99; Gadamer's italics).[11]

---

[9] See Bury, *Littérature et politesse* 152: "L'aune de la vérité morale de la fiction sera alors beaucoup plus la *reconnaissance* d'une expérience individuelle et particulière [...] que le partage complice d'une *doxa* et d'une mémoire communes."

[10] Gadamer places this challenge, and ultimate defeat, of imitation by expression in the eighteenth century. I would move the challenge back to the seventeenth century, to the shift from resemblance to representation described by Foucault in *Les Mots et les choses*.

[11] Compare Gadamer's statement about imitation and essence to the quotation from Lindenberger (*Extravagant Art* 40) in the introduction (31), "the essence of a narrative situation in musical terms." Apostolidès (*Prince sacrifié* 35, 134) speaks of an "identification du spectateur au personnage" facilitated by the presentation of an essence." See also Schiller's critique of naturalistic art and his praise of opera for concentrating on an intrinsic truth, on ideals (Flaherty 296-300).

Gadamer presents this view of mimesis as Aristotelian and then, in an effort to make it more adaptable to the modern world, goes back to Pythagoras, where the process of recognition involves relations, the *as* that links the sign to the something we have already seen. As Gadamer reads Pythagoras, "the earliest concept of imitation thus implies all three manifestations of order: the order of the cosmos, the order of music, and the order of the soul" (102). Gadamer's conclusion is that true art

> succeeds in elevating what it is or represents to a new configuration, [...] a new order of unity in tension [...]. Mimesis in its most original sense [is] the presentation of order, [...] that spiritual ordering energy that makes our life what it is. (103)

Gadamer sees this type of imitation as "a far cry from [...] any kind of classicism" (99). My point is that this recognition of order, of the essence of things, this deeper understanding of the self, this "order of unity in tension" is exactly what one finds in the Quinault-Lully operas as well as in the great French classics such as Racine. This order exists on at least five not always separate levels:

1. plot;
2. politics and ideology, as the official view of Louis XIV's reign is established through art;
3. similarities to current events;
4. emotions, as the spectator undergoes catharsis and perceives harmony;
5. archetypes and the unconscious, suggesting a new order.

The first three levels correspond to more traditional views of drama and of the *tragédie lyrique,* where a work's dramatic and representational worth is judged mainly from the point of view of its plot and where interpretation often does not go beyond the recognition of ideas or current events that contemporaries would have found mirrored in the libretto. One cannot deny the importance of these first three levels, but the lasting value of the *tragédie lyrique* is found in the last two.

If an opera such as *Atys* can be so successful in 1676 in Paris and in 1989 in Brooklyn, where advertisements called it the "hottest ticket of the season," it is because, regardless of how little what happens on stage corresponds to "real" life, the spectator recognizes emotions both for what they are and for what they do to him/her.[12] These recognizable emotions are no more raw than is the nature in the gardens of Versailles, nor is their presentation any less beautiful. They are effective and their presentation is beautiful precisely because this (re)presentation is organized, put together in a way that is pleasant to the ear and eye but that is also true to how we react to these emotions. Furthermore, if we are willing to accept that different ages have different conventions and to look and listen beneath the surface, these spectacles—whether or not they conform to our idea of French classicism—are true to the essence of things. Is this not what classicism is all about?

---

[12] When Racine makes a similar point about his *Iphigénie* and that of Euripides, and then goes on in the next sentence to criticize Quinault's *Alceste* because the "modernes" felt it necessary to change some things in Euripides's *Alcestis,* he is being illogical and disingenuous. If spectators in Athens and in Paris shed tears over the same thing, it is not because Racine did not make any changes to Euripides's *Iphigenia at Aulis:* he begins the preface by detailing "les principales choses en quoi je me suis un peu éloigné de l'économie et de la fable d'Euripide." The tears come from emotional reactions to basic situations, not from attention to details in the plot.

Appendix I

Quinault Libretti Modified by Other Librettists

There were constant revisions to the Quinault libretti as the operas on which he collaborated with Lully were revived after their lifetimes. This appendix contains only revisions for which new music was composed or for which there were major changes to the libretto, such as shortening it from five to three acts. It does not include revisions that were limited to new music for the *divertissements;* see, for example, the 1771 *Amadis* in Schmidt, *Catalogue*, LLC 11-36.

TITLE	REVISER	COMPOSER	DATE
Alceste		Floquet[1]	never performed
Thésée		Mondonville[2]	1767
Thésée	Morel de Chédeville	Gossec	1782
Thésée	Marmontel	no setting survives	
Atys	Marmontel	Piccini	1780
Isis	Marmontel	no setting survives	
Proserpine	Guillard	Paisiello	1803
Persée	Marmontel	Philidor	1780
Amadis	Devismes	J.C. Bach	1779
Amadis	Marmontel	no setting survives	
Roland	Marmontel	Piccini	1778
Armide	Marmontel	no setting survives	
Armide		Gluck[3]	1777

---

[1] Floquet apparently set Quinault's libretti without any major changes.

[2] Mondonville made some changes to Quinault's text.

[3] Gluck made minor changes to about a dozen lines of Quinault's text and added four lines to the end of act III.

Appendix II

Biographical Sketch

Philippe Quinault was baptized in Paris on June 5, 1635. His father, Thomas, was a master baker, but some of his relatives, such as young Philippe's godparents, held important administrative posts. It is often said that Quinault entered the service of the poet Tristan l'Hermite as a page around 1643, but a recently discovered document states that in 1646 Quinault's father enrolled him as a boarding student under Philippe Mareschal, a *maître écrivain* in Paris, "pendant cinq ans ou environ [...] pendant lequel temps il lui aurait enseigné les principes de la langue latine et l'aurait rendu capable d'entrer comme il fit lors en quatrième au Collège du Cardinal Lemoine." It is true that the document was drawn up at Quinault's request in 1671, but the documented presence of Quinault at the baptism of Mareschal's son in 1656 confirms their earlier relationship. It seems most likely, then, that Quinault was in the service of Tristan from about 1643 to 1646 and that he continued his relationship with his mentor while he received a more formal education.

Quinault began practicing law in 1655, the same year in which his first play, *Les Rivales,* was produced, with the help of Tristan. According to an anecdote in the Parfaict brothers' *Histoire du théâtre français* (7: 428-30), this was the first play for which the author was paid a percentage of the box office revenues, rather than a fixed fee. By the time he was in his mid-twenties, Quinault enjoyed a considerable reputation for well-crafted plays and for the elegant expression of tender sentiments, the *tendresse* that became his trademark.

In all, Quinault wrote fifteen plays for the spoken stage, the last being *Bellérophon* (with a subject similar to that of Racine's *Phèdre*) in 1671. These works include seven tragi-comedies, five tragedies, three comedies, and *La*

Comédie sans comédie, which includes one-act works in four different genres. He quickly became a favorite with the public and with many critics; he was elected to the Académie Française in 1670, and in 1674 he was one of the first members of the "Petite Académie," the Académie Royale des Inscriptions et Médailles.

On April 29, 1660, Quinault married Louise Goujon, a rich young widow, and he continued to improve his social status: described as an attorney ("avocat en la cour de Parlement") in the marriage contract, by the baptism of his first daughter (March 23, 1661) he could claim a position at court, "escuyer, valet de chambre du Roy." It was also in 1660 that he began to work, as he wrote to Louis XIV in 1684, "pour les divertissements du roi," beginning with *Lysis et Hespérie*, in celebration of the Spanish alliance and the marriage of the king with Marie-Thérèse. He would continue to write for the spoken stage—his tragedy *Astrate* (1665) was one of the greatest box office successes of the century, and his comedy *La Mère coquette* (1666) enjoyed great success up through the nineteenth century—but he was becoming more involved with the ballets and other spectacles involving poetry, music, and dance that were so popular with Louis XIV's court. He wrote more than 60 airs that were published in various collections between 1660 and 1674, and he collaborated on several court ballets, in particular *Le Ballet des Muses* in 1666 and 1667. It was therefore natural that Lully would think of Quinault in 1671 to write the poetry for the sung sections of *Psyché,* for which Molière and Corneille wrote the spoken sections, and to be his librettist when he launched his Académie Royale de Musique in 1672 with *Les Fêtes de l'Amour et de Bacchus.*

By this time Quinault was in an even higher position at court, having obtained the important—and expensive—rank of Auditor in the Chambre des Comptes on September 18, 1671, in spite of the resistance of some members of the group who did not like the idea of having a playwright of humble origins in their august company. The part of his career that would bring him the greatest fame, however, was just beginning; he would remain Lully's librettist (except for *Bellérophon* and *Psyché* in 1678 and 1679, for which the king's mistress Mme de Montespan had Quinault replaced by Thomas Corneille and Fontenelle, because of negative allusions that courtiers found in the libretto to *Isis*) until he retired in 1686, because of his health and of religious scruples. He died, a famous and relatively wealthy man, on November 26, 1688.

Appendix III

Quinault's Works for the Theater[1]

Les Rivales (comédie), 1653
La Généreuse Ingratitude (tragi-comédie pastorale), 1654
L'Amant indiscret, ou le maître étourdi (comédie), 1654
La Comédie sans comédie, 1655
Le Coups de l'Amour et de la Fortune (tragi-comédie), 1655
Le Fantôme amoureux (tragi-comédie), 1656
Amalasonte (tragi-comédie), 1657
Le Feint Alcibiade (tragi-comédie), 1658
Le Mariage de Cambyse (tragi-comédie), 1658
La Mort de Cyrus (tragédie), 1659
Stratonice (tragi-comédie), 1660
Lysis et Hespérie (pastorale allegorique), 1660 (lost)
Agrippa, roy d'Albe, ou le faux Tibérinus (tragi-comédie), 1662
Astrate, roi de Tyr (tragédie), 1665
La Mère coquette, ou les amants brouillés (comédie), 1665

La Grotte de Versailles (églogue) 1668; revised as L'Eglogue de Versailles, 1674
Pausanias (tragédie), 1668
Bellérophon (tragédie), 1671
Psyché, with Molière and Pierre Corneille (tragédie-ballet), 1671
Les Fêtes de l'Amour et de Bacchus (pastorale), 1672
Cadmus et Hermione (tragédie lyrique), 1673
Alceste (tragédie lyrique), 1674
Thésée (tragédie lyrique), 1675
Atys (tragédie lyrique), 1676
Isis (tragédie lyrique), 1677
Proserpine (tragédie lyrique), 1680
Le Triomphe de l'Amour (ballet) 1681
Persée (tragédie lyrique), 1682
Phaéton (tragédie lyrique), 1683
Amadis (tragédie lyrique), 1684
Roland (tragédie lyrique), 1685
Le Temple de la paix (ballet) 1685
Armide (tragédie lyrique), 1686

---

[1] The exact nature of Quinault's contribution to court spectacles in the 1660s, and in particular to Le Ballet des Muses of 1666 and to its revival in Paris in 1667, is unclear; see Couvreur, "La Collaboration de Quinault et Lully avant la 'Psyché' de 1671."

Bibliography

BOOKS AND ARTICLES

Abbate, Carolyn. *Unsung Voices: Opera and Musical Narrative in the Nineteenth Century*. Princeton: Princeton University Press, 1991.

Abraham, Claude. "Farce, ballet, et intégrité: les dernières comédies-ballets de Molière." *Offene Gefüge*. Ed. H. Krauss. Tübingen: G. Narr, 1994. 65-73.

_____. *On the Structure of Molière's Comedy-Ballets*. Biblio 17. Paris/Seattle/Tübingen: PFSCL, 1984.

Adam, Antoine. *L'Époque de Pascal*. 1948. Vol. 2 of *Histoire de la littérature française*. Paris: Del Duca, 1962.

Anthony, James R. *French Baroque Music from Beaujoyeulx to Rameau*. New York: Norton, 1974. Revised and expanded edition. Portland: Amadeus Press, 1997.

_____. "Lully." *The New Grove Dictionary of Music and Musicians*. Ed. Stanley Sadie. London: Macmillan, 1980. 11: 314-29. *New Grove French Baroque Masters*. New York: Norton, 1986. 1-70.

Anton, Herbert. *Der Raub des Proserpine: Literarische Traditionen eines erotischen Sinnbildes und mythischen Symbols*. Heidelberg: Carl Winter Universitätsverlag, 1967.

Apostolidès, Jean-Marie. "From Roi Soleil to Louis le Grand." *A New History of French Literature*. Ed. Denis Hollier. Cambridge: Harvard University Press, 1989. 314-20.

_____. *Le Prince sacrifié: théâtre et politique au temps de Louis XIV*. Paris: Minuit, 1985.

_____. *Le Roi machine: spectacle et politique au temps de Louis XIV*. Paris: Minuit, 1981.

Ariosto, Ludovico. *Orlando furioso*. Ed. Nicola Zingarelli. 1532. Milan: Hoepli, 1959.

_____. *Orlando furioso*. Trans. William Stewart Rose. Ed. Stewart A. Baker and A. Bartlett Giamatti. Indianapolis: Bobbs-Merrill, 1968.

Aristotle. *Poetics*. Trans. George Whalley. Montreal: McGill-Queens University Press, 1997.

Arnauld, Antoine, and Pierre Nicole. *La Logique, ou l'art de penser*. Paris: Charles Savreux, 1662. Paris: P.U.F., 1965.

Aronson, Nicole. *Mademoiselle de Scudéry*. Twayne World Authors Series. Boston: Twayne, 1978.

Aubignac, François Hédelin, abbé d'. *La Pratique du théâtre*. 1657. Ed. Pierre Martino. Paris: Champion, 1927.

Auld, Louis. *The Lyric Art of Pierre Perrin, Founder of French Opera*. Henryville (PA): Institute of Medieval Music, 1986. 3 vols.

Bacilly, Bénigne de, ed. *Recueil des plus beaux vers, seconde et nouvelle partie*. Paris: Ballard, 1668.

_____. *Remarques curieuses sur l'art de bien chanter*. 2nd ed. 1679. Geneva: Slatkine Reprints, 1971.

Baker, Susan Read. *Dissonant Harmonies. Drama and Ideology in Five Neglected Plays of Pierre Corneille*. Tübingen: Gunter Narr, 1990.

Baret, Eugène. *De l'Amadis de Gaule et de son influence sur les mœurs et la littérature au XVIᵉ et au XVIIᵉ siècle*. Paris: Durand, 1853. 2nd ed. Paris: Firmin-Didot Frères, 1873.

Barnett, Dene. "La Rhétorique de l'opéra." *Dix-septième Siècle* 132 (1981): 335-55.

_____. *The Art of Gesture: The Practice and Principles of Eighteenth-Century Acting*. Heidelberg: C. Winter, 1987.

Barras, M. *The Stage Controversy in France from Corneille to Rousseau*. 1933. New York: Phaeton Press, 1973.

Barthélemy, Maurice. *Métamorphoses de l'opéra français au siècle des lumières*. Arles: Actes Sud, 1990.

_____. "L'Opéra français et la Querelle des Anciens et des Modernes." *Lettres Romanes* 10 (1956): 379-91.

Barthes, Roland. *Degré zéro de la littérature*. Paris: Seuil, 1953.

_____. *Sur Racine*. 1960. Paris: Seuil, 1963.

Bassenne, M. *La Vie tragique d'une reine d'Espagne. Marie-Louise de Bourbon-Orléans, nièce de Louis XIV*. Paris: Calmann-Lévy, 1939.

Bassinet, Stéphane. Introduction. *Atys*. By Philippe Quinault. Geneva: Droz, 1992.

Batteux, Charles. *Les Beaux arts réduits à un même principe*. Paris: Durand, 1747.

Bayle, Pierre. *Lettres*. Ms. 12771. Paris. Bibliothèque Nationale, fonds français.

_____. *Œuvres diverses de Pierre Bayle; contenant tout ce que cet auteur a publié sur des matières de théologie, de philosophie, de critique, d'histoire, et de littérature, excepté son Dictionnaire historique et critique*. La Haye: P. Husson, 1727-31. 4 vols.

Beasley, Faith E. *Revising Memory: Women's Fiction and Memoirs in Seventeenth-Century France*. New Brunswick: Rutgers University Press, 1990.

Beaussant, Philippe. *Lully ou le musicien du soleil*. Paris: Gallimard/Théâtre des Champs-Élysées, 1992.

_____. *Versailles, opéra*. Le Chemin. Paris: Gallimard, 1981.

_____. *Vous avez dit "baroque"?* Arles: Actes Sud, 1988.

_____. *Vous avez dit "classique"?: sur la mise en scène de la tragédie*. Arles: Actes Sud, 1991.

Beffara, Louis-François. *Dictionnaire de l'Académie Royale de Musique*. 1783-84. Ms. Rés. 602-603. Paris. Bibliothèque de l'Opéra.

Benoît, Marcelle, ed. *Dictionnaire de la musique française aux XVIIe et XVIIIe siècles*. Paris: Fayard, 1992.

Benserade, Isaac de. *Ballets pour Louis XIV*. Ed. Marie-Claude Canova-Green. Toulouse: Littératures Classiques, 1997.

Bernard, Catherine. *Inès de Cordoue, nouvelle espagnole*. 1696. Ed. René Godenne. Geneva: Slatkine Reprints, 1979.

Bernet, Charles. *Le Vocabulaire des tragédies de Jean Racine*. Geneva/Paris: Slatkine/Champion, 1983.

Berrone, Carlo. "Du théâtre parlé à la tragédie lyrique: Médée, héroïne noire de Quinault." Mazouer, *Recherches* 75-87.

Betzwieser, Thomas. *Exotismus und "Türkenoper" in der französischen Musik des Ancien Régime*. Laaber: Laaber Verlag, 1993.

Biet, Christian. "De la Veuve Joyeuse à l'individu autonome." *Dix-septième Siècle* 187.2 (1995): 307-30

_____. *Œidpe en monarchie: tragédie et théorie juridique à l'âge classique*. Paris: Klincksieck, 1994.

_____. "La Passion des larmes." *Littératures Classiques* 26 (1996): 167-83.

_____. *La Tragédie*. Paris: Armand Colin, 1997.

Blanchard, Jean-Vincent. "Le Baroque a-t-il cru à ses machines? Fétichisme de l'artifice au XVIIe siècle." *Cahiers du Dix-septième* 6.1 (1992): 23-36.

Blaze, François-Henri-Joseph, dit Castil. "Lully." *Revue de Paris* 8 (Aug. 1834): 73-98, 145-69.

Bluche, François. *Louis XIV*. Paris: Fayard, 1986.

Boileau, Nicolas. *Œuvres*. Ed. Georges Mongrédien. Classiques Garnier. Paris: Garnier, 1961.

_____. *Odes. Poésies diverses*. Ed. Charles-H. Boudhors. Les Textes Français. Paris: Société Les Belles Lettres, 1960.

Bonnet, Jacques. *Histoire de la musique et de ses effets*. 1715. Geneva: Slatkine Reprints, 1969.

Boscheron. *La Vie de Philippe Quinault de l'Académie Françoise*. Quinault. *Théâtre*. Paris: Pierre Ribou, 1715. Paris: Veuve Duchêne, 1778. 3-62. Geneva: Slatkine Reprints, 1970.

_____. *Vie de M. Quinault de l'Académie Françoise avec l'origine des opera en France*. Ms. 24329. Paris, Bibliothèque Nationale, fonds français.

Bouhours, Dominique. *Recueil de vers chosis*. Paris: G. et L. Josse, 1683.

Bouissou, Sylvie. *Vocabulaire de la musique baroque*. Paris: Minerve, 1996.

Bourciez, Édouard. *Les Mœurs polies et la littérature de cour sous Henri II*. Paris: Hachette, 1886.

Bray, René. *La Formation de la doctrine classique en France*. Paris: Nizet, 1957.

Brécourt, Guillaume Marcoureau de. *L'Ombre de Molière*. Paris: Barbin, 1674. *Les Contemporains de Molière*. Vol. 1. Ed. Victor Fournel. Paris: Firmin Didot, 1863. 519-48.

Brégy, Charlotte Saumaise de Chazan, comtesse de Flecelles de. *Les Œuvres galantes de Madame la Comtesse de B*. Paris: J. Ribou, 1666.

Brereton, Geoffrey. *French Tragic Drama in the Sixteenth and Seventeenth Centuries*. London: Methuen, 1973.

Brody, Jules. "What *Was* French Classicism?" *Continuum* 1 (1989): 51-77.

Brooks, William. *Bibliographie critique du théâtre de Quinault*. Biblio 17. Paris/Seattle/Tübingen: PFSCL, 1988.

_____. "From Lazzi to Acrobats: The Court's Taste after 1680." *Cahiers du Dix-septième* 6.2 (1992): 45-53.

_____. "Lully and Quinault at Court and on the Public Stage." *Seventeenth-Century French Studies* 10 (1988): 101-21.

_____. "Perrin, Corneille, and the Beginnings of French Opera." Carlin 339-48.

_____. "Quinault Criticism, Boileau and the Problem of Racine." *Actes de Las Vegas: Théorie dramatique, Théophile de Viau, Les Contes de Fées*. Actes du XXIIe colloque de la North American Society for Seventeenth-Century French Literature, University of Nevada, Las Vegas (1-3 mars 1990). Ed. Marie-France Hilgar. Biblio 17. Paris/Seattle/Tübingen: PFSCL, 1991. 37-48.

_____, ed. *Le Théâtre et l'opéra vus par les gazetiers Robinet et Laurent (1670-1678)*. Biblio 17. Paris/Seattle/Tübingen: PFSCL, 1993.

_____, and P. J. Yarrow. *The Dramatic Criticism of Elizabeth Charlotte, duchesse d'Orléans*. Lewiston, NY: Edwin Mellen, 1996.

_____. "Observations sur la datation de quelques lettres de Madame, princesse palatine." *Dix-septième Siècle* 45 (1993): 131-38.

Brunetière, Ferdinard. *Les Époques du théâtre français*. Septième conférence. Paris: Hachette, 1896.

_____. *Manuel de l'histoire de la littérature française*. Paris: Delagrave, 1921.

Buijtendorp, Johannes B. A. *Philippe Quinault: sa vie, ses tragédies et ses tragi-comédies*. Amsterdam: H. J. Paris, 1928.

Bury, Emmanuel. *Le Classicisme. L'avènement du modèle littéraire francais, 1660-1680*. Collection 128. Paris: Nathan, 1993.

_____. *Littérature et politesse: l'invention de l'honnête homme, 1580-1750*. Paris: P.U.F., 1996.

Bussy, Roger de Rabutin, comte de. *Correspondance avec sa famille et ses amis (1666-1693)*. Ed. Ludovic Lalanne. Paris: Charpentier, 1858. 6 vols.

Butler, Philip. *Classicisme et baroque dans l'œuvre de Racine*. Paris: Nizet, 1959.

Cahusac, Louis de. *La Danse ancienne et moderne, ou Traité historique de la danse*. The Hague: Neaulme, 1754. 3 vols.

Callières, François de. *Histoire poëtique de la guerre nouvellement déclarée entre des anciens et des modernes*. Amsterdam: Pierre Savouret, 1688.

Campardon, Emile. *L'Académie royale de musique au XVIIIe siecle; documents inédits découverts aux Archives nationales par Émile Campardon*. Paris: Berger-Levrault et Cie, 1884. 2 vols.

Canova-Green, Marie-Claude. "Ballet et comédie ballet sous Louis XIV ou l'illusion de la fête." *PFSCL* 17.32 (1990): 253-62.

Cardy, Michael. *The Literary Doctrines of Jean-François Marmontel*. Oxford: Voltaire Foundation, 1982.

Carlin, Claire, ed. *La Rochefoucauld, Mithridate, Frères et sœurs, Les Muses sœurs*. Actes du 29e congrès annuel de la North American Society for Seventeenth-Century French Literature. Biblio 17. Tübingen: Gunter Narr Verlag, 1998.

Cave, Terence. "Corneille, Œdipus, Racine." *Convergences: Rhetoric and Poetic in Seventeenth-century France. Essays for Hugh M. Davidson*. Ed. David Lee Rubin and Mary B. McKinley. Columbus: Ohio State University Press, 1989. 82-100.

_____. *Recognitions: a study in poetics*. Oxford: Clarendon Press, 1988.

Cessac, Catherine. *Marc-Antoine Charpentier*. Paris: Fayard, 1984.

_____. "La Musique de Marc-Antoine Charpentier pour les pièces à machines (1675-1682)." *Littératures Classiques* 21 (1994): 115-24.

Charavay, Étienne. "Jean-Baptiste Lully." *Revue des documents historiques* 2 (1875): 108-16.

Chavardès, Maurice. *Histoire de la librairie*. Paris: Pierre Waleffe, 1967.

Christie, William. "Lully réévalué." *L'Avant-Scène Opéra* 94 (1987): 114-19.

Christout, Marie-Françoise. *Le Ballet de cour de Louis XIV: 1643-1672*. Paris: Picard, 1983.

Clément, Catherine. *Opera, or the Undoing of Women*. Trans. Betsy Wing. Minneapolis: University of Minnesota Press, 1988. Trans. of *L'Opéra ou la défaite des femmes*. Paris: Grasset, 1979.

Clément, Jean-Marie-Bernard, and Joseph de Laporte. *Anecdotes dramatiques*. Paris: Veuve Duchesne, 1775. 3 vols.

Clément, Pierre, ed. *Lettres, instructions et mémoires de Colbert*. Paris: Imprimerie impériale, 1861-82. 10 vols.

Corneille, Pierre. *Andromède*. Ed. Christian Delmas. S.T.F.M. Paris: Didier, 1974.

_____. *Trois Discours sur le poème dramatique*. Ed. Bénédicte Louvat and Marc Escola. Paris: Flammarion, 1999.

Corneille, Thomas. *Timocrate*. 1656. Ed. Yves Giraud. Textes Littéraires Français. Geneva: Droz, 1970.

Cornic, Sylvain. "*Ad limina templis Polymniae:* les fonctions du prologue d'opéra chez Quinault." Mazouer, *Recherches* 47-62.

Courville, Xavier de. "Quinault, poète d'opéra." *La Revue musicale* 6 (1925): 74-88.

Couvreur, Manuel. "La Collaboration de Quinault et Lully avant la 'Psyché' de 1671." *Recherches sur la Musique Française Classique* 27 (1991): 9-34.

_____. *Jean-Baptiste Lully: musique et dramaturgie au service du Prince*. Brussels: Le Cri, 1992.

Cowart, Georgia, ed. *French Musical Thought 1600-1800*. Ann Arbor: UMI Research Press, 1989.

_____. "Lully *enjoué*: Galanterie in Seventeenth-century France." *Actes de Baton Rouge*. Ed. Selma Zebouni. Biblio 17. Paris/Seattle/Tübingen: PFSCL, 1986. 35-51.

_____. *The Origins of Modern Musical Criticism: French and Italian Music, 1600-1750*. Ann Arbor: UMI Research Press, 1981.

Crapelet, G.-A. "Notice sur la vie et les ouvrages de Quinault." *Œuvres choisies de Quinault*. Paris: Crapelet, 1824. 1: i-xxxiv.

Cuénin, Micheline. Introduction. *Les Désordres de l'amour*. By Mme de Villedieu. Geneva: Droz, 1970.

_____. *Roman et société sous Louis XIV: Mme de Villedieu*. Paris: Champion, 1979.

Dangeau, Philippe de Courcillon, marquis de. *Journal du Marquis de Dangeau*. Ed. Soulié, Dussieux, de Chennevières, Mantz, et de Montaiglon. Paris: F. Didot, 1854-60. 19 vols.

DeJean, Joan. "Amazons and Literary Women: Female Culture during the Reign of the Sun King." Rubin, *Sun King* 115-28.

_____. *Ancients against Moderns: Culture Wars and the Making of a Fin de Siècle*. Chicago: University of Chicago Press, 1997.

_____. "Lafayette's Ellipses: The Privileges of Anonymity." *PMLA* 99.5 (1984): 884-900.

_____. *Tender Geographies: Women and the Origins of the Novel in France*. New York: Columbia University Press, 1991.

Delmas, Christian. Introduction. *Andromède*. By Pierre Corneille. xi-civ.

_____. *Mythologie et mythe dans le théâtre français (1650-1676)*. Paris: Droz, 1985.

_____. *Recueil de tragédies à machines sous Louix XIV*. Toulouse: Université de Toulouse-le-Mirail, 1985.

_____. "Le Théâtre musical et *Psyché* de Molière." *Littératures Classiques* 21 (1994): 221-36.

_____. *La Tragédie de l'âge classique (1553-1770)*. Écrivains de toujours. Paris: Seuil, 1994.

Denécheau, Pascal. "*Thésée* de Lully, partitions et livrets." La Gorce and Schneider, *Quellenstudien* 223-47.

_____. "*Thésée* de Lully et Quinault: histoire d'un opéra (1675-1779)." D.E.A. Université de la Sorbonne, Paris IV, 1997.

Denis, Delphine. *La Muse galante: poétique de la conversation dans l'œuvre de Madeleine de Scudéry*. Lumière Classique. Paris: Champion, 1007.

Descartes, René. *Les Passions de l'âme*. Paris: Henri Le Gras, 1649. Ed. Geneviève Rodis-Lewis. Paris: Vrin, 1966.

Deshoulières, Antoinette du Ligier de la Garde, Madame de. *Poësies de Madame Deshoulières*. Paris: Veuve de Sébastien Mabre-Cramoisy, 1693.

Deshoulières, Christophe. "*Atys*: la révélation." Prassoloff. 37-44.

_____. Entretien avec Ph.ilippe Beaussant. "Mais que faire des ballets?" Prassoloff. 69-75.

Dictionnaire de l'Académie Française. Paris: Coignard, 1694.

Donington, Robert. *The Opera*. New York: Harcourt Brace Jovanovich, 1978.

_____. *Opera and Its Symbols: The Unity of Words, Music and Staging*. New Haven: Yale University Press, 1990.

_____. *The Rise of Opera*. London: Faber and Faber, 1981.

Du Baroque aux Lumières: pages à la mémoire de Jeanne Carriat. Mortemart: Rougerie, 1986.

Du Bos, l'Abbé Jean-Baptiste. *Réflexions Critiques sur la Poësie et sur la Peinture*. 1719. 7th ed. Paris: Pissot, 1770. Geneva: Slatkine Reprints, 1967.

Duchêne, Roger. *La Fontaine*. Paris: Fayard, 1990.

_____, and Pierre Ronzeaud, ed. *Ordre et contestation au temps des classiques*. Biblio 17. Paris/Seattle/Tübingen: PFSCL, 1992.

Du Crest, Sabine. *Des Fêtes à Versailles: les divertissements de Louis XIV*. Paris: Aux Amateurs du Livre, 1990.

Durey de Noinville, Jacques-Bernard. *Histoire de l'Académie Royale de Musique en France depuis son établissement jusqu'à présent*. Paris: J. Barsou, 1753. 2nd ed. Paris: Duchesne, 1757. Geneva: Minkoff, 1972.

Ducrot, Ariane. "Les Représentations de l'Académie royale de Musique à Paris au temps de Louis XIV (1671-1715)." *Recherches sur la Musique Française Classique* 10 (1970): 19-55.

Dufourcq, Norbert, ed. *La Musique à la cour de Louis XIV et de Louis XV d'après les Mémoires de Sourches et Luynes (1681-1758)*. Paris: Picard, 1970.

Duron, Jean. "*Atys*. Commentaire musical et littéraire." *L'Avant-Scène Opéra* 94 (1987): 32-80.

_____. "L'Instinct de M. de Lully." *La Tragédie lyrique* 65-119.

Durosoir, Georgie. *La Musique vocale profane au XVIIe siècle*. Paris: Klincksieck, 1994.

_____. "Pastorales avec musique et pastorales en musique en France au milieu du XVIIe siècle." *Littératures Classiques* 21 (1994): 237-48.

Du Tralage, Jean-Nicolas. *Notes et documents sur l'histoire des théâtres de Paris au XVIIe siécle*. Ca. 1687. Ed. Paul Lacroix. Paris: Librairie des Bibliophiles, 1880.

Edelman, Nathan. *The Eye of the Beholder*. Essays in French Literature. Ed. Jules Brody. Baltimore: John Hopkins University Press, 1974.

Eliot, T. S. *Poetry and Drama*. Cambridge: Harvard University Press, 1951.

Ellis, Helen Meredith. "The Dances of Jean-Baptiste Lully." Diss. Stanford, 1967.

Emelina, Jean. "Racine et Quinault: de *Bellérophon* à *Phèdre*." *Hommage à Jean Onimus*. Paris: Les Belles Lettres, 1979. 71-81.

Fajon, Robert. "La comédie-ballet, fille et héritière du ballet de cour." *Littératures Classiques* 21 (1994): 207-19.

_____. "Les Incertitudes du succès: étude du répertoire de l'Académie Royale de Musique des origines à 1750." *L'Opéra au XVIIIe siècle*. Actes du Colloque [...] les 29, 30 avril et 1er mai 1977. Aix-en-Provence: Université de Provence, 1982. 287-344.

_____. *L'Opéra à Paris du Roi Soleil à Louis le Bien-Aimé*. Paris: Champion, 1984.

Favart, Charles Simon. *Thésée, Parodie nouvelle de Thésée*. 1745. *Théâtre de M. Favart*. Vol. 7. Paris: Duchesne, 1763. 8 vols.

Félibien, André. *Les Fêtes de Versailles: chroniques de 1668 et 1674*. Ed. Martin Meade. Paris: Maisonneuve et Larose, 1994.

Fénelon, François de Salignac de la Mothe. *Les Aventures de Télémaque*. Ed. J.-L. Goré. Paris: Garnier, 1994.

_____. *Lettre à Louis XIV*. Ed. Henri Guillemin. Neuchâtel: Ides et Calendes, 1961.

Ferrier-Caverivière, Nicole. "1664-1686: Le genre lyrique, miroir de la société de cour." *Du Baroque aux Lumières* 92-95.

_____. *L'Image de Louis XIV dans la littérature française de 1660 à 1715*. Paris: P.U.F., 1981.

Flaherty, Gloria. *Opera in the Development of German Critical Thought*. Princeton: Princeton University Press, 1978.

Fleck, Stephen H. *Music, Dance, and Laughter: Comic Creation in Molière's Comedy-Ballets*. Biblio 17. Paris/Seattle/Tübingen: PFSCL, 1995.

Forestier, Georges. *Essai de génétique théâtrale: Corneille à l'œuvre*. Paris: Klinck-sieck, 1996.

Foucault, Michel. *Les Mots et les choses*. Paris: Gallimard, 1966.

Fumaroli, Marc. *L'Age de l'éloquence: Rhétorique et "res literaria" de la Renaissance au seuil de l'époque classique*. Geneva: Droz, 1980.

_____. "Le Corps éloquent: théorie de l'action du héros cornélien." *Héros et orateurs: rhétorique et dramaturgie cornéliennes*. Geneva: Droz, 1990. 414-48.

Furetière, Antoine. *Dictionnaire universel [...]*. 1690. Paris: Robert, 1978. 3 vols.

_____. *Factums*. 1685-94. Ed. Charles Asselineau et P. A. Cap. Paris: Poulet-Malassis, 1859.

Gadamer, Hans-Georg. "Art and Imitation." *The Relevance of the Beautiful and Other Essays*. Ed. R. Bernasconi. New York: Cambridge University Press, 1986. 92-104.

Gethner, Perry. "La Fonction des sentences dans les livrets de Quinault." *C.A.I.E.F.* 41: (1989): 129-44.

_____. "La Magicienne à l'opéra, source de subversion." Duchêne and Ronzeaud 1: 301-07.

_____. "La 'Morale lubrique' dans les opéras de Quinault." *Les Visages de l'amour au XVIIe siècle*. Toulouse: Université de Toulouse-le Mirail, 1984. 145-54.

_____. "The Roles of the Chorus in Late Seventeenth-Century Opera." *Ars Lyrica* 91 (1998): 41-49.

Giles, Patrick. "Leap of Faith: Embracing *Tosca*." *Opera News* (March 1999): 48-51.

Ginguené, P.-L. *Notice sur la vie et les ouvrages de Nicolas Piccini*. Paris: Veuve Panckoucke, 1800-01.

Giraud, Yves. *La Fable de Daphné*. Geneva: Droz, 1968.

_____. Introduction. Montalvo 1: [3]-[28].

_____. "Quinault et Lully, ou l'accord de deux styles." *Marseille* 95 (1973): 195-211.

Girdlestone, Cuthbert M. *La Tragédie en musique (1673-1750) considérée comme genre littéraire*. Geneva: Droz, 1972.

_____. "Tragédie et tragédie en musique." *C.A.I.E.F.* 17 (1965): 9-23.

Goodkin, Richard. *The Tragedy of Primogeniture in Pierre Corneille, Thomas Corneille, and Jean Racine.* Philadelphia: University of Pennsylvania Press, 2000.

Grannis, Valeria Belt. *Dramatic Parody in Eighteenth-Century France.* New York: Publications of the Institute of French Studies, 1931.

Graves, Robert. *The Greek Myths.* 1955. New York: George Braziller, Inc., 1959.

Green, Eugène. "Le lieu de la déclamation." *Littératures Classiques* 12 (1990): 275-91.

Grimal, Pierre. *Dictionnaire de la mythologie grecque et romaine.* Paris: P.U.F., 1951.

Grimarest, Jean-Léonard le Gallois de. *Traité du récitatif.* Paris: Jacques Lefèvre et Pierre Ribou, 1707. New York: AMS Press, 1978.

Groos, Arthur, and Roger Parker. *Reading Opera.* Princeton: Princeton University Press, 1988.

Gros, Etienne. "A propos de Lamartine et de Quinault." *Revue d'Histoire Littéraire de la France* 36 (1929): 590-91.

_____. "Les origines de la tragédie lyrique et la place des tragédies en machines dans l'évolution du théâtre vers l'opéra." *Revue d'Histoire Littéraire de la France* 35 (1928): 161-93.

_____. *Philippe Quinault, sa vie et son œuvre.* Paris: Champion, 1926. Geneva: Slatkine Reprints, 1970.

Gros de Boze, Claude. *Histoire de l'Académie royale des Inscriptions et Belles-Lettres, depuis son establissement jusqu'à présent.* Paris: Guerin, 1740. 3 vols.

Grout, Donald J. "Seventeenth-Century Parodies of French Opera." *Musical Quarterly* 27 (1941): 211-19, 514-26.

_____. *A Short History of Opera.* 2nd ed. New York: Columbia University Press, 1965.

Guiffrey, Jules-Joseph, ed. *Colbert, 1664-1680.* Vol. 1 of *Comptes et bâtiments du roi sous le règne de Louis XIV.* Paris: Imprimerie Nationale, 1881.

Harris-Warwick, Rebecca. "Contexts for Choreographies: Notated Dances Set to the Music of Jean-Baptiste Lully." La Gorce and Schneider, *Jean Baptiste Lully* 433-55.

_____, and Carol G. Marsh. *Musical Theater at the Court of Louis XIV: the Example of "Le Mariage de la Grosse Cathos."* Cambridge: Cambridge University Press, 1994.

Hazard, Paul. *La Crise de la conscience européenne, 1680-1715.* 1935. Collection Idées. Paris: Gallimard, 1968. 2 vols.

Henriet, Maurice. "La Fontaine aux archives de Chantilly." *Revue Bleue* (19 August 1899): 232-37.

Hertel, Carola. "'Sans avoir égard à la mesure des vers, ni au caractère de l'air, ni au sens des paroles'? Observations sur des parodies de récitatif de Lully." *Timbre und Vaudeville. Zur Geschichte und Problematik einer populären Gattung im 17. und 18. Jahrhundert.* Ed. Herbert Schneider. Hildesheim: Olms, 1999. 42-56.

Heyer, John Hajdu, ed. *Jean-Baptiste Lully and the Music of the French Baroque: Essays in Honor of James. R. Anthony*. New York: Cambridge University Press, 1989.

_____. *Lully Studies*. New York: Cambridge University Press, 2000.

Hibbard, Lloyd. "Mme de Sévigné and the Operas of Lully." *Essays in Musicology: a Birthday Offering for Willi Apel*. Ed. Hans Tischler. Bloomington: Indiana University School of Music, 1968. 153-63.

Hilgar, Marie-France. *La Mode des stances dans le théâtre tragique français 1610-1687*. Paris: Nizet, 1973.

Hilton, Wendy. *Dance and Music of Court and Theatre: The French Noble Style, 1690-1725*. Princeton: Princeton University Press, 1980.

Himelfarb, Hélène. "Source méconnue ou analogie culturelle? des livrets d'opéras lullystes au décor sculpté des jardins de Versailles." *Gazette des Beaux-Arts* (Nov. 1992): 179-94.

_____. "Versailles, fonctions et légendes." Nora 235-92.

Hoffmann, Kathryn A. *Society of Pleasures: Interdisciplinary Readings in Pleasure and Power during the Reign of Louis XIV*. New York: St. Martin's Press, 1997.

Howard, Patricia. "The Académie Royale and the Performance of Lully's Operas." *The Consort* 31 (1975): 109-15.

_____. "The Positioning of Women in Quinault's World Picture." La Gorce and Schneider, *Jean Baptiste Lully* 193-99.

Isherwood, Robert. *Music in the Service of the King: France in the Seventeenth Century*. Ithaca, NY: Cornell University Press, 1973.

Jackson, W. T. H. *The Hero and the King: An Epic Theme*. New York: Columbia University Press, 1982.

Jacquiot, Josèphe. *Médailles et jetons de Louis XIV d'après le manuscrit de Londres*. Paris: Imprimerie Nationale/Klincksieck, 1968. 4 vols.

_____. "Philippe Quinault, membre de la Petite Académie." *Mélanges d'histoire littéraire offerts à Raymond Lebègue*. Paris: Nizet, 1969. 305-20.

Journal de L'Opéra [*Théâtre de l'Opéra: Journal*]. Ms. Usuels 201. Paris, Bibliothèque de l'Opéra.

Karro, Françoise. "L'Empire ottoman et l'Europe dans l'opéra français et viennois au temps de Lully." La Gorce and Schneider, *Jean Baptiste Lully* 251-69.

_____. "Marques de royauté dans les livrets de l'Académie Royale de Musique entre 1672 et 1687." *Revue de la Bibliothèque Nationale* 49 (1993): 12-25.

_____. "Le Prologue d'*Armide*." *Les Écrivains français et l'opéra*. Ed. Jean-Paul Capdevielle and Peter-Eckhard Knabe. Cologne: dme-Verlag, 1986. 39-47.

Kerman, Joseph. *Opera as Drama*. 1956. 2nd ed. Berkeley: University of California Press, 1988.

Kintzler, Catherine. "De la pastorale à la tragédie lyrique: quelques éléments d'un système poétique." *Revue de Musicologie* 72 (1986): 67-96.

_____. *La France classique et l'opéra.* Paris: Harmonia Mundi, 1998.

_____. *"Platée*: la comédie, vérité de la tragédie." *L'Avant-Scène Opéra* 189 (1999): 44-49.

_____. *Poétique de l'opéra français de Corneille à Rousseau.* Paris: Minerve, 1991.

_____, ed. *La Pensée de la danse à l'âge classique.* Cahiers de la Maison de la Recherche. Lille: Université Charles-de-Gaulle - Lille III, 1997.

_____, and Jean-Claude Malgoire, ed. *Musique raisonnée.* Paris: Stock, 1980.

Kivy, Peter. *Osmin's Rage: Philosophical Reflections on Opera, Drama, and Text.* Princeton: Princeton University Press, 1988.

_____. *Sound and Semblance: Reflections on Musical Representation.* Princeton: Princeton University Press, 1984.

_____. *Sound Sentiment: An Essay on the Musical Emotions, Including the Complete Text of* The Corded Shell. Philadelphia: Temple University Press, 1989.

Knight, R. C. "The Evolution of Racine's 'poétique.'" *Modern Language Review* 35 (1940): 19-39.

Labie, Jean-François. *William Christie: sonate baroque.* Paris: Alinéa, 1989.

La Bruyère, Jean de. *Les Caractères ou les Mœurs de ce siècle.* Ed. Robert Garapon. Classiques Garnier. Paris: Garnier, 1962.

Lachèvre, Frédéric. *Bibliographie des recueils collectifs de poésies publiés de 1597 à 1700.* 1901-05. Geneva: Slatkine Reprints, 1967.

La Fontaine, Jean de. *Fables, contes et nouvelles.* Ed. René Groos and Jacques Schiffrin. Bilbiothèque de la Pléiade. Paris: Gallimard, 1954.

_____. *Œuvres.* Ed. Henri Régnier. Grands Écrivains de la France. Paris: Hachette, 1883-97. 11 vols.

_____. *Œuvres diverses.* Ed. Pierre Clarac. Bilbiothèque de la Pléiade. Paris: Gallimard, 1958.

La Gorce, Jérôme de. *Berain, dessinateur du Roi Soleil.* Paris: Herscher, 1986.

_____. "Les Débuts de l'opéra français: origines et formation de la tragédie en musique." Mamczarz 133-40.

_____, ed. *Lully: Un Age d'or de l'opéra français.* Catalogue d'exposition. Paris: Cicero, 1991.

_____. *L'Opéra à Paris au temps de Louis XIV: histoire d'un théâtre.* La Mesure des choses. Paris: Desjonquères 1992.

_____. "L'Opéra français à la cour de Louix XIV." *Revue d'Histoire du Théâtre* 35 (1983): 387-402.

_____. "Un proche collaborateur de Lully, Philippe Quinault." *Dix-septième Siècle* 161 (1988): 365-70.

_____, and Herbert Schneider, ed. *Jean Baptiste Lully. Actes du colloque / Kongreßbericht.* Laaber: Laaber-Verlag, 1990.

_____. *Quellenstudien zu Jean-Baptiste Lully / L'Œuvre de Lully: Études des sources.* Hildesheim: Georg Olms, 1999.

La Harpe, Jean-François de. *Cours de littérature ancienne et moderne.* Paris: C. Didot, 1863. 3 vols.

Lajarte, Théodore de. *Bibliothèque Musicale du Théâtre de l'Opéra.* Paris: Librairie des Bibliophiles, 1878.

Lancaster, Henry Carrington. *French Dramatic Literature in the Seventeenth Century.* Baltimore: Johns Hopkins University Press, 1929-42. 4 vols.

La Laurencie, Lionel de. *Lully.* Paris: Alcan, 1911. Paris: Éditions d'Aujourd'hui, 1977.

Lancelot, Francine. *La Belle danse: catalogue raisonné fait en l'an 1995 sous la direction de Francine Lancelot.* Paris: Van Dieren, 1996.

Laporte, Joseph de. *Dictionnaire dramatique [...].* 1776. Geneva: Slatkine Reprints, 1967. 3 vols.

Laurent, Jacques. *Lettres en vers à leurs altesses royales Monsieur et Madame.* Paris, 1677-1678. Brooks, ed., *Le Théâtre et l'opéra vus par les gazetiers Robinet et Laurent (1670-1678)* 161-71.

La Vallière, Louis-César. *Ballets, opéra et autres ouvrages lyriques par ordre chronologique.* Paris: Bauche, 1760.

Le Brun, Antoine-Louis. *Théâtre lyrique: avec une préface, où l'on traite du Poëme de l'Opéra.* Paris: Pierre Ribou, 1712. Preface rpr. Lesure (no continuous pagination).

Lecerf de la Viéville, Jean-Laurent, sieur de Freneuse. *Comparaison de la musique italienne et de la musique françoise.* 1704-06. Geneva: Minkoff Reprints, 1972.

Legrand, Raphaëlle. "*Persée* de Lully et Quinault: orientations pour l'analyse dramaturgique d'une tragédie en musique." *Analyse musicale* 27 (1992): 9-14.

Lesure, François, ed. *Textes sur Lully et l'opéra français.* Geneva: Minkoff, 1987.

*Lettre de M. de ***. à madame de ***. sur les opéra de Phaéton et Hippolite et Aricie.* Paris: C. F. Simon, Fils, 1743.

Lindenberger, Herbert. *Opera: The Extravagant Art.* Ithaca, NY: Cornell University Press, 1984.

_____. *Opera in History from Monteverdi to Cage.* Stanford, CA: Stanford University Press, 1998.

Loewenberg, Alfred. *Annals of Opera.* Geneva: Societas Bibliographica, 1943.

Louvat, Bénédicte. "De quelques créateurs mineurs: l'opéra français avant Lully." *Littératures Classiques* 31 (1997): 81-97.

_____. "Les Spectacles musicaux en France et en Angleterre: des formes baroques?" *Littératures Classiques* 36 (1999): 271-92.

_____. "Le Théâtre musical au XVIIᵉ siècle: élaboration d'un genre nouveau?" *Littératures Classiques* 21 (1994): 249-64.

Malgoire, Jean-Claude. "L'Analyse ramiste du monologue d'*Armide*, commentaire musical et esthétique." Kintzler and Malgoire 201-15.

Mamczarz, Irène, ed. *Les Premiers opéras en Europe et les formes dramatiques apparentées*. Paris: Klincksieck, 1992.

Marie, Alfred. *Naissance de Versailles*. Paris: Vincent, Fréal & Cie., 1968.

Marin, Louis. *Le Portrait du roi*. Paris: Minuit, 1981.

Marmontel, Jean François. "Opéra." *Éléments de littérature*. 14: 407-56. *Œuvres complètes*. Paris: Verdière, 1818-20. 19 vols.

Marsan, Jules. *La Pastorale dramatique en France à la fin du XVIᵉ et au commencement du XVIIᵉ siècle*. Paris: Hachette, 1905. New York: B. Franklin, 1971.

Martin, Henri-Jean. *Le Livre français sous l'Ancien Régime*. Paris: Promodis (Éditions du Cercle de la Librairie), 1987.

Martinoty, Jean-Louis. *Voyages à l'intérieur de l'opéra baroque: de Monteverdi à Mozart*. Paris: Fayard, 1990.

Masson, Chantal. "Journal du marquis de Dangeau, 1684-1720: extraits concernant la vie musicale à la Cour." *Recherches sur la Musique Française Classique* 2 (1961): 193-223.

Maurice-Amour, Lila. "Comment Lully et ses poètes humanisent Dieux et héros." *C.A.I.E.F.* 17 (1965): 59-95.

May, Georges. *Les Mille et une nuits d'Antoine Galland*. Paris: P.U.F., 1986.

Mazon, Paul. Introduction. *Prometheus Bound*. By Eschylus. Paris: Belles Lettres, 1966. 1: 151-57.

Mazouer, Charles. *Molière et ses comédies-ballets*. Paris: Klincksieck, 1993.

_____, ed. *Recherches des jeunes dix-septiémistes*. Actes du Vᵉ colloque du Centre International de Rencontres sur le XVIIᵉ siècle. Bordeaux, 28-30 janvier 1999. Biblio 17. Tübingen: Gunter Narr, 2000.

McGowan, Margaret M. *L'Art du ballet de cour en France, 1581-1643*. Paris: C.N.R.S., 1978.

_____. "Les Échanges entre le ballet de cour et le théâtre au milieu du XVIIᵉ siècle." Mamczarz 154-69.

_____. "Racine, Ménestrier, and Sublime Effects." *Theatre Research International* 1 (1975): 1-13.

McIntyre, Bruce. "Armide ou le monologue féminin." *Australian Journal of French Studies* 36.2 (1999): 157-72.

_____. "Éros et merveilleux: les tragédies lyriques de Quinault." Diss. MacQuarie University, 1997.

_____. "Quinault's Lyric Tragedies: a Genealogical Sketch." *Essays in French Literature* 34 (1997): 1-22. (University of Western Australia)

Melzer, Sara, and Kathryn Norberg. *From the Royal to the Republican Body*. Berkeley: University of California Press, 1998.

Mélèse, Pierre. *Répertoire analytique des documents contemporains d'information et de critique concernant le théâtre à Paris sous Louis XIV*. Paris: Droz, 1934.

Ménagiana, ou Bons mots, rencontres agreables, pensées judicieuses, et observations curieuses, de M. Menage, de l'Academie Françoise. 1693. 2nd ed. Paris: P. Delaulne, 1694. 2 vols.

Ménestrier, Claude François. *Des Ballets anciens et modernes*. Paris: René Guignard, 1682. Geneva: Minkoff, 1972.

_____. *Des Représentations en musique anciennes et modernes*. Paris: René Guignard, 1681. Geneva: Minkoff, 1972.

Miller, Dean A. *The Epic Hero*. Baltimore: Johns Hopkins University Press, 2000.

Milner, Jean-Claude, and François Regnault. *Dire le vers*. Paris: Seuil, 1987.

Moine, Marie-Christine. *Les Fêtes à la cour du Roi-Soleil, 1653-1715*. Paris: F. Lanore, 1984.

Molière [Jean-Baptiste Poquelin]. *Théâtre complet*. Ed. Robert Jouanny. Paris: Garnier, 1962. 2 vols.

Mongrédien, Georges. *Recueil des textes et des documents du dix-septième siècle relatifs à La Fontaine*. Paris: C.N.R.S., 1973.

Montaiglon, Anatole de. *Dépenses des Menus Plaisirs et affaires de la Chambre du roi pendant l'année 1677*. Paris: Dumoulin, 1857.

Montalvo, Garci Rodríguez de. *Le Premier livre d'Amadis de Gaule*. Trans. Nicolas de Herberay, Seigneur des Essarts. 1540. Ed. Hugues Vaganay and Yves Giraud. S.T.F.M. Paris: Nizet, 1986. 2 vols.

Morambert (Antoine-Jacques Labbet), abbé de. *Amadis, parodie nouvelle de l'opéra, meslée d'ariettes*. Paris: Cailleau, 1760.

Morel, Jacques. "Philippe Quinault, librettiste d'*Atys*." *L'Avant-Scène Opéra* 94 (1987): 22-25.

Moureau, François. "Haendel et l'opéra français." *Du Baroque aux Lumières* 117-123.

_____. "Lully en visite chez Arlequin: parodies italiennes avant 1697." La Gorce and Schneider, *Jean Baptiste Lully* 235-250.

Naudeix, Laura. "Par où commencer une tragédie lyrique?" Mazouer, *Recherches* 63-73.

Nédélec, Claudine. "Galanteries burlesques, ou burlesque galant." *Littératures Classiques* 38 (2000): 117-37.

Nelson, Robert J. "French Classicism: Dimensions of Application." *Continuum* 1 (1989): 79-104.

Néraudau, Jean-Pierre. "Du Christ à Apollon." *La Tragédie lyrique* 5-21.

_____. *L'Olympe du roi-soleil: mythologie et idéologie royale au Grand Siècle*. Paris: Les Belles Lettres, 1986.

Newman, Joyce. *Jean-Baptiste de Lully and His Tragédies Lyriques*. Ann Arbor: UMI Research Press, 1979.

Niderst, Alain. "*Mithridate* opera?" Carlin 125-36.

_____. "La Tragédie à intermèdes musicaux (1650-1670)." Mamczarz 141-51.

Nora, Pierre. *La Nation*. Part 2. Vol. 2 of *Les Lieux de mémoire*. Paris: Gallimard, 1986. 3 vols.

Norman, Buford. "Actions and Reactions: Emotional *Vraisemblance* in the *Tragédie-Lyrique*." *Cahiers du Dix-septième* 3.1 (1990): 141-54.

_____. "Ancients and Moderns, Tragedy and Opera: The Quarrel over *Alceste*." Cowart, *French Musical Thought* 177-96.

_____. "Le Héros contestataire dans les livrets de Quinault: politique ou esthétique." Duchêne and Ronzeaud 289-300.

_____. "Les Styles d'Alceste." *Papiers du Collège International de Philosophie* 16 (1993): 39-54.

_____. "'Le Théâtre est un grand monument': l'évocation du passé et des passions dans l'*Alceste* de Quinault." *Les Lieux de mémoire et la fabrique de l'œuvre*. Biblio 17. Paris/Seattle/Tübingen: PFSCL, 1994. 321-29.

_____. "Trailing Clouds of Glory: Operatic Elements in Racine's *Mithridate*." *Cahiers du Dix-septième* 1.2 (1988): 21-36.

Nuitter, Charles-Louis-Étiennne [Charles-Louis-Étienne Truinet], and A.-E. Thoinan [A.-E. Roquet]. *Les Origines de l'opéra français*. Paris: Plon, 1886. Geneva: Minkoff, 1972/New York: Da Capo, 1977.

O'Connor, John J. *Amadis de Gaule and its Influence on Elizabethan Literature*. New Brunswick, NJ: Rutgers University Press, 1970.

Orcibal, Jean. "Racine et Boileau librettistes." *Revue d'Histoire Littéraire de la France* 49.3 (1949): 246-55.

Otis, Brooks. *Ovid as an Epic Poet*. 1966. 2nd ed. Cambridge: Cambridge University Press, 1970.

Ovid [Publius Ovidius Naso]. *Les Métamorphoses*. Trans. Nicolas Renouard. Paris: Veuve Langelier, 1619.

_____. *Les Métamorphoses*. Trans. Pierre Du Ryer. Paris: 1666.

_____. *The Metamorphoses*. Trans. Rolfe Humphreys. 1955. Bloomington: Indiana University Press, 1972.

_____. *Metamorphoses*. Ed. F. J. Miller. 3rd ed. Loeb Classical Library. Cambridge: Harvard University Press, 1977-84. 2 vols.

_____. *Les Métamorphoses*. Ed. Jean-Pierre Néraudau. Trans. Georges Lafaye. Folio. Paris: Gallimard, 1992.

The Oxford Companion to Musical Instruments. Ed. Anthony Baines. Oxford/New York: Oxford University Press, 1992.

Parfaict, Claude, and François Parfaict. *Dictionnaire des théâtres de Paris*. Paris: Rozet, 1767. 7 vols. Geneva: Slatkine Reprints, 1967. 2 vols.

_____. *Histoire de l'Académie Royale de Musique, 1645-1742*. Ca. 1741. Ms. 12355. Paris, Bibliothéque Nationale, Manuscrits français. Partial transcription annotated by Renée Girardon-Masson, Vmb.47. Paris, Bibliothèque Nationale, Département de Musique. Manuscript copy by Beffara, Rés. 536. Vol. 1. Paris, Bibliothèque de l'Opéra. 2 vols in 1.

_____. *Histoire du théâtre françois depuis son origine jusqu'à présent*. 1734. 3rd ed. Paris: P.-G. Le Mercier, 1745-49. 15 vols. New York: B. Franklin, 1968.

Pascal, Blaise. *Pensées. Œuvres complètes*. Ed. Louis Lafuma. Paris: Seuil, 1963.

_____. *Pensées*. Ed. Philippe Sellier. Paris: Mercure de Frane, 1976.

Paul-Harang, Pascal. "Phaéton ou la volonté de briller." Booklet accompanying Lully, *Phaéton*, 22-25.

Pausanias. *Graeciae Descriptio*. Ed. Friedrich Spiro. Leipzig: Teubner, 1903. 3 vols.

Pavillon, Étienne. *Œuvres d'Étienne Pavillon*. Amsterdam: Zacharie Chatelain, 1750. 2 vols.

Pelous, Jean-Michel. *Amour précieux, amour galant (1654-1675)*. Paris: Klincksieck, 1980.

Perrault, Charles. *Critique de l'opéra, ou examen de la tragédie intitulée Alceste, ou le Triomphe d'Alcide*. Paris: Barbin, 1674. *Alceste, suivi de La Querelle d'Alceste*. By Philippe Quinault. 79-102.

_____. *Les Hommes illustres qui ont paru en France pendant ce siècle, avec leurs portraits au naturel*. Paris: Antoine Dezallier, 1690-1700. 2 vols.

_____. *Parallèle des Anciens et des Modernes*. Paris: Coignard, 1688-97. Geneva: Slatkine Reprints, 1979.

_____. *Recueil de divers ouvrages en prose et en vers*. Paris: Coignard, 1675.

Pesqué, Jérôme. "*Renaud et Armide:* opéra des princes, opéra des peuples." Mazouer, *Recherches* 89-97.

Picard, Raymond. *La Carrière de Jean Racine*. Paris: Gallimard, 1956.

_____. *Nouveau Corpus Racinianum*. Paris: CNRS, 1976.

Pitou, Serge. *The Paris Opera: An Encyclopedia of Operas, Ballets, Composers and Performers. Genesis and Glory, 1671-1715*. Westport, CT: Greenwood Press, 1983.

Pocock, Gordon. *Boileau and the Nature of Neoclassicism.* Cambridge: Cambridge University Press, 1980.

Poizat, Michel. *L'Opéra ou le cri de l'ange.* Paris: A. M. Métailié, 1986.

Plutarch. *Lives.* Dryden edition revised with an introduction by Arthur Hugh Clough. London: J. M. Dent, 1910.

Pommier, Édouard. "Versailles, l'image du souverain." Nora 193-234.

Pommier, Jean. "Le Silence de Racine." *Aspects de Racine.* Paris: Nizet, 1954. 47-85.

Pougin, Artur. *Les Vrais créateurs de l'opéra français, Perrin et Cambert.* Paris: Charavay, 1881.

Powell, John S. *Music and Theatre in France, 1600-1680.* Oxford Monographs on Music. Oxford: Oxford University Press, 2000.

_____. "Music, Fantasy and Illusion in Molière's *Le Malade imaginaire.*" *Music and Letters* 73.2 (1992): 222-43.

_____. "Musical Practices in the Theater of Molière." *Revue de Musicologie* 82 (1996): 5-37.

_____. "'Pourquoi toujours des bergers?' Molière, Lully, and the Pastoral *Divertissement.*" Heyer, *Lully Studies* 198.

Prassoloff, Annie, ed. *Opéra baroque et théâtralité. Textuel* 26 (1993).

Primi Visconti, Jean-Baptiste. *Mémoires sur la cour de Louis XIV, 1673-1681.* Ed. Jean-François Solnon. Paris: Perrin, 1988.

Prunières, Henry. *Le Ballet de cour en France avant Benserade et Lully.* Paris: H. Laurens, 1914.

_____. "La Fontaine et Lully." *La Revue Musicale* 2 (1921): 97-112.

_____. *Lully.* Paris: Laurens, 1909. 2nd. ed. Paris: Laurens, 1927.

Racine, Jean. *Œuvres complètes.* Vol. 1 (Théâtre - Poésie). Ed. Georges Forestier. Bibliothèque de la Pléiade. Paris: Gallimard, 1999.

_____. *Œuvres.* Ed. Paul Mesnard. Grands Écrivains de la France. Paris: Hachette, 1865-73. 9 vols.

_____. *Principes de la tragédie en marge de la Poétique d'Aristote.* Ed. Eugène Vinaver. Paris: Nizet, 1951.

Racine, Louis. *Mémoires contenant quelques particularités sur la vie et les ouvrages de Jean Racine. Œuvres complètes.* By Jean Racine. 1: 1114-1205.

Rameau, Jean-Philippe. *Observations sur notre instinct pour la musique, et sur son principe.* 1754. *Musique raisonnée.* Ed. Catherine Kintzler. 150-200.

Ranum, Patricia. *The Harmonic Orator: The Phrasing and Rhetoric of the Melody in French Baroque Airs.* Stuyvesant, NY: Pendragon Press, 2001.

Rapin, René. *Réflexions sur la Poétique d'Aristote et sur les ouvrages des Poètes anciens et modernes*. Paris: F. Muguet, 1674.

_____. *Réflexions sur la Poétique de ce temps et sur les ouvrages des Poètes anciens et modernes*. Paris: F. Muguet, 1675. Ed. E. T. Dubois. Geneva: Droz, 1970.

Reckow, Fritz. "Der inszenierte Fürst. Situationsbezug und Stilprägung der Oper im absolutischen Frankreich." *Die Inszenierung des Absolutismus: politische Begründung und künstlerische Gestaltung höfischer Feste im Frankreich Ludwigs XIV*. Ed. Fritz Reckow. Erlangen: Universitätsbund Erlangen-Nürnberg, 1992. 71-104.

Recueil des harangues prononcées par messieurs de l'Académie Françoise, dans leurs receptions, & en d'autres occasions, depuis l'establissement de l'Académie jusqu'à present. Vol. 1. Amsterdam: Aux dépens de La Compagnie, 1709.

Regnault, François. *La Doctrine inouïe: Dix leçons sur le théâtre classique français*. Paris: Hatier,1996.

_____. "Que me parlez-vous de la musique?" *Cahiers de la Comédie-Francaise* 17 (1995): 63-82.

Rémond de Saint-Mard. *Réflexions sur l'Opéra*. La Haye, 1741. Geneva: Minkoff, 1972.

Reynier, Gustave. *Thomas Corneille: sa vie et son théâtre*. Paris: Hachette, 1892. Geneva: Slatkine Reprints, 1970.

Richelet, Pierre. *Dictionnaire françois*. 1680. Geneva: Slatkine Reprints, 1970.

Richter, [Rudolf] Erich. *Philippe Quinault, sein Leben, seine Tragödien, seine Bedeutung für das Theater Frankreichs und des Auslandes*. Leipzig: Bomboes & Schneider, 1910.

Rigal, Eugène. *Alexandre Hardy*. Paris: Hachette, 1989.

Ripa, Cesare. *Iconologie*. Trans. Jean Baudouin. 2 vols. Paris, 1636. New York: Garland, 1976.

Robinet, Charles. *Lettres en vers à Madame. Le Théâtre et l'opéra vus par les gazetiers Robinet et Laurent (1670-1678)*. Ed. William Brooks. 23-155.

Robinson, Paul. "A Deconstructive Postscript: Reading Libretti and Misreading Opera." Groos and Parker 328-46.

_____. *Opera and Ideas from Mozart to Strauss*. Ithaca, NY: Cornell University Press, 1985.

Rolland, Romain. *Musiciens d'autrefois*. Paris: Hachette, 1908.

Rosen, Charles. *The Classical Style*. New York: Norton, 1972.

_____. "The Fabulous La Fontaine." Review of Marc Fumaroli, *Le Poète et le roi: Jean de la Fontaine en son siècle* (Paris: Editions de Fallois, 1997). *New York Review of Books* December 18, 1997. 38-46.

Rosow, Lois. "The Articulation of Lully's Dramatic Dialogue." Heyer, *Lully Studies* 72-99.

_____. "French Baroque recitative as an expression of tragic declamation." *Early Music* 11 (1983): 468-79.

_____. "How Eighteenth-century Parisians Heard Lully's Operas: The Case of *Armide*'s Fourth Act." Heyer, *Lully and the Music of the French Baroque* 213-37.

_____. "Lully." *New Grove Dictionary of Opera* 1: 242-44.

_____. "Lully's *Armide* at the Paris Opera: A Performance History." Diss. Brandeis University, 1981.

Rothschild, James de, and Émile Picot, ed. *Les Continuateurs de Loret. Lettres en vers de la Gravette de Mayolas, Robinet, Boursault, Perdou de Subligny, Laurent et autres (1665-1689)*. Paris: Damascène Morgand, 1881-99. 3 vols.

Rougemont, Denis de. *L'Amour et l'occident*. Paris: Plon, 1939.

_____. *Love in the Western World*. Trans. Montgomery Belgion. Rev. ed. 1956. New York: Harper and Row, 1974.

Rousseau, Jean-Jacques. *Lettre sur la musique française*. 1753. *Essai sur l'origine des langues, où il est parlé de la mélodie et de l'imitation musicale; Lettre sur la musique française; et, Examen de deux principes avancés par M. Rameau*. Ed. Catherine Kintzler. Paris: Flammarion, 1993. 129-84.

Rousset, Jean. *La Littérature de l'âge baroque en France: Circé et le paon*. Paris: José Corti, 1965.

Rubin, David Lee. *A Pact with Silence: Art and Thought in The* Fables *of Jean de La Fontaine*. Columbus: Ohio State University Press, 1991.

_____, ed. *Sun King: The Ascendancy of French Culture during the Reign of Louis XIV*. Washington: Folger Shakespeare Library, 1992.

Saint-Evremond, Charles de Marquetel de Saint-Denis de. *Œuvres en prose*. Ed. René Ternois. S.T.F.M. Paris: Didier, 1962-66. 4 vols.

_____. *Les Opéra* (1676). *Œuvres meslées*. Paris, 1705. Ed. Robert Finch and Eugène Joliat. Geneva: Droz, 1979.

_____. "Sur les opéra. A Monsieur de Bouquinquant." *Œuvres meslées*. Paris: Claude Barbin, 1684. 11: 77-119. Lesure (no continuous pagination).

Saint-Simon, Louis de Rouvroy, duc de. *Mémoires; Additions au Journal de Dangeau*. Ed. Yves Coirault. Bibliothèque de la Pléiade. Paris: Gallimard, 1983-88. 8 vols.

Sartori, Claudio. *I Libretti italiani a stampa dalle origini al 1800*. 5 vols. Cuneo: Bertold e Locatelli Musica, 1991.

Schmidgall, Gary. *Shakespeare and Opera*. New York: Oxford University Press, 1990.

Schmidt, Carl B., ed. *The Livrets of Jean-Baptiste Lully's* Tragédies Lyriques: *A Catalogue Raisonné*. New York: Performers' Editions, 1995.

_____. "The Geographical Spread of Lully's Operas During the Late Seventeenth and Early Eighteenth Centuries: New Evidence from the Livrets." Heyer, *Lully and the Music of the French Baroque* 183-211.

Schneider, Herbert. "Les Monologues dans l'opéra de Lully." *Dix-septième Siècle* 161 (1988): 353-63.

_____. *"Persée."* Benoît 549.

_____. *Die Rezeption der Opern Lullys im Frankreich des Ancien Régime.* Tutzing: H. Schneider, 1982.

_____. "Tragédie et tragédie en musique: querelles autour de l'autonomie d'un nouveau genre." *Literatur und die anderen Künste* (Universität Bayreuth). *Komparatische Hefte* 5-6 (1982): 43-58.

Seneca, Lucius Annaeus. *Tragedies.* Vol. 1. Ed. F. J. Miller. Cambridge: Harvard University Press, 1968. 2 vols.

Sénecé, Antoine Bauderon de. "Lettre de Clément Marot à M. de *** touchant ce qui s'est passé à l'arrivée de Jean Baptiste de Lully aux Champs Elysées." 1688. *Œuvres choisies de Sénecé.* Ed. Emile Chasles and P. A. Cap. Paris: P. Jannet, 1855.

Sévigné, Marie de Rabutin Chantal, marquise de. *Correspondance.* Ed. Roger Duchêne. Bibliothèque de la Pléiade. Paris: Gallimard, 1974-78. 3 vols.

Shattuck, Roger. *Forbidden Knowledge: from Prometheus to Pornography.* New York: St. Martin's Press, 1996.

Sonneck, O. G.-Th. *Catalogue of Opera Librettos Printed Before 1800.* Washington, D.C.: Government Printing Office, 1914.

Sourches, Louis-François du Bouchet, marquis de. *Mémoires sur le règne de Louis XIV.* Ed. Gabriel-Jules, comte de Cosnac, Arthur Bertrand, and Ed. Pontal. Paris: 1882-93. 13 vols.

Spiegelman, Willard. "Opera: Handel With Musical Care." *Wall Street Journal* December 8, 1998. A20.

Spielmann, Guy. "Spectacle, théâtre, texte: esquisse d'une problématique." *L'Esprit Créateur* 39.3 (1999): 76-88.

Stanton, Domna. "The Ideal of 'repos' in 17th-Century French Literature." *L'Esprit Créateur* 15 (1975): 79-104.

Sweetser, Marie-Odile. "La Création d'une image royale dans le théâtre de Racine." *PFSCL* 29 (1988): 657-75.

Tasso, Torquato. *Gerusalemme liberata. Poesie e prose.* Ed. Siro Attilio Nulli. Milano: Ulrico Hoepli, 1955. 3-500.

Tessier, André. "Un document sur les répétitions du *Triomphe de l'Amour* à Saint-Germain-en-Laye (1681)." *Actes du Congrès d'Histoire de l'Art [...] Paris [...] 1921.* Paris: P.U.F., 1923-24. 3: 874.

_____. "Les Répétitions du *Triomphe de l'Amour* à Saint-Germain-en-Laye." *La Revue Musicale* 6.4 (1925): 123-31.

Thomas, Downing. "Opera, dispossession, and the sublime: the case of Armide." *Theatre Journal* 49 (1997): 168-88.

Todorov, Tzvetan. "Introduction au Vraisemblable." *La Notion de littérature et autres essais*. 1971. Paris: Seuil, 1987. 85-94.

La Tragédie lyrique. Paris: Cicero/Théâtre des Champs-Élysées, 1991.

Turnbull, Michael. "La Tragédie en musique considérée ..." *Newsletter of the Society for Seventeenth Century French Studies* 1 (1979): 32-35.

Turnell, Martin. *The Classical Moment: Studies of Corneille, Molière and Racine*. New York: New Directions, 1946.

Van der Cruysse, Dirk. *Madame Palatine, princesse européenne*. Paris: Fayard, 1988.

Vanuxem, Jacques. "Racine et le baroque." *Europe* 453 (1967): 165-81.

_____. "Racine, les machines et les fêtes." *Revue d'Histoire Littéraire de la France* 54.3 (1954): 295-319.

_____. "Sur Racine et Boileau librettistes." *Revue d'Histoire Littéraire de la France* 51 (1951): 78-81.

Vaunois, Louis, ed. *L'Enfance et la jeunesse de Racine. Documents sur la vie de Racine. Iconographie racinienne*. Paris: Del Duca, 1964.

Verschaeve, Michel. *Traité de chant et mise en scène baroques*. Paris: Zurfluh, 1997.

Viala, Alain, ed. *L'Esthétique galante. Paul Pellison. Discours sur les Œuvres de Monsieur Sarasin et autres textes*. Toulouse: Littératures Classiques, 1989.

_____. *Naissance de l'écrivain: sociologie de la littérature à l'âge classique*. Paris: Minuit, 1985.

_____. "'Qui t'a fait minor ?' Galanterie et Classicisme." *Littératures Classiques* 31 (1997): 115-134.

_____. "Racine galant, ou l'amour au pied de la lettre." *Cahiers de la Comédie-Française* 17 (1995): 39-48.

_____. *Racine: la stratégie du caméléon*. Paris: Seghers, 1990.

Vialet, Michèle, and Buford Norman. "Sexual and Artistic Politics Under Louis XIV: The Persephone Myth in Quinault and Lully's *Proserpine*." *Images of Persephone: Feminist Readings in Western Literature*. Ed. Elizabeth T. Hayes. Gainesville: University Press of Florida, 1994. 45-74.

Voltaire [François-Marie Arouet]. "Art dramatique." *Questions sur l'Encyclopédie*. 1770. *Dictionnaire philosophique. Œuvres complètes*. Vol. 7. Paris: Th. Desoer, 1817. 360-85. 13 vols.

_____. *Commentaires sur Corneille. Complete Works*. Ed. David Williams. Geneva: Voltaire Institute, 1974-75. 3 vols. (numbered 53-55)

_____. *Correspondence*. *Complete Works*. Ed. Theodore Besterman. Geneva: Voltaire Institute, 1968-77. 51 vols. (numbered 85 to 135)

Vuillemin, Jean-Claude. "Histoire et dramaturgie classique au XVIIe siècle." *Actes de Columbus: Racine; Fontenelle: Entretiens sur la pluralité des mondes; Histoire et littérature*. Actes du XXIe colloque de la North American Society for Seventeenth-Century French Literature, Ohio State University (6-8 avril 1989). Ed. Charles G. S. Williams. Biblio 17. Paris/Seattle/Tübingen: PFSCL, 1990. 229-44.

Wagner, Marie-France. "Le 'miroir sans tache' dans l'*Andromède* de Pierre Corneille." *Perceptions of Values in French Literature*. *FLS* 22 (1995): 163-75.

Walton, Guy. *Louis XIV's Versailles*. Chicago: University of Chicago Press, 1986.

Weigert, Roger-Armand. *Notes de Nicodème Tessin le Jeune relatives à son séjour à Paris en 1687*. Extrait du *Bulletin de la Société de l'Histoire de l'Art Français*, année 1932. Paris: n.p., 1933.

Wine, Kathleen. "Romance and Novel in *La Princesse de Clèves*." *Approaches to Teaching Lafayette's* The Princess of Clèves. Ed. Faith E. Beasley and Katharine Ann Jensen. New York: MLA, 1998. 146-57.

Winn, James Anderson. *Unsuspected Eloquence: A History of the Relations Between Poetry and Music*. New Haven: Yale University Press, 1981.

Wolf, John B. *Louis XIV*. New York: Norton, 1968.

Wolfe, Phillip J. Introduction. *Choix de Conversations de Mlle de Scudéry*. Ravenna: Longo Editore, 1977.

Wölfflin, Heinrich. *Renaissance and Baroque*. 1888. Trans. Kathrin Simon. Ithaca, NY: Cornell University Press, 1966.

Wood, Caroline. *Music and Drama in the* Tragédie en Musique, *1673-1715*. *Jean-Baptiste Lully and His Successors*. Diss. U. of Hull, 1981. Revised ed. New York: Garland, 1996.

_____. "Orchestra and Spectacle in the *Tragédie en Musique* 1673-1715: Oracle, *Sommeil*, and *Tempête*." *Proceedings of the Royal Music Association* 108 (1981-82): 25-46.

Wright, Terrence C. "Lully and Quinault: Musico-dramatic Synthesis in the Tragédie en musique." Diss. U. of Kansas, 1983.

Yates, Frances. *The French Academies of the Sixteenth Century*. London: Wartburg Institute, 1947.

Zanger, Abby. "Lim(b)inal Images: 'Betwixt and Between' Louis XIV's Martial and Marital Bodies." Melzer and Norberg 32-63.

Zebouni, Selma. "Rhetorical Strategies in *L'Art poétique*, or What is Boileau Selling?" *FLS* 19 (1992): 10-18.

Zweig, Paul. *The Adventurer: The Fate of Adventure in the Western World*. Princeton: Princeton University Press, 1974.

EDITIONS OF PLAYS AND LIBRETTI BY QUINAULT[1]

Complete libretti or plays:

Livrets d'opéra. Ed. Buford Norman. Toulouse: Littératures Classiques, 1999. 2 vols.

Le Theatre de M' Quinault. Contenant ses Tragedies, Comedies et Opera. Derniere édition, Augmentée de sa Vie, d'une Dissertation sur ses Ouvrages, & de l'origine de l'Opera. Le tout enrichi de Figures en taille-douce. Paris: Pierre Ribou, 1715. 5 vols.[2]

Le Théatre de Monsieur Quinault. Contenant ses Tragédies, Comédies, et Opéra. Nouvelle édition, enrichie de Figures en taille-douce. Paris: Compagnie des Libraires, 1739. 5 vols.

Théatre de Quinault. Contenant ses Tragedies, Comedies et Opera. Nouvelle édition, Augmentée de sa Vie, d'une Dissertation sur ses Ouvrages, & de l'origine de l'Opéra. Paris: Veuve Duchêne, 1778. 5 vols. Geneva: Slatkine Reprints, 1970.[3]

Recueil général des opéra, représentés par l'Académie Royale de Musique, depuis son Établissement. Paris: Christophe Ballard, 1703-45. Geneva: Slatkine Reprints, 1970. 16 vols. in 3.[4]

Petite Bibliothèque des Théatres, contenant un Recueil des meilleures Pieces du Théatre François, Tragique, Comique, Lyrique & Bouffon, depuis l'origine des Spectacles en France, jusqu'à nos jours. Paris: Au Bureau, 1783-89. 75 vols.[5]

---

[1] These do not include the hundreds of editions and reprintings of Quinault's libretti for performances during the seventeenth and eighteenth centuries. For details on editions during Quinault's lifetime, see Schmidt's catalogue and the *notices* of my edition.

[2] The libretti for Quinault's operas and ballets are found in volumes 4 and 5 of this edition, as they are in the 1739 and 1778 editions of his complete theater.

[3] This edition was also published by Les Libraires Associés. Only the title pages are different.

[4] The libretti for Quinault's operas and ballets are found in volumes 1-3 of the original edtion and in volume 1 of the Slatkine reprint. See appendices 1 and 2 of Schmidt's catalogue for details on similar collections printed in Amsterdam and on the numerous *recueils factices*, which consist of pages of previously printed   libretti.

[5] The libretti of Quinault's operas and ballets are in the four volumes of the series "Opéra," published from 1784 to 1787. The copy in the Bibliothèque Nationale in Paris, Yf.5064-5079, vol 1. (Yf.5064-5067), contains libretti from *Les Fêtes de l'Amour et de Bacchus* to *Thésée* (the printed catalogue and the spine give this as vol. 5). Vol. 2 (Yf.5068-5070) contains libretti from *Atys* to *Proserpine*. Vol. 3 (Yf.5071-5074) contains libretti from *Le Triomphe de l'Amour* to *Amadis*. Vol. 4 (Yf.5075-5079) contains libretti from *Roland* to *Armide*.

Selected libretti or plays:

Œuvres choisies de Quinault. Paris: Didot, 1811-17. 2 vols.[6]

Œuvres choisies de Quinault. Paris: Crapelet, 1824. 2 vols.[7]

Théâtre choisi. Ed. Victor Fournel. Paris: Laplace, Sanchez et Cie, 1882.[8]

Chefs-d'œuvre lyriques de Quinault. Paris: Au Bureau général des Chefs-d'œuvre dramatiques, 1791. 3 vols.[9]

Suite du Répertoire du théâtre français. Ed. Lepeintre. Paris: Veuve Dabo, 1822-23. 81 vols.[10]

Théâtre du dix-septième siècle. Ed. Jacques Truchet and André Blanc. Bibliothèque de la Pléiade. Vol. 3. Paris: Gallimard, 1992.[11]

Individual libretti or plays:

Alceste, suivi de La Querelle d'Alceste: Anciens et Modernes avant 1680. Ed. William Brooks, Buford Norman, and Jeanne Morgan Zarucchi. Geneva: Droz, 1994.

Armide. Paris: Stock, 1923.

Astrate. Ed. Edmund J. Campion. Exeter: University of Exeter, 1980.

Atys. Ed. Stéphane Bassinet. Geneva: Droz, 1992.

Bellérophon. Ed. William Brooks and Edmund J. Campion. Geneva: Droz, 1990.

---

[6] Vol. 1 contains *Alceste, Thésée*, and *Atys*. Vol. 2 contains *Proserpine, Persée, Amadis, Roland*, and *Armide*.

[7] Vol. 1 contains *Alceste, Thésée*, and *Atys*. Vol. 2 contains *Isis, Proserpine, Persée, Phaéton, Amadis, Roland*, and *Armide*.

[8] Contains *Cadmus et Hermione, Alceste, Atys, Amadis, Roland*, and *Armide*.

[9] Vol. 1 contains the Boscheron *Vie, Roland, Armide*, and *Le Temple de la paix*. Vol. 2 contains *Proserpine, Persée*, and *Amadis*. Vol. 3 contains *Phaéton, Isis*, and *Le Triomphe de l'Amour*.

[10] Vols. 12-13 ("Grands-Opéras" I and II) contain all of Quinault's libretti, except for *Cadmus et Hermione*. The inclusion of Quinault's complete text in this edition, even though several of the libretti had been reduced to three acts or otherwise "retouchés" for performance during the eighteenth century (see Appendix I), is indicative of the continuing importance of Quinault's libretti for the reading public: "Nous avons ajouté des variantes à ceux des opéras réduits, où ce qui a été supprimé à la représentation est bon à conserver à la lecture" (12: 33).

[11] Contains *Atys* and *Armide*.

MODERN EDITIONS OF SCORES[12]

Chefs-d'œuvre classiques de l'opéra français. Paris: T. Michaelis, 1878-83. New York: Broude Brothers Limited, 1971. 40 vols.[13]

Lully, Jean-Baptiste. *Œuvres complètes.* Ed. Henry Prunières. 1930-39. New York: Broude Brothers Limited, 1966-74. 11 vols.[14]

_____. *Œuvres complètes.* Ed. Jérôme de La Gorce and Herbert Schneider. Paris: Musica Gallica.[15]

_____. *The* Tragédies lyriques *in Facsimile.* Prefaces by François Lesure et al. Williamstown, MA: Broude Brothers Limited, 1998-.[16]

_____. *Armide.* 2nd ed. 1713. Béziers: Société de Musicologie de Languedoc, n.d.

_____. *Atys.* 2nd ed. 1709. Béziers: Société de Musicologie de Languedoc, 1987.

_____. *Proserpine.* 2nd ed. 1714. Florence: Studio per edizioni scelte, 1994. 2 vols.

Piccini, Niccolò. *Atys.* Ed. Julian Rushton. French Opera in the 17th and 18th Centuries 55. Stuyvesant, NY: Pendragon Press, 1991.

RECORDINGS

Complete operas:

Handel, George Frideric. *Teseo.* Les Musiciens du Louvre, dir. Marc Minkowski. Erato 2292-45806-2, 1992. 2 CD.

Lully, Jean-Baptiste. *Alceste.* La Grande Écurie et la Chambre du Roy et l'Ensemble Vocal Sagittarius, dir. Jean-Claude Malgoire. CBS 79301, 1975. Out of print.

_____. *Alceste.* La Grande Écurie et la Chambre du Roy et l'Ensemble Vocal Sagittarius, dir. Jean-Claude Malgoire. Disques Montaigne 782012, 1992. Astrée-Auvidis, 1994. 3 CD.

---

[12] Scores of several Lully operas are available on the University of North Texas Music Library's Lully Collection website: http://www.library.unt.edu/projects/lully/lullyhom.html. I have also been able to consult performing editions of *Alceste, Isis,* and *Roland,* thanks to the generous cooperation of friends and colleagues mentioned in the acknowledgments.

[13] These are piano-vocal scores. Vols. 16-18, 20-24, 26, and 29 contain ten of the eleven Quinault-Lully operas: *Alceste* (16), *Armide* (17), *Atys* (18), *Cadmus et Hermione* (20), *Isis* (21), *Persée* (22), *Phaéton* (23), *Proserpine* (24), *Thésée* (26), and *Roland* (29).

[14] Vol. 1 contains *Cadmus et Hermione.* Vol. 2 contains *Alceste.* Vol. 3 contains *Amadis.*

[15] This new edition will include all of Lully's operas, beginning with *Isis* in 2001.

[16] This series will include all the Lully operas. Quinault-Lully works available as of mid 2001 are *Cadmus et Hermione, Thésée, Atys, Persée, Phaéton, Roland,* and *Armide.*

_____. *Armide.* Ensemble vocal et instrumental de la Chapelle Royale, dir. Philippe Her-rewegghe. Actes I-III, V. Erato STU 715302, 1984. Out of print.

_____. *Armide.* Chœur et orchestre du Collegium Vocale et de la Chapelle Royale, dir. Philippe Herrewegghe. Harmonia Mundi 901456.57, 1993. 2 CD.

_____. *Atys.* Les Arts Florissants, dir. William Christie. Harmonia Mundi 401257.59, 1987. 3 CD.

_____. *Phaéton.* Ensemble vocal Sagittarius et Les Musiciens du Louvre, dir. Marc Minkowski. Erato 4509-91737-2, 1994. 2 CD.

Excerpts:

Charpentier, Marc-Antoine. *Musique de théâtre pour "Andromède" et "Circé." Sonates.* London Baroque, dir. Charles Medlam. Harmonia Mundi 1901244, 1986, 1993. 1 CD.

Lully, Jean-Baptiste. *Pièces élaborées pour clavecin par Jean-Henry d'Anglebert.* Kenneth Gilbert, clavecin. Harmonia Mundi 901267, 1987. 1 CD.[17]

_____. *Divertissements.* Guillemette Laurens; Capriccio Stravagante, dir. Skip Sempé. Deutsche Harmonia Mundi 77218-2-RC, 1990. 1 CD.[18]

_____. *Le Bourgeois Gentilhomme; Les Nopces de Village; Cadmus et Hermione.* André Danican Philidor, *Le Mariage de la Grosse Cathos.* Marie-Ange Petit, percussion; London Oboe Band, dir. Paul Goodwin. Harmonia Mundi 907122, 1994. 1 CD.

_____, et al. *Concert de danse.* Howard Crook; La Petite Bande, dir. Sigiswald Kuijken. Accent 96122D, 1996. 1 CD.[19]

_____. *Musiques à danser à la Cour et à l'Opéra.* Les Talens Lyriques, dir. Christophe Rousset. La Simphonie du Marais, dir. Hugo Reyne. Erato 0630-10701-2, 1995. 2 CD.[20]

_____. *Musiques aux États du Languedoc.* Françoise Masset; La Simphonie du Marais, dir. Hugo Reyne. Astrée E8560, 1999. 1 CD.[21]

_____. *The World of Lully.* Patrice Michaels Bedi; Chicago Baroque Ensemble. Cedille 09999 043, 1998. 1 CD.[22]

---

[17] Contains exceprts from *Cadmus et Hermione, Roland, Phaéton, Thésée, Proserpine, Atys,* and *Armide.*

[18] Contains excerpts from *Amadis* and *Armide.*

[19] Contains excerpts from *Armide.*

[20] Contains excerpts from *Thésée, Persée, Phaéton,* and *Roland.*

[21] Contains excerpts from *Thésée.*

[22] Contains excerpts from *Alceste, Persée, Phaéton, Amadis,* and *Armide.*

Indexes

The first of these indexes includes key concepts discussed in the book and the names of seventeenth- and eighteenth-century writers and other historical figures. It contains the major eighteenth-century commentators on opera, such as Lecerf and Du Bos, but not the numerous more recent critics to whom I am greatly indebted. It also includes individual works by Racine, Molière, and Charles Perrault, but not characters found in the works discussed. References for Lully are to pages where he and/or his music are mentioned specifically, but it is of course not always possible to separate his contributions from those of Quinault.

The second index lists references to works by Quinault, either to the work as a whole or to specific passages. It includes all passages cited, but not references that are more a guide to the plot than discussions of the passage in question. See also works to which Quinault is known or thought to have contributed, such as Molière's *Psyché* and *Ballet des Muses* and Lully's *Carnaval*, *Bellérophon*, and *Psyché*.

I. NAMES AND CONCEPTS

II. WORKS BY QUINAULT